Local Literacies
Theory and Practice

Volume Editors

Marilyn A. Mayers
Bonnie Brown

Production Staff

Laurie Nelson, Production Manager, Compositor
Hazel Shorey, Graphic Artist

Local Literacies

Theory and Practice

Glenys Waters

A Publication of
The Summer Institute of Linguistics
1998

Library of Congress Catalog No: 96-72066
ISBN: 1-55671-038-0

08 07 06 05 04 03 02 01 00 99 10 9 8 7 6 5 4 3 2 1

Printed in the United States of America

Copies of this and other publications of the Summer Institute of Linguistics may be obtained from

International Academic Bookstore
7500 W. Camp Wisdom Road
Dallas, TX 75236-5699

Voice: 972-708-7404
Fax: 972-708-7433
Email: academic_books@sil.org
Internet: http://www.sil.org

Contents

Preface

What! Me write a book? Impossible! Before this I had never written anything but letters to friends. The idea was absurd. But during my first three years of literacy consulting work in Papua New Guinea (PNG) I often felt that there was a need for a literacy resource manual and someone ought to write it!

But what kind of book does it need to be? It needs to be a book that gives some of the background that people need to know if they are going to train others to teach people to read and write in their own language. It needs to be a book that sets out different ways of doing things, for there are many different ways to teach others to read and write. It needs to be a book that tells why certain ways are better than others without forcing literacy workers to follow one particular way. It needs to be a book that is practical and gives examples of ideas that can be tried in the village. It also needs to be a book that talks about some of the theory behind what literacy workers do. Then those people who really want to understand things on a deeper level can do so. Yes, someone ought to write a book like that. It is needed.

Time and again things would happen in my literacy work in PNG and I would go home and complain strongly to my husband. And time and again his response was, "Write the book! Write the book, no one else will!"

And so I started.

I never thought it would get finished. There was so much I should put in it. In Australia, libraries have shelves and shelves of books about teaching people to read and write and here I was trying to put all the things I thought were important into one book. It was an enormous job and hard to do. But my husband kept saying, "Write the book."

I would say, "The language I need to use to talk about some of the things is just too complicated, and some of the ideas seem too hard to explain unless people know a lot of other things first. Maybe I should leave that part out?" But he would say, "No, just write the book!"

So I wrote the book.

My journey as a literacy worker started in teachers college, moved to teaching in Australian schools for three years, continued as I worked for twelve years in the Australian Aborigines and Islanders Branch of the Summer Institute of Linguistics, included teaching my two daughters on School of the Air (what a long term study that was!), stretched across the ocean to PNG for a little over three years, and was further stretched during the year I taught migrant adults in Australia to read, write, and speak English. My journey has also been affected by my university studies (1992–1993). Most of my literacy work in PNG has been as a consultant and teacher of other literacy workers. All these experiences influenced what I have written in this book.

I have not written this book with any intended bias towards one gender or the other. However, it will be apparent that male gender is often used, especially for pronouns, throughout the text. There are two reasons for this. One reason is that literary gender is not an issue to many of those for whom this book is intended. A second, and probably the most important reason, is that it is simply not possible to meet the goal of a clear communicative style of English for second-language speakers, and also to use gender-inclusive language.

This is not a book that you have to read from cover to cover. It has, however, been written in an order where each chapter should flow on to the next. It is a book that is like a market. Each stall holder has something to offer and shoppers walk from one stall to the next and choose what is wanted according to their needs at the time. So happy shopping. Feel free to browse and to choose what is wanted to meet whatever need you have at the time. If there are things that are too difficult to understand or are not useful, then pass over them, and keep looking until you find the things that you need.

The first two chapters deal mostly with theory. The rest of the chapters are a mixture of theory and examples of how to put the theory into practice.

There are not as many examples and ideas in the book as I would like. My collection of stories is limited because of the type of journey I have had as a literacy worker. Also, I ran out of time and I had to stop somewhere. If you have ideas of things that you would like to see added to the book, or if you have actual examples from your teaching practice that would be good to share with others I would love to hear from you.

I hope that you find things in this book that are helpful to your work.

Glenys Waters
Summer Institute of Linguistics
Papua New Guinea 1995

Acknowledgements

I could not have written this book without a lot of support, help, and encouragement from my husband, Bruce. He also assisted with the editing to help make the book more readable and numerous other tasks to help me get it finished. His belief that I could and should do it often kept me going. Without his contributions the book would never have been finished. He helped me push on to the end. A special coach indeed.

I would also like to thank Dr. Tom McCormick for his regular encouragement, for his belief that I could do it and his assurance that there was a need for my book. He helped me with the section on critical literacy and taught me much through his workshop on reading theory and his continuing mentoring.

Thanks also to my two daughters who put up with their mum working too hard and too often, but who were nevertheless interested in what I was doing. We would trade my literacy stories for their school stories.

I would also like to thank my God, who encouraged me to keep going when I wanted to give up, who inspired me and gave me ideas on how to say things, put things at my finger tips at the right time, brought people across my pathway at the right time, and guided me each step of the journey.

I also want to acknowledge the invaluable assistance of Marilyn Mayers in editing the final draft and the assistance of Dr. Steve Walter with the pre-publication processes.

I am a great believer that every picture tells a story and that teachers often learn as much from the pictures in a manual as they do from the text. Pictures also give ideas of how principles can be put into practice and often stimulate alternative ideas about a similar topic. So when I dreamed about what this resource manual would be like it included lots of pictures. I would like to thank the following people for their help with the illustrations. Without them the finished product would have been very different from my dream and quite boring. Thanks to my daughter Natashia Waters who time and again has been asked to draw just one more picture, and who was always willing to tell me when my dreams needed to make way for reality! Thanks to Nozomi Kume, Adelle Walter, and Hazel Shorey who came along at opportune times and were willing to help. To my dear friend Yasuko Nagai, whose illustrations I borrow regularly, I say thanks very much and keep up the good work. And Barbie Hynum, I still think her transfer primer illustrations are THE best! Special thanks to Jessie Bennett whom the Lord sent at the right time to complete the art work, and who did an excellent job. Without her it would not have gotten done. Her willingness and cheerfulness in doing the task was a great encouragement to me, at a time when I needed it.

It is my hope and prayer that this book will be a useful resource for those who train village people to teach other people to read and write in their own language.

I dedicate this book to the people of Papua New Guinea, a people whom I have come to love as we have served as guests in their country.

1

How Learning Takes Place

"Learning is a natural process, a process of making sense of things."[1]

What is teaching really about? Is it about teaching well? Or is it about people learning well? Is it about knowing lots of good teaching techniques? Or is it about supporting people as they learn? Most people would probably say it is about both. But where should this book start—by looking at teaching or looking at learning?

I have chosen to start by looking at learning because I think this is the most important part of literacy work. A teacher can have all the right kinds of techniques to help students learn, he can have good materials and the latest equipment, but all these things will not make sure that students learn. It might cause the students to have a good time in class, and others might be impressed. But is real learning taking place? I have sat through all kinds of workshops and conferences, courses and training sessions, and there have been many times that I have not really learned anything, despite the teaching that took place.

So, for me, the crucial place to start when talking about teaching is to begin by looking at learning. How do people learn? Once there is a clear understanding about how people learn, then the kinds of methods teachers use can be looked at.

1.1 How children learn

Joe laughed uncontrollably as he got out of the car. He then turned to us and said, "What is it?" We were in the capital city for a translation workshop and it was the first time our Djinang friend had seen such an animal and he didn't know what it was. "It's a kind of

---

[1] *Victorian Mathematics Frameworks* 1988:22 Melbourne, Australia: Victorian Department of Education.

dog," Bruce replied. The animal that stood before us did not fit any ideas that Joe had about what a dog was like. This one was a very large, round, and hairy English sheep dog. It looked like a huge ball of long hair.

Joe had grown up in a different culture, and the dogs he knew were small, skinny, hunting dogs which had to fend for themselves. Those dogs to us seemed to be just bags of bones. But if there was food about they were quick, agile, and first in line. I am sure it was hard for Joe to imagine the English sheep dog hunting animals in the bush. It looked too large and clumsy.

Joe had built up an idea, a concept, of what a dog was and the English sheep dog did not fit his concept of dog.

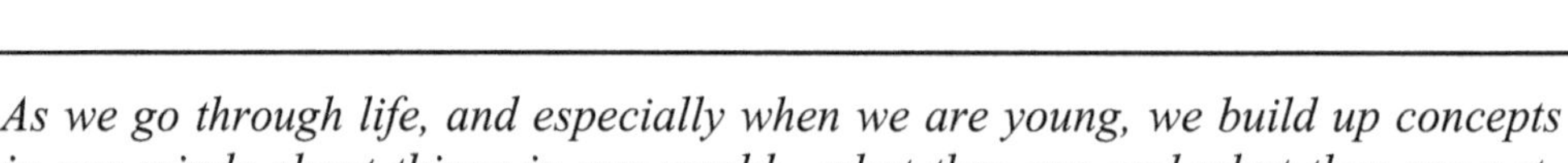

As we go through life, and especially when we are young, we build up concepts in our minds about things in our world—what they are and what they are not.

We build up concepts through our senses, that is what we see, smell, hear, feel, and sometimes taste. Our senses send messages to the brain and the brain organises them. We also build concepts about things through our experiences.

People who study how we come to understand our world are known as cognitive psychologists.[2] Cognitive psychologists would say that,

> the brain "constructs" meaningful patterns from the information it receives...it "decides" how best to organise meaning in memory; it "determines" what meanings to expect in the future on the basis of the meaning it has already constructed and stored; and it "intends" what to do next on the basis of its expectations and purposes. (Bussis 1985:10)

Cognitive psychologists differ among themselves in their views about how people come to know about things. Some are called behavioral psychologists. They believe people learn in response to stimuli. Stimuli are happenings from the world which prompt the human body to react in some way. For example, a new baby learns to respond to light and dark and shapes and gradually learns to see and follow things with his eyes. When he is a little older, he learns not only to follow the stimulus but grab onto it. Some cognitive psychologists are called constructivists. They see people constructing their knowledge stage by stage. Others

[2] "The aim of cognitive science is to understand how people think and comprehend; how they learn and remember and how they solve problems and come to be creative" (Francis J. Di Vesta 1987:204).

look at knowing in terms of information processing, that is, how we structure the knowledge we have in our minds.

Each group of cognitive psychologists has developed its own ways of talking about how people come to know things.

> All of these complex terms and approaches amount to the simple concept...that, based on one's experience of the world in a given culture (or combination of cultures) one organises knowledge about the world and uses this knowledge to predict interpretations and relationships regarding new information, events and experiences. (Tannen quoted by Bussis 1985:11)

So, even though people have different ways of looking at how we come to know about things, there are things that they agree on. As Tannen says, they agree that people organise their knowledge about the world on the basis of their experience of it in their culture, and then they use their knowledge to help them deal with new information and experiences.

People's minds organise knowledge and use that organised knowledge to deal with new information. One of the strong factors which shape how people organise knowledge in their mind is the culture in which they live.

How do children learn and develop in your culture? What are the sorts of words people use in the village to talk about children's learning? Do they recognise different stages of development? What are those stages? How do they encourage children to develop? It would be good to think about these things in your situation.

New ideas and information are learned when they are linked in some way to the knowledge structure that a person already has. A structure is something that is built from many parts in an ordered way. Ausubel, a well known cognitive psychologist, talks about a person's knowledge being organised in structures. These structures are a bit like trees. Think back to the example of the concept of dogs. Knowledge about dogs can be structured on a tree. There are certain features that make an animal fit the category of 'dog-ness'. This category can be further divided into groups: dogs that are wild, dogs that are pets, dogs that work for man, and dogs that are used in sport.

Even though I do not know much about dogs, I know a little about some of these dogs. And so my knowledge of dogs can be structured like a tree. As I learn new information, I will link it to things that I already know.

My nephew recently bought a whippet, and I did not know what it was. After talking to him and seeing the dog, I worked out it was like a greyhound dog, but smaller, and used for racing. So I was able to link whippet into my structure of knowledge about dogs used in sports and races.

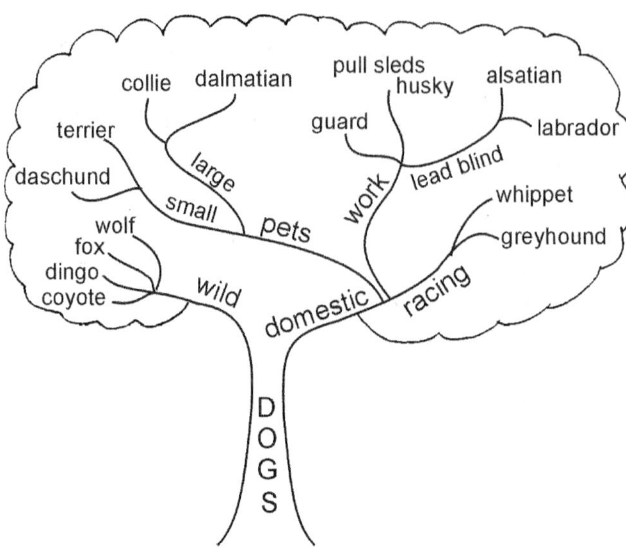

My knowledge of dogs can be structured like a tree.

When I was young, the dogs used to lead blind people were always labradors, but lately I have seen a few alsatians doing the job. I added that new information to what I already knew about dogs used to lead blind people. As I learn new things about dogs, I add them to my existing knowledge structure about dogs.

Someone else who knows more about dogs would structure their knowledge differently. Instead of grouping their knowledge around categories like, 'wild' and 'domestic', and 'pets' or 'workers', they might structure their knowledge on the different breeds of dogs, things which I know nothing about. If one day I learn more about the different breeds of dogs, I may want to reorganise the way I have structured my knowledge of dogs. For the moment, however, I will stick with what I know! Each person has experiences which differ from those of others, and each person's knowledge structures will differ to some extent from other people's knowledge structures. However, every person will have their knowledge of the world structured in some way.

> *As new information comes to a person and is processed, it interacts with the knowledge structures a person already has and is added into those structures.*

Learners have to relate new information to the ideas they already have in their own knowledge structure. They look for things which are the same and for things which are different. They try to work out how the new information is related to what they already know.

They may even need to create new ideas or structures. Or they may need to reorganise knowledge structures that they already have.

> *Learners have to be willing to get involved in the learning process and be willing to work hard at doing so.*

If not, then the learning he does becomes rote learning, that is, things are memorised but are not added into existing knowledge structures and are soon forgotten.

Ausubel (1985) says that our existing knowledge structures have a big influence on our future learning. He also says that the way our knowledge about a particular topic is organised will affect our learning of new things that are related to that topic.

And so Ausubel sees the learner as having structures of knowledge that are constantly being added to and reorganised in slightly different ways. He also says that new structures are being built when needed, and that if people want to improve or help others in their learning they need to know the following things.

- what the learner already knows
- how that knowledge is structured
- what new information needs to be introduced
- what concepts need to be built from ideas that the learner already has

1.2 Informal learning styles

A lot of our learning in life takes place informally. It is not in a school type of situation and it is not necessarily done in planned ways, for example, babies learning to speak, toddlers learning to walk, children learning to swim, or learning to ride a bicycle.

From his study of how traditional Aborigines in the north of Australia come to know things, Stephen Harris (1977) characterized several major features of their informal learning as follows:

- learning by observation
- learning by doing
- learning by imitation
- learning by personal trial-and-error
- learning through real-life performances
- learning by persistence and repetition

So Harris found that more Aboriginal learning is done by looking and watching rather than through talk. He found they learn by doing rather than by hearing or talking about things. They learn by imitating or copying, and by trying things for themselves rather than by someone combining talk and demonstration. They learn more through doing real things rather than practicing in pretend situations. When they are learning they do something over and over again until they do it well.

Harris (1977) found that they give little attention to breaking down something into ordered parts; rather learning takes place through successive approximations to the efficient end products. He found that, when Aborigines learn something they practice the whole thing that they are wanting to learn over and over again. Each time they do it, they get nearer and nearer to a good performance of the thing they are learning. It could be things like learning to make a string bag, learning to spear fish, or learning to play football. They do not break the task down into small parts—how to catch the ball, how to drop-kick the ball, how to hand pass the ball and so on, and practice each part. Rather, they play a game of football and practice the whole thing. And the next time they practice, they play a whole game of football again.

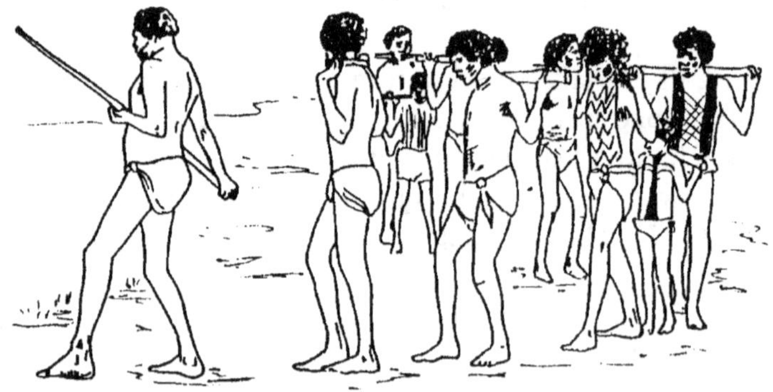

Young men learn to dance in the Aboriginal ceremonies. No one takes them aside and teaches them sets of steps and then how to put the sets of steps together into a dance. They grow up attending ceremonies and watching the men dancing. When they feel confident to try, the boys join the end of the line of male dancers and imitate what the men are doing. No one takes much notice of them at first. As they get older and better at their dancing, people reward them with claps when they dance well and shame them with laughs if they make mistakes. But they are never taken aside and told, "here watch my feet," or "do it like this." Gradually they polish their dancing skill to fit the skills of the older men that are dancing. They have learnt by watching, imitating, doing, trying for themselves in real-life situations, doing it over and over again till they get it right.

Informal styles of learning, like those discussed above, apply to cultures other than the Australian Aborigines. In my time in Papua New Guinea I have found that in village situations people use similar informal learning styles.

When my Papua New Guinea neighbour taught my daughter how to kill, pluck, and clean a chicken, she assumed Rachel and I would learn using informal learning styles similar to those I have mentioned. However, we have been brought up in a different way of learning and we had to stop from time to time and talk about the process. Then we had to break the task up into stages. I found myself adding a lot of talk to my neighbour's demonstration, drawing Rachel's attention to important points. Experiences like these highlight clearly the difference between western learning styles and the kind of learning styles which are common among Aborigines in Australia and Melanesians in Papua New Guinea.

1.3 Formal learning styles

In Papua New Guinea, the schooling process is one that has come from a western country and brings with it western ideas of formal learning.

Harris (1987:43) summarizes the major features of formal learning processes as follows:

- (i) It is decontextualised[3]—with its content having little application to everyday life and survival.
- (ii) It follows from (i) that it will therefore deal largely with abstractions, that is, information abstracted or taken out of any real-life context.
- (iii) It follows from (i) and (ii) that it will therefore need to be conducted verbally, which includes both the written and spoken forms.
- (vii) It is a conscious process. Before something can be talked about the speaker must be conscious of it.
- (v) It must be purposeful.

---

[3]Decontextualized means something has been taken out of the context in which it normally occurs.

Harris is saying that formal learning is often done in situations that are not natural, and with lots of talking, for example, talking in a classroom about how to catch fish rather than going down to the beach and doing it. He also says formal learning involves dealing with representations of the real thing rather than the real things themselves, and that the learner actively plans to take part and his attention is strongly focused.

It is important when teaching people to read and write that we understand how they best learn things and try and fit our way of teaching to their preferred ways of learning. Teaching people to read using real books and the shared reading approach (see §8.3) is often a useful method in the situations I have talked about in §1.2.

However, if people are going to continue with their learning by entering into formal schooling, then teachers need to think of ways to help the students move from being competent learners within their own culture to being competent learners in a western style education system.

> A particular style of learning is neither 'good' nor 'bad' in itself, but is effective if it helps the learner adapt to his situation and survive in it. The traditional Aboriginal economy and technology...was served by a largely informal non-verbal learning style. Western technological society and cash economy is well served by a higher proportion of formal, verbal learning style. (Harris 1984:3)

Teachers in traditional cultures should build on the strengths of the main learning styles of the people they are teaching. This is important. However it must also be recognised that formal schooling is mostly verbal, conscious, and is largely divorced from real-life situations. So if students are to do well at school they need to be taught how to learn in such situations.

1.4 Encouraging purposeful learning

Harris claims that informal learning styles are usually the best way to introduce reading and writing or any classroom skill or understanding. But he points out that eventually there is a need to move into the use of formal learning styles.

> *Students must progress from learning to read to reading to learn.*

They must also learn to predict, judge, evaluate, and reflect on what they have read.

> It is a good rule to begin with experiences, and then talk about and record those shared experiences...This approach involves beginning in an "Aboriginal way"

> and ending up in a more conscious, verbalised "school" way of transmitting and reviewing knowledge. (Harris 1984:18)

It is important to help the student use formal learning strategies not merely because it is the 'school way' but because it is a good way of learning in formal learning situations.

> It is highly efficient in terms of allowing for out-of-context learning, allowing immediate feedback, promoting the formation of generalised principles and creating consciousness about what is known and unknown, which in turn increases the chance of applying knowledge or principles in new settings. (Harris 1984:18)

Teachers also need to begin training the students to interact more in the classroom.

> It is not being implied that there was and is no formal verbal instruction in Aboriginal society. Mothers certainly name people and things a lot to their children and there is verbal instruction at ceremonial times and there is much telling and reciting but all of these examples of verbal teaching are different from the two-way process of student and teacher being verbally involved and responding to each other. (Harris 1984:20)

It is this talking back and forth between two people in the classroom that students are not used to. One of the Madang Teachers College lecturers I spoke with said he found it extremely difficult to get his students to talk back and forth in the classroom. They were not used to the western way of talking in education.

Students also need to be trained to be more actively involved in their education rather than just "being there."

Students need to try hard to be involved in the lesson. To westerners, taking an active role in their education is taken for granted. However, it does not come easily to children raised in traditional cultures.

> Yolngu [Aboriginal] children do not expect to and do not participate in the school program in an active purposeful self-conscious way, but rather participate passively in the school learning process...They are happy to co-operate passively with virtually anything that occurs in the classroom but have enormous difficulty in taking initiative in any school or learning situation...[they] copy endlessly from the blackboard, but have much difficulty where active thoughtful and self-conscious participation is required. (Christie 1982:11–12)

At Ramingining where I first worked, I am sure that some students' goals in school learning were very different from those of their teachers. Some children felt that by sitting in the desk they were doing school and would learn. The Aboriginal Teaching Assistants at Ramingining often completed the children's worksheets for them, colored their pictures and so on. I am sure they felt they were helping the children achieve their goal—completing the page of work. But how much did the children learn from the activity?

If students with backgrounds and attitudes such as these are to continue in western style schooling successfully, they need to take a more active role in their learning. Teachers must design and use activities which aim specifically at helping the students do this. Students need to understand the goals of the lessons, to take personal control over learning, and to make judgments about what they are doing (Christie 1982:19–25).

For example, students need to understand that you do not learn to read by following a ritual or just sitting in class. They should be encouraged to be more active in their learning. This can be done, for example, by encouraging them to persist with practicing the skills being taught outside of the teaching context. Give them tasks to take away from the class situation to work on independently outside of the class. Give them materials to practice reading at home several times, encourage them to read things to several different people each day. Encourage them to set their own reading and writing goals each week and then help them to reach those goals. Doing lots of activities like these will help the students to stop thinking that learning will be done to them, and they will come to understand that learning is something they have to be actively involved in.

Students also need to be told and shown that learning to read takes a long time and a lot of practice, and that they have to work hard at it. At the same time, many "learning to read-by-reading" opportunities should be given to the students, especially in the early lessons, so that the link between what they are doing in class, and what real reading (or real writing) is like, is very obvious. In some cases, early reading lessons seem to have little or nothing to do with what fluent reading is like. When that happens, students often become frustrated because they do not think they are really learning to read.

1.5 Helping students construct meanings effectively

So far I have mentioned several ways of thinking that different people have about how people come to learn or come to know things. There are many ways to talk about this subject and most of them have something helpful to say to people who want to teach others. Indeed many books have been written and much work and research about learning has been carried out. It is impossible to mention all the important works here. But it is important to mention a few other ideas about learning that are currently highly respected by teachers and by trainers of teachers: one from Kelly, the other from Vygotsky.

George Kelly in 1955 approached the study of how we learn (cognitive psychology) very differently from the mechanistic approaches of his day. His theory was called a PERSONAL CONSTRUCT THEORY.

> This title announced the central importance he gave to the idea that each of us creates our own reality, that we can know the whole world we live in only through the personal interpretations, or constructions, that we make of it. (Salmon 1988:11)

Kelly would say that each of us construct our own reality, that we are constantly constructing and reconstructing it as we learn. He places the importance on the learning process, a process which is often hard for the learner and sometimes causes changes to the learner which affect him deeply.

Some of the differences between Kelly's way of looking at learning and teaching and those that were commonly held in 1955 are listed below.

Mechanistic versus Personal Construct Approach

Mechanistic approaches	Personal construct theory
People can be explained by externals, their histories, their circumstances.	People can be understood only by their personal construct system.
Learning:	Learning:
• painless, limitless personal growth	• often hard, sometimes costly
• divorced from personal stance and social engagements	• depends on stance taken towards becoming involved in learning, often defined by previous experience and knowledge
• reception of ready-made facts	• building of new personal meanings
• acquisition of isolated bits of knowledge	• sees things as depending on each other, and unable to be fully separated; a change in one idea means that it might be necessary to rethink other ideas
	• involves risk taking

Teaching	Teaching
• handing out ready-made facts	• a meeting between the teacher's and student's personal constructions of reality • helping students in the construction of meanings • consideration of each student's personal stance towards becoming involved in learning • all learning is personal, which means that each learner must be treated as an individual • pupil-teacher, pupil-pupil relations are important so that each can understand the others' personal worlds • depends on a shared social reality; the sense we make of our lives must also make sense to others

A good example of the differences of these two approaches can be seen in the movie, "To Sir With Love." This story is about an Afro-Englishman who went to teach at one of the most difficult schools in London. The teenagers at this school came from poor families. The early part of the movie shows the teacher trying to use the approaches to teaching and learning outlined in table 1 as mechanistic approaches. He works with the textbooks and ready-made facts that are to be taught. However, the class he is in charge of are not at all interested in learning or playing the 'school game'. They had decided to resist learning in the school context. They had worked out ways of making their situation at school as bearable as possible for themselves and had worn other teachers down by the way they acted and behaved.

Part way through the movie, their teacher, "Sir," comes to the understanding that because of the situation he is not able to teach them anything. He also comes to understand the teenagers better, to understand their backgrounds and where they are headed once they leave school at the end of the year. He throws away the ready-made facts and isolated bits of knowledge and starts to help them build personal understandings and values for themselves that will help them when they leave school and have to face the real world. He shows them that to learn and to do better in life, they have to work hard, take risks, and take on a positive attitude to learning. He helps them in many different ways to build understandings of things related to what their everyday living will be like in the future. He helps them to personally construct their own meanings and understandings.

As you can see, teaching ready-made facts is less complicated from the teacher's point of view. The facts are set out, it is up to the student to commit them to memory. But if teachers are to help students construct meanings then their job is more difficult. Teachers must come to know what meanings students have already constructed in their minds. They must know the best ways each student constructs new meanings for himself and they must work out how they can best help each student construct meanings for himself. Teachers working in this way must work hard to support students in their learning.

> *It is important for the teacher to support students in their learning by helping them to build knowledge which is meaningful for them. It is not easy but it is what the students need if they are to learn well.*

Another psychologist who focuses on supporting students in their learning is the Russian, Vygotsky. Vygotsky talked about *the zone of proximal development.* In talking about a zone of development he is referring to the stage in a person's learning when that person moves from not knowing something to knowing something. Vygotsky talks about the actual development that has taken place already in the learner, what he already knows and can do. He also talks about a level of potential development—what the learner may be able to do tomorrow but is now just beginning to develop. He uses the picture of a fruit tree to help explain his idea. The buds or the flowers of the fruit tree are like the buds or the beginnings of a learning process, and the fruit of the tree represents learning that has already taken place, learning that has come to maturity. Just as the buds develop into fruit, so the learner develops from someone who is beginning to know something to someone who really knows it.

So, in helping students learn, Vygotsky (1978:87) talks of teachers working in the zone of proximal development, that is, working in a middle area which is close to what students can already do on one side, and also close to what they are just beginning to learn but have not yet mastered on the other side.

People who follow Vygotsky's theories would say that it is important for teachers to create a zone of development when helping people to learn, and that the teachers should work with people now on things that they are able to do with a little bit of help so that soon they can do those things alone.

1.6 Two case studies on learning

Case study 1. My university friend

The following story is part of an essay a friend of mine wrote about her learning experiences.

When I was thirteen I was in a class at Our Lady's Sunshine. It was called the scholarship grade and only certain students were admitted. I was eligible because I had qualified according to the criteria set by Sister Sebastian. We called her Basher because she literally bashed us. As well as her usual teaching tasks she was also the choir mistress. At the Catholic church in Sunshine the clergy and the congregation were well and truly into praising the Lord at Sunday Mass. Basher loved me because I could pronounce the Latin words and sing *Panis Angelicus* in parts which wasn't bad considering I didn't have a clue what it all meant. I did know one thing. Basher didn't hit me on Mondays after she had heard me sing and she always gave me a lolly from her tin that she kept hidden in the cupboard in the old tennis club room which served as our classroom. She told me that I had a beautiful voice and she also told me that I was sensible.

Now to be sensible meant a great deal to Basher. One afternoon she had me working on the board. I was trying to work out a mathematical problem and I just couldn't solve it. She came over to the board and put her arm around my shoulders. She told the class publicly that I was a 'sensible' person because I could see that I was doing something wrong but I just couldn't work out what that was.

I would try to understand the algebra and geometry, but it made no sense to me and I wept over the fact that I couldn't understand. The year wore on and she despaired of me because of these maths and finally the exam time came and of course I failed the test. I was brokenhearted and Basher was too.

To compensate she taught me how to knit really intricate patterns and I spent the rest of the year out on the steps of the vestry knitting baby clothes which the nuns would raffle to raise money for the school.

I got over my disappointment fairly quickly because I knew my place in the scheme of things. The construction of gender had taken place in my life. By the time I had reached my teens I knew that all I was good for was being a wife and mother. Although even that was questionable because I was such 'an ugly bugger' as my brothers told me constantly.

It was many years later that I realised that something had happened between Basher and me. She tapped into my inner self, and I know intuitively that if we had been fortunate enough to have had time and a curriculum that did not make huge demands on this very old and sick woman, we would have engaged in 'learning'.

Many years passed before I had the privilege of meeting another woman who inspired me to believe in myself. Because of her own passion for literature she kindled in me a burning desire to unravel the mysteries that had kept me in bondage for what had seemed like an eternity. My close friend took me under her wing and basically loved me into learning. She encouraged me to have a go; she told me that I could think, and she encouraged me to stop pretending I was somebody that I was not.

No amount of scientific experimentation could possibly measure the process of learning that has taken place within this brain's network. How do you measure love?

Case study 2. How did I "come to know" and how then should I teach?

The following story is part of an essay I wrote about a learning experience of mine and how it helped me think about what was important in teaching others.

I have always thought of myself as an academic failure. I couldn't write essays at school for beans. I failed my Higher School Certificate (HSC). I wasn't good at the school game. I was the quiet mouse in the back of the class that the teacher never knew. I was the one who would swallow tablets before exams to calm my nervous stomach. I was the one, according to my mother, who could never write essays. I was the average plodder that plodded all the way to HSC but couldn't plod through those final exams.

It didn't bother me as I don't get my feelings of self-worth from such things. I have succeeded in plenty of other areas. Academic disciplines, however, had not been my thing. I went on from attempting HSC to train as a Primary School Teacher, years ago when it was a more practical rather than academic course. I loved teaching, I loved kids, and I knew what I was doing and why I was doing it. Looking back I feel I was a good teacher. Since then, I've enjoyed the last eighteen years working as a literacy worker with SIL. I feel I know my subject area and can deal well with the practicalities. People have enjoyed my practical help as a consultant and I can often see creative ways of doing things rather than sticking with the status quo when it is not working. I get a buzz out of my literacy work.

But writing academic papers—that's not me. So why at this very moment is my spare time taken up with writing—not just an academic paper but a whole book, a village literacy workers' manual? It's quite an academic exercise and requires a lot of technical writing. How did I come to be writing such a volume? How did I come to know that I could do this? Indeed that I must do it? Given my feelings of failure in the essay-writing game of school, how did I come to this point? How did I come to know I could have a go at technical writing and succeed?

Five keys

As I look back over my life and reflect on my coming to know that I could write technical articles, I can see that it has been quite a complex and dynamic process. I can see five key factors that have affected this process:

- having something that I wanted to say (strong motivation),
- having people encourage me to believe it is a worthwhile thing to do and that I can and should do it,
- coming to an understanding of the structure of technical articles and how to communicate with an audience,
- gaining confidence with the abilities needed—computer skills and the writing process, and
- having an excellent editor who was willing to ensure that I succeeded in communicating effectively in the world of technical article writing.

Learning is a life-long process along a continuum. From my experiences with technical writing I can see that my "coming to know" has not been determined by formal teaching, exams, assessments, etc. It has been brought about by the five things mentioned above.

Five principles

Generalising from my experience, I can see five principles which are important for helping people to learn something.

A strong motivation fueling the desire to learn. I wanted to communicate my ideas about literacy work which were often different from what others were teaching. I wanted to show the sound foundations that my ideas were built on. I had something I wanted to say, and to a wider public audience than just my friends.

Being exposed to lots of the finished product. Over the nineteen years that I have been in SIL I have had to read lots of technical papers. Through these experiences I have noticed things about the articles that communicated well, and other things which did not. I have built up a "personal construct" about how I think articles should be written.

Encouragement by significant people. Through all my work, my entire family has cheered me on and taken an interest in my work. They have told me I could do it and should do it. Another close friend with a doctorate in reading theories also encouraged me to write the book. He kept assuring me there was a need for it and that I could do it.

The learner has confidence that he has sufficient skills to make an attempt. Over the years I have had to do a lot of writing related to my literacy work. I have had to write course outlines, lecture notes, literacy reports, class handouts, and so on. In doing these jobs I have come to learn a lot about the writing process, to do lots of drafting, and to use the computer to help me turn out a good finished product.

A key supporter who ensures success. The learner needs a special person or persons willing to help him improve in his efforts. My husband helps me with all my editing and makes sure that my finished products are the best they can be. He continually encourages me that what I have to offer others is worthwhile and helpful for them. He always works on the assumption that I will succeed in my writing, and has no doubts about it.

These five things were important in my learning. Now that I know this, how then should I teach others? Thinking about these things has emphasised for me the things that are important in teaching others.

When teaching others my main task should be to encourage and assist the learners with their goals. I must help them become active in learning whatever they need for the task they have set themselves. I should build an atmosphere of encouragement and support for them in their efforts. They should feel comfortable enough to be willing to take risks in order to learn something new.

I should help learners get to a stage where they feel confident with each of the skills they need for a particular task, confident enough to eventually have a try at the ultimate goal, and go on trying. I should immerse them in the task they are seeking to master. For example, if a person wants to improve his writing, then I need to give him plenty of opportunities to write. I should also make sure he is reading and being exposed to lots of examples of good writing so he can absorb the language structures, techniques, and ways of saying things that are used by good writers.

I should be there to help with any parts of the task that they are not yet confident about doing. I should be training them in strategies that will help them cope with the things they find difficult. I should be drawing their attention to the things they have done well. I must continually be expecting them to succeed in the learning task. I should be a key supporter.

But above all, I must base my teaching on the motivations of the learners. The learning process must be fired up and maintained by their strong personal motivations—whatever it is that they want to learn, or whatever task they want to be able to do.

1.7 Strategies for building a good learning environment[4]

- Create a supportive atmosphere in which students can relax and be themselves.
- Use materials that will provide an experience of success.
- Focus on what the students can do and talk about what they did well.
- Make sure that students can succeed at the task.
- Expect to make changes in your teaching program. If you find things are too difficult for students, don't be afraid to change them or abandon them. But if you do that, then explain why you do not like the activity.
- Encourage the students to take risks in their efforts to learn. Always support them when they do and help them succeed.
- Talk about their learning problems and share stories with them of times that you have had the same or similar problems.
- Talk about methods the students are using to solve problems in whatever they are learning.
- Talk about ways others have solved similar problems.
- Talk about the fact that end products done perfectly are achieved through lots of trial and error.
- Encourage the students to take their time and keep trying.
- Talk about how the students feel about their learning.
- Allow time for students to work in groups or with partners. Working alone can be stressful.
- Use materials, situations, and examples which are relevant to students' needs, goals, and interests.

---

[4]Some of the ideas presented here are adapted from a handout from Marr and Helme 1991, *Growing in Numbers.*

2

The Learning Context

A context is a situation in which something takes place. For example, in chapter 1, informal and formal learning contexts were discussed. They are two different situations in which certain kinds of learning happen. Formal contexts include situations such as school classes, Sunday school classes, women's classes, Bible study classes, and so forth. Informal contexts are situations like teaching your neighbour on the verandah of your house or showing your child how to do something. So in this book when I talk about a context I am talking about the learning situation in which people are involved.

As seen from chapter 1, there is more to teaching than just what the teacher does, and it is necessary to look at both sides of the coin—teaching and learning. Teaching-learning situations are typically complex, with many factors affecting them, and some of those factors are not very obvious at all. The teaching-learning situation can be looked at from four viewpoints that are all related to one another.

The viewpoints are those of:

- the learner,
- the teacher or facilitator,
- the context, and
- the learning event or learning task.

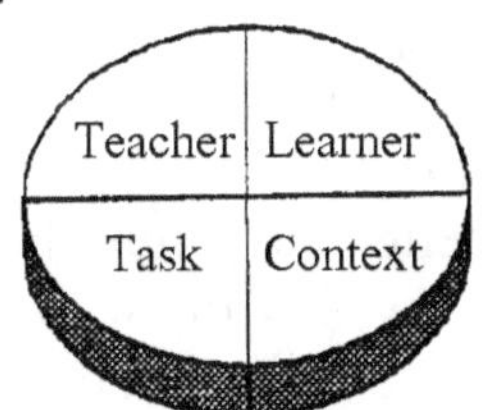

The teaching-learning situation can be compared to the wheel of a cart. This wheel has four main parts. All four parts are connected and related to each other and work together to make the wheel turn smoothly. In looking at each of these viewpoints it should always be remembered that the viewpoints are always connected and related to each other.

2.1 The learner

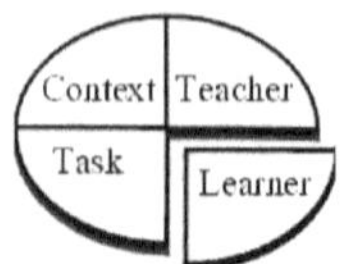

Debbie's story

Debbie, very thin and very angry, joined my class in the family center together with her screaming nine month old baby. Debbie lived on her own, all her family were in the country. She depended on people at the Children's Hospital when she had problems. But this wasn't without its problems because she was always in trouble for missing appointments and disobeying their instructions. She had the same troubles with other places that she had dealings with. Eventually, someone realised that they may be having all these problems with her because she had a literacy problem. She couldn't read their directions, instructions, or letters. So she was told to come to my literacy class.

The first thing I wanted to do was to stop the baby screaming. I hoped to do this by making his stomach happy. He had been fed on whatever tinned baby food was at hand, most of which he was not supposed to be eating because of his medical problems. Together we went to the shop and I copied the labels of foods which were all right for her baby to eat. I talked about Timmy's diet and wrote the names of these foods on cards. We built these cards into sentences about Timmy and his food, what he ate, what he liked, and what he disliked. Later we collected the actual labels from the foods and practiced reading those.

We also worked on telling the time, reading the date, and reading appointment cards. Another tutor worked with her on shopping, budgeting, operating a bank account, and measuring the milk powder for his bottle.

We were a team of professionals working together on various needs, but what we were actually doing was putting Debbie to rights. We were doing things to her and for her. She was going along with us, but it would be an exaggeration to say she was enthused. She quickly became bored with what we were doing even though I could see she was beginning to be able to read.

One day, she had had enough, or was sufficiently confident to assert herself, and said what she really wanted to do was to write to her brother who had sent her a message through a friend suggesting that she was deliberately ignoring him. So I helped her to write a letter. She told me what she wanted to say, I wrote it for her and she copied it. He wrote back to her, I read it, and together we wrote him another letter.

Even though she was overwhelmed by what she saw as the hopelessness of her position—she felt she would never be able to read his handwriting—there was new energy in the learning situation when we moved on to her agenda where she was doing what she wanted to do, using her voice, saying things in the way she wanted to.

Adapted from a class handout written by Aileen Treloar

The learner has goals

The story about Debbie had a powerful impact on me when I first read it, especially the sentence "We were doing things to her and for her." So often in my teaching I have been the one to decide what to do and how to do it. This story was a strong reminder to me that the learner needs to have equal input into the lesson about what is done and how it is to be done, and I should not take a position in which I am always the one who decides what is to be learned.

As Aileen thought about what had happened to Debbie she said,

> It was all done in the name of doing good to her, but the only power she had was in rejecting them and all their words and works...Debbie's baby does need an improved diet, but as his mother she has to be able to make that choice meaningfully.

Debbie's story illustrates that teachers working with learners need to work hard at not doing things to them and for them. Instead, find out what it is that they want help with, and then support them in doing the things they want to do. The teacher should find out what their goals are and help them work towards reaching them, not impose someone else's goals upon them.

The learner has expectations

When working with students, particularly adults, teachers must also take into account the students' expectations. Teachers of Aborigines in Arnhem Land, Australia, have commented to me that the Aboriginal children often expect to learn to read just because they walk through the door and sit in the classroom. They do not realise they have to put individual effort into the process. They think that just by going to school and following the rituals they will learn.

The Hewa in Papua New Guinea expected to learn to read straight away when they went to literacy classes. So they were not happy to spend time working on syllable drills; like *ba bu bi, ma mu mi.* And when they did not learn to read in the first few lessons they stopped coming to classes.

The Umanikaina people of Papua New Guinea were keen to come to literacy classes, but they were not sure the literacy classes were being taught correctly because the lessons had no syllable drills in them. In the old days, reading classes always had syllable drills, so they expected the new reading classes to be the same.

My adult literacy students in Australia expected to have formal English grammar lessons because they thought those kinds of lessons would help them to learn to speak the language properly.

Every student will have expectations about the teaching-learning situation. It is important that the teacher understands these expectations and works with the students. Either the students need to adjust their expectations to something that is more realistic, or the teacher needs to adjust what is done in the lessons to fit in with their expectations; or perhaps both need to adapt.

The learner has fears

Rosa was an older lady, a grandmother. She taught me a lot about various things and I knew she was a very capable lady. She had migrated to Australia when she was eighteen years old, she had had a terrible marriage and lived in very difficult circumstances. She had struggled all her life to have enough money to put food on the table for her children. She had supported several members of her family through many serious illnesses such as kidney operations, cancer, etc. She was a loving, caring, kind person. I really admired her. She had been orphaned when she was four and was never allowed to go to school, because in those days in her culture girls just stayed at home and helped with the house work. And now as a Granny she was determined to learn to read and write—a thing she had always wanted to do, something that had been denied her so far.

Even though she was strongly motivated and worked hard at learning to read, Rosa had to battle her fears that she would not learn. She would never join in group reading with the rest of the class for fear that she would be wrong, or that she might make a mistake. She felt this way even though we were often reading stories she had written herself, even though we were in a supportive group where others made mistakes, and even though mistakes were accepted as part of learning. When she was reading stories to me she would read along, repeating the words to herself over and over, checking and rechecking to see if it made sense and often saying, "Oh, that's not right" when it was right. She was afraid to read aloud, afraid to commit herself, afraid that it would not be right. If I tried to support her in her efforts, she seemed to get more flustered and nervous, afraid of the extra attention I was paying to her.

Even though I saw Rosa as a capable lady, a lady whom I admired greatly, and even though our class worked in a supportive friendly atmosphere, Rosa's learning was still affected by her fears. All students bring some fears with them to the learning-teaching situation. Teachers need to take these into consideration.

Positive and negative experiences of the learner

Hakan completed his university education in Turkey and then taught for seven years. When he came to Australia and could not speak English he was unable to get a teaching job, so he went to work in a factory. Rosa also went to work in a factory when she came to Australia because people did not need to speak English to work in a factory. But she had never been to school or learned to read and write. Hakan and Rosa both came to my literacy class, but each had different learning experiences behind them. Hakan was fairly confident in the learning experiences in my class—he had studied a lot before and done well, he knew he could do it again. If he was not sure of a word he could look it up in his Turkish dictionary. He could already read well in Turkish and it would not take long to apply those reading skills to a language he was learning to speak. Rosa had been working with a home tutor. She was beginning to see progress and had some successes. But she was very lacking in confidence about her learning since she had not been able to learn to read and write all her life. She was nervous about her attempts and, if she was unsure of something, she was unable to look it up in the dictionary—she had to depend on others.

Each learner brings with them feelings about the learning experiences they have had, and these feelings can affect their learning in good or bad ways.

The learner already has knowledge

At the first adult literacy class that I conducted in Australia I was reminded that even though people cannot read they still know many things. My first student came in and as we introduced ourselves he handed me his business card. He was a successful businessman in the building industry. My second student came in carrying his mobile phone! Just because people cannot read and write does not mean they are ignorant of the world around them. And it also does not mean that they are not competent in their daily lives.

For many years we lived in an Aboriginal community in Australia. Very few of the Aboriginal people there could read. But they were very clever people. Often I felt incompetent despite all my training and my education. Ten-year-old Aboriginal girls could function better in the community than I could. I was a dead loss when we went hunting. When we went fishing I was hopeless at lighting a fire to cook the fish we caught. I could not follow the intricate dance steps that were performed so easily by the women in the ceremonies. My efforts at making a 'dilly bag' were laughed at. "Throw it away and I will make you one," my illiterate Granny said.

When we moved to live on Karkar Island (Papua New Guinea), I tried to be involved in village activities. But I could not even cook the food properly when the Baibel Komiti came for their meeting. When the women came to cut the grass around our house, I lasted only a few minutes in the heat and humidity. They could work all morning.

Although the people mentioned above cannot read, they have a lot of knowledge and are very capable people. Anything that is done in the teaching-learning situation should build on and use the knowledge, skills, and abilities possessed by the learners. Such things should never be ignored.

Even young children coming to school for the first time have knowledge, knowledge that will help them learn to read and write. For example, they already know a lot about their language. They know many of the words, what the order of words should be to make sentences, how spoken stories are structured, how they begin and end. They know a lot about their culture and the way people do things, and how people should behave in their culture. They know some of the history of their society. They have also learned things about the world around them. They recognise many things in their world and know how to do things that are relevant to their way of life.

So if Angor (Papua New Guinea) children are learning to read the story about Cockatoo and Crow—how one came to be white and the other black—they have a lot of knowledge that will help them read that story (see the full story on page 113). They already know the story, having heard members of their family tell it. They know all about sago making—the processes involved, where people make sago, and the importance of having the water at the right temperature. Their knowledge helps them in their efforts to learn to read the story, and it helps them recognise certain words in the story. Their knowledge helps them understand why the cockatoo was annoyed with the crow, and why he did what he did at the end of the story.

The learner already has knowledge that will help in the learning of new things.

2.2 The teacher or facilitator

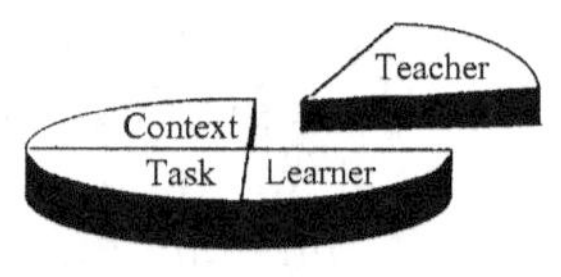

The facilitator, or the person doing the teaching, comes to the teaching-learning situation with many different experiences. He might feel unsure or afraid. He has certain goals he wants to achieve, he has certain skills and abilities. He has his own ideas about how to teach, and about how to teach that subject in particular. He may have had good teaching experiences in the past, or bad ones. All these thoughts, feelings, and ideas that the teacher brings with him to the situation influence what happens in that situation.

Some teachers are more skilled than others, can control the class better, and can respond better to things that happen in class. They find it easier to make things clear to the students. Some people have been teaching longer and are more experienced than others. People new to teaching may be unsure of themselves and what they should do. Teachers who are experienced are more comfortable about changing what they are doing in the lessons to fit in with the learner's goals, abilities, and needs. Teachers who are unsure of themselves tend to stick closely to the teaching program that has been set up, rather than feeling free to make changes.

Teachers, even experienced ones, bring many fears with them to teaching-learning situations. Even though I have taught and spoken in public many times, every time I come to a new teaching situation I get very nervous. Will it work this time? Will the people understand what I am trying to teach them? Will they learn? Will they feel the classes have been helpful and worthwhile? Can they see they are progressing in their learning? Maybe my ideas will not work in this situation. Maybe I am wrong about the way people should be taught to read and write after all? It worked when I taught at the other place, but that was different. And some days I just have an off day—things that normally work well for me end up as a flop.

I often do things when I am teaching because of my ideas about how to teach or because of my ideas about teaching that particular subject. For example, the materials I have written about in §5.1 were developed when I was asked to teach literacy workers about reading readiness activities. I was uncomfortable with the course outline that I was given to follow because I believed that it was not adequate for getting students ready for reading. So I designed a different course from what was being taught by others in Papua New Guinea at the time.

Different teaching styles

Teachers have different styles and ideas about how to teach which affects what they do in teaching-learning situations.

Some teachers look at teaching as something like banking, they keep putting deposits of knowledge into the students. The students are empty vessels to be filled up with information. So the teacher's job is to spend his time putting information into the students.

Others believe in discovery learning, where the students discover things for themselves. The teacher's role is to set up situations that will help the students discover things.

Other teachers believe in using a style of teaching which focuses on giving the students experiences from which they can learn things. So they provide lots of different experiences for their students.

Others believe students learn best when a teacher models the real thing for his students, and then gives the students opportunities to do the same thing that the teacher has just done.

Other teachers believe very strongly in group learning. So they set up situations in which students can do things in groups—learning together and learning from each other.

Other teachers try to support their students in the learning process by teaching at the point of need, when students are involved in authentic tasks.

Many teachers use a combination of several of these styles of teaching. All these beliefs, styles, fears, skills, and expectations that the teacher brings to the learning-teaching situation influence what happens there.

2.3 The context

The social and cultural influences that operate in teaching-learning situations have an effect on what happens in those situations. These influences may hold back effective learning so they must be taken into consideration.

The people who are in the teaching-learning situation have an effect on how things are structured and on what can be done there. For example, some cultures have rules about who is allowed to do things together and about how people relate to one another.

Among Australian Aborigines there are very strong rules about whom a person can speak to, whom he must avoid speaking to, whom he may joke with, whom he may marry, and so forth. Also certain activities within their culture are carried out by groups of women, but other activities are done only by groups of men. There are some men's activities that women are forbidden to attend; and women would be seriously punished if they accidentally happened to see those activities taking place. These restrictions mainly concern things related to traditional ceremonies.

It is also considered bad manners for younger people to be in positions of authority over older people. So it is important to select the right people to be teachers and to make sure that women do not teach men unless the men make it clear that it is okay to do so. In this kind of situation, formal classes probably need to be held for men and for women separately.

Another cultural issue to consider when teaching in the Australian Aboriginal context is that it is very easy to cause people to be shamed in public situations. Causing shame should be avoided. In such situations, for example, it is better to work on tasks together as a group rather than call for individuals to come up with answers. It is better to call for information to be volunteered than to ask individuals specifically. The teacher would not bring one person out to the front of a class for any reason. Instead, he would work carefully at maintaining a group feeling.

Also, teachers should not decide who should be in a group. That decision should be left to others who know the group members well and who know how everyone is interrelated. It is important that groups be formed around those who already do things together. It is also important that people who are supposed to avoid one another should not be placed in uncomfortable situations. At the local school, run by Europeans, children were often placed in groups with people they should not be with or with people who were traditional enemies. The European teachers then wondered why certain children did not come to school very often!

In the Australian Aboriginal context it is also important not to direct praise to one person too often. To do better than everyone else is looked upon as a bad thing. I heard a story of an

Aboriginal boy who was winning a running race. When he saw that he was winning, he slowed down to let the others in the race catch up so that they could all finish together. I have also seen Aboriginal people be quite hurtful in their attempts to bring people who were doing too well back down to the level of the rest of the group. This was talked about as 'leveling' people, keeping people on the same level.

These issues of how people relate to one another and how things are done in certain cultures are all important and must be taken into consideration when teaching in such situations. The details will be different in every new situation. There always needs to be discussion with those involved. Sometimes what people want to do might be quite different from what the facilitator expects. I was surprised to hear of one group in Papua New Guinea who wanted to have their literacy students all working together—youth, adults, men, women, children, and the old people. In this way the young could help the old when appropriate, and in acceptable ways, and they would all learn things together at the same time. This was a decision the people made themselves, and it suited their situation well.

2.4 The learning task

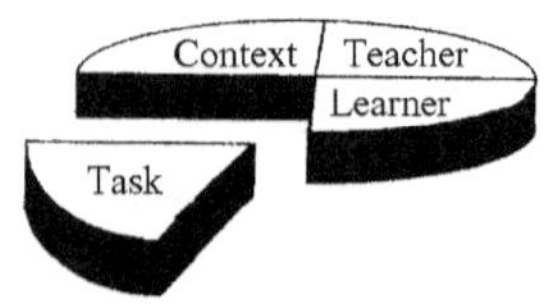

The fourth viewpoint to consider is what is actually being done in the teaching-learning situation. This is called the task—what it is that is being done. The following kinds of things need to be considered when looking at the learning task

- Is the task an appropriate one for the particular student involved? Is it at the right level of difficulty?
- Are the materials which are in use the right ones for that situation?
- Are the students actively involved in the learning task or is the teacher doing too much of the work, that is, too much of the talk, too much of the effort of making connections and building meanings?
- Do the students' responses show they understand what is going on?
- Does the lesson have the right pace? Is it flowing quickly or smoothly enough?
- Does the task or activity in the lesson start from what the student already knows? Does it cause him to progress to a new point in his understanding? That is, does it build on what is known and lead on to more learning?

Tasks that are appropriate

It is important that the tasks are suited to the needs of the learners. When I reflect on the reading lessons that I have taught, I believe that some have not been very helpful for my students! This, however, is part of the process by which I learned what is helpful for them. For example, sometimes things I have given my students to read have turned out to be far too difficult for them at their present stage of learning. All they learned from that part of the lesson was that they were not very good at reading and it made them feel they probably never would be any good at reading! It had the effect of making them very anxious about their reading ability. That was definitely not what I wanted them to feel!

Sometimes students are given activity sheets or activities to do as part of the reading lesson, especially when teachers are busy working with other students. However, if you look carefully at what the sheets ask students to do, you discover that these activities may involve very little reading or practicing of reading skills.

Some of the things that are done in reading lessons, while not being helpful for teaching reading, are still worth doing for other reasons. That is fine. They just should not be called reading tasks!

When I was teaching my daughters on School of the Air,[5] I had a lot of trouble getting Rachel interested in reading. I could not understand this as her older sister always had her nose in a book, especially when I wanted her to do housework! And we had spent a lot of time in our family encouraging the girls to be interested in books. But every time a new batch of books arrived from the school, Rachel would have fights with me about what she was not going to read. Eventually her teacher and I worked out what the problem was. It was not so much the reading that was the problem, it was all the work Rachel had to do about the reading once she had finished the book—writing essays about it and writing answers to many questions. For her, reading a book was something she did not want to do because of all the other school work that had to be done with each book she read.

This is often the case in school classes. People who read are rewarded with having more work to do about the reading, rather than just being allowed to enjoy the book and go on to the next one. Teachers often have lists of questions the student has to answer about the story. These are then marked right or wrong and students are graded accordingly. The task becomes too heavy for the student, and in some cases it works against what it was originally designed for—to give some practice in reading.

It is not wrong for teachers to want to check up on students' reading to see how they are doing, but they need to do this in ways that do not go against their other goals of getting children to enjoy reading and helping them to read fluently and frequently. So instead of Rachel having to write essays about the books she had read or answer endless questions about them, we did other things. Sometimes she drew a picture of her favourite part of the story,

[5]School of the Air is a system of schooling set up by the Australian government for children who live in remote areas of Australia and cannot go to a local school. Sets of lessons are posted to the students. A set is completed and returned to the school every two weeks by post. The children's mother or a paid governess tutors them. Each weekday the children join a half hour two-way radio conversation with the rest of their classmates and have lessons over the air with their class teacher. Our two daughters did most of their primary schooling through School of the Air.

and while she was drawing we would talk about the book. Other times I would say: "tell me about a favourite part," "pick what character you would like to be and tell me why," "give me a different ending to the book," or "read me your favourite part." We would do things like that. By doing these things I was able to see if she had understood what she had been reading, and it did not give her a lot of extra work.

What teachers expect students to do must fit in with the learning task and not work against it.

Providing a range of tasks

In Australia I taught an adult migrant literacy class. Their early lessons were mostly readings of stories which they or other students had written. I did this so they could read things at a level that was not too difficult for them to read. When writing their own stories, the students used words they knew and wrote about things that were familiar to them.

They also enjoyed reading stories that I had copied or adapted from magazines and books. These stories often used words they were not familiar with and talked about things they had not experienced. Although some of these stories were quite a challenge, they introduced the students to words and expressions they would otherwise not have met. Once the students were familiar with the new words and expressions, they began to use them in their own writings. It also opened their minds to new things which they found interesting. They appreciated the comfort of being on familiar ground when reading the stories written by the students, but they also enjoyed being stretched a little beyond the known into the unknown. They appreciated having a range of materials to work with.

Appropriate materials

It is important that the materials used in the learning-teaching task are appropriate ones. The following stories illustrate the importance of having the right materials in the reading lessons.

In my adult literacy classes mentioned above I had to be very careful that the stories they were learning to read were not too difficult, and that they were appropriate for their skills and abilities. When the pieces I had chosen were too hard, it was very difficult for them to learn new things.

One translator came to me and said he wanted to begin a literacy class. But he also said that in the area where he worked the literacy classes needed to be like Bible studies, otherwise the people would not come. My response was, "that is good, why not build those reading lessons on the scripture passages they want to study?" He and his wife did this and it has been a most successful programme. In some countries, it would not be appropriate to use religious materials in literacy lessons because of government policy or restrictions.

When my daughter Natashia was young, if I wanted her to do anything around the house I would have to hide from her the books she was reading. So we were surprised one day to get a report from her teacher saying that she needed to read more at school. Why was she not reading books at school? After thinking about this we asked Natashia why she did not read much at school since she was always reading at home. Her response was, "there is nothing worth reading at school." She had read all those books a long time before.

And then there were the Hewa who, as I mentioned earlier, did not want to come to reading classes and do all those reading exercises. But they were still very interested in learning to read the published translation of the book of Mark.

Actively engaging the student in the task

Another thing to consider about the learning task is how much the student is actively engaged in the activity. For example, some teachers divide their classes into reading groups and the teacher works with one group while the other groups do reading activities. This is common practice. However, studies of what goes on in these groups have brought to light some disturbing facts.

One study showed that the teachers conducted these groups in different ways for students with different abilities. The study showed that students in the slower group spent a lot less time actually involved in reading. Teachers would spend a lot of time organizing the group and maintaining discipline—both in the group and with the rest of the class, making sure everyone in the group was at the same place in the book, and so on. Also, when the slower group was reading, teachers tended to interrupt them more often and would not allow the readers to self-correct their mistakes as often as they did for the good readers. The teachers made the slower groups spend more time sounding out words, rather than allowing them to use the surrounding meaning in the story to work out the unknown words. They concentrated on getting the students to read perfectly word by word.

The same teachers would work quite differently with a group of good readers. They gave these students more turns at reading. The teacher did not interrupt when they made a mistake but allowed them to self-correct. Students were encouraged to use the surrounding meaning to help them work out unknown words, and so on.

So the study showed that the slower students actually did less reading, when what they needed was to do more. The quality of their reading activities was poor. The gaining of meaning was not top priority, and they were not encouraged to use the reading strategies that good readers use.

Another teacher tried having the students in his class work together in groups more often so they could learn from each other as well as from him. He was pleased with how much work the students seemed to do when they were in groups. He decided to tape record a group and see how they were going. His study showed that the students, even though they looked busy, were actually spending very little time on the work that he had set. They spent a lot of time talking about things they had done outside of class, pulling other students down because of their writing or because of how they were doing things, and so on. Every now and then they would get back to the task he had set, but then their attention would wander off again on to other things. When he considered what the tape of the session had revealed, he realised that the students spent very little time actively engaged in the task he had set for them.

So it is important for teachers to consider whether or not the student is actively involved in each part of a lesson. How much time is spent sitting back and letting others do the work? How much time is actually spent in being involved in the thinking and doing which is related to the learning task.

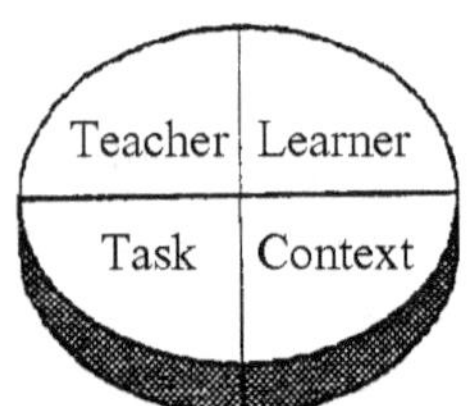

In summary, as seen by looking at these four areas of the teaching context, the situation is a very complex one. Many things influence what happens. The ideal situation is to be able to structure what the teacher does, the task that is undertaken, and the context, so that the student can learn as well as possible.

The teacher also should take into account what the student brings to the situation. This is easiest to do in one-to-one situations which are structured by very experienced teachers.

Literacy program coordinators face many problems working with previously unwritten languages. They usually have modest training and few resources. They work in isolated areas and often work with under-trained literacy class teachers. Because of these facts, what happens in classes will often have been planned well in advance. However, it is important not to loose sight of the four interrelated viewpoints that influence the teaching-learning situation, that is, the learner, the facilitator, the context, and the learning task. These four viewpoints should be taken into account in all that is done; adapting as much as possible, so that these viewpoints guide what takes place in the lessons.

3

Planning a Literacy Programme

3.1 Determining the needs

Before beginning a literacy programme it is important to find out about the literacy needs in the area so the programme can fit the needs that exist.

Sometimes it is very time consuming and unprofitable, especially in large language groups, to do literacy surveys of all locations. It is more effective to spend time doing other literacy related activities. However it is also important that the literacy program be structured to meet the needs of the community. Those needs should be real, not just things which people guess might be needed.

For example, people often say they can read, but their level of reading ability is very low and it would not be possible for them to read any scripture booklets that might be produced as part of a translation programme. Or people would say that they can read, but in actual fact they rarely pick up something and read it. Or sometimes people have told me they can or cannot read but, when I have observed them, they have done better or worse than they said they could.

There are many things a person can do to discover the literacy needs in a particular area. Some of those things are as follows.

Ask people

Often people in the local area already realize what many of their needs are. They also have a good understanding of the level of literacy in the area. They would be able to provide a lot of the information needed in order to plan a literacy programme.

Observations and 'gut' feelings

A person can learn a lot about a culture just by living in it and watching how and when people do things. Because of my experiences and involvement, I often have a gut feeling inside of me but cannot explain why I know certain things need to take place in certain ways if they are to work. I may not be able to explain my feelings until many years later when I read something about it or until I really sit down and think things through. But often my gut feelings give me good guidance.

Literacy observations may also take a more formal shape as in keeping a literacy practices diary or log. Make a note in it of anything observed that is connected with literacy. Choose a time period of say one month. Keep a diary of all literacy practices observed in daily interactions with people and in visiting people in the village. Include such things as the date, where the observations were done, what were the literacy practices observed, and what language was in use.

Here are some samples from my literacy log book that I kept in May 1994 in Midan village.

3rd May
Tok Pisin
Fellowship on our first night home.

While we were waiting for our family line to turn up for a small meal together on our return to the island after over two and a half years absence, a group of kids sang to us for about twenty minutes. There was not a songbook or piece of paper in sight. They had no need of it as they knew many many songs off by heart, with the actions...both Pidgin, English and Takia. Besides that, most of the time they were singing in the pitch dark, until the large lantern arrived from Simion's house. Even little Anna who was just over three years old was keeping up with them.

After tea, Koris and the kid's group did a family devotions for us. In our previous stays evening worship had usually been run by adult males only, using the old church hymn book in Gedged (the Church language that only the old people know), the Lutheran calendar with daily readings listed, and a Pidgin Bible. Tonight all the kids sang and Lucille read a little from what seemed to be an order of service. Then Malang read a scripture verse from the Pidgin New Testament and gave a brief talk on it. An older woman being involved was also unusual. However she is one of the few women I see reading.

Sat 7th May
Tok Pisin
TBBK Meeting

The Takia Buk Baibel Komiti met at Midan. The agenda that Malio had written out was used. Basen Babob, one of the Tok Ples Prep Skul (vernacular preparatory school) supervisors was appointed secretary. He read out the agenda points as they were needed for the Chairman and he took notes for the minutes. Most discussion was in Tok Pisin because we were present and we do not speak much Takia yet.

Tuesday May 10
Tok Pisin

I interrupted Malio at home to ask him to help Bruce to lift the logs for the top of the septic hole. He was typing a report to take up to the Circuit Conference at Bafur.

Sunday May 15th
Takia and Tok Pisin
Church service

Bubun came to visit and worship with us at the Midan church service. I took the three Takia song books with me. Malang was saying she used to have Book 3 but its cover came off and they lost all the pages. She had the Bel song book and a Tok Pisin pocket New Testament. She can read all of them well—Takia, Bel and Tok Pisin.

Bubun was cross with Bruce for not having a Calendar (Lutheran diary). How could he know the Bible readings for each day without a calendar? Bubun and Malio checked with the Calendar to get the readings for the service and Malio who chaired the service wrote notes as to hymns, etc., to use. Bubun gave the sermon, with no notes of course, and talked about the passage then handed on to Bruce and Malio to add to what he had said.

Monday 16th May
On my verandah
English

Runie came for some help with learning to read in English...Because she was shy she came with a friend and we both read together from one of the readers that were here.

Lots of folk wanted to stand around and join in but because Runie was shy I sent them away. But there was a lot of interest in what they were doing and some onlookers joined in the reading. Malang's daughter came halfway through and Malang too. When I brought out paper and pencils for the girls to write one of the sentences we had learned to read, Malang insisted her daughter wanted to join in too. I told her I was not sure I had another pencil but I was able to find one and she joined in. The girls worked much better together than individually and each helped the other.

It showed me that the minute you produce books, paper or pencils, there is a great interest in reading and writing. But as I have been seeing this week few have access to books, paper and pencils.

Friday 20th May
Afternoon, on my verandah
Takia

Tatu returned my copy of 'Big Mouth Frog' and took 'Malu and Kangkoi'. He said the children at the TPPS had enjoyed the book and he had done some activities with the sentences from the book. [Days later he told me that the other TPPS teachers in the area wanted him to bring the book to their weekly inservice and show what he had done.]

Sunday May 22nd
Church service at Simeon's
Waiting for church

Simeon gave me two stories he had written in Takia and told me what they were about in Tok Pisin. They will be very good stories for pre-school…He also edited two more stories for me.

During church

The four Bible readings were read in Tok Pisin. As the lay pastor had come to take the service all the hymns were in Bel from the Kanam book. Some of the young girls were trying to follow along in their parent's Kanam books. Kuab read the reading from Ezekiel. There were a few parts where he got hung up and some parts he had to reread. I am not sure what was causing the hassles as he seemed fluent in the other parts. It may have been that parts were not translated well, distractions from his young daughter, the pig standing right next to him, or the unfamiliar story.

Junior spent the time during the sermon going through his aunty's Tok Pisin Bible looking at all the pictures. She also had some Tok Pisin tracts inside it—one on the four spiritual laws. He counted the four numbers several times. They are learning their Takia numbers in pre-school!

After church

Simion got out an exercise book to record the offering in it. He is the keeper of the money and the records. It was neatly ruled up in columns.

May 26/28
Tok Pisin
Our house

Malio worked on the funding proposal, doing it on the computer. He polished it with Bruce...Saturday and Sunday, he worked on another funding proposal for the Midan TPPS with Tatu, one of the teachers.

These entries in my diary illustrate some of the different kinds of literacy practices that I observed. I observed people reading scripture, local stories, agendas, and minutes of meetings. I observed people writing Takia stories, agendas and minutes of meetings, reports for meetings, and funding proposals. These are just some of the things I observed.

From my literacy log book I was able to write up a summary of my observations and use examples from my log book to back up my points. Here are a few paragraphs from my summary.

Most literacy practices observed in Midan village have strong links with the Christian faith that pervades the people's lifestyle. They see God as the creator of all things, the giver of the rain and the sun to grow the crops and the provider of all food needed to sustain their bodies and make them strong for working gardens. Each evening devotion (lotu) finishes with a prayer including thanks to God for looking after them that day and providing such things for them. Other literacy practices observed outside of lotu services often seem to be related in some way to the Church work—notices of meetings, minutes, agendas, etc.

At this time, the language used in most literacy practices observed is Tok Pisin—even pre-school timetables, workshops schedules, and so on are in Tok Pisin. This could be because the language of instruction at teacher training courses is Tok Pisin. The instruction is done by non-Takia people. Also the things being written about are not local concepts but English or Tok Pisin concepts. Also none of the local typewriters have the symbol '*ŋ*' on them so if things are typed then Takia cannot be used.

Four Takia scripture portions have been published—Mark, Luke, Acts and Genesis but they were published a long time ago. Also people mention various problems about using them...There are very few of the books still around because it is at least ten years since they were published, so few people still have access to them. Also some people have not become fluent readers and writers of Takia as there have been no classes or literacy programs to support this happening for a long time. In the early mission days the mission used to teach literacy using a related vernacular and people could switch to Takia easily, but this has not been done for many years.

There seems to be little use of English literacy in the community despite community school being entirely in English and despite most children attending community school for at least 6 years. This could be because English is a foreign language and there is little need for its use here or in Madang. Takia is still the common language of communication within the language group and Tok Pisin is used when people do not speak Takia. Many of the older people do not even speak Tok Pisin. We have been told we will learn Takia much quicker if we sit with the older people because they do not use Tok Pisin and we would be surrounded by Takia.

...Most literacy practices observed were in situations of shared reading. Groups of people would read together and construct meanings of texts as they went along. The first day when I was teaching the three girls their English catch up class many others grouped around and joined in the reading, helping them along. Many others wanted to join in and it was distracting for the girls so I had to, against my better instincts, ask them to leave. But obviously reading together and learning to read together across all age groups would be an excellent strategy here—as long as the boys who misbehave were under the authority of adults.

The sharing of Lucille's letter after fellowship also demonstrated well the group construction of meanings. Because the letter was written in "Pinglish" according to Malio (a mixture of Tok Pisin and English), it was difficult to read and so people worked together to work out the meanings. When the quoted Bible reading was not found, (Mark 28 does not exist!) people started talking about what verse was meant in the letter and why, etc. People talked about the events that had led to the young man being away from the community and what had happened to him since.

...In summary then, the observations made in this time period and in this location would suggest that any literacy program that denied the existence of strong Christian values, beliefs and church work would be overlooking the majority of opportunities for the exercising of literacy practices in Takia villages. The observations also suggest that encouraging shared literacy practices and shared constructions of meanings would also be very important. The observations would suggest therefore that these two factors are vital in any Takia literacy program which wishes to encourage the use of literacy practices in normal village life.

A representative sample

Another alternative to surveying the whole area would be to survey a representative sample. For example, choose three or more households in the language group and do a household literacy profile based on those families. Use the ideas presented in the chapter on assessment and how to build a picture of students' reading abilities. Be careful when choosing the households. They should be average households for the area. The people in the households should have had about the same amount of education as others, the same amount of church training as others, and have the same amount of money and resources as others. For example, the families of pastors would not be a good example of an average household. They usually have had extra education from the church and may have had access to more books than anyone else. Families who have been able to send many of their children to schools would probably have more people in them that can read and write. Families who have more money than others may be able to afford to have more books in the home than others.

Some of the things that can be done in order to find out about the literacy abilities of the household members are listed below. Most of them are described in more detail in chapter 10.

- Familiar reading: Have the person read something of their choice, or something that they have written.
- Guided silent reading of a passage: Have a sample text that you would like them to read. Before they begin to read, tell them what the topic of the text is, and ask them to find the answer to a question about the text.
- Cued reading of a text: Ask them to read a text, but first give them a little idea of what the passage is about.
- Known words: Ask them to write down a list of words that they already know.
- Known sounds: If they are new literates, ask them to circle the sounds in the alphabet that they know.
- Text response: Ask them to read a text and write some sentences about it. Or ask them to write a text about something that has happened to them.

Talk to the members of the households about what type of reading they do. When do they use reading? For what purposes do they read? How often do they read? Record their responses. Doing these things will help build a picture of actual literacy use in these households.

It is also important to remember that household members may be literate in other languages, e.g., English, Spanish, or in PNG it may be Tok Pisin or Motu. It may be necessary to profile people's abilities in these languages. If someone can already read fluently in another language, it is much easier for them to learn to read in their own language.

Once a literacy worker has been involved in literacy in the area for quite a while and is well accepted in that role, it may be good to train local people to do a representative sample at various locations throughout the language group, especially areas where dialects change.

There is a danger in saying that because the houses surveyed did one thing then everyone in the language group will do that. There will be many other factors that influence literacy abilities and use. Closeness to schools, towns, and mission stations will influence these things. But a sample will give a good idea of how things are in a particular language area, enough to do basic planning. Remember to work closely with each community when planning literacy activities. They know their needs well.

Doing a literacy survey

A literacy survey can take many forms and the information can be collected in many ways. Some surveys require people to go from house to house collecting information. Others require people to visit perhaps five houses in each village. Some surveys ask people if they can read, in what languages, and what grade they finished at school. Other surveys expect that people will read certain texts and write certain things. While they are doing this, the surveyor observes how good that person's reading and writing skills are. Other surveys require that the surveyors make lists of the kinds of literacy practices they actually see people using.

Before doing a survey, decide what kind of information is needed and what is the best way of getting it. For example, the main goal of the survey that the Clarks did (*Read* magazine 28(1):10–17) was to find out how accurate people were in estimating their own ability to read. In doing this survey the Clarks found out that the people's self assessment was usually close to what their actual ability was. They also found out that men are better readers than women, that more men read than women, that young men are more likely to be readers than older men, and that younger women are better readers than older women. The survey also helped the Clarks make some changes to their alphabet. But the survey did not find out when people used their reading and writing skills or what types of reading and writing they were doing or needing. The survey was not designed to find out these things. After doing the survey the Clarks thought of some ways they could have improved the survey.

When thinking about doing a literacy survey, it is good to read about what others have done, what they have found helpful and what things they would do differently if they had to do a survey again.

Topics and questions that might be helpful for a literacy survey

The following list of topics and questions may be helpful in carrying out a literacy survey. These questions may bring other questions to mind. Add them to the list. If any of these questions are not applicable for an area, cross them off the list.

1. Population and dialects
   What are the approximate population figures for the language group?
   Are there different dialects of the language?
   Approximately how many people speak each dialect?
   Is it necessary to publish books in each dialect?

2. Who can read and write
   From observations of the village what appears to be the level of literacy in the language group? High? Medium? Low?
   How many people out of every hundred can read?
   How many people in each household can read and write?
   Is it just the men who can read?
   Is it just the young people?
   Can older women read?

3. Use of reading and writing skills
   How many people are seen using their literacy skills? About half of the village? About a quarter of the village? Only a few people? Often people say they are literate but do not use their literacy skills very much.
   How often are people seen reading or writing? Everyday? Only at Church?
   In what kinds of situations are people reading or writing? (See Partial List of Literacy Activities at end of this section.)
   What language were they using?

4. Previous and present schooling
   How did those who can read learn their skills?
   Have literacy classes been held in the area before? Who were they for? Were they well attended? Were they successful? Did they have any problems?
   How many community schools or government schools are there in the language area?
   How many students in the area complete Grade 6? Grade 10? Grade 12?
   Would separate literacy classes be needed for men and women?
   Do men and women do things together?
   Can men teach women? Can women teach men?

5. Feelings about books and literacy
   Are people interested in buying books?
   Do people have enough money to spend some of it on books?
   What are some general statements that are made that show people's attitudes towards literacy. Some examples of things that I have heard are: "She's too lazy to learn." "They say yes, but they do not turn up to class." "The women are too busy in the gardens."

6. Motivations for reading and writing
   Are people interested in learning to read?
   What seems to be their motivations for learning to read?
   What are the motivations among the youth? Among the men? Among the women?
   What literacy needs are people talking about?

7. Alphabet
   Is there an alphabet for the community language?
   Does the alphabet work properly?
   Are people happy with it?
   Are there any problems with it?

8. The community and the value of literacy
   What groups in the community encourage reading and writing in the community language? The village literacy committee? Bible studies? The church? Local schools?
   How do they do this?

9. Local resources
   Do the people want literacy classes?
   How do they think they could organize the classes?
   Who would teach the classes?
   Would the teachers need to be paid?
   How would the community raise the money needed to pay for literacy programmes?
   What local resources could be used to help with literacy?

Partial list of literacy activities[6]

Communication
- Writing letters to family
- Writing letters to friends
- Writing letters to society members
- Writing letters to government officials
- Writing notes and letters for others
- Reading letters received
- Writing invitations to a feast or event
- Writing down radio messages for others
- Writing graffiti

Economic
- Writing letters to ask for economic help: loans, purchases, funding proposals
- Contracts
- Mail order purchases
- Account keeping for business
- Writing receipts
- Writing checks
- Signing checks and receipts
- Keeping record of personal assets
- Keeping record of family assets

Educational
- Reading school materials (as a student)
- Writing school lessons (as a student)
- Writing educational materials (primers, etc.)

Entertainment
- Reading comics
- Reading novels, stories
- Reading poetry
- Writing stories
- Writing poetry
- Written messages in decorative art

Informational
- Reading to learn about a topic: health, agriculture, animal husbandry, etc.
- Reading a newspaper
- Reading a community bulletin board
- Writing articles for a newspaper
- Writing advertisements
- Reading advertisements
- Writing down mythology
- Writing down traditional productive lore: how to hunt, trap, grow vegetables
- Recording genealogies
- Writing down magical knowledge
- Writing announcements
- Writing one's name

Medical
- Reading medicine labels
- Reading medical texts
- Writing down traditional medical recipes
- Writing medical records

Memory supportive
- Writing lists for shopping
- Writing "To Do" lists
- Writing a diary
- Recording 'secret' knowledge, often in coded form

Social and administrative
- Keeping records of town, village affairs
- Keeping rolls/census of town, village, or area
- Writing minutes of meetings
- Reading minutes of meeting
- Writing or dictating a will
- Writing to government officials
- Keeping membership rolls of clubs, committees, societies
- Writing laws and regulations
- Reading laws and regulations
- Working out taxes

---

[6]This list was compiled by Steve Barber who works with the North America Branch of the Summer Institute of Linguistics. He emphasizes that it has been compiled to stimulate thinking. It is not by any means a complete listing.

Religious
- Public reading of scripture
- Family reading of scripture
- Private reading of scripture
- Writing sermons
- Reading sermons
- Singing from a hymnal
- Writing hymns and songs
- Writing translated scriptures
- Writing memory verse cards
- Reading religious books
- Reading prayers
- Writing prayers
- Writing down dreams, visions
- Writing spiritually encouraging letters, epistles
- Writing charms: healing, protection, love, harming enemies
- Reading charms

3.2 Designing a literacy programme: Some factors to consider[7]

There are many factors to take into account when designing a literacy program, when choosing a method of teaching reading, and when designing primers to fit these choices and situations. These factors will be different in their importance in each situation. The following list does not cover everything. Other situations may require some extra factors. But it is necessary to think through these types of things when planning a programme.

Geography of the area

The geographical features of an area will affect the planning of a literacy program. These features differ from one language group to another. Some people in PNG live on islands, some in the highlands. Some areas have road access, others need to travel by plane or helicopter. Some live on remote islands where boats call maybe once every couple of months. All these things affect what can be done in literacy and how it should be done. The Jesudasons, working with the Umanikaina people in a very remote mountainous area of PNG, were careful to choose a method that required minimal teacher training and which could be carried out under minimal supervision. They made these choices because people live in very rugged mountains and many of the walking trails have dangerous river crossings. Thus, it is difficult to get people together for long, complicated training courses and for supervisors to visit classes in remote areas.

[7]This section is part of what I presented at the Second International Literacy Consultants Seminar in Dallas in 1991. The paper has since been published (Waters 1992a).

Social organization

How people groups live affects the design of primers and literacy programmes. Some PNG groups live in large villages. On Karkar island, villages often have 400 to 600 people living in them, the largest has 1,600. In other areas of PNG people do not live in villages but live near their gardens. Others live in small hamlets, and others in small clusters of houses scattered through the bush. Some areas are organized more on a 'town' basis.

In East New Britain, the SIL team worked with the provincial government overseeing four Tok Ples Skuls and helped other SIL literacy work in the area. So the primers and materials used there are quite different from those used with the Hewa, Southern Highlands Province, where people live individually in the bush and do not live together in larger groups. Field workers there chose to live at the junction of several trails. Since the Hewas never go past a house without dropping in, the SIL team has good access to the people and opportunities for literacy work, but formal classes and programs are difficult to arrange.

It is helpful to bear in mind that such cultures as these generally have ways of organising themselves to accomplish things. We should not assume from the outset that to do literacy work it is necessary to set up additional structures. Often it is possible to work with structures that already exist and function smoothly. On Karkar the women could be encouraged to teach literacy skills through the women's groups, Sunday school teachers to teach their classes to read, motivated people within clan groups to take responsibility for teaching within their clan, and pastors to practice reading together when they meet together as part of their circuit duties, and so forth. Working this way avoids having to set up new structures. It also means that it is not necessary to find large amounts of money and personnel to get programmes off the ground and to supervise them.

History

Each people group has a history of its own, and what has happened in the past affects what is done and how it is done in the present. Many parts of PNG have had mission schools for up to a century, and many people are already literate. When they are teaching a literacy class they tend to teach the way they were taught. Many people learnt by saying something over and over again many times. In areas where this is common, it may be good to use something like repeated readings as a method of teaching reading.

When teachers trained by the Jesudasons started teaching, they used a whole language approach. However, some people outside the classes complained that the classes were not being taught properly because they were not using syllable charts. In the people's view that was the right way to teach reading because that was the way they were taught many years ago. So syllable charts were included in their readers (primers). The students often find these charts boring and skip over them to read the interesting parts of the books, but now everyone is happy.

I have heard that there have been problems with teachers drilling the story track of multi-strategy method; and in my own experience I have watched painfully as teachers drill a shared reading experience with a Big Book (sometimes called "blown up books").

Because of these kinds of historical factors, it might be necessary to fit in with the ideas people have about how things should be done as the Jesudasons did by adding the syllable charts. It may be necessary to modify programmes slightly by, for example, putting in less repetitions in the shared book times since people will tend to repeat or drill them anyway.

Educational levels

On Karkar Island, the Takia have had mission contact for one hundred years and lots of people have been taught to read, but they are not choosing to read the scripture portions that are available to them. So I have designed Takia (transfer) primers using accounts from Genesis. People there should be able to pick up the primers and teach themselves because many of them can already read in Tok Pisin or English.

Pat Lillee works with the Girawa, also of Madang Province. That language group had a literacy rate of about four percent, so she needed to start right at the beginning with basic instructional materials.

On the other hand, the Hewa of West Sepik Province took six months to learn how to "read" a picture on a page and had to be taught basics such as how to hold a pencil. This made it necessary for the Vollraths to add a prewriting booklet to the Hewa Genesis primers.

So the educational level of the people will affect the contents and approaches of both primer and programme design.

Educational levels of potential teachers also affecs the complexity of methods chosen. If there are many people with grade ten education available to train as literacy teachers and supervisors, then more complicated ways of teaching or combinations of different teaching methods can be chosen. For example, multi-strategy method combines the story track and a syllable method (workbook track); for the Dami program I recommended a combination of shared book, repeated readings, and a syllable approach. In some areas teachers have had little or no schooling, and if that is the case, methods and materials need to be kept simpler and easier for them to manage.

Another thing to remember is that if nationals are going to be designing the primers, it is necessary to choose methods of primer construction that can be easily handled by them. This is especially important where governments are calling for literacy programmes in schools or communities and there are no expatriate people involved in literacy who can help. Primers that can be easily designed are also important for National Bible Translation Organizations (NBTO) teams who do not have expatriate advisors.

Local politics

Sometimes the methods and programme choices depend on decisions made by a local committee and on how well such committees can function. On Karkar I am reluctant to get involved with Tok Ples PreSchools (TPPS) for various reasons, but I may be forced to do so if the Takia Buk Baibel Komiti decides I should.

At the time of writing, some literacy programmes in the Madang region are struggling because the committees set up to oversee them are not functioning well. Because the programmes were designed to function in a formal way under the control of the committee, this is causing problems. How well local politics functions to get things done can affect literacy programmes and should be considered before beginning work on a literacy plan. If local committees exist, then work with them and make sure there is good communication. If local committees have trouble getting things done, it may be better to structure the literacy programme more in an each-one-teach-one style. The programme must be designed to fit the situations in the area.

National politics

It has been very encouraging to see the PNG government endorsing vernacular literacy, with over 850 languages within its borders! This has not always been the case. Attitudes have shifted in recent years. At the time of writing, the government is actively promoting the use of community languages particularly in the first three years of school.

> The language of instruction for these early years of education must be common to all agents, and must not exclude the parents as educators. Research evidence indicates that children acquire literacy more effectively when they first learn to read and write in their own languages. (*A Philosophy of Education for PNG,* p. 18)

Some provinces are making it a priority to commit manpower and money to training programmes, TPPS, and vernacular components in community schools. In other provinces, governments acknowledge the national government's desire to promote vernacular literacy but are not committing resources such as people and money to help it happen yet. Progress in implementing government policies vary from area to area.

It is important to take into account national and provincial (state) policies and politics when planning literacy programmes as these can strongly affect funding, resources, training programmes, continuity, and how literacy programmes are run. In some nations governments are against community language reading programmes in the formal education system. Situations vary from place to place and country to country and must be taken into account.

Economics

The amount of money people have and are willing to spend in order to learn to read will affect what teaching methods are chosen. If people are willing to pay teachers then it is possible to plan on having formal classes and things like TPPS. In these situations, more complicated methods which require more training can be used compared with situations where there is dependence on voluntary workers. (TPPS requires more finances to set up properly.)

Gardening societies, especially those that are involved in cash cropping, are restricted as to when the people can be involved in literacy activities. Originally, the Dami decided that they would have only three terms to their school year—terms 1, 2, and 4. Third term is the season for planting gardens, so teachers and pupils are heavily involved in these activities. Communities in the highlands of PNG never run formal courses nor classes during coffee harvest season. In other areas, people hold their literacy classes first thing in the morning so that people are free to go off to the gardens for the rest of the day. Others hold classes at night because people are too busy during the day.

It is important to design programmes that fit in with local economic activities. This means things like: materials which are flexible enough to be put aside during periods when people have to be busy doing other things; and scheduling of lessons for formal teaching situations needs to be at times acceptable to the community.

Can the people afford to pay for books, or is their income totally used in meeting their basic needs? In one area the teachers give out the readers for the students to use, but the students do not get the next one until the first has been returned. In another area, people trade garden produce or artifacts for books. If people cannot afford to buy books then books that can be used over and over again need to be designed.

Motivation

The people's motivation for learning to read[8] will affect the contents of the primer and the design of the literacy programme as well as the teaching method. If their motivation is to read the scriptures then scriptures should be used in the primers. If people want to read so that they can better their lifestyle, then it would be good to use topics such as health, farming, and banking information in the primers. If people want to learn about the world around them, then primer stories need to be about other villages, other countries, other cultures and news items.

If learners do not see the link between the reading lessons and their personal motivations for learning to read, they will often give up in frustration. The Hewa started reading classes

[8]Some alternatives for BTA Literacy Programmes in Madang Region presented later in this chapter (§3.3) give suggestions for literacy programs taking into account the target audience's motivation.

using Gudschinsky-style primers, but they saw no relation between classes and learning to read the book of Mark, which was what they really wanted to do. When a whole language approach was tried using scripture as primer text, they could see the connection and got excited about reading classes.

Another translator, Bob Bugenhagen, said to me that his literacy programme had to look like Bible Studies or the people would not be interested. Dawn Clark has used Sunday school lessons for teaching vernacular literacy skills with the Sio people.

It is important to take into account the motivation of those who want to learn to read when designing primers and literacy programmes.

Target groups

The method choosen and the kinds of primer texts to be used will depend on who is going to use the primers—adults, teenagers, children, or family groups.

It is also important to know if instruction is to be in classes of people the same age, in family groups, or individually with a friend. If people are going to be teaching their friends, then choose a method that most people can handle without too much trouble and training, that is, a method in which self-teaching is the dominant strategy. If teachers are to be trained formally, more difficult methods can be used.

In early literacy classes, the Umanikaina people worked really well in mixed groups. Those learners that caught on quickly would help the slower ones without shaming them because they knew the culturally appropriate ways to help in such circumstances. In other situations, adults may wish to learn separately from children because they become embarrassed by their lack of knowledge or skill in reading.

It may also be necessary to have different reading materials for different age groups. Children may enjoy reading repetitive stories about different animals, whereas youth or adults may find them too babyish.

Learning styles

Every culture has its own way of passing on knowledge, information, and abilities. When my daughter Rachel was learning how to kill, clean, and gut a chicken, Anastasia (a national lady) came to our house. She took the chicken, showed her how to cut its throat, put it in hot water, pull the feathers, etc. She showed her rather than told her what to do. When we, being

Westerners, wanted to teach Rachel we told her how to do it. We broke the tasks down into small chunks and talked about it very exactly. Our children do not always observe, unless we focus their attention verbally.

When I was learning to make a Miwini (dillybag) at Ramingining, the women said, "You do it like this." And then they demonstrated. I found it hard to learn. They went very fast and did not explain anything. It took me a long time to work out what their fingers were doing. I am sure they thought I was a bit slow mentally. If I was teaching you to make a Miwini, I would tell you very detailed instructions. I would then show you very slowly how to do it, repeating my instructions as I did it. I would do it several times, then get you to do it again as I repeated my instructions.

Westerners tend to analyze the task that needs to be done, break it down into small chunks, talk about it a lot and sometimes demonstrate it.

The children at Ramingining, and PNG children too, learn new skills by: watching, watching, watching, imitating (copying), copying, copying, watching, imitating. They are very good at observing. They are willing to try many times and gradually get better and better at doing the things they need to do (learn by doing). Learning is done in the real life situation, not in made up or artificial situations.

How people learn best is important when choosing reading methods, primer, and programme design. Fit what needs to be taught with the ways people teach naturally. When Yasuko Nagai worked with the Maiwala and Labe people using a shared book model, they commented that the shared book approach was the way they themselves like to teach, and that it suited their style better than other methods taught in vernacular literacy workshops within the province at the time. Shared book approaches fit well in cultures that teach by doing, by observation, and by trying many times.

There are probably many other key factors that are important for any particular country or area. Literacy programme designers have always been encouraged to consider such factors in literacy programme design, but people often forget to make decisions about teaching methods and what goes in the primers with these things in mind also.

It is a good idea to summarize the key factors for a particular area so these can be kept in mind when planning. The following chart shows an example summary of a language group in PNG. An empty chart is included for the reader's use.

This chart gives an example from a language group I am familiar with.	
Geography	2 islands, road access on one island. People do get together for courses, etc. 2nd island remote, needs simpler method, less supervision
Social organisation	Will need to be village based programme, work through existing church and school structures
History	100 years of mission, some can read, don't see many people (other than pastors) reading Want TPPS for their children to learn as they used to learn in the old mission days
Education levels	Community schools to Gr 6 on island. High School other side of island. Common that students complete Gr 10. A few go further. People say the Sunday School Teachers will train to teach TPPS.
Community support	A lot of talk, not sure how much action, varies from community to community.
Provincial/State support	Province very supportive, Non Formal Education Officer all for it. Some funds may be available. Beginning its own teacher training programmeme, need to fit in with them.
National support	Government is very supportive and encouraging vernacular in first three grades of school.
Economics	People spend most of their money on salt, kerosene, rice, tin fish, clothes, school fees. Not much money for anything else. Will trade food for books. Will build schools free. Some will teach without pay.
Motivation	Adults: want to read scripture. Children: to improve their education
Target groups	Women: low literacy rate. Grade 6 completers. First three years of school. Pastors.
Learning styles	Learn by doing, successive approximations of the real thing, informal, supported learning—a friend or relative.

This chart is for you to write about your area's literacy needs.

Geography	
Social organisation	
History	
Education levels	
Community support	
Provincial/State support	
National support	
Economics	
Motivation	
Target groups	
Learning style	

3.3 A typical programme

There are many different kinds of literacy programmes so it is hard to talk about a typical programme and give examples of all the things that need to be done and planned. But in thinking about planning a literacy programme, it is good to consider what things are usually done in literacy programmes in order to decide what needs to be done and what does not need to be done

Considerations when planning a total literacy programme

The following list gives examples of things that should be considered in a literacy programme in Papua New Guinea. The list is not necessarily complete. It was written in early 1991 and since then government policy has changed to include more vernacular in the first three years of school. The list does show that it is necessary to think of all members of the local community when planning a programme and make sure that the needs of each group will be met—children, women, youth, adults, people who can already read in one language and want to transfer to another, and people who need to read in public situations such as church. It may be helpful to go through the list and use it to make a list of the things that need to be done in a specific area.

1. Vernacular preparatory school (Tok Ples Prep School)
    - meaning-based pre-reading materials
    - primers and 10 to 20 books per term
    - teacher's guides
    - teaching aids
    - full teacher training
    - non-literacy subjects—curriculum, materials and training
2. Vernacular component in schools
    - approximately 2 hours per week in community schools
    - books to read to the students, grades 1–6
    - primer materials for early grades
    - materials for older grades
    - some teacher training
3. Adult reading class
    - primers (approximately 5)
    - supplementary readers
    - scripture portions
    - teacher training

4. Reading fluency
    - adult reading clubs
    - youth reading clubs
    - new materials available
5. Transfer of reading skills from one language to another
    - primers for youth
    - primers for adults
    - transfer to national or trade language
    - transfer from national or trade language
6. Using literacy in daily living
    - for some communities the focus may be on Scripture-in-use (encouraging people to read and use scripture materials). This could be done through Bible study materials, Sunday school materials, pastors classes, cassettes and non-print media, hymn book and liturgy, non-biblical materials like "How the Jews lived," and so on.
    - For some communities the focus may be on agriculture, forestry, small scale village industries, education, information, health, or social aspects.
    - or a combination of these things.
7. Courses
    - teacher training courses
    - writer's workshops
    - literature production training courses

After thinking about these things, it is also necessary to consider if the community has the manpower, the willingness, and the ability to do each of these things. Sometimes it is necessary to settle for less than the ideal, or less than what should be done. It is better to bite off a mouthful that a community can chew rather than to choke by trying to bite off too much. Also remember that these things do not all have to be done at once. A planner may choose to start with one thing that can be achieved and make it successful and then gradually add the other things that need to be done as people become trained and available to help.

For example, some SIL teams do not feel they have the time or ability to help foster literacy programmes that cover so many things. Others do not feel it is necessary in their area.

Maybe the people who want to learn to read already know how to read and just need a little help here and there. For a literacy programme to be finished or successful, there must be opportunities and materials available to those who want to learn to read now and also for future generations. There should be a plan that will enable the programme to keep on going on its own for as long as is needed.

Adequate literacy programme

Again, the following list is just a suggestion. It was compiled with people in mind who do not feel they can do a full literacy programme for various reasons and attempts to answer the question, "What *must* I do?"

1. Village or household classes
   - primers based on what it is that people want to read using an each-one-teach-one method
   - two hours teacher training, with refresher courses and apprenticeship-style of training
   - some cultural stories and news item type stories
   - hymn book
   - scripture portions
2. Literacy clubs
   - or some way of encouraging people to keep using literacy skills in their daily lives
3. Vernacular component in grade 6 (optional)
   - This encourages those who are learning to read in another language to transfer their reading skills to the community language.

BTA[9] literacy programmes in Madang

In 1990 I was asked, "What should BTA teams be doing in literacy work in the Madang region of PNG?" I developed the following list, "Some alternatives for BTA literacy programmes in Madang Region." I have included the list in this section because it may be helpful in planning other literacy programmes. My response to the question was that "it depends." It depends on a lot of factors, some of which are mentioned in §3.2. The BTA list takes into account the motivation of the groups who have been identified as wanting literacy, the ages of the people involved, and what materials would be needed to provide programmes for them, given their age and motivation.

---

[9]The Papua New Guinea Bible Translation Association.

Some alternatives for B.T.A. literacy programmemes, Madang Region, Papua New Guinea

TARGET GROUPS

MOTIVATION		ADULTS	PASTORS	YOUTH	CHILDREN
	SCRIPTURES	Scripture-based primers Hymn book Bible study materials Continuing trickle of translated scriptures	Scripture-based primers Hymn book Liturgy Topical studies and sermon outlines	Scripture-based primers Hymn book and chorus book Scripture-in-use materials such as scripture studies, puzzles, activities Bible studies Christian biographies	Sunday school primers Hymn book, chorus book, song charts Bible society new reader series
	CULTURE	Primers based on cultural stories Reading clubs		Primers based on cultural stories Continuing trickle of books to read and game and puzzle books Reading clubs	Phonics reader Alphabet books Primers based on cultural stories Follow-up reading books
	EDUCATION	Transfer to English materials Some mathematics	Transfer to English How to use English commentaries and sermon helps	Transfer to English	*Tok Ples Prep Skul:* Literature-based reading programme: 10–20 stories/term Big Books, song charts - - - - - - - - *Vernacular Component:* Big Books, song charts 10 stories per term 1 writing or activity book

3.4 Literacy for adults

Adult literacy work is quite different from teaching children to read and write. Children's literacy classes are often formal ones in a school setting. Adult classes are often informal ones on a village house verandah, on a rug under a shade tree, or in the village church. Children usually attend their classes very regularly, but adults have many other responsibilities so that they often miss classes or can only attend classes for a short time in the day. Children come to class because that is what children do at a certain age, and they are willing to 'waste' time doing things that do not seem to be connected with reading and writing. Adults come to class with a specific purpose in mind, and if they cannot see the relevance of what they are doing in class to what they want to learn, they will soon stop coming. Children enjoy different types of reading games and materials. Adults will come to reading classes wanting to read specific types of books. They may think some books are too childish for them. They may think some books have been written in a way that is all right for children but not for adults. For example, many Australian easy-reading books are about things that only teenagers are interested in. Adult learners are not interested in reading these.

Children come to classes expecting they will eventually learn to read and write. Adults often come to class wondering if they will ever be able to learn to read and write. After all they have not learned in all their earlier years, so they think that maybe their heads are too hard to learn now. Some adults have tried to learn to read before and have not been able to.

> Their memories are often ones of failure, of humiliation, when they could not read out loud, when they could not spell a word, when they got no meaning from what they were supposed to be reading. Gradually their sense of alienation from the printed word became cemented and they began to receive the message that they were failures, and to perceive themselves that way. (Campbell 1991:10)

Children come to class because it is what children do. Adults come to class because they enjoy the time of being together as a group and doing things together.

In §2.1 I told the story of Debbie. Her story reminds those of us who are involved in adult literacy classes that adults need to be in charge of their learning.

> We were doing things to her and for her. She was going along but it would be an exaggeration to say she was enthused...One day, she had had enough, or was sufficiently confident to assert herself, and said what she really wanted to do was to write to her brother. (Aileen Treloar, class notes)

Adult learning situations should not be ones where the person teaching is seen as doing things to and for the students in the manner in which they were done to Debbie. Care should be taken to think about the backgrounds of the students. What has made them come to learn? What are their goals? How can the teacher help them? They are adults and the person teaching has no right to make decisions without talking things over with them. Teachers should remember that although these people do not know how to read or write, they are very capable at operating in the world around them, in making decisions, in knowing their minds.

> ...because the Blues [those in the blue group, the poor readers] of this world must depend heavily on the spoken word and wordless communication to get to know themselves and their fellows, it does not follow that their world is lacking in strength and colour. (Nelson 1989:6)

Before any learning situation can be planned, the literacy worker should spend time thinking about the adult learners who will be participating in the programme. What have been their previous experiences with formal learning, with reading, and with writing? What are their expectations, misunderstandings, and fears?

One headmaster at a school in Arnhem Land, Australia, attempted to provide classes for Aboriginal adults in the community. He organised the building of a small covered classroom area with lockable storage shed and blackboard for their use. It was built in the school grounds but off to one side for easier access for the adults. The community advisor said that it would never be used because the adults would never go inside the school ground for lessons. They would not put themselves into a situation which they felt was for children. His comments proved to be accurate, and adults never went there for classes.

When working with adults it is important to understand how they feel and think about things. This might affect such things as where and when classes are held and who attends classes together. It is important that the classes are held where the adults are comfortable, a place where they feel no shame about being involved. This will be different for different people and different cultures. The Aboriginal people in Arnhem Land worked best in the groups in which they usually hunted together or worked together or in kinship groups. Bob and Salme Bugenhagen found that the Siasi people of PNG wanted literacy instruction in all-age, all-level groupings.

Sometimes people feel that they will learn just by sitting in class and being present during class activities. People who have come from cultures where their usual learning styles are informal ones often feel this way. Informal learning is fairly passive and happens without them thinking much about it. This leads some people to expect that by following the rituals in the class, they will learn. They won't have to "think about it."

Adults who think this way need to be shown that learning requires them to do some hard work.

Adults often have an idea in their minds of what class will be like, especially when it comes to reading and writing. Daniel and Wei Lei Jesudason found this to be the case with one group in PNG. They had chosen to use a whole language approach to the teaching of reading, but had to modify their approach to include syllable charts. The lessons were changed to fit in with the people's ideas of what the lessons should be like, and those who wanted to do the drills did them.

We found the people of North East Arnhem Land were very hesitant to write without having a dictionary at hand. They were very worried that they might make a spelling mistake. They thought that pieces of writing must be spelled perfectly the first time they wrote them. Mary Stringer found a similar thinking in her adult literacy classes in PNG. She worked very hard to overcome this barrier and eventually did so. The people began to write more freely. It is very important to know what adults are thinking about the learning tasks, and to help them understand what they need to do. It is also important to help them realize that their efforts will not always be perfect but are steps to learning the task at hand.

As well as having ideas about how classes should be run and what is done in class, adults may also be worried about their success. Any worries students may have need to be understood and talked about. Teachers need to be sensitive in what they do and expect their students to do. There needs to be a lot of encouragement and an expectation that they will learn. Group learning can be a real help here. Learning and doing things as a group takes a lot of pressure off the individual to do things totally on their own ability. Beth Marr has found that this has been really helpful with adult math classes in the inner suburbs of Melbourne. She has found students working in a group are more willing to attempt learning tasks which require skills that are harder than what they feel capable of, or harder than what they would attempt if they were working independently. People can help each other in whatever needs to be done.

At all times when working with adults, remember that they have their own ideas, their own worries, and their own goals, and that the teacher is there to help them in the best way possible.

When planning a literacy programme, who are the people who should be given most consideration? Adults, or children? The answer to this question is always "the adults." They are the decision-makers of the community. They may not be the easiest group to start with, but once they have become successful readers they will then make sure that others learn too.

3.5 Literacy for children

As I said before, children's literacy classes are often formal ones. It depends on the situation in each area as to what the classes will be like.

In Papua New Guinea, some villages choose to run a Tok Ples Prep Skul (TPPS), a school in their community that children attend before they go to the schools run by the government. In these schools they concentrate on teaching the children how to read and write in the language of the community first before they go to the government school where teaching is done in a national or trade language. It is much easier to teach someone to read in their own language first and then for them to learn in other languages. TPPS's are good ways of doing this. But it should be remembered that prep schools need a lot of time, money, and commitment both to set up and to keep them running.

The people of some villages choose to teach their children to read and write in the village language during their Sunday school classes. The scripture lessons for the day and the activity sheets are all in the village language and the children are taught to read them.

Children's literacy classes need different materials than those materials used for adults. The stories and books need to suit the children's interests. They need to be ones that hold the children's attention. They need to be shorter. And they need to have interesting illustrations in them that help the children to understand the story and also capture and hold their interest. Sections 5.1 and 8.3 of this book give ideas of different kinds of materials that are suitable for use with children.

Some village people feel the children will learn to read and write at the government schools and that it is easy enough for the children to teach themselves how to read in the village language later on. Or they think that the children will learn informally from family members who can already read. In cases like these, a formal literacy programme for children would probably not be needed.

It is important, when planning a literacy programme, to consider how the children are going to learn to read in their own language. Are they already learning without formal programmes in place or do they need some type of formal programme? All these things need to be discussed with the decision-makers in the targeted area.

3.6 Literacy for youth

The youth in the village have often learned to read in another language and have taught themselves to read in the community language. The main focus in working with youth in these types of situations is to give them opportunities to maintain and improve the reading skills that they already have. They may need help to become fluent readers. It is also good to build a group that focusses on reading and writing as a shared activity—something the youth can do together and enjoy.

The types of materials the youth need will be different again from those that children enjoy. A favourite Tok Pisin book in our village on Karkar is the story of Nicky Cruz. The young people enjoy the book as it talks about a rascal who became a Christian, how his life was changed, and how he started to help others. When the Gulf War was going on in 1991, everyone was following the radio news and talking about what would happen and whether a world war would result. When planning a literacy programme for youth, find out what they are interested in reading about. Young people are interested in stories from other areas, other cultures, and other countries, especially stories that are true.

If possible involve the young people in writing books in the village language. These books could be designed for children to enjoy or they could be for other youth to enjoy. They may like to read books in the national language and re-tell the stories in their own language for others to read.

Sometimes the youth like to get together for weekly Bible studies and singing. This presents a good opportunity for them to use Bible study materials that are based on the scriptures that have been translated. They might like to be involved in the actual preparation of Bible study materials—taking the scriptures, discussing them, and coming up with questions or focus sentences that could be used as the starting point for discussions by themselves or by other groups. On Karkar I suggested that one fellowship group prepare studies on one book and then swap them with those prepared by a neighboring group on a different book. Each group can then give suggestions for improvements in the work of the other group and talk about the things that were good in the studies.

When planning a literacy programme do not forget the youth of the area. They are the future decision-makers. But remember when working with youth it is important to find out what their goals and interests are and use materials and activities that fit in with them.

Do not prepare materials thinking that they will meet everyone's needs because probably they will not. Think about the target groups, whether or not they need materials, and if they do, what materials would be suitable.

3.7 Transfer materials

In some literacy programmes it is necessary to develop transfer materials. Often people learn to read in one language but want to be able to transfer their reading skills to other languages that they speak. In some language groups people have been taught to read in a trade language or church language and they want to read in their own community language. In some groups, people have learned to read in their community language and they also want to read materials in a trade language, or they want to be able to read and write in the language used in the schools.

Sometimes people do not make special books for transfer lessons. They just hold fluency classes or reading clubs. People who can already read get together in small groups and practice reading together. They start with easy stories first and as they build up their confidence they gradually try harder and harder texts.

Sometimes people design primers to help people transfer their reading and writing skills from one language to another. These are called transfer primers. In doing this, remember to start with what the students already know, and build on that. Gradually introduce the things that they do not know. Sometimes it is not possible to do this, because the new letters may be ones which occur very frequently in any text.

Start by talking about the letters that are the same sounds in both languages.

Give the students practice in using the letters that they already know in the language that they are learning.

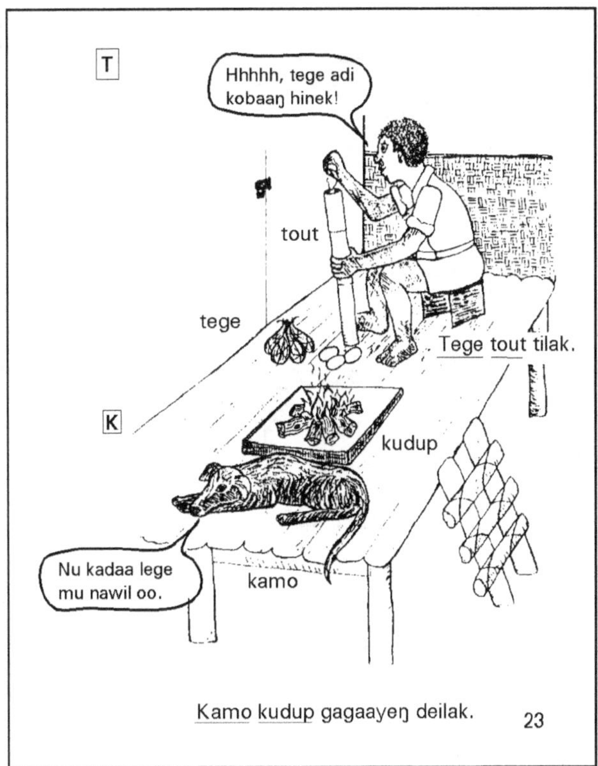

Have some easy-to-read stories for them to practice reading.

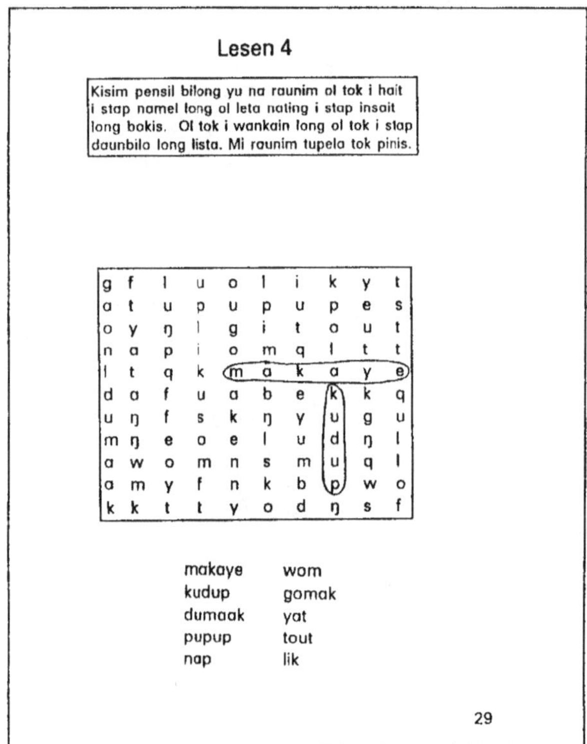

Lesen 4

Kisim pensil bilong yu na raunim ol tok i hait i stap namel long ol leta nating i stap insait long bokis. Ol tok i wankain long ol tok i stap daunbilo long lista. Mi raunim tupela tok pinis.

g f l u o l i k y t
a t u p u p u p e s
o y ŋ l g i t o u t
n a p i o m q l t t
l t q k m a k a y e
d a f u a b e k k q
u ŋ f s k ŋ y u g u
m ŋ e o e l u d ŋ l
a w o m n s m u q l
a m y f n k b p w o
k k t t y o d ŋ s f

makaye	wom
kudup	gomak
dumaak	yat
pupup	tout
nap	lik

29

Include some activities that are fun to do.

Gradually introduce new letters of the alphabet of the language the students are learning.

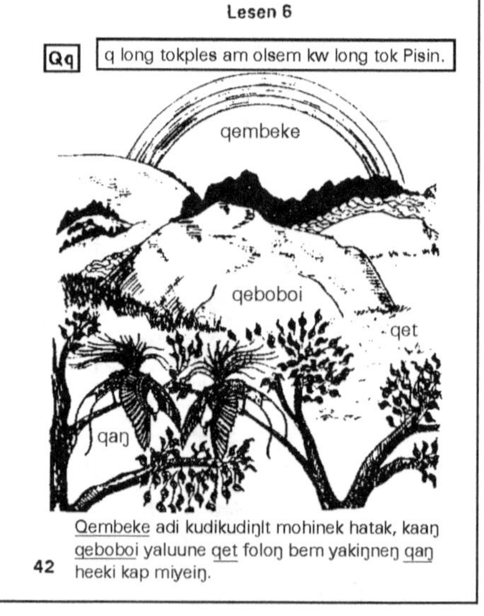

Lesen 6

Qq q long tokples am olsem kw long tok Pisin.

Qembeke adi kudikudiŋlt mohinek hatak, kaaŋ qeboboi yaluune qet foloŋ bem yakiŋneŋ qaŋ heeki kap miyeiŋ.

42

Include some short stories for the students to practice reading.

Lesan 15 (pgs 53, 54)

Nau ritim dispela tok

1. Du nak yaawiyat ye baalé viyaadén viyat. Viyaatake déku duwat waadéka yaadatan. Yna baalé kérae yaate waabule gayot kure yédatan. Kure ye taakadaraka gaan kwaagéidéka waabule kérae yaate kure ye yaawi maaléba yan saamuke waba tudaran. Tulake kaata kérae kure ye raadaran. Raatake matu tuwe baakaaran. Baake kadoran.

Sometimes people want to transfer their reading, writing, and speaking skills to another language that they do not speak. This is much harder. They are learning to read in another alphabet and they are learning another language at the same time.

4

Reading

4.1 The reading debate

In 1820, in Hartford, Connecticut in the United States, Rev. Thomas Gallaudet was nearing the end of a long and dedicated teaching career with deaf and dumb children. He had worked hard to find a way of teaching these children to read so that they could read the Word of God. When he retired, he thought the method that he had developed would work well in the common schools that were being set up at that time. This led him to write the book, *A Mother's Primer*, in which he set out the whole-word method of instruction.

The book found its way to the city of Boston, Massachusetts. The people there were setting up and expanding a school system for children of people in the poorer section of the community. Some of these classes used his method but there was a lot of debate about it. The popular way of teaching reading at the time was for the children to learn the names of the letters and their sounds, then gradually blend the sounds into words and learn all the phonic rules about those sounds. Gallaudet's word method taught children to recognize words by sight only. Some schools experimented with his method. Others were very critical of it.

In 1885 and 1886 Catell published two papers, the results of his research. The first was on reaction time, the second on letter and word perception. From this time on, scientific research began to influence the way reading was taught and the debates about teaching reading.

It wasn't until the 1950s that the reading wars heated up. Rudolf Flesch's book *Why Johnny Can't Read* (1955) brought it all to the surface. In 1967 Jeanne Chall published her study, *Learning to Read: The Great Debate*. She had looked at several different reading approaches. From her studies she recommended a concentration on decoding skills, that is, teaching the child phonics and the blending of sounds to help them work out what the words were saying.

Predictably, those who preferred the whole-word or sight-word approach to teaching reading replied with research and statistics of their own to show they had good reasons for teaching reading their ways.

From then on a number of people from the discipline of Linguistics joined the debate. In 1968 Kenneth Goodman published *The Psycholinguistic Nature of the Reading Process.* In 1971 Frank Smith published *Understanding Reading*. These two writers and others who have followed their thinking have had a profound impact on the teaching of reading and have supported the use of whole language approaches.

In 1983, The National Institute of Education created a Commission on reading and issued its report in 1985, titled *Becoming a Nation of Readers*. It was answered by a book *Counterpoint.* These two books represented the two sides to the argument-which is the best way to teach reading-phonics or whole language

Similar things were happening in Australia and New Zealand. In the 1970s people such as Don Holdaway and Marie Clay promoted the whole language approach to teaching reading, and many teachers have followed their example.

And so the controversy that started in the 1830s continue!

4.2 Ways of teaching reading

People have been arguing over what is the right way to teach reading for years and years. Many people have written books about it, done research about it, governments have funded commissions about it, and the great debate continues. But I think through these debates and arguments people have lost sight of the overall goal.

There is a saying that there is more than one way to skin a cat. Not that I have ever seen anyone skin a cat. But I do believe there is more than one way to teach people to read. Some of these ways are represented on the continuum below.

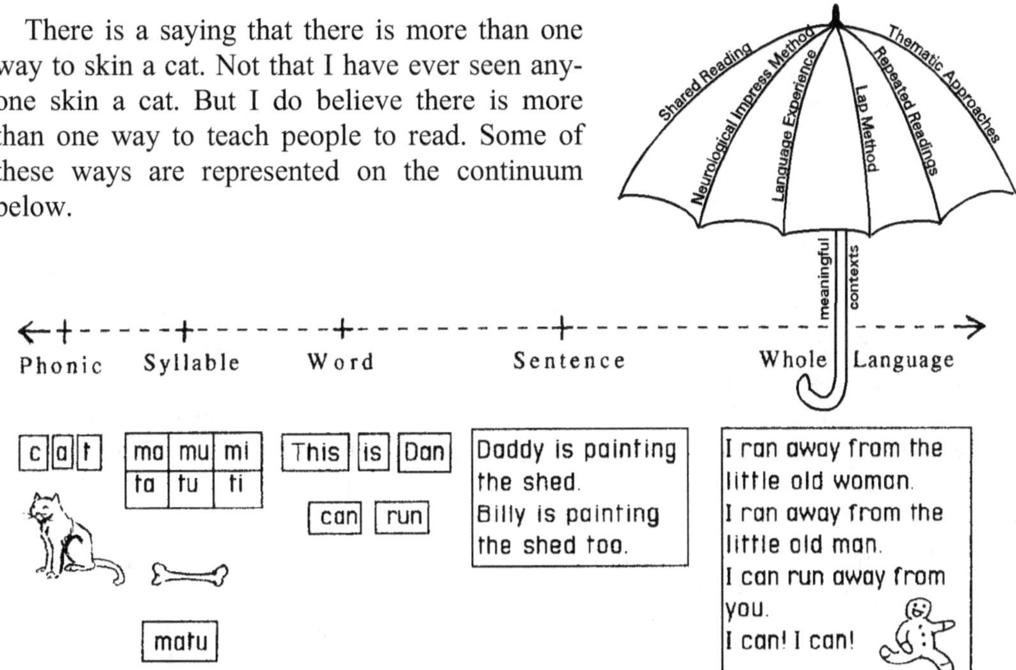

At a reading theory workshop in PNG in 1991, I set the participants the task of planning a reading program using just the phonics approach. They were very frustrated and concluded that no program uses only one way of teaching reading. They all use many ways combined together.

Marilyn Jager-Adams, a strong supporter of the teaching of reading using phonics, also stresses the need for teaching that reading is gaining meaning from print. McCracken and McCracken would class themselves as belonging to the whole language side of the continuum, but they encourage a five-minute session every day where they teach spelling through phonics. (They do this in an uncomplicated way that I feel would be excellent for village literacy classes. See §12.2.) So although they promote whole language they still teach phonics.

I think that such educators as these have helped to put things in proper perspective. It should not be phonics versus whole language, or phonics versus word, or syllable versus whole language, but a recognition that each way of teaching reading has something important to contribute. The different reading skills need to be taught in a balanced way, i.e., skills linked with reading for meaning.

Many literacy teachers and literacy programmes use combinations of these ways of teaching. When they are combined, they are often known as eclectic methods. For example, Sarah

Gudschinsky's method[10] combines the syllable method, word method, and the use of connected reading material. The multi-strategy method[11] combines the syllable method and word method in the workbook track and also uses various whole language strategies in the story track. Teachers who use mainly whole language methods often teach phonics, especially when it comes to the spelling lesson.

When my eldest daughter wanted to learn to read, I taught her with the word method using the *Ladybird* books. She learned to read very quickly and has been an avid reader ever since. When it came time for her sister to learn to read, she was taught at school with the "Break Through to Literacy" method, also a word method. She was totally frustrated until she had a change of teachers. The new teacher used some phonics teaching (learning of sounds) and then she was alright.

When I was teaching in the classroom I tried to use as many different approaches as possible as I knew that some children learn to read more easily with one approach than others. I used phonics, language experience approach, word approach, shared reading, etc. It is good to combine several ways of teaching reading in a reading programme.

New ways of teaching reading come and go and every few years there seems to be something new that is supposed to be better than all the others. Sometimes they are just things that teachers have been doing naturally for years called by another name, or new combinations of old things. Sometimes some really good things have been developed.

Sometimes people show me their reading materials that have been developed by a lot of hard work over a long period of time and say they feel that they should throw it all away and start over, using more modern methods. My first question to them is, "Does it work? Are people learning to read using your materials?" Often they look at me with relief in their eyes and say, "Yes, they do." "Then why throw out all that hard work?" is my response. "But can you see ways the materials can be improved? Can you add more time for shared reading here and process writing there?" Existing materials and programmes can be improved to make them work better, but there is no need to throw them away and start over again whenever a new fashion comes along.

When new things come along and people are pushing them with great enthusiasm, it is easy to feel one must do things the new way. Maybe they have the right answers. But remember that there is no **one** right way of teaching reading. The question is, what is the right way for any one community given all the factors involved. (This is discussed in chapter 3, Planning a Literacy programme.)

---

[10]See *A Manual for Pre-Literate People,* a collection of lectures and seminars given by Gudschinsky on how to use the method she developed.

[11]Mary Stringer and Nicholas Faraclas present their method in their book, *Working Together for Literacy.*

Do not get caught up in the reading methods controversy. Instead, try to understand how students learn to read, some good ways of teaching them to read, and know what kind of balance is needed in the reading lesson. Think about how much time should be devoted to each part in the reading lesson to give the students the best chance of achieving their goal of learning to read.

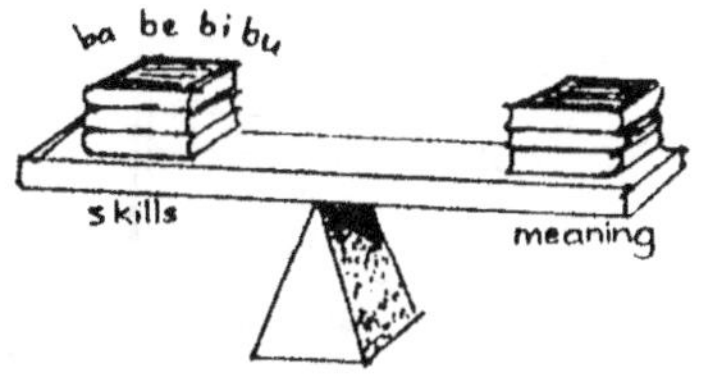

A balanced reading programme

4.3 What is reading?

Reading is deciphering an abstract code

The marks on the page of a letter, a newspaper, a magazine, or a book represent a message that someone has put there for someone else. The marks are sometimes called the code. Those marks carry meaning and it is this meaning, the communication, that is conveyed from one person to another that is important. The skill of getting meaning from symbols on a page is sometimes called decoding. While a student may be able to sound out some of the words of the message and decode the letters to make sounds, unless he can decode the total message that the writer is sending, then reading has not taken place. Reading is about getting meaning from the printed page, and understanding the message that is being communicated by the print.

Reading is like driving a car[12]

When you drive a car, in order to get from one place to another, a lot of things are happening at the same time. Reading is like that too. When you read a book or a message, a lot of things are happening in order for you to be able to understand the message of the marks on the page.

In order to drive a car and in order to read, there are a few things that need to be available. See the following comparisons:

[12]This idea came from reading Adams 1991:3-5.

<table>
<tr>
<td>Driving
No fuel,
no driving
</td>
<td>Reading
No print,
no reading

</td>
</tr>
<tr>
<td>• You can have a good car, a licence, know how to drive well, and have a map showing you where to drive, but without fuel in the car you cannot drive very far.</td>
<td>• Similarly you can have people who are really keen to read, classes set up, teachers trained but if you have no print, then no reading can take place.</td>
</tr>
<tr>
<td>• Fuel is very important in the driving process.</td>
<td>• Print is very important in the reading process.</td>
</tr>
<tr>
<td>• The more fuel you have the further you can drive.</td>
<td>• The more print you have, the further you can go in the reading process.</td>
</tr>
<tr>
<td>• It is important to have the right quality fuel.</td>
<td>• It is important to have the right quality books.</td>
</tr>
</table>

Driving	Reading
No driver, no driving	No reader, no reading

• Without a driver the car does not get very far.	• Without a reader, the message stays in the book, magazine, or letter.
• The driver brings various things to the driving task.	• The reader brings various things to the reading task.
• He brings the key that unlocks the system and allows the car to be started up.	• His eyes are like the key, they unlock the system and allow information to start flowing.
• He brings certain knowledge with him about the driving task.	• He brings certain knowledge with him about the world and the reading task.
• He brings his knowledge of how to drive and the driving skills that he has learned.	• He brings knowledge of how to read and the reading skills that he has learned.
• All his experiences of past driving as a passenger and as a driver are there to help him, especially in difficult circumstances.	• All his past experiences of getting meaning from messages, spoken and written, are there to help him, especially in difficult circumstances.

When driving or reading is in progress there are various things happening at the same time, a lot of systems working together.

Driving	Reading
Systems working together	Systems working together
 	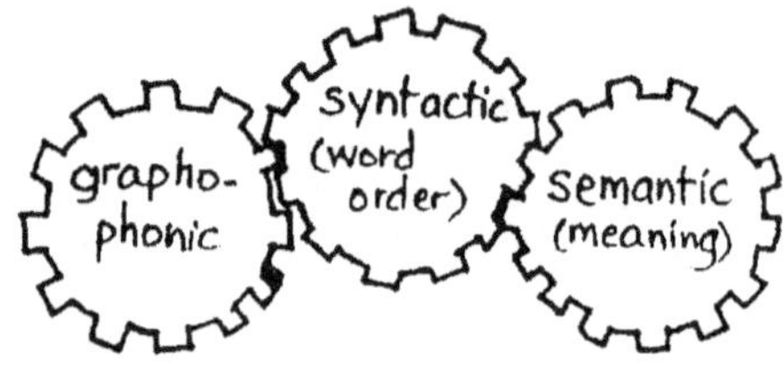
There are a lot of things working together underneath a car to keep it running-pistons, spark plugs, crankshaft, battery, starter motor, wheels, radiator, fan belt, differential, etc. Some of these things can malfunction a little and the car will keep going with a little effort, but sooner or later there will be a breakdown.	There are a lot of things working together in the head of the reader to help him gain meaning out of the print-what is seen with the eye, the sounds that the symbols bring to mind (grapho-phonic correspondences), knowledge of the language, word order, meaning of the rest of the print surrounding that word, predictions that can be made about that word, etc.

Providing the fuel and giving the driver access to the vehicle are the first steps in being able to drive. After that, if driving is to continue, then the vehicle's systems and the driver's skills must keep working smoothly; there must be no breakdowns in either of these. Have you ever driven with a new driver? Sometimes he has not worked out all the systems and got them running smoothly together. To improve, new drivers need practice.

Reading is like that. For students to continue reading there must be a lot of things for them to read. Also, the systems and skills that are used in reading must work smoothly with no breakdowns. If readers never learn to read smoothly, they will not enjoy reading and will soon get tired of trying. practicing the skill of driving over and over ensures it becomes smooth, effortless, and enjoyable. The same is true for reading.

The goal of reading is for the reader to construct meaning by looking at print. When a reader does this he uses many systems. Teachers of reading should encourage students to use all of the skills and systems that are involved in this task. (Some of the systems he uses are his knowledge of phonics, letter shapes, grammar of the language, word order, and so forth.)

So far in this section, I have covered the topic "What is reading" very briefly in order to give you an overview. There are many complex, interrelated issues that affect reading and people's learning to read.

4.4 How do people learn to read?

The four reading stages

There are four stages involved in the reading process. They can be called: reading readiness, reading with someone else's help (sometimes called mediated reading), the magic moment, and fluency. I discuss each of these stages below.

Reading readiness. The first stage is when the students are getting ready to read. They are learning things about reading but not actively engaged in trying to work out what the marks on the page are saying, that is, they are not breaking the code of the printed message (decoding).

With young children, this stage can begin at about six months of age and may extend for many years depending on factors which vary from child to child, from village to village, and from country to country. How long adults take to move through this stage depends on factors such as how much exposure they have had to the world of print and books, their motivation, and the opportunities open to them to be involved in reading-like activities.

In chapter 5 I discuss the types of things that can be done to help students become ready to learn to read. All the activities mentioned in that chapter lead up to the moment when the students themselves are ready to learn how to break the code and get meaning from the print. They need to learn such things as:

- how to hold the book the right way
- how to turn the pages carefully
- print has meaning
- the pictures say the same things as the text
- the need to look at the print when reading
- the print is in chunks, words, and sentences and each chunk has meaning
- the same print always says the same thing
- the print goes from one side of the page to the other
- reading is fun

When the students have come to understand these things about the reading task, they are then ready to move on to the next stage.

Reading with someone else's help (mediated reading). Seymour Itzkoff uses the term "mediated reading" in his book *How We Learn to Read.* He states that "mediated reading is a...stage in the process of learning to read that follows reading readiness...Through mediated reading the child is acquainted with the visual-letter-word equivalents of his/her natural language" (1986:83).

It is during this stage that the student begins to understand the relationships between letters and their sounds, between groups of letters and the word they make up, and between words and the meanings that they bring to the reader. Usually these connections are taught by a teacher or someone who can already read. That is, the teacher is the go-between, the mediator.

The magic moment. Itzkoff uses the term "the magic moment" to talk about the time when the many systems involved in the reading process have developed to a stage when they begin to function well together and the student is suddenly able to read. For the student, this is definitely a magic moment.

Fluency. Once things have 'clicked into place' for the student and he has become able to read, then the student can become a fluent reader. He can learn to read smoothly, can gain meaning from the print without a lot of trouble, and can use the meaning gained to understand the next part of the text. Fluency is gained from a lot of practice in reading.

Three essentials for gaining fluency

Each of the above four stages require three things without which it is very difficult for students to achieve the final goal of fluent reading. Holdaway says that sharing books is the main ingredient in teaching children to read. He maintains that it is necessary to provide a supportive literacy environment for this task, one which includes a large supply of reading materials, regular opportunities to hear books read aloud, and an adult who enjoys reading and responds to the readers' questions about books and print.

For reading programmes to be successful, it is important to have the three essentials listed below to help students learn to read.

- a large supply of reading materials
- regular opportunities to hear books read aloud
- an adult who enjoys reading and responds to the reader's questions about books and print

There should be things worth reading so that people will want to learn to read. If materials are few, or not worth reading, then people will have no desire to read. There should be a lot of things to read so people can keep practicing their reading skills and gain good levels of fluency. If not, they will revert to illiteracy after the initial literacy campaign has ended. An adult who enjoys reading and reads well can help others learn to read and will continue to motivate, encourage, and help people along the path to independent fluent reading.

Five helps for teaching reading

The following five suggestions have been found to be helpful when teaching reading.

Read to the learner. "A large part of the educational research and practice of the last twenty years confirms conclusively that the best way to produce a reader is to read to him, both in the home and in the classroom" (Anderson et al. 1985:23).

"There is no substitute for a teacher who reads good stories to children. It whets the appetite of children for reading, and provides a model of skillful oral reading. It is a practice that should continue throughout the grades" (Anderson et al. 1985:51).

In many developing countries, people are not exposed very much to print nor to reading in the home or village. Reading programmes in such areas should take this into account and build times into the reading programme for reading aloud to the student. This should be done even more than is the case in programmes in developed countries. The teacher needs to help make up for all the experiences that are not available in the home. Trelease (1989:3) states that:

> To sell a product called reading:
> 1. You read to children while they are still young enough to want to imitate what they are seeing and hearing.
> 2. You make sure the readings are interesting and exciting enough to hold their interest while you are building up their imaginations.
> 3. You keep the initial readings short enough to fit their attention spans and gradually lengthen both.

Phonics is a helpful decoding strategy. Phonics should be taught and it should be taught early and quickly. The United States Department of Education booklet *Research about Teaching and Learning,* 1986, states that generally children who are taught phonics get off to a better start in learning to read than children who are not taught phonics. It states that: "Children get a better start in reading if they are taught phonics. Learning phonics helps them to understand the relationship between letters and sounds and to 'break the code' that links the words they hear with the words they see in print" (p. 21). This conclusion is also backed up by the 1984 research report of Anderson et al. (1985:37).

A lot of phonics research has been done, and it indicates that teaching phonics is a very helpful thing for beginning readers. For that reason it is good to include some phonics activities in the reading lesson. These need to be balanced, however, by teaching other types of reading strategies also, and the teaching of phonics should not be extended too long in any one lesson nor in the total teaching package.

> Phonics ought to be conceived as a technique for getting children off to a fast start in mapping the relationships between letters and sounds...Once the basic relationships have been taught, the best way to get children to refine and extend their knowledge of letter-sound correspondences is through repeated opportunities to read...A number of programmes try to teach too many letter-sound relationships and phonic instruction drags out over too many years...The right maxims for phonics are: Do it early. Keep it simple. (Anderson et al. 1985:38, 43)

Some primers I have seen in PNG have 180 lessons or more, spanning over 4 or 5 primers. Sounds are often taught many times over in every position in which they occur in the word and in every syllable type. But it is often only necessary for students to do half of those lessons to pick up adequate phonics skills and be able to start on the road to independent reading.

Decoding involves more than letter by letter analysis. Identifying words is not just identifying each letter and its sounds.

> A possible interpretation of a word usually begins forming in the mind as soon as even partial information has been gleaned about the letters in the word. The possible interpretation reinforces the analysis of the remaining information contained in the letters. When enough evidence from the letters and the context becomes available, the possible interpretation becomes a positive identification. (Anderson et al. 1985:11)

When a person is trying to read a written message (decode), many things are happening at once. As he reads a sentence, ideas begin to form in his mind as to the meaning behind these groups of letters and words. The reader is continually sampling (looking at parts), predicting (making an informed guess as to what they say), and confirming (checking that he is right, meanings are making sense, and the word fits with the rest of the sentence). With all this and more going on, the reader is not looking at every mark on the page and sounding them all out. For example, read the passage below.

> A language does not use all possible arrangements of the sounds or letters comprised in its system. If accidentally a forbidden combination appears, we automatically correct it to what we think it should be, e.g., if we transpsoe some of hte lettres in a text, it sitll remians surprisingly intleligible. One cuold even get used to htis sort of thing aeftr a hwile.
>
> Or one cn lve out ltrs nd the msg will be nvrthlss qte understndbl. Ths is abrvtn. Smthg lke ths is dne in Hbrw wrtg, whr only the consnts ar wrtn.
>
> Eaven extry lettchrs kan bee ritten, withaoutt mutch harm beaing dun. (from Dilena)

The passage is still quite readable even though it is full of mistakes, letters are left out, and so forth. As I read the passage, I use cues other than phonics to help decode and gain meaning from the print that is there.

It can, therefore, be seen from the above illustration that it is not necessary to teach total sounding out of every word, as the reader does not usually read that way. Instead, encourage the reader to give attention to the beginning sounds of words (and in some languages, the ending sounds also) along with the context of the story in order to work out the meaning of a word, phrase, or sentence.

Matching teaching to a person's beliefs about reading. What goes on in the reading lesson should match the teacher's beliefs about what is important in learning to read. Many teachers go to a lot of trouble to understand what happens when people learn to read and to know all the methods of teaching reading. However, what they know and believe about teaching reading is often not backed up by what they do in the classroom, in the primer lesson, and in other parts of the reading lesson.

For example, many teachers believe that it is important to teach phonics and, at the same time, to give the students practice using these sound and letter correspondences in their reading materials. Adams (1990:286) looked at many phonic reading programmes that had been developed by experts. She found they did not match the reading material with the sounds that were being taught in the phonics part of the reading lessons, even though the people designing and using them believed they should do so.

Another example: Teachers believe that for people to become good readers they need to read a lot of story material. Yet, when students are having trouble with reading, these same teachers go back and spend most of their teaching time drilling phonic skills. They give students less practice in reading for meaning, fewer chances to make their own corrections from the context, and less time to enjoy meaningful reading experiences. Gumperz describes some observations made:

> With the slow readers she [the teacher] concentrated on the alphabet, on the spelling of individual words...Her enunciation was deliberate and slow. Each word was clearly articulated with even stress and pitch...Pronunciation errors were corrected whenever they occurred, even if the reading task had to be interrupted.
>
> With the advanced group on the other hand reading became much more of a group activity and the atmosphere was more relaxed...Words were treated in context, as part of a story...There was no correction of pronunciation although some deviant forms were also heard. (Quoted from Gumperz by Cazden 1985:128-129)

The teacher taught each group of children differently even though she believed certain things about teaching reading were important. What she did, did not match what she believed.

Teachers and reading programme designers believe that learning to read by doing a lot of reading is a very important thing. But often when reading programmes are implemented, the amount of time the student is actively involved in reading is very limited. Often students spend their time on exercises, on waiting for other students to behave or get ready, on getting organised, and very little time on actual reading.

It is important to understand what happens in the reading process, know what is important when teaching people to read, and make sure that what you **do** matches your beliefs and understandings.

Good attitudes towards reading. One of the most important things that affects whether students learn to read well or not is attitudes. The attitudes of the teacher and of the students strongly influence the success of the reading programme.

> Every teacher and every coach will tell you how important attitude is. Indeed when 101 reading teachers listed their nine most important instructional priorities, improving attitudes toward reading was rated second only to comprehension. But when those same teachers assessed their instructional day, they found attitude was next to last with only 8.6% of their time devoted to it. (Trelease 1989:17)

Children learn to talk well because their parents expect them to.

> You will expect your child to learn to talk. You will not expect failure-that your child won't be able to learn to talk. This expectation of success meant that everything you do to help is geared towards success...All attempts at talking are acceptable, children even get praised for being close. There can be gentle correction of errors, but they are more likely to be treated as partial successes (nearly right) than as failures. (Cutting 1982:8)

Students will learn to read well if those teaching them expect them to learn to read well and assist them to do so in a caring, encouraging manner.

Teacher's attitudes to reading and the reading process affect the student's attitudes, and determine whether the student will continue to practice reading and growing towards being a fluent independent reader or not. Also, many people who have learned to read in literacy campaigns face the danger of slipping back into illiteracy because, although they have learned to read, they are not choosing to read and thereby do not maintain their reading skills.

> Obviously, if we are spending large amounts of money and time in successfully teaching children to read, but they in turn are choosing not to read, we must conclude that something is wrong. In concentrating almost exclusively on teaching the child how to read, we have forgotten to teach him to want to read. And there is the key: desire. (Trelease 1989:8)

A teacher, therefore, must not only have the attitude of expecting students to learn to read well but they must also pass on a love of books and a love of reading to their students so that they continue to choose to read and practice their skills.

> Children cannot fall in love with drill and skill because they are lifeless. But not pointless. They serve the same purpose-when used in moderation-as spring training in the baseball season. Every spring for a century we've taken these grown men to Florida and drilled them in the mechanics of baseball skills. But no one believes for a second that spring training is what inspires people to become baseball players or fans. You know what does it? Being taken to real games, the taste of hot dogs, seventh-inning stretches, watching your older brother rush for the box scores in the sports page, and playing catch in the yard.
>
> The same thing is true with reading. You become a reader because you saw and heard someone you admired enjoying the experience, someone led you to the world of books even before you could read, let you taste the magic of stories, took you to the library, and allowed you to stay up later at night to read in bed. (Trelease 1989:9)

The attitude of the student is also important. If students are highly motivated and expect to learn to read, they will work hard and over long periods of time in order to do so. Teachers can help keep them interested and give them good experiences. "The attention and cooperation that any student invests in reading activities depends on the degree to which her or his interests and sense of progress are engaged" (Adams 1990:6).

Adams also says: "More than anything else, the student engagement depended on the atmosphere-momentum, support and expectations-created by the classroom teacher" (Adams 1990:35).

If the students work hard and experience success in a positive and helpful atmosphere, they will be willing to practice their reading skills more and more. The more they practice the more successful they will be.

5

Reading Readiness

When students have had little or no involvment with books, we cannot expect them to be able to pick up one and be immediately ready to learn to read. When you teach children in the village to work in the gardens or in the community, you know they will not be able to do the work without learning how to do it first. There are some jobs you do not ask very young children to do. You wait until you think they are ready to learn to do them. When you think they are ready or able to do the work, then you begin to teach them. It is the same with learning to read. We have to give students opportunities to get ready to learn to read. We have to give them time to develop the ability to be able to learn to read. There are things we can do to help students become ready. These are called reading readiness activities.

When children are growing up in the village they learn a lot by watching other people and often play at doing things they have seen others do. They like to be 'helpers' with those who are doing the work. Well before the children are ready to do jobs around the village, they have already spent a lot of time watching, mimicking, copying, and playing at those jobs. To learn how to wash the clothes, the girls do not go hunting. To learn how to work in the garden, the children do not go swimming. To learn how to make houses, the boys do not go for a ride on a truck. When they are learning a task, the children do things that are very much the same as the task they want to learn.

- To learn how to wash clothes, the girls go with their mothers to the place where clothes are washed.
- To learn how to garden, the children go to the gardens with someone who is going to work in the garden.
- To learn how to swim, the children go to a place where there is a lot of water, with someone who can swim.

- To learn how to build a house, the boys go with their fathers, uncles, and brothers when they build a house.

It is the same with reading. Some people say that children learn to read by reading and learn to write by writing. The things children must do to get ready to read must be like things they will do when they actually read. They must copy reading-like behaviours.

How can students become ready to learn to read? What things do they need to learn before they can read? They need to learn:

- to hold the book the right way up
- to turn the pages carefully one by one
- to look at the print
- to read the print from the left side of the page to the right side of the page
- that the pictures say the same things as the print
- that the print is in chunks, words, and sentences and that these parts have a meaning, which together make sense
- that words have beginnings, middles, and ends and are made up of letters
- that the same print always says the same thing
- how to 'read' the pictures if they have never seen pictures or illustrations before
- that reading can be fun

So activities that help students become ready to learn to read should include all these types of things. And when thinking about reading readiness activities the teacher must ask, "Is that activity teaching the things they need to learn or is it just keeping them busy?" Also, "Does the student see that what they are doing is part of learning to read?" Questions like these should be in the minds of the teachers as they plan reading readiness activities.

5.1 Reading readiness activities

Reading readiness activities are activities that get students ready for reading. It is good to know as many activities as possible in order to have a range of activities to choose from to suit the students or the situations in which you teach. It also means you can have variety in your lessons so the students do not get tired of doing the same thing every session. Then they will be excited about doing their work. Happy, excited students work better than bored students. Following are some different ways to help children get ready for reading.

- read a lot of books to them
- have boxes of books available for them to handle or borrow

- talk about the pictures as you read the story so they can see that the pictures say the same things as the words
- point to the words as you read them so they learn to focus on small chunks of speech and so they see that you read from left to right
- ask questions about the story as you read so they learn to predict what comes next
- have charts or words written on blackboards that start with the same sound
- make alphabet books or wall hangings about beginning sounds
- write known songs, poems, and chants on charts; sing or read them together, pointing to the words as you go
- re-read and re-read favourite stories so students begin to pick out words they know
- write the students' personal sentences regularly so they can enjoy reading and re-reading the things that are important to them

Following is a more detailed discussion of different activities that I have been able to think of. You may be able to add to the collection.

Alphabet chart or books

Many people use alphabet charts or books to help get students ready for reading. There are different kinds of alphabet books. The teacher can make one up or can use what other people have done and change it to fit his language. Here are some examples:

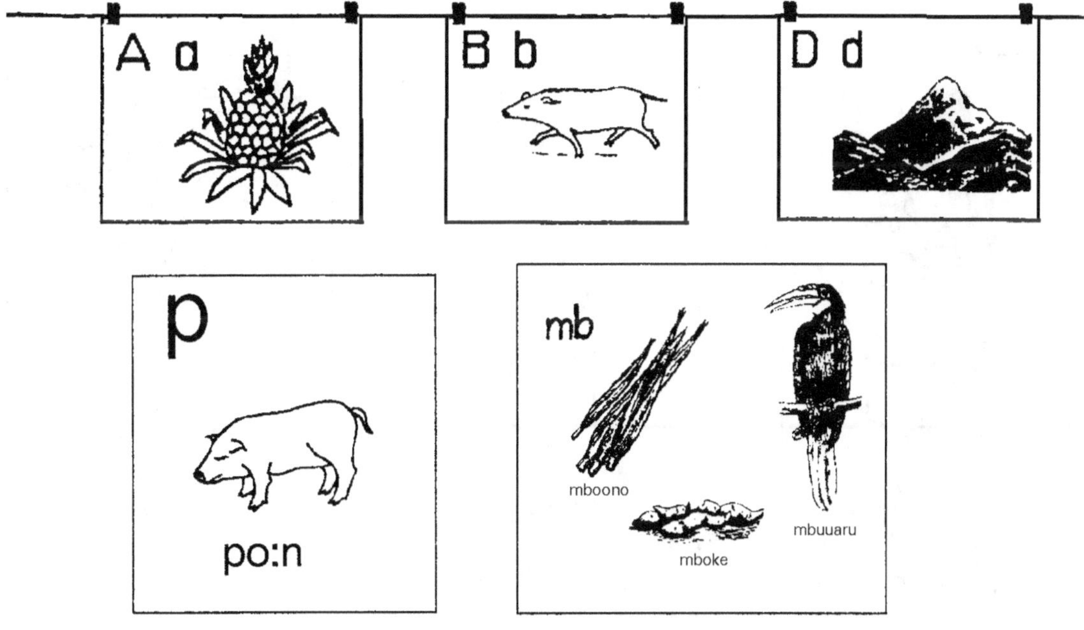

When using an alphabet book, I suggest doing the following activities.

- read and talk about it as a class
- let groups of students read it together and talk about it
- let individual students read through it during times of free reading
- draw pictures of other words that start the same, write the words near the pictures, underline the beginning sound
- make charts of other words that start the same
- use it to get the students familiar with important words for the first book they will read; use key words from primers
- make little story books for each key word for each sound in your alphabet
- make puppets as did the Kriol (Australia) teachers to represent each sound of their alphabet, e.g., Sally Snake (for the 'S' sound)
- make up an alphabet song as did the Numangang (PNG) teachers to go with their alphabet chart and books

Instant readers

Instant readers are books that are very easy to read. The students read the pictures carefully. The text for each page is usually one sentence long. On each page the sentence changes only by one or two words, which can be read with the help of the picture. Some examples are shown below.

Book 1:

Em i karim kaikai.

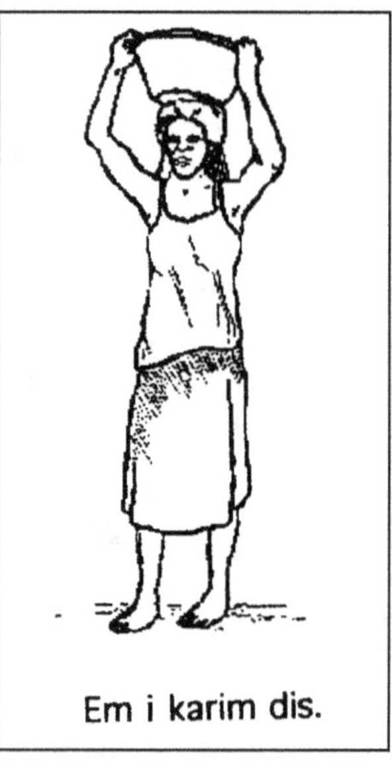

Em i karim dis.

Em i karim diwai.

Book 2:

Em i wokim kanu.

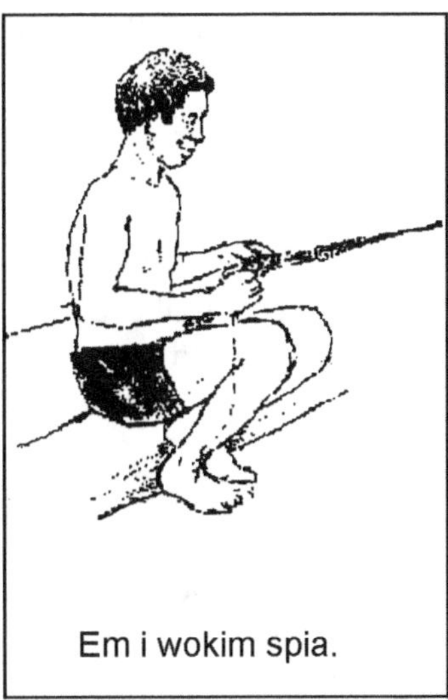
Em i wokim spia.

Em i wokim mat.

You can make sentence strips for the instant readers. Get the students to match these to the text, and eventually after practice they will be able to put these together to make the whole story without using the book. Sentence strips for Book 1 examples would be as follows:

Em i karim pikinini.

Em i karim kaikai.

Em i karim bilum.

Em i karim dis.

Em i karim diwai.

When the students are familiar with these sentences, you can make word cards. Get the students to make each sentence by matching the cards to the sentences in the book. Word cards for Book 1 would be:

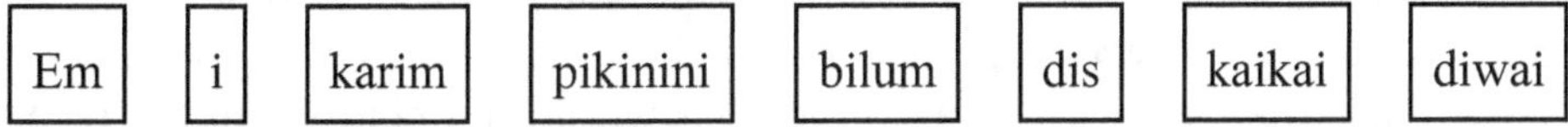

The students can then begin to make their own instant readers. Keep these for all the other students to read. The students can draw the pictures for the book, and the teacher can write the sentences.

Keep the instant readers in a box or on a shelf in the classroom and give the students plenty of opportunities to read them. They can read them individually or in groups, before or after class, or when they have finished their work and are waiting for the others to finish. The more the students read and handle books, the more they will learn about reading.

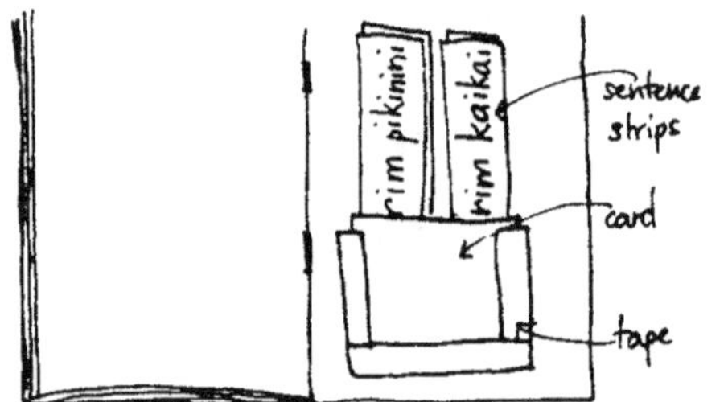

You can make a pocket in the back of the book to keep the sentence strips or word cards in.

The students will learn to read more easily if there is not a lot of print to read. (If you use books with a lot of print when a child starts to learn to read, the child may think the work of learning to read is too hard and may give up trying.)

Well-known songs

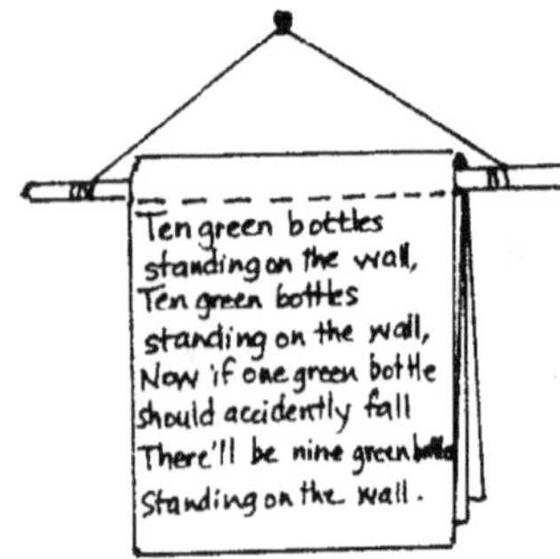

Charts of well known songs are good ways to help students get ready for reading, especially if the songs have a lot of repetition in them. Make collections of the song charts and have them hanging in the room. They can be used at different times throughout the day.

Have a student or the teacher use a pointer to follow the lines of words and point to each word as the class sings. Pointing helps the beginning reader to focus on each word. The songs should be ones that are suitable for the age group you are working with. They can be traditional songs, church songs, school songs, or made up songs.

If a hymn book in the local language is available, it is a good tool for teaching adults about reading. You can use the hymn books in either classes or with individuals. Start and finish each lesson time together singing a hymn. Make sure the students try and follow the song in their hymn books by pointing with their fingers. This helps them to concentrate their attention on each word as they sing. For a while they will sing from memory but gradually they will begin to pick out words and phrases. In the meantime they are learning pre-reading or reading readiness skills.

Songs written by students

Some teachers encourage the students to make up their own songs to well-known tunes. These often become the students' favourite class songs. The following is a fun song made up by the teenagers at Ukarumpa, PNG. The tune is one they know, called *Country Road.*

Almost heaven, Ukarumpa,
Slide the *kunai*, gummy down the river.
Life's a blast there, better than the States
Finer than Australia, hurry don't be late.
Dusty roads, take me home
To the *ples bilong mi*
Ukarumpa, near perfection,
Take me home, dusty roads.

Pictured below is one of the verses of the made-up song, *Five Frogs*. It is sung to the tune of *Ten Green Bottles*. I have used this song when doing a theme on frogs along with the story of the *The Frog with the Big Mouth*.

A teacher can make song books or charts to be used in classes. If the students are using song books, make sure they follow the habit of pointing out the lines and words as they sing. This helps them to focus on the print. When making charts, make them attractive by putting illustrations on them. It is best to put each verse of a song on a separate page and have an illustration to match each verse. Once the students have become familiar with the song, draw their attention to special words and phrases that are the same, such as the following.

This part says *Faivpela Rokrok*. Can you find another part that says the same?
Which part do you think says *Rokrok*?
Can you find the word card that says *Rokrok*?
Can you see how it starts?
Let's sing this part again.

Or you can talk about the verse as follows:

What did the frog eat?
Which part tells us what he ate?
Can you point to the word that says *binatang*?
Let's sing the song again.

The next day you can teach the second verse in the same way. And so on.

The teacher can make sentence strips and word cards for the verses and have the students match them to the chart. When they know the song well, they may be able to take turns in making up each verse just using the cards. They can do this individually, in small groups, or as a class.

Well-known poems

Some villages have well-known poems that children say when they walk about or sit down or play in groups. You can make charts of these poems or write a different poem on the blackboard each week. You can make up your own poems or get the students to help you make them up. Following is a translation of a Nembi (PNG) poem made up to use with the theme on frogs.

Rokrok i stap
Rokrok i stap
I stap long wara
I stap long wara
Em i kalap i go long wara
Em lus long wara.

Use this poem to show the students that the words *Rokrok i stap* are the same in the first two lines. The words look the same and sound the same. "Here is the word that says *Rokrok*. Can you find another word that looks the same and says the same thing?"

Have the students find the word (teacher points to word) that says w*ara* as many times as they can. "What other things start with the same sound?"

In these ways the students' eyes are being trained to look for things that look the same and ears are being trained to hear the sounds that are the same. After students have seen this poem many times, they will begin to pick out words that they know. You can write the poem on the board with some parts missing or cover words over and see if they can work out what is missing as they recite the poem from memory.

Riddles

Riddles can be fun to make up as a class. Then write them on charts and read them together.

I live in the sand near the sea.
I have eight legs.
I have two strong nippers.
I eat any scraps I can find.
I have a hard shell.
I walk sideways.
What am I?

Well-known stories

In the village there are a lot of stories that fathers and mothers, grandparents, aunts and uncles tell children many times. Some of these stories are ancestral stories, some are stories of things that happened to people when they were young, or stories from the first time the white man came, such as "The first time I saw a mirror," and other stories like that.

It is good to collect such stories in books, on charts, or write them on the blackboard and use them to help people learn to read. They can share them in groups, as a class, or on their own. These stories often have a children's version and an adult's version. It is best to match the version you use with the age of the people you are teaching to read. The stories should be short enough to be read at one sitting by the teacher, over and over again, so that the print becomes familiar.

Funny stories

People always enjoy reading funny stories. They can be local stories that people always laugh at or they can be funny stories from other places that have been translated into their language. (If translating humour from one language to another, check that people think it is a funny story. What people laugh at is very different from place to place.)

Keep the stories short with a lot of pictures. Read these stories to the class often, let the students pretend to read them to each other and play with the stories in small groups.

Funny stories help students enjoy learning to read and shows them that reading can be fun. They can also teach many things about reading such as how to turn the pages and what the marks on each page means.

Bible stories

Some places have a lot of Bible stories already translated into the local language. These stories can be used to help students learn about reading, especially if they are stories that are well-known to them. Break the stories down into small pieces and illustrate each page to make the stories easier to read.

Such simplified Bible stories can be used in groups, in pairs, or in a class. If each story is simple and interesting, students will gradually learn to read it themselves after they have seen it many times.

Comics

Children (and many adults) love to read comics. It is not necessary to be a good reader to read comics because much of the story is made clear by the picture.

Health comics, Bible comics, and so on can be used. They can be comics that other people have printed with the vernacular language pasted over the English, Tok Pisin, or whatever words are already there for each picture. You can make up the comics yourself or have the students help you draw the pictures for a class comic. You can make books or charts out of comics, or stick them together in a long line and hang them in the classroom.

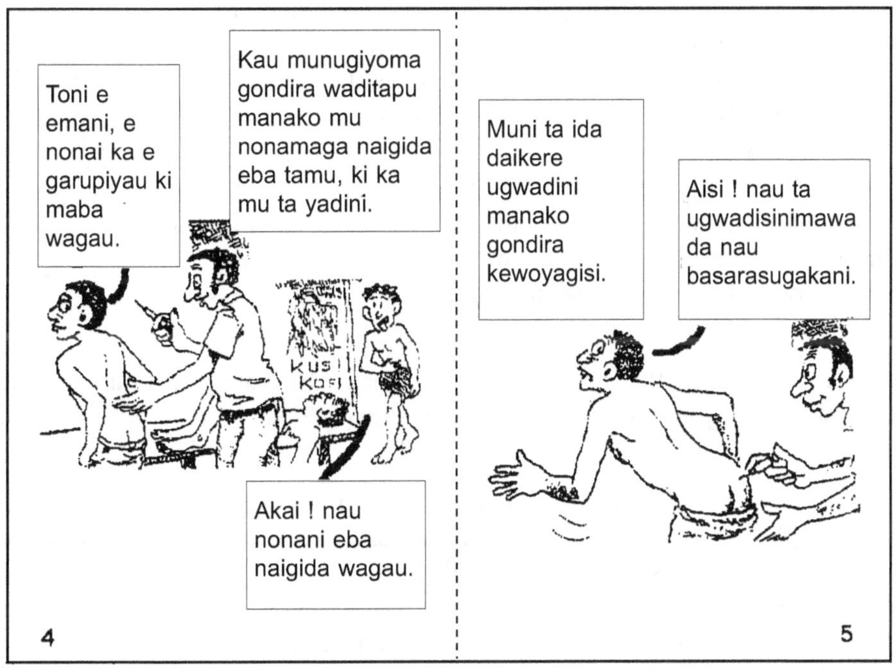

Experience Stories

Students, children in particular, are good at helping to make their own reading materials. They can illustrate or dictate stories of things that have happened to them. These stories are called experience stories. There are a lot of things happening in village life that can be recorded in print, such as things to do with gardening, house building, killing pigs, chasing wild pigs, making canoes, and going fishing.

Adults can dictate writings about village issues—decisions made about the walk-about-sawmill, about the community sewing machines, about village work projects, rosters for Sunday school or church work, legal actions planned, letters to local politicians, things that can be done to prevent malaria, and issues like these.

Get the students to talk about the issue first and to decide what they would like written on their paper. (Children will often draw a picture about it and then the teacher will write their sentence under the picture.) The teacher then writes the text for each person or for the group if you are doing group writing. As the teacher writes, he talks about what is being written, drawing the attention of the students to what is happening on the page.

> I'll start this sentence with a capital letter. The next word starts with an 's' sound. To make an 's' you put your pencil here and draw a snake. Be careful to sit it on the line.

The teacher then reads what has been written several times pointing to each word as he reads. The student then tries to repeat what the sentence says pointing to each word as it is said. This process is repeated several times until the student can remember what the print on his page says. These stories can then be shared with others in the class, taken home and read to the family, or collected into books to be kept and re-read over and over again. There should be some kind of picture clues on the page to help trigger the students' memory as to what the writing is about. The story should only be one or two sentences or thoughts.

The teacher can also give the students experiences to draw and dictate stories about. Take the class for a walk to see something that is happening in the village. Come back to the classroom and talk about it before dictating and drawing. Because the student has been involved in the choice of words that are on the page they usually find it easy to remember. (Be careful not to alter their words too much. If you make changes, students may find it difficult to remember your way of saying it.) Because the writing is about things that the student has experienced, experience books often become popular books to read and often get worn out because they are used so frequently.

For example, the class could make a book about a village feast. Discuss the feast and all the things that happen as people prepare for it. Have the class discuss what will be written on each page. Then the teacher writes each sentence on a separate piece of paper. It may look something like the following:

Title Page:	Getting ready for a big feast.
Page 1.	The women got up early and went to the gardens.
Page 2.	The men got up early and caught the pig.
Page 3.	The men dug a big hole for the mumu.
Page 4.	The boys collected the stones.
Page 5.	The girls collected the firewood.
Page 6.	The women came back from the gardens with all the food.
Page 7.	They brought kaukau, greens, pumpkin, taro, corn, and yam.
Page 8.	The men killed the pig and cut it up.
Page 9.	The men made the fire.
Page 10.	The women got the food ready for the mumu.
Page 11.	Today the people in our village will eat a big feast. It is a special time.

Each page is then illustrated by a group of students. When completed, the pages are stapled together to make a book and the story is shared with the class several times. The book is then read by the teacher each day during that week. The students join in as they are able, mainly using the picture clues to help them remember the story but focussing on the print as the teacher points to each word as he reads. Then the book can be placed in the class library along with other class books to be read by groups of students in free reading times.

Big Books

Big Books are popular stories that have been made into large books so that they can be used with small groups or a whole class.[13]

The teacher usually has a stand or ledge to put the book on and a stick to point to the words. The writing and pictures of the Big Books is large enough so that it can be easily read by all who are sitting nearby. As the teacher reads the story, she points to the words with the pointer so the students learn to look at the words as units and eventually are able to read along with the teacher. The teacher reads the whole story through once, then talks about it with the class.

Big Books can be read many times to the class but be careful not to read the same story too often or the students will lose interest in it. The teacher can use a word mask to cover up all the words near the word she wants the students to concentrate on. Then she can talk about the word, discussing things like, what it starts with, what it says, and what other words are like it.

Big Books are made to be read and enjoyed in groups or as a class. Reading them should be a fun thing to do together. They get the student used to what books are like, help them to follow the print from left to right as the teacher points, and so on. It is good to start with Big Books that have repetitive stories with predictable phrases. These are easier to read.

Blackboard reading

Sometimes the only thing that a teacher has in a classroom is a blackboard. A blackboard can be used in many ways to help students learn to read.

- One part of the blackboard can be set aside for stories. Each week write a new, short story on this part of the board. The students will be interested to get to class at the beginning of a new week to see what the new story is. Different students in the class can illustrate the story each week. You can also write poems or songs on the blackboard to teach to the class.
- On the last day of class that week, erase one of the important words from each sentence and see if the students can work out which word is missing. They should do

[13]For more information on Big Books and their use see §8.3 "Literature-based reading programmes for Papua New Guinea" and §8.4 "Making Big Books."

this by reading through the text and using the clues from the rest of the story. You could write the words that are missing in a box at the bottom of the story for the students to choose from.

- The blackboard can also be used to write down experience sentences or stories that the class dictate to the teacher. Then the teacher uses a stick or pointer to point to the word that says '____' or the word that starts with *m,* or whatever it is the teacher wants to focus on.
- Teachers can use the blackboard to talk about words that sound the same (see Sally snake and slimy snail), or list words that belong to a theme (see tree below).

All of the activities I have mentioned in this section about reading readiness activities are related to real reading. They teach the students all the things listed at the beginning of this chapter that students need to know before they are ready to learn to read.

Some groups may not need to have as much time spent on readiness activities as others. They may have already worked out a lot of these things and be ready to learn. Other groups need to have longer because they come to class not knowing very much at all about the world of books and print. The amount of time spent on these activities should match the needs of the student.

When are students ready to progress to learning to read? The following check sheet may be helpful as you review each student.

From the first day, does the child (during shared book):

- ask questions about character and plot?
- predict what might happen next?
- repeat words, sounds, and phrases?
- relate what is happening to their own experience?
- join in with reading or re-reading?
- comment about the story or other children's responses?
- smile, laugh, or look delighted at the right places?
- point to illustrations?
- open eyes wide?
- imitate actions of the story?
- choose to read the book again?

After a month, is the child:

- familiar with how to handle a book?
- aware that print conveys a message?
- aware that speech can be written down?
- capable of writing his name?

Does the child understand:

- the concept of a word?
- the concept of a letter?
- that words in a sentence have an order?
- that the order of the letters is important?
- that you read from left to right, and at the end of the line you go to the line beneath?
- that spaces separate words in a sentence?
- show in his writing any understandings about print, i.e., are his letters written in the right direction, is he writing any words?

And once he has started reading:

Does the child during independent reading:

- expect text to make sense?
- read to identify meaning and not just read words and letters?
- employ strategies like:
  reading on to end of the sentence,
  guess,
  start again,
  use picture clues,
  use initial letter clues,
  self-correct?
- predict what might happen next?
- predict on the basis of knowledge of the language?
- process in chunks?
- enjoy reading?

These lists are adapted from the teachers' manual of the Story Box reading programmes. See the Story Box manual for more details.

5.2 A skills-based approach to reading readiness

Teachers all over the world do things differently. They choose to teach in ways that fit their beliefs about how students learn and how students should be taught. Many teachers and researchers have spent a lot of time trying to find out how children learn to read and what is the best way to teach them. There are many different approaches to reading readiness. It is all right to do things the old ways, if we know those ways work well. It is also good to try new ways and see if they are better.

Some of the traditional methods of teaching reading reflects a skills-based approach. Teachers who teach this way tend to separate out the different skills they believe are important in learning to read. They focus on teaching each skill separately. They believe that when the students have mastered each separate skill, then they are ready to learn to read.

The skills these teachers tend to isolate are things like auditory discrimination skills (listening skills—using the ear to hear sound differences) and visual discrimination (using the eye to see differences in letter shapes).

When teaching auditory discrimination teachers encourage students to listen carefully for differences in sounds, especially sounds that are alike such as *m* and *n, f* and *v,* for example.

In the exercise below, students are asked to circle the pictures of things that start with the same sound.

When teaching visual discrimination teachers encourage the students to look carefully for differences in the written symbols. They start with shapes and then go to letters and finally word shapes. Students are asked to point to, or circle, the pictures of things that are the same or circle those that are different. Examples of this approach are pictured below. (Details on designing these types of activities can be found in *Working Together for Literacy.*)

Pictures

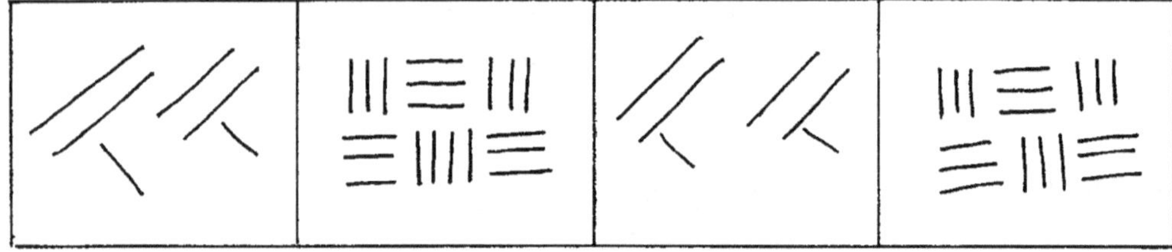

Symbols

Letters

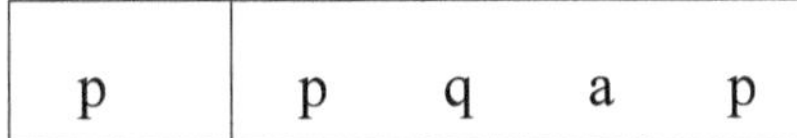

Words

papa	mama papa brata

If these types of activities are used for reading readiness, be aware that they are often very different from the reading-like behaviours new reading students must learn. Research has shown that they are not helpful in preparing students for reading. Students often like doing the activities, and teachers like to get students doing them so they can use that time to do reading activities with other groups. Reading readiness activities should mirror what real reading is like; they should involve the student in reading-like behaviours.

6

Principles of Primer Construction

Literacy workers face many difficult problems when working in vernacular languages. They usually have modest training and few resources, and work in isolated areas, often with teachers who have not had a lot of training. Because of this, literacy workers usually use primers in their programmes. Primers are reading books which contain pre-packaged, pre-determined materials for reading lessons. These materials lock students into doing what the class teacher is comfortable with which means that they must pursue the reading course as it has been set and use the materials that have been provided.

Although this approach is less than ideal, there are, in addition to the primers, things which can be done to help meet the needs and goals of the students. Also, more consultation and communication with the target group before primers are designed will help the designers to develop materials that are more suited to the needs of those who will use them.

The village literacy teachers need to understand that they can change the pre-packaged lessons to better fit the expectations of their students. In order for them to do this, they need to be better trained. They need to understand the processes learners go through when acquiring literacy, rather than just knowing how to follow the primer lesson plans that they have been given. There is nothing magical about these lesson plans. They need to know they have the freedom to add other activities into each lesson that will help learners achieve their goals. Teachers need to be shown how to adapt the lesson plans and be encouraged to do so.

Having said all that, the primer is still an important resource for village literacy teachers, and the primer lesson is important in vernacular literacy classes. The remainder of this chapter looks at how primers are constructed.

6.1 Look at the sound system of the target language[14]

Before beginning to make primers (some people call them readers), it is necessary to spend some time looking at the sound system of the language. Each language has its own system and its own way of putting sounds together to make words. Some languages have few letters in the alphabet, others have many.

Usually, each sound has its own symbol or letter but sometimes sounds are represented by more than one letter. These are known as DIGRAPHS. There are quite a few digraphs in English, for example:

th in 'this', 'that'
ng in 'sing' (some languages write this sound as *ŋ*)
oo in 'choose'
kn in 'know', 'knew', 'knit'
ph in 'photo', 'paragraph'

Some alphabets use digraphs like:

mb, nd, nt for sounds like *b, d, t* which have a short nasal sound before the stop.

Some languages put marks above or below some of their letters or symbols, for example:

French	*à la femme*
Gupapuyngu	d̲, t̲, n̲ (Underlining means the tongue tip is curled upwards when this sound is made.)

Some use marks under the vowels, *ą, ų, ǫ, ę, į,* to show that they are made with nose air (nasalisation). Marks written above or below letters are called DIACRITICS.

Digraphs or sounds with diacritics should always be taught as a whole, never separated. For example, the sound [gʷ], written as *gw*, should not be separated to teach *g* or *w* but always kept as a unit. Different words would be used to teach the *g* sound or the *w* sound as they are different from the *gw* sounds.

For example, in Golin (PNG), *gwi* 'wind' could be used to teach the *gw* sound. A different word like *gal* 'string bag' would be used to teach *g,* and another different word to teach *w.* It would be wrong to use *gw* to teach either *g* or *w* because a word beginning with *gw* starts with a different sound altogether.

[14]Sarah Gudschinsky, 1973, covers many of these aspects in chapter 4, pp. 36–48, of her book. Bob Litteral and Susan Malone, 1991, also cover some aspects mentioned here in a similar way.

Students need to be taught all sounds, letter combinations, and extra marks that they will encounter when learning to read in their language. Thus, the worker preparing the primers needs to know what the sounds of the language are.

It is also helpful in preparing a primer to know which sounds occur most frequently, how they fit in a syllable pattern, which words with the more frequent sounds can be illustrated easily, and how to choose key words. I now discuss each of these points.

Frequency counts

A frequency count (or sound count) determines how often each sound occurs in written language. It is used as a guide to help decide which sounds should be taught first in primers and reading lessons.

The frequency count is only a guide. It should never be used to set a rigid order of introducing sounds in primer lessons. It does not have to be followed slavishly and can be changed to suit other needs. It is good, however, to teach the most common letters first in early reading lessons. More words can be made using these letters, and so stories can be read more easily.

Following is an example of how to do a frequency count using a sample story from Tok Pisin (PNG). It is taken from page 2 of the booklet, *The Sounds of Your Language*, put out by the Department of Education (PNG, 1991).

Pasin bilong wokim nupela gaden na banis.

Sapos papa bilong mi i laik wokim nupela gaden, pastaim em i katim kunai na pitpit na bus samting. Olgeta samting i drai pastaim, orait em i kukim.

Em i save tumas long pasin bilong ol pik. Olsem na em i kisim diwai i gat strong. Em i brukim na sapim bilong wokim banis pik. Em i pasim banis long rop. Olsem na ol diwai i paspas na pik i no inap brukim.

Banis i pinis, orait papa bilong mi em i tokim sampela man, na ol i go kamautim as bilong pitpit na rausim rop bilong diwai. Ol i wok pinis, na papa bilong mi em i mumuim sampela kaikai bilong ol, na ol i go kaikai.

Long narapela taim em i singautim sampela man i go brukim graun long stik bilong ol. Ol i putim sampela kunai na lip bilong diwai i go daunbilo. Ol i karamapim na hipim graun antap na ol i planim kaukau. Long sampela hap ol meri tasol i save hipim graun na planim kaukau.

Arere long gaden mipela i save planim sampela pitpit na sampela kon na sampela aibika na kumu na bin. Banana tu, sampela taim. Tasol banana em i save planim klostu long haus. Mi liklik yet na mi wantaim papa bilong mi, mitupela i save mekim wok olsem.

To do a sound count for this Tok Pisin story, go through the story word by word. Each time you come to a new sound, write the sound in the first column (under Sound) in the following chart and put one mark in the second column (Number of times in story). Then, every time you see that sound again, put another mark in the second column next to that sound. After you have gone through the entire story, count up the number of marks for each sound and put the total for each sound in the last column (Total). This chart will then show the order of sounds as they occurred in the sample story, the number of times the sound occurred, and thus which were the most frequent sounds in the story.

After counting the sounds in the two words *Sapos papa,* the sound count chart would look like the following:

Sounds	Number of times in story	Total
s	𝍷𝍷	
a	𝍷𝍷𝍷	
p	𝍷𝍷𝍷	
o	𝍷	

When a sound has four marks against it like this 𝍷𝍷𝍷𝍷, the fifth mark is used to 'tie the bundle' like this 𝍸. Continue marking the chart and tie the sticks in bundles of five. At the end of the Tok Pisin text the sound count chart would look like this:

Sounds	Number of times in story	Total
s	𝍸 𝍸 𝍸 𝍸 𝍸 𝍸 𝍸 𝍸	40
a	𝍸 𝍷𝍷𝍷	113
p	𝍸 𝍸 𝍸 𝍸 𝍸 𝍸 𝍸 𝍸 𝍸 𝍷	46
o	𝍸 𝍸 𝍸 𝍸 𝍸 𝍸 𝍸 𝍸	40
ng	𝍸 𝍸 𝍸 𝍷𝍷	17
b	𝍸 𝍸 𝍸 𝍷𝍷𝍷𝍷	19
i	𝍸 𝍸 𝍸 𝍸 𝍸 𝍸 𝍸 𝍸 𝍸 𝍸 𝍷	51
l	𝍸 𝍸 𝍸 𝍸 𝍸 𝍸 𝍸 𝍸 𝍸 𝍷𝍷𝍷	48
n	𝍸 𝍸 𝍸 𝍸 𝍸 𝍸 𝍸 𝍸 𝍸	45
g	𝍸 𝍷𝍷𝍷𝍷	9
m	𝍸 𝍸 𝍸 𝍸 𝍸 𝍸 𝍸 𝍸 𝍸 𝍸 𝍸 𝍷𝍷	57

k	𝍸 𝍸 𝍸 𝍸 𝍸 IIII	29
r	𝍸 𝍸 𝍸	15
v	𝍸	5
w	𝍸 II	7
u	𝍸 𝍸 𝍸 𝍸 𝍸	25
e	𝍸 𝍸 𝍸 𝍸 𝍸 𝍸 𝍸	35
d	𝍸 II	7
t	𝍸 𝍸 𝍸 𝍸 𝍸 II	27
y	I	1
h	IIII	4

Now the sounds can be listed in order of their frequency.

a	113	e	35	d	7
m	57	k	29	w	7
i	51	t	27	v	5
l	48	u	25	h	4
p	46	b	19	y	1
n	45	ng	17	j	0
o	40	r	15	f	0
s	40	g	9		

This chart shows that the sounds *j* and *f* were not in the sample story. It is, therefore, important to do sound counts on several different stories in order to get a good sound count. Also, some letters may be more frequent in this story than in other stories. For these reasons, it is good to do sound counts for 3–5 different stories to get a more accurate count.

Sounds	Text 1 Papa	Text 2 fishing	Text 3 frog	Text 4 gardens	Text 5 how to...	Total
a						
m						
i						
l						

When the counts from 3–5 stories or more are totalled, list the sounds in order of their frequency. Group the sounds as follows:

most frequent
next frequent
next
next
least frequent

> *Remember, the sound frequencies are just a guide for designing primers.*

The sound counts I did in Takia resulted in the following list:

most frequent: a, i, o, u.
next frequent: b, g, d, l, n, t
next: ŋ, y, e
next: f, k, m
least frequent: s, p, r, w

I used this list as a guide when doing primers but I also changed the order around a little to fit in with the stories I was using in the lessons and the design of the primer. For example, I introduced the letter *i* before the letter *a* because the key word in the story for the lesson was *ilalang*, which means 'light'. And I introduced *y* in the third lesson instead of the twelfth because the word *you* 'water' was an important word in that part of the story. The sound counts are only a guide.

Yasuko Nagai did sound counts on all the stories that were written for use in the Maiwala prep school. Then she ordered the use of the stories according to the sound counts. This meant that the story matched well with the sound being taught in each lesson.

Syllable patterns (adapted from the booklet, *The Sounds in Your Language*)

Each language has its own rules for the way that sounds can be put together into words. Alphabets are made up of vowels, such as *a, e, i, o, u* and consonants such as *t, s, m, l, y.* Vowels and consonants combine together to make syllables.

What is a syllable? A syllable is a vowel sound together with the consonants which closely surround that vowel. Think of the consonants in the syllable as belonging to that particular vowel rather than to some other vowel. The consonants which usually belong to a vowel are the ones which come before the vowel. In some languages it may also include consonants following the vowel. A syllable does not have meaning, it is just a combination of sounds. Combinations of syllables make words and words carry meaning.

People seem to know how to divide words into syllables, especially when they speak very slowly. For example, if a person says the English word *motor* very slowly, it is divided into the two syllables *mo* and *tor*. The Tok Pisin (PNG) word *mama* has two syllables *ma* and *ma* and the Hiri Motu word *masini* has three syllables *ma, si,* and *ni.*

Syllables are of different types depending on the patterns of vowels and consonants. The patterns are different in different languages. In some languages, a syllable may have two vowels in it rather than one because the pair of vowels act like a single vowel. For example, in the Tok Pisin word *kaukau* the ***au*** acts like a single vowel so we get ***kau kau***. Some other Tok Pisin words with two vowels in the syllable are ***kaikai*** and ***boi.***

Sometimes two vowels next to each other are from two different syllables. The Tok Pisin word *stia* is like that. It has the syllables *sti* and *a*.

In Tok Pisin, sometimes two consonants occur together in the same syllable such as ***st**ap,* ***sk**in,* ***sp**et,* ***sn**ek,* and ***sw**it.*

Occasionally, three consonants occur together in the same syllable, for example ***str**et.*

It is necessary to know the common combinations of sounds in a language. In Tok Pisin, for example, *s* combines with a lot of other consonants in a syllable but *f* rarely does. The common combinations for a language should be taught in the primers so students can practice reading them.

Words easily illustrated

No matter what type of primer is made, it is helpful to make a list of words that can be easily illustrated. All beginning primers depend heavily on using picture clues, especially in the early stages when a student is just beginning to get meaning from print. Many primers use a picture and a word to teach each new sound. Words that can be illustrated are usually a noun, that is, a person, place, or thing. It is difficult to illustrate a verb (an action) or a feeling.

Whenever I design primers, I make a list of words that can be easily illustrated. The following list is part of my Takia list of words that can be illustrated.

s	*sasam* 'shark', *sabai* 'prawn', *sis* 'grass hopper', *suwir* 'parrot', *sisei* 'clam shell'
t	*tamol* 'man', *tatu* 'bone'
u	*ul* 'breadfruit', *urit* 'octopus', *ut* 'weeds', *ut* 'lice'
w	*wos* 'aibika', *walu* 'pumpkin', *woi* 'mango', *wagudum* 'bush berry'

It is also important that the pictures prompt the response that you desire from the students. For example, at Ramingining, Australia, a certain picture of a kangaroo never received the response of *garrtjambal,* the general word for female kangaroo. People would try and work out the specific type of kangaroo by the particular features which were obvious in the picture. Their responses would not necessarily start with *g* and often caused great discussions about what type of kangaroo it was. This happened because the artist did not draw an accurate picture of what the real animal looked like. This distracted the people and stopped them from associating the picture with the letter *g.*

Again, at Boroloola, Australia, Judy Knowles had to redraw her primer pictures of a girl many times as she would get a variety of responses from "baby," "young child," "child of marriageable age," to "young woman" depending on her drawing.

All illustrations should be checked with the village people. Check that they can recognize them and that their initial response to them is the word wanted in the lesson. This is particularly important for the pictures that are used in the early primer lessons.

A list of words that can be illustrated, and sound counts from several texts are important tools for the literacy worker who designs primers or readers.

Choosing key words

Many primers use a picture and a word to teach each new sound or syllable.
Key words must be chosen carefully.

- They should be chosen from words that can be illustrated.
- They should contain the letter or syllable being taught in the initial position in the word, if at all possible.
- They should be words that have a simple syllable structure. (If CV syllables are common they are usually best for key words.)
- If possible they should be an important word or theme word in the story material that is the focus of the lesson.

kesu
ke
k

Be careful not to place an improper emphasis on a key word. Use it to demonstrate that "this is the part of *kesu* that says *ke* or *k*" as the case may be and move on.

Some years ago, the following key words and pictures were used in Mexico to teach *sa* and *la.* Gudschinsky's comments follow.

> Unfortunately what the pupils learned was that the syllable and word were one and the same, so that when they attempted to read the unfamiliar word *sala* 'lounge room' they came out with a meaningless word *sapo-lata*.
>
> There can be a danger in the use of a key word if the teacher continually refers back to it and too strongly equates a single syllable with the key word used to teach it. (Gudschinsky 1973:36)

6.2 Consider principles from reading research and experience

Have meaningful contexts

Reading research tells us that reading is more than just sounding out letters and putting them together to make words.

> Reading is the process of constructing meaning from written texts. It is a complex skill requiring the coordination of a number of interrelated sources of information. (Anderson et al. 1985:7)
>
> Other non-phonic processes are necessary for ariving at meaning from texts, and are naturally active in all reading, even beginning reading. In particular, the use of context—at all levels—is a necessary non-phonics reading process. (McCormick 1990a, §V, p. 1)

These authors tell us that reading is more than just being able to sound out words. It is making meaning out of the print on the page. Readers decode for meaning in more than one way and, when they make meaning out of print, they do so by using all the information they have at hand. If reading is more than just phonics (sounding out), then teaching people to read should involve more than just teaching people how to sound out words (phonics). If there are ways other than phonics that are important for helping the reader make meaning from texts, then students should be taught such ways and given opportunities to use them.

One thing that helps readers work out meanings of words is the clues they pick up from the context, that is, from the words and ideas surrounding the word they are trying to read. Therefore, all primer reading activities should be within meaningful print contexts.

> What makes meanings and individual words become transparent to us is context, which means the general sense in which the difficult element is embedded. Provided that what we are trying to read has the possibility of making sense to us the parts that are unfamiliar can usually be deciphered because of all the other clues available. (Smith 1978:123)

Frank Smith is saying here that when we read we are able to work out the meanings of difficult words because of the other meanings already understood from the rest of the context.

Reading some words without their context, or on their own (reading words in isolation), is very difficult for some students. We do not know how to read some words in English until we see them among other words. The words around them can change the way we read them. For example:

Last night I read a book.
I will read you a story today.

The word *read* in these two examples is said differently even though they are spelled the same and have similar meanings. Another example:

Mary had a little lamb.

This sentence can mean Mary had a little piece of lamb meat to eat, or it can mean that Mary owned a baby sheep, a lamb. It is not until we see the word in context that we know if Mary ate the lamb or if it was her pet.

Mary had a little lamb
Its fleece was white as snow
And everywhere that Mary went
The lamb was sure to go.

Mary had a little lamb, mint sauce, roast potatoes, and vegetables.

Or take the word *drive*: I can talk about driving a golf ball and driving a car. If I drive a golf ball, I hit the golf ball with a golf club and it flies through the air, hopefully towards the hole and the flag. If I drive a car, I sit behind the wheel of the car and make it move from one place to another. I don't hit the car. To understand the meaning of driving I need to read it in context, that is, read the other words around it or know what kind of story I am reading. The context helps me work out the meanings of the words.

Context also builds expectations about the words which might come next in a group of words or in a sentence. This can be illustrated by the following Angor story of the Cockatoo and Crow.

> One day Cockatoo told crow, "Hey, let's go down and scrape sago." Crow said, "All right, let's go."
>
> So the two of them left the village and went down to the place for scraping sago. Cockatoo scraped sago but Crow went looking for insects in the water and made the water dirty.
>
> After Cockatoo finished scraping sago he washed it. When he had finished washing it he later went to find firewood and stones. He made a fire for heating the stones in order to make hot water. When all the stones were hot, Cockatoo called out, "Aya, bring some water here." But Crow answered, "Pi, wait, the water is dirty."
>
> Later cockatoo called out again, "Aya, bring some water here."
>
> But crow answered, "Pi, wait, the water is dirty."
>
> The fire burnt out and the stones were no longer very hot. Cockatoo kept on waiting and waiting. Then, he got some water himself. Crow too, brought some dirty water.
>
> Well, Cockatoo put all the hot stones into the water, "Ts! Ts!" He poured the water over the sago and rolled it over and over but the sago would not thicken because the water was not hot.
>
> Cockatoo was angry and he poured the dirty water over Crow. Crow paid him back by pouring the sago water over Cockatoo.
>
> "Pi", Crow flew away and perched on the branch of a *dabure* tree. "Aya", Cockatoo flew away and perched on the branch of a *galip* tree.
>
> That's the reason why Cockatoo is a white bird and Crow is black.

When an Angor student is learning to read the story of the Cockatoo and Crow and they come to "After Cockatoo finished scraping sago he," they will expect that the sentence will to go on to say "washed it," because in their language, these are the only words that could follow after "scraping sago" and make sense.

The Angor have a good knowledge of sago making, the subject of this text. Every Angor has this background information in their minds because sago is the main food of their area. So it is easy for the Angor student to get the correct meaning from this piece of text because making sago is known and understood, and the steps for doing it are familiar. For that reason readers know what to expect next in the story, and the words used in the text will be easily predicted by the person trying to read it.

It is important that reading activities use the knowledge that the reader has. It is also important that reading activities are surrounded by meaningful contexts. These two things are important when teaching reading and also in doing the primer activities. It is helpful in early reading lessons if the stories are about things that are well-known to the student.

Use real language

Using natural texts, rather than artificial or controlled texts, is helpful to new readers. An artificial text is one that someone would never say, one in which only a few carefully chosen easy words are used. An example might be something like: "Hello dog. Dog is big. Hello big dog."

> Merely shortening words and sentences to improve readability is like holding a match under a thermometer when you want to make your house warmer...Indeed dividing long sentences into shorter sentences and substituting familiar words for less familiar words can make a text more difficult to understand. (Anderson et al. 1985:63–64.)

Short words and simple sentences are not always easy to read. Often it is the complicated words that students either remember, or can read because it comes naturally to them in that situation. Sometimes they become frustrated when it is not the word they expect, even if it is a simpler word.

Harold McCracken in his video "The McCracken Philosophy" (1990), used the following example to illustrate this point. First he used a little story about a skunk and a farmer and shows how at every point that he pauses the reader can predict what the next word is going to be. At points where there are alternatives to choose from, the reader uses his knowledge of the language patterns being used and a small amount of phonics to choose between the alternatives. Then McCracken tries to do the same thing using a text that he has taken from a grade reader, one that is similar to those used throughout the United States. Without looking at the words outside the box, try to read the passage and fill in the missing words.

A cat on a bus	
Tom had a ____ . Tom had to get to ____ ____	(job, his, job)
on a bus. Tom's pet cat, Rob, sat by him.	
A red bus ran ___ to Tom and Rob.	(up)
A big man ran ____ ____. The bus man said to	(the, bus)
Tom, "Men can get on ___ bus. But cats cannot	(my)
____ ___.	(get, on)
So Tom said to Rob, "No, Rob, cats cannot get	
on the bus. Go and sit on the ___ and ___."	(rug, nap)

You can see that many of the missing words are not what you expected. Also some of the words you would expect are not there. For example, the story says, "A big man ran the bus" instead of "A driver drove the bus." Tom tells the cat to go and sit on a rug and take a nap. This does not fit in with what we know about bus stops. Thus, using short, simple words does not necessarily make the story easy to read.

> This is not language. It is a book written in order to have kids pronounce words. Reading is not pronouncing words…No one would tell a cat to go and sit on a rug and take a nap at a bus stop! (McCracken 1990, video)

Therefore, a new reader's knowledge of the language, how it works, and what patterns of words go together, help the reader to predict and decode.

Let me give another example: If I were writing a primer in Takia, I might make the mistake of writing a story like the following one.

John bought the food.
John took the food home.
John gave the food to Betty.
Betty cooked the food in a pot.
John and Betty ate it.

Even though this story is written with a lot of repetition and uses simple sentences, Takia students would find it very difficult to read because it does not fit their way of saying things. People do not speak like that. It is unnatural text and therefore not predictable. It does not conform to the patterns of normal everyday speech. In PNG hundreds of languages have what are called serial verb constructions. These are strings of action words (verbs) with few or no naming words (nouns). The things being referred to by the naming words are understood from the context. The above story should then read something like the following:

John food he bought,
got, came to wife gave.
She cooked, they ate.

Similarly, many PNG languages have a word pattern which linguists call head-tail linkage, which is important for signaling the time sequence of events. Sentences in these languages often look like the following:

John bought food at the market.
Buying, he went home.
Arriving gave it to wife.
Giving, she cooked.
Cooking, they ate.

Every language has its special ways of ordering words and its own special linguistic features and patterns. These patterns must be reflected in the texts in primer stories. Then students can use their knowledge of their own language to help them learn how to read.

A well-structured text helps the student to work out the meanings of the words in the text and helps them understand the text as a whole.

> The most important text characteristic for comprehension and learning is textual coherence. The more coherent the text, the more likely the reader will be able to construct a coherent cognitive model of the information in the text. (Armbruster 1984:203)

Some people design early reading materials by severely limiting the vocabulary used, thinking that this will make it easier for the beginning reader. This is not, however, always helpful. Texts such as these, called 'considerate text', can make mental processing of the print more difficult. McCormick (1990b:9) lists the following four practices which are unhelpful as far as students are concerned.

- reducing sentence length by destroying interclausally explicit connectives
- selecting simpler, but less descriptive vocabulary
- altering the flow of topic and comment relations in paragraphs
- eliminating qualifying statements that specify the conditions under which generalizations are thought to hold

Primer texts that are used for teaching reading need to be natural texts and whole texts that are easily understood, using words that are well-known and expected in the context. When writing stories for primers, also use the normal joining words (connectives) which join clauses together, even if it makes the sentence longer.

Approximate reading behaviours

The reading lesson and the primer page material must be seen by the student as being relevant to real reading.

> From the onset, the question repeatedly asked by the students was, "when are we going to read?" By the time we finished lessons in the pre-reader and began work in the first primer, interest and enthusiasm had waned and more students were absent for longer periods of time in order to handle their normal social and economic responsibilities. The remaining students were happy to do the drills, but after only eight primer lessons general interest in continuing faded almost completely...It was obvious to us that...these students were not grasping the materials as steps building up to reading. (Vollrath 1990:6–7)

As mentioned in the section on learning styles (see §1.2), learning by doing and learning by imitating the real thing is often how skills are learned in the types of cultures in which we work. In PNG, breaking the task down into small steps, learning the steps first, and then putting them together is not the usual way of learning something.

> One of the more out-of-date ways to approach the teaching of reading was to emphasise the teaching of letters first, then words, then comprehension skills, then later to expose the learner to lots of easy reading practice. More recently, the tendency is to reverse this emphasis; to expose the child to lots of reading first and foremost…and then to teach smaller parts in a more informal way in the context of meaningful material. The theory is that although children do need to be taught word-attack skills, it is more important to realise that children learn to read by approximating reading behaviour. (Harris 1987:45)

Have a positive focus rather than a negative one

In some methods in which linguistic insights have influenced the way reading is taught, consonants are not presented in isolation as they often cannot be pronounced correctly on their own. This has led to the practice of teaching by negative focus. Aboringinal teachers in Australia have found this negative focus very confusing. And when it is combined with complex syllable boxes (see the following illustration), teachers and students alike are confused as to what exactly is being taught. I suspect this type of problem is not confined just to Australia.

Compare the two different ways of teaching *k* in the following sample primer page.

Using negative focus

Using positive focus

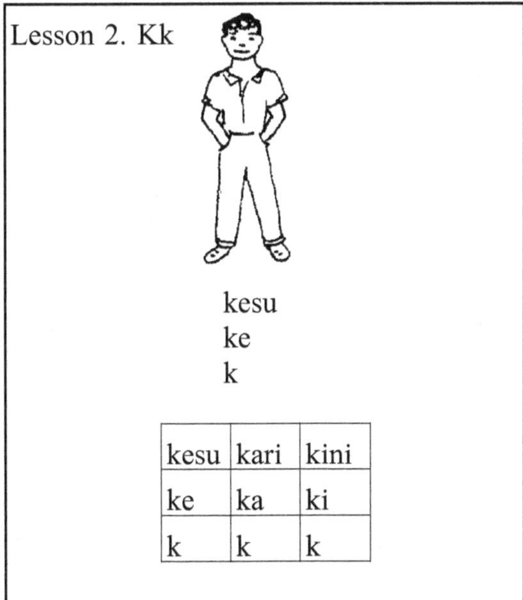

It is important that the teacher and the student are both clear on what is actually being taught in the primer lesson. In the Gudschinsky-style lesson above (on the left), some people are not sure if *k* is being taught or *e*. In the alternative lesson (on the right), it is more obvious that *k* is being taught. The sound *k* is given a positive focus since it is stated at the top of the page, and it is the sound at the end of all the drills.

Teach phonics early and quickly

Phonics is a helpful decoding strategy. The 1986 United States Department of Education booklet *Research about Teaching and Learning* says that children who are taught phonics get off to a better start in learning to read than those who are not taught phonics. It states:

> Children get a better start in reading if they are taught phonics. Learning phonics helps them to understand the relationship between letters and sounds and to "break the code" that links the words they hear with the words they see in print. (p. 21)

This conclusion is also backed up by the research report of the National Institute of Education's Commission on Reading (1985:37).

Phonics teaches what each letter of the alphabet is and what sound it makes. Then students are taught to blend the sounds together to say words. A lot of phonics research has been done, and it shows that teaching phonics to beginning readers is very helpful. If that is the case, then it would be good to include in the primer lesson some phonics type activities. These need to be balanced, however, by teaching other types of reading strategies as well, and the teaching of phonics should not be dragged out for too long in any one lesson nor in the total teaching package.

> Phonics ought to be conceived as a technique for getting children off to a fast start in mapping the relationships between letters and sounds...Once the basic relationships have been taught, the best way to get children to refine and extend their knowledge of letter-sound correspondences is through repeated opportunities to read...A number of programs try to teach too many letter-sound relationships and phonic instruction drags out over too many years...The right maxims for phonics are: Do it early. Keep it simple. (Anderson et al. 1985:38, 43)

Decoding

Decoding involves more than looking at words one letter after another. Readers form ideas in their minds as to what the word might be, using many different pieces of information.

> A possible interpretation of a word usually begins forming in the mind as soon as even partial information has been gleaned about the letters in the word...The possible interpretation reinforces the analysis of the remaining information contained in the letters...When enough evidence from the letters and the context becomes available, the possible interpretation becomes a positive identification. (Anderson et al. 1985:11)

Now look at the example below from Mike Dilena's *The Active Reader* which illustrates that it is not necessary to teach total syllabification or sounding out of every word, but rather to encourage the use of clues from beginning sounds of words along with clues from the context of the story to help in decoding.

> A language does not use all possible arrangements of the sounds or letters comprised in its system. If accidentally a forbidden combination appears, we automatically correct it to what we think it should be. Eg. If we transpsoe some of hth lettres in a text, it sitll remians surprisingly intleligible. One cuold even get used to htis sort of thing aeftr a hwile.
>
> Or one cn lve out ltrs nd the msg will be nvrthlss qte understndbl. Ths is abrvtn. Smthg lke ths is dne in Hbrw wrtg, whr only the consnts ar wrtn.
>
> Eaven extry lettchrs kan bee ritten, withaoutt mutch harm beaing dun.

Link content to motivation

Below is a page from a primer designed for students who want to learn to read the Bible. It is from the creation story and is the part about God making light. It is important that people learning to read, especially adults, are taught using materials that they want to read.

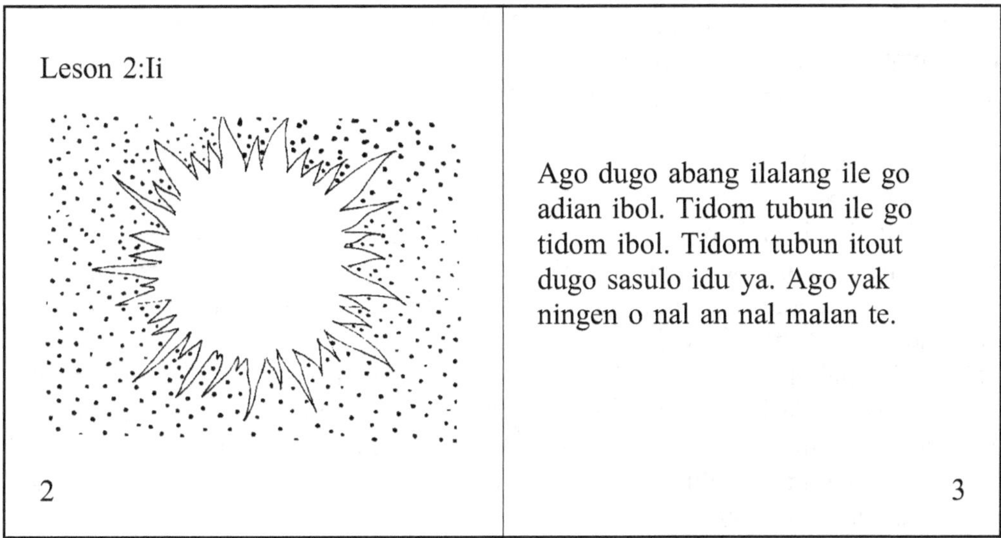

Leson 2:Ii

Ago dugo abang ilalang ile go adian ibol. Tidom tubun ile go tidom ibol. Tidom tubun itout dugo sasulo idu ya. Ago yak ningen o nal an nal malan te.

2 3

The Vollraths with the Hewa in PNG, and Borneman with Kriol in Australia, found that the people felt their expectations were being fulfilled much better when the reading lessons were connected to the actual things that they wanted to learn to read. After the Vollraths initially tried a traditional Gudschinsky approach, Karen Vollrath wrote:

> It was obvious to us that...these students were not grasping the materials as steps building up to reading...The objectives that we had set for the course...had been accomplished, but the student's expectations of being able to read had not been met, and there was no interest in resuming further study. (Vollrath 1990:7)

Some years later the Vollraths decided to develop a whole language approach in their literacy work, using Scripture text as the foundation for reading and writing lessons.

> Returning from furlough in August, 1989, we found that there continued to be a general coolness towards literacy, but the desire to acquire more knowledge about Scripture was extremely high.
>
> The whole-language approach has proved ideal in the Hewa context because each student can determine and control his own material and the pace at which he

> prefers to handle it in order to meet his own unique set of expectations. (Vollrath 1990:7, 16)

It is a good idea to base the primer lessons on something that the people actually want to learn to read. Mack Graham (Western Highlands Province, PNG) designed the Kandawo primer to teach the people to be able to read three local legends.

> By the time they finish the primer they will be able to read these three books. Hopefully they will be able to feel confident to try other books, but at least they will be able to read these three. (personal communication)

Keep lesson format simple

The lesson format should be simple so that untrained teachers can understand the principles behind the format, handle the teaching of the lessons easily, and yet be able to adapt and add to the lessons in meaningful ways if necessary. Teachers should be able to control the materials well and be comfortable with them.

If this design principle is followed, any person who has learnt to read using the primers should be able in turn to teach someone else to read using the same materials. The simpler and more understandable the format, the less need for complicated training programmes and teacher's manuals. If natural teaching strategies are used, then lesson formats and guide books are simplified considerably.

The lessons themselves need to have a natural flow that leads the teacher through the necessary stages fluently. McCormick states:

> The lessons should have a natural flow (to some extent this is "logical," to some extent it is "cultural")
>
> This "natural flow" should be evident at all levels/stages of the program, i.e., within each lesson (from one activity to another), from term to term, from prep school to community school, etc.
>
> Part of the "naturalness" is the coherence within each lesson, within each term, within the program as a whole, with regard to the relation between prep school and community school.
>
> There should be a progression ("flow") from known to unknown, from simple to more complex at every transition: within each lesson (from one activity to another), from term to term, from prep school to community school, etc. (McCormick 1990b)

The primer lesson design that I developed for use in a training course at the Madang Teachers College some years ago did this to some extent. See the following sample page.

Naa taka boun Gono keus lori boun disilen. Disil oun Naru; tetek boun Sonde an lori naanu; disil genen.

tetek
kesu
kari
kini

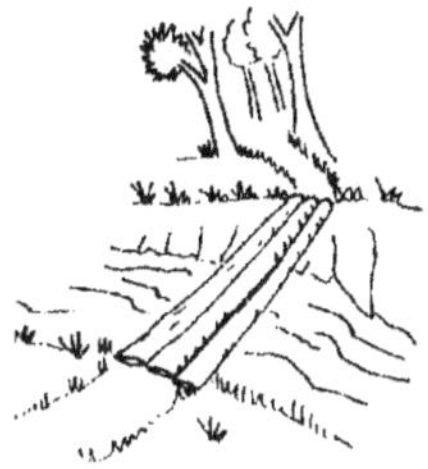

Gono kesu lori boun disilen
Gono **k**esu lori boun disilen
Gono ____ lori boun disilen

kesu
ke su
k

kesu tetek kari

1. Tama ______ bulu; fi yen.

2. _____ beleb boun dale di, laa fen.

3. Tamo _____ boun so; yen.

kesu	kari	kini	kuku;
ke	ka	ki	ku

kesu
kari
kini
tete**k**

kesu	saki
kari	kodol
saki	kari
kodol	kesu

Naa taka _____ gono kesu _____ boun disilen. Disil oun Naru; t____ boun Sonde an lori _____ disil genen.

The lesson started with a chunk of whole language (meaningful text) from a story that had been written and made into a book. The focus of attention then moved from the chunk to the sentence level, word level, individual sounds, and then built back up to word level, sentence level, and finally returned to the whole piece of text. I designed it that way so that the student teachers would be forced to follow the design when constructing a similar primer of their own. In this way I tried to ensure they would keep a natural flow throughout the lesson from whole to part and back to whole again.

The teacher must understand the reading process

Too often literacy programmes neglect their most valuable resource—the intelligence and skill of the teachers themselves.

> One most important application is that inasmuch as the teacher him or herself is the most important factor in reading instruction (and there is excellent research support

> for this conclusion), the teacher who understands the reading process best (whether intuitively or self-consciously) will be the better teacher. (McCormick 1990a:4)

The teacher who understands the reading process best will be the better teacher. Assuming that is true, then it is important that trainers of teachers spend time helping them to understand what teaching reading is all about. Two things are helpful. One is to understand the reading process. The second is to know what is helpful to students who are learning to read. Knowing these two things helps teachers think about what they are doing, understand why they are doing it, and helps them think of changes that need to be made so that lessons will fit better with the culture and the needs of the students. Teachers who understand what they are doing get better results.

Control the amount of time engaged in meaningful reading

Studies have shown that, although teachers think students are busy with their work during class, all kinds of things interrupt them and keep them from giving their full attention to the task at hand. Also, a lot of their work is seat work or busy work, that is, work they are given to do to keep them busy while the teacher is doing something else. This work is not necessarily helpful.

McDermott's study (1976, 1977) of two reading groups in the same classroom is one of the more well-known studies. His observations showed that:

> Children in the high group were found to spend three times as much time on tasks as those in the low group...The circumstances under which the low group had to get organized and on task were not the same as for the high group. (p. 103)

A lot of time in the low group was spent on getting organised and this group had twenty times more interruptions than the high group. Therefore, they got a lot less practice at reading. Also, the teacher focused more on phonic strategies with the low group and less on things like gaining meaning from reading, encouraging self-correction, and prediction.

When designing primers, literacy workers need to keep in mind how much of the students' time is going to be involved in practicing helpful reading strategies and how much time is going to be spent on other things.

6.3 Choose a method and design a layout

Now that you have looked at the sounds of your language and their frequencies (§6.1) and considered which information from reading research and education writings is important for your reading lessons (§6.2), it is time to think about choosing the reading methods you are going to use, what kind of a primer you will need, and designing a primer layout that will suit your situation. It is possible, and some people would say it is preferable, to use several different methods when teaching reading as some students find one method more helpful than others.

I have mentioned different reading methods in chapters 7, 8, and 9. There are many ways of teaching reading, and for each possible method there are people who say that is the best way to teach. The many different methods can be grouped into three types. One group start with a whole text, concentrates on helping the student to read the whole text, and gradually teaches the students to read the parts. We can think of this group of methods as starting with the whole and moving to the parts (whole to part). The second group starts with parts of words and teaches the students how to build the parts together making sense of each word as they go and gradually building up to reading a whole story (part to whole). The third group does both at the same time. It teaches the student to read the whole and at the same time to focus on some of the parts in the whole and learn them. This approach is called an interactive or integrated approach.

The main question as far as the primers are concerned is are you going to start with wholes or parts or do both?

Starting with wholes has the advantage that you can use interesting texts straight away. The words and sentences in primer and reading lessons, and the things students are learning to read, can be real language, written like they speak. Starting with parts first often results in unnatural and uninteresting texts. It can result in texts like those pictured below (taken from *First Aid in Reading, Writing and Spelling* by Theodore MacDonald).

A man ran.
Dan ran.
A fat cat ran.
Can Nan pat a cat?
A fat cat ran at a fat rat in a bag.

After many such lessons, students can read:

If you were learning to read for the first time, you might feel encouraged at being able to decode the words in the story about Dan and Nan. However, the stories are not very exciting or interesting. The things that happen do not happen in real life. Have you ever seen a fat cat run at a fat rat in a bag, or a cat bagging a rat? Also, in English, we never say sentences like these in real life. We often say if such and such, then so and so, but we would never link "Hal hitting a pig" with his "cat bagging a rat." Those two actions have no meaningful connection. Also, we would not be able to predict any of those things from what we have read earlier in the sentence, and once we have read them I am not sure that we would feel they had much meaning or made sense. Remember we are trying to teach that reading is making meaning of print and that it is fun.

So, if you choose to start with parts and build to wholes, make sure that the stories (texts) in your primer lessons make sense and that the language in them is what people would really say in day-to-day conversation.

On the other hand, you can teach the same kinds of sounds and words in the above texts starting from whole stories. Note the following.

This text is one often used in Australia to teach young children to read. It is usually well-known to children because it is a very old well-known folk tale. The text does not quite match the way we talk, but children love the story and find the poetic style very interesting. (There are a lot of stories that are used that do fit all these characteristics—meaningful, interesting, and matching the way we speak, for example, stories like "Who is the strongest?" "Are you my mother?" "Just this once," and many others.)

The children are interested in finding out what happens to the gingerbread man in the end. From this story the children learn the words *am, can, ran, man, woman*. Teachers can then build on this knowledge and extend it to other words such as *cat, rat, mat*. Teachers and students can make up sentences about other things that the gingerbread man ran away from.

Teaching can start by using the whole story and then moving from the whole to looking at the parts.

So, you will need to decide where you are going to start in your primer lessons—with whole text, or with the small parts that make up the text, or if you are going to do both and interrelate the two approaches.

You also need to decide if you are going to teach phonics (single sounds of the language) or syllables (combinations of sounds) when you are looking at the small parts that go together to make up a word. (See the second subsection under 6.1 and chapter 7.) Teachers generally prefer to teach phonics. Phonics has the advantage that only a few sounds need to be taught; this way of teaching has proven to be effective all over the world.

It is important, therefore, to take into account all the above considerations when you plan your primer. Having done that, then fill out something like the following checklist so you can keep in mind clearly what are going to be your guiding ideas in constructing your primers.

Teach using	
• phonics	____
• syllable	____
• word	____
• sentence	____
Include meaningful reading in the primer	____
Whole to part or part to whole	____
Size of pages	____
Number of pages per lesson	____
Built-in review	____
Number of sounds or syllables to teach	____
Use key words	____
Use pictures	____
For children or adults	____
Controlled vocabulary or free text	____

Teach using	
phonics	✓
syllable	
word	
sentence	
Include meaningful reading in the primer	✓
Whole to part or	✓
part to whole	
Size of pages	A4
Number of pages per lesson	1
Built-in review	✓
Number of new sounds or syllables per lesson	1
Use key words	✓
pictures	✓
For children or adults	children
Controlled vocabulary or free text	✓

If you choose the options listed next, then your design may look something like lessons 3 and 4 in the next chart.

Lesson 3. M, m

I am a gingerbread man.
I ran away from the little old woman,
I ran away from the little old man,
I can run away from you, ! I can!

Lesson 4. Revising M, m.
(Read the story from lesson 3.)

I ran away from the man.
I ran away from the mouse.
I ran away from the woman.
I can run. I can! I can!

Man
m

gingerbread man
man
m

(Look for 'man' and 'm' in the story above and below.)

My mother makes marvelous gingerbread men.

(Match the pictures and words)

man

mouse

moth

mat

Man
m

moth
m

mat
m

mouse
m

Reread the story.

6

(Find the words that are the same)

man	man	mat	mouse
moth	mop	moth	mouse
mat	mat	man	mat

(Read the complete gingerbread man story together)

7

If you choose the options shown in this next chart, then your design for lesson 5 may look something like the one following it. You can use more pages per lesson if you need to. In the Takia, I used six small pages (see §8.3).

Teach using	
phonics	
syllable	✓
word	
sentence	
Include meaningful reading in the primer	some
Whole to part	✓
or part to whole	
Size of pages	half A4
Number of pages per lesson	2
Built-in review	✓
Number of new sounds or syllables per lesson	1
Use key words	✓
pictures	✓
For children or adults	adult
Controlled vocabulary	✓
or free text	

Lesson 5. M, m

ma mu
mama mumu

ma	mu
pa	pu
sa	su

mama
ma

mama papa mumu
susa mama papa

10

mouli maus

meri moni

Mama na papa em i mas karim ol pikinini long haus sik na kisim sut.

11

If you are not sure about whether you want to use phonics, syllables, or whole language or choose parts of each method, chapters 7, 8, and 9 have examples of what others have done with these different methods.

Once you choose a lesson format it is good to keep using it throughout the primer. That makes it easier for you to design the lessons and easier for the teacher to teach them.

When designing lessons, it is good to keep a checklist as you proceed through the lessons. Then you will know at a glance what you have already covered and what still needs to be covered, and you can make sure there is a good progression through the primer(s). A sample check sheet is included below but it is best if you design your own to suit your own needs.

Lesson No.	Teaching	key word	Revising	possible picturable words	practice reading suggestion
1	a	ant	—	ant, axe, alligator	story about alligators
2	r	rabbit	a	rabbit, rock	
3	m	man	a, r	man, mop, moth, mat, mouse	gingerbread man story
4 etc.					

6.4 The primer as part of the reading lesson

The primer lesson is, however, just part of a reading programme. There needs to be time set aside for other reading activities such as shared reading, time for Uninterrupted Sustained Silent Reading (USSR), guided readings, readings of poems and songs, and reading texts to get information.

In §5.1 using well-known songs in reading readiness programmes is mentioned. They can also be used in the reading lesson. Hymn books, song books, and song charts are one of the most valuable resources teachers can use.

It is also good to include times when the class reads a book together (shared reading §8.2), or the teacher or a student reads a story or text to the whole class. Sharing reading together shows the students the value of reading, that reading is all about understanding the message that is printed on the page, and that reading can be enjoyed and talked about.

Students should be given the opportunity to read and reread books and articles that are of interest to them. A time of USSR should be included in reading lessons if there are enough books for students to each have one.

Some teachers like to include guided reading as part of their lessons. Guided reading is done by first asking the students a question that needs to be answered from a text, and then giving students time to read the text to find the answer. This helps students to focus on certain parts of the text and to learn to read for information. The questions can be varied to suit the ability of the students. It is good to start with easy questions and ones that concentrate on the main point of the article.

For example, when Nick was reading "The Rescue," I asked him, "What were the two ways the rescue team searched for the buried skier?" This was a fairly easy question as the answer was in the text, and it was one of the main points in the story.

Questions can be made more difficult as the students improve in their reading ability. For example, later in the year, Nick was reading "You are what you eat," and I asked him "Are you a carnivore, herbivore, or omnivore?"

This was a more difficult question as Nick had to read the text to find out what a carnivore, herbivore, and omnivore were and then he had to decide which category humans fitted into before answering my question. The answer was not directly in the text.

Questions like these get students thinking more carefully about the meanings of the stories they are reading. It shows them that getting the meaning is the important thing about reading. Guided reading also helps students learn to skim—read parts of the story and focus carefully on detail in other parts of the story. Both are good reading skills to develop.

Reciprocal questions are when the student and the teacher take turns to ask and answer questions about a story they have read. Students usually enjoy doing this as it gives them a chance to try and outsmart the teacher. Again the questions can be varied in difficulty according to the students' skills and the level of difficulty of the passage they are reading.

Lesson frameworks

I find when I am teaching that it is very helpful to develop my own lesson framework or routine. Actually, after a few sessions I tend to do this automatically. I start out with a rough outline of what I want to do and gradually this gets modified by the specific situation, by the class needs, by what seems to work well and what does not work, and by acting on my reflections of various aspects of my teaching practice.

These frameworks help give an overall structure to what I do and free me as a teacher to concentrate on the interaction with the students rather than having to worry about what it is that I need to do next. The lesson framework also helps speed up planning of future lessons and allows me to spend the time saved on other important aspects of teacher preparation.

The following pages give some examples of different lesson frameworks. You need to think about what is needed in your situation and work with the teachers to help them develop a lesson framework that fits their needs.

When I consulted with the Dami TPPS programme, the following framework for the reading and writing lessons was developed.

Greetings

Welcome on arrival, sharing of news, mark the roll

Devotions or moral teaching

Songs

These would be from the collection of songs that the teachers had previously written up on charts. Teachers use a pointer to direct the students' attention to the words as the song is sung together.

Reading

Shared reading experience

This could either be doing a shared book lesson, or shared reading of wall chart, story murals, blackboard stories, or class books.

Paired reading

USSR (using the library corner)

Teacher read story

(related to day's theme or lesson)

Break time

Song

Writing

Letter formation lesson

Dictated writing or process writing

When I taught adult migrant literacy in Australia I developed, over time, the following framework for my lessons.

Greetings and announcements

Reading

Familiar reading

students' choices

-
-
- last week's main text

Shared readings

-
-
-

Serial Story—an episode

Paired reading

Conversation practice

Writing

Spelling

Revise:

Look/cover/write/check practice

Blackboard dictation

Personal writing

This lesson framework was just a guide and I changed it when I needed to because of a particular situation. I added things like reciprocal questions, writing story summaries, ordering story summaries, retelling stories, group writing, and teacher demonstrations of writing.

The following reading lesson framework uses a Gudschinsky primer:

Discussion

Teacher reads a story with the class

Introduction of key word and illustration

Learning the new sound

Word building

Reading exercises

Writing
- letter formation exercises
- dictation
- creative writing

Song

6.5 The primer as part of the literacy programme

Just as the primer is only part of the reading lesson, so the primers are only part of a literacy programme. Primers are often used in the initial stages. Then students move on to small books with collections of stories in them and finally to longer books. Primers are only one kind of literacy books. You need to prepare other books at each level for the students.

If you just teach students to read the primers and leave them there, they will soon lose the reading skills that they have learned. It is important that students continue to read, becoming fluent, and choosing to read as a part of their lifestyle.

The following chart gives an overview of the suggested reading programme for the Dami TPPS. The primers are just one part of the programme.

Reading Activities				Writing
	Formal	Big Book	USSR	
Term 1	Readiness	A new book each week.	Instant readers, alphabet book	Pre-writing all letter shapes, own names
Term 2	Primer 1 introduces alphabet 2 sounds per week plus revision	A new book each week	Alphabet stories*	Formation of all letters dictated and copied writing
Term 3	Primer 2 reviews alphabet 2 sounds per week	A new book each week	village stories and humorous stories	writing own sentences with help
Term 4**	Language experience	Some new Big Books and some old favourites	class books individual books	writing own stories with help

* a story written about the key word for each letter of the alphabet

** Originally the Dami did not plan to have a fourth term leaving students and teachers free to work in their gardens, but others asked me what I would suggest for term 4 if they did!

The following chart gives an overview of the literacy programme that was developed in the Maiwala/Labe TPPS programme (PNG).

Term	Theme (Big Books)	Spelling	Individual writing and drawing	Group writing and drawing
1	Familiar animals	All the sounds	Watch as teacher models writing; encourage students to try and write own name and captions.	Class book: Rewrite a story (teacher and children make story together. Teacher writes text; children draw pictures).
2				
3	Family and self	Review	Write own captions	
4	Experience, various feelings		Conference writing	

The Big Books are as follows.

Term 1	Term 2
theme: familiar animals 1. Big mouth frog 2. Are you my mother? 3. Who sank the boat? 4. I shone the torch 5. Crocodile daydreams 6. Whose friend is he? 7. If I were a mother pig 8. Let's play	theme: familiar animals 1. If I were a butterfly 2. You must be my friends 3. If I were a bird 4. Who will help me? 5. If I were a rooster 6. You belong in the water 7. If I were a big fish 8. Bossy dog 9. If I were a big dog 10. If I were a mother cat
Term 3	**Term 4**
theme: self, family, legends 1. During school holidays (boy) 2. During school holidays (girl) 3. When I grow up (boy) 4. When I grow up (girl) 5. I love (like) my father 6. I love (like) my mother 7. What is your mother doing? 8. Where is your mother? 9. Ant and Crab (legend) 10. Egret and Turtle (legend)	theme: feelings, experience 1. Our sides ached 2. Fishing first time 3. I caught something white 4. Help! Cassowary is chasing me! 5. Slingshot 6. Getting pineapples 7. Getting *dulubi* fruit 8. Paddling a canoe 9. You are caught! 10. Bush fowl

This section has given two examples of literacy programmes to give you some ideas in shaping your own.

7

Phonics, Syllable, Word, and Sentence Approaches

Chapters 7, 8, and 9 give examples of various ways of teaching reading and designing primers. Some ways suit some situations better than others. Some ways fit teachers' personal beliefs about the reading and learning process better than others.

All methods have things that are useful in teaching reading. All have their advantages and disadvantages. Even though one particular method is used primarily, there is no reason why things from other approaches cannot be used whenever there is an advantage in doing so.

7.1 Phonics approach

Phonics is defined as "the method of teaching reading which focuses on teaching letter-to-sound correspondences and the subsequent ability to 'sound out' words" (McCormick 1990:1).

In other words, when people teach phonics they teach what the symbol or letter looks like, and the sound which that letter stands for. In some languages, sometimes two letters stand for one sound, for example, in English *ph* in 'photograph', *oo* in 'book' and *ng* in 'sing'. Once the letters have been taught, then students are taught to blend (run together) the sounds of each letter into the next and come up with the word. For example, the sounds *m, a, n* blend together and are read as the word 'man'.

A man ran.
Dan ran.
A fat cat ran.
Can Nan pat a cat?
A fat cat ran at a fat rat in a bag.

People who teach reading by teaching the learners to **only** sound words out, assume several things.

- They assume that readers need to sound out a word to get meaning from it.
- They assume reading means learning to say words out loud.
- They assume readers need to sound out every letter in every word.

Sometimes, however, we know words without sounding them out. Sometimes we only need to look at a word carefully or sound out only part of it. Often we read without sounding out words at all.

Also, we know from English that just being able to sound out letters in words or say words is not all there is to reading. Some people can do this and still not understand the meaning of words. (This is often called 'barking at print'. Such people can make the right noises but do not understand the meanings.)

Furthermore, it is necessary to know the context of some words in order to know how to say them or to understand their meaning. This is especially so in English. For example, how would you say the three words below?

wind read live

Unless these words are placed in a context within a sentence or story, a beginning reader would not know how to sound the words out, nor would he know their meanings. Consider the following sentences which have these words in them, but in different contexts.

The *wind* blew through the trees.
Wind the cord around the top of the mower and then pull it hard to start it.

I *read* his story with interest.
I would like to *read* his story.

Fish *live* in the sea.
Live fish wriggle and flap when you try to hold them.

Some words have double meanings so it is necessary to see or hear them with other words around them to know which meaning is being used. This is the case in Djinang, the Australian Aboriginal language I worked with. An English example of this is:

My daughters play in a *band.*
I need an elastic *band.*

So reading is more than phonics, more than just learning to sound out and blend words together. But phonics is a good thing to teach along with other things. It has been found that students "get a better start in reading if they are taught phonics" ("What Works" 1986, U. S. Department of Education).

Learning the names of the letters is a good thing too. It is good for students to have a way of talking about the letters. But reading is more than this.

Spelling in vernacular languages is often easier than spelling in English. In vernacular languages, there is usually only one way to write each sound (phonemic alphabets). So teaching phonics is easier than teaching phonics in English where one sound may be written in several different ways. Stellan and Eivor Lindrud chose to prepare reading lessons in the Kol language of East New Britain Province (PNG) using a phonics approach. That is, they wanted to concentrate on teaching the sounds and symbols (letters) first. After two or three months when the learner knows the letters and knows how to attack words, they encourage teachers and students to spend more class time on reading whole texts.

The method of teaching reading used with the Kol has three stages. It is designed to help the learner become an independent reader and writer after just sixteen weeks of schooling. The three stages are as follows (Lindrud 1994a:30–31):

> **Stage 1**
>
> This stage lasts about 8 weeks. During that time all of the letters are taught. Word attack is also thoroughly practiced on 75 words. The learner both writes and reads those words. One letter and three new words are taught each day. Each new word is discussed together by the learners and the teacher. Then the sounds of the word are determined by saying the word slowly and listening to the sounds. The students write down the letters corresponding to the sounds. The new words contain only known letters and the new letter for the day. A story time lasting for three minutes is also included in each lesson.
>
> **Stage 2**
>
> This stage is also about 8 weeks long. During the first two weeks, 18 sentences are studied. Each sentence is 4 words long. Three of the sentences are taught each day. These are taught in two different ways. They are taught by tracking, that is, the instructor points to the words (written on the blackboard for the entire group to see) and the class follows the reading. The sentences are also taught by fast syllable analysis of each word in the sentence. The learners also write the sentences and read them from their lapboards.
>
> After two weeks, the learners are given cards to read. These cards have the same sentences that were taught from the blackboard. The students write these sentences from memory. The next two weeks, the same procedure is repeated with another

set of 18 sentences which are six words long. The sixth and seventh weeks, the students read short stories. They also write messages and letters together with the teacher. These messages are familiar to learners because they are of the sort that are commonly sent by people in the area. Stories from the culture are also read. All of these stories are printed on durable cards.

Stage 3

This stage lasts for the rest of the year (and the rest of the student's life). The learners apply the skills they have gained in literacy. In Prep Schools, reading and writing can be integrated with the other subjects.

(For more details see Lindrud and Lindrud 1994. Available from: Box 233, Ukarumpa via Lae, PNG.)

Below are pages 20 and 21 of an early Kol Primer, based on a phonics approach to teaching. This primer has since been replaced by handboards (see §12.3). The primer pages are included here to show what a phonics primer may look like. This lesson focuses on teaching the letter *p* and using it with other letters that have already been taught.

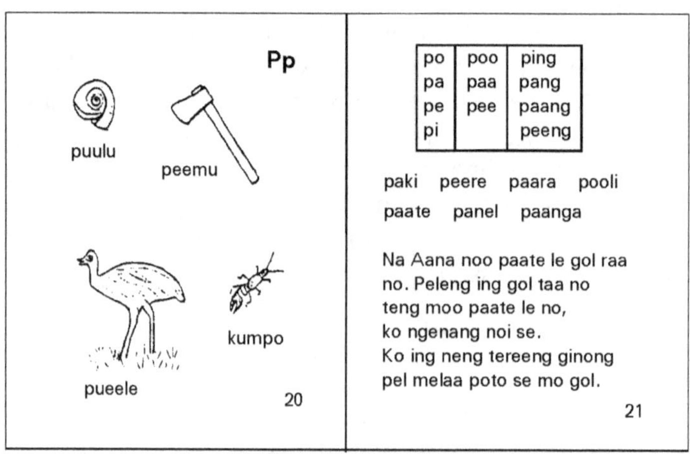

Pp

puulu

peemu

pueele

kumpo

20

po	poo	ping
pa	paa	pang
pe	pee	paang
pi		peeng

paki peere paara pooli

paate panel paanga

Na Aana noo paate le gol raa
no. Peleng ing gol taa no
teng moo paate le no,
ko ngenang noi se.
Ko ing neng tereeng ginong
pel melaa poto se mo gol.

21

Paul and Marcia Heineman working with the Lembena language, Enga (PNG) also designed primer materials that have a focus on phonics. Each lesson focuses on one letter or sound. The lesson starts with a story about the key word which begins with the letter that is being taught. This is followed by two questions about the story. Then a phonics lesson follows the story using a key word taken from the story. For example, the lesson that teaches the letter and sound *y* is given below.

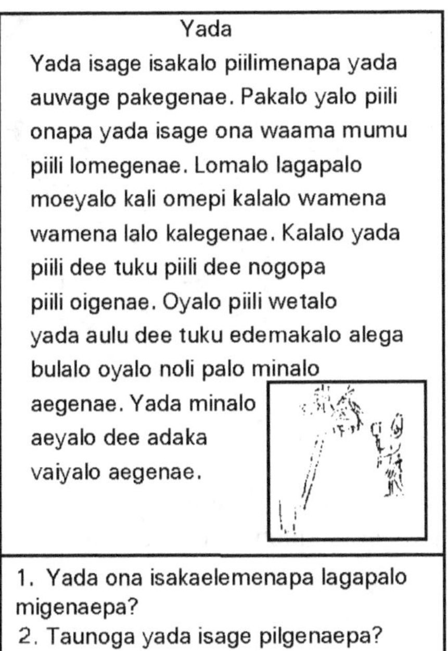

Yada

Yada isage isakalo piilimenapa yada auwage pakegenae. Pakalo yalo piili onapa yada isage ona waama mumu piili lomegenae. Lomalo lagapalo moeyalo kali omepi kalalo wamena wamena lalo kalegenae. Kalalo yada piili dee tuku piili dee nogopa piili oigenae. Oyalo piili wetalo yada aulu dee tuku edemakalo alega bulalo oyalo noli palo minalo aegenae. Yada minalo aeyalo dee adaka vaiyalo aegenae.

1. Yada ona isakaelemenapa lagapalo migenaepa?
2. Taunoga yada isage pilgenaepa?

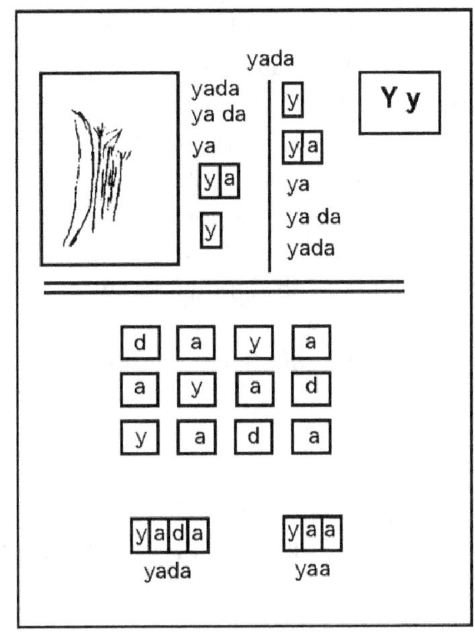

There are many ways of making phonic primers. The above are just two of the possibilities.

7.2 Syllable approach

Some people choose to use a syllable method when teaching others to sound out words and read. A description of syllables is given in §6.1. Syllables are made up of vowels and consonants. In their Nankina transfer primer, Craig and Pat Spaulding (1991) liken the sound of vowels to the sound of a conch shell, that is, a continuous kind of sound. In Nankina there are six vowels: *a,* , *e, i, o,* and *u.*

They liken the consonants to the sound of the *kundu* drum. A drum gives a brief sound, and the sound cannot be made to go on continuously. In Nankina these would be sounds and letters like *b, d, p, w, g, j, n, ŋ, m, t, r, s, j,* and *y.*

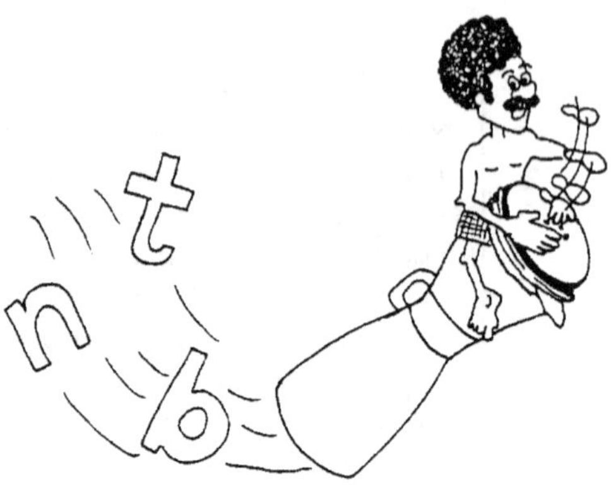

People who use the syllable method of teaching believe it is better for students to sound out syllables rather than to sound out each letter, especially when working with languages which have long words. Working with syllables enables students to break words into smaller "chunks."

Syllable primers

The early Daga primers (Milne Bay, PNG) followed a syllable approach in teaching reading. In primer 1, three of the vowels which occur most frequently in the language, *a, o,* and *u,* are taught first.

These vowels are then combined with *t, n, y,* and *p.* Vowels *i* and *o* are taught later on in this primer. There are five primers altogether in the series.

On the next page are pages 10 and 11 from primer 1 which focuses on the letter *n* and teaches the *na* and *nu* syllables. The syllables *ni, no,* and *ne* are taught in later lessons.

The lesson starts by using two key words and pictures (p. 10) to teach the new syllables. Then on page 11 the new syllables are compared and contrasted with syllables that have been taught previously. Then syllables are put together to make words, for example, *a* and *nu* making *anu.* The lesson concludes (p. 12) with a short story for the student to read. All the words in this story are made up of syllables which the students have been taught previously. Charts, flashcards, and exercises on the blackboard are used to supplement the primer materials.

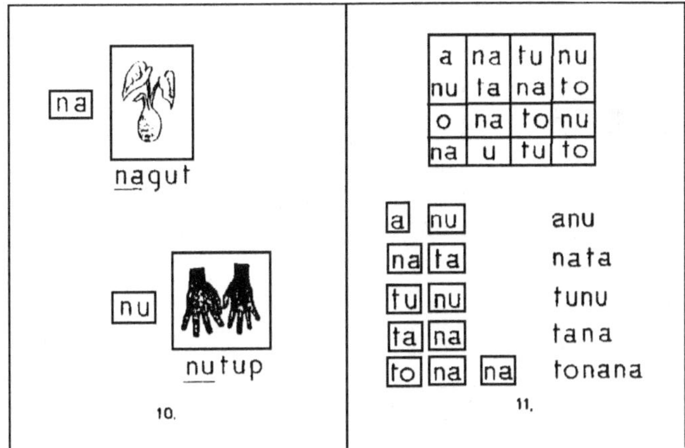

na

nagut

nu

nutup

10.

a	na	tu	nu
nu	ta	na	to
o	na	to	nu
na	u	tu	to

a nu anu

na ta nata

tu nu tunu

ta na tana

to na na tonana

11.

Included below are sample pages from other primers () which use the syllable approach.

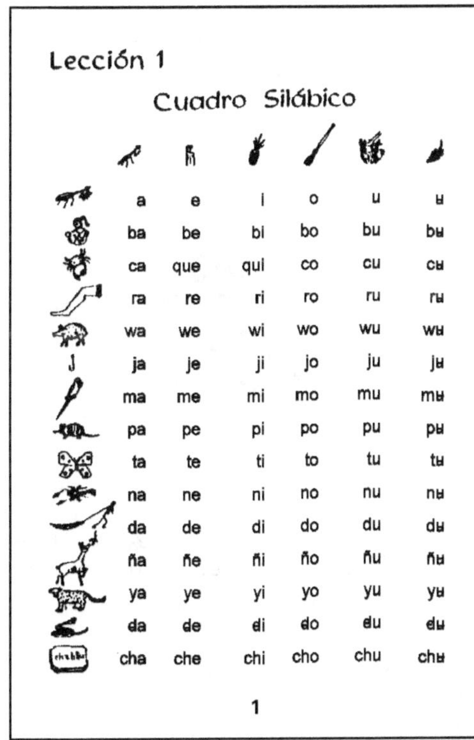

Lección 1

Cuadro Silábico

a	e	i	o	u	ʉ
ba	be	bi	bo	bu	bʉ
ca	que	qui	co	cu	cʉ
ra	re	ri	ro	ru	rʉ
wa	we	wi	wo	wu	wʉ
ja	je	ji	jo	ju	jʉ
ma	me	mi	mo	mu	mʉ
pa	pe	pi	po	pu	pʉ
ta	te	ti	to	tu	tʉ
na	ne	ni	no	nu	nʉ
da	de	di	do	du	dʉ
ña	ñe	ñi	ño	ñu	ñʉ
ya	ye	yi	yo	yu	yʉ
đa	đe	đi	đo	đu	đʉ
cha	che	chi	cho	chu	chʉ

1

Lección 3

beibo

ba	be	bi	bo	bu	bʉ
Ba	Be	Bi	Bo	Bu	Bʉ

o bi

obi

be i bo

beibo

bu ʉ

buʉ

bʉ be bo

bʉbebo

5

Unidad 3

M m

Ma	ma
Me	me
Mi	mi
Mo	mo
Mu	mu
Mʉ	mʉ

emu
mu
u

ma	me	mi	mo	mu	mʉ

a	e	i	o	u	ʉ
ma	me	mi	mo	mu	mʉ

10

u
mu
emu

i
mi
imi

emu pa'imʉ
Emu pa'imʉ.

i
mi
miu

a
ma
mami

miu pa'imʉ
Miu pa'imʉ.

Escriba:

m

M

emu

11

emu	mami
umu	mai
imi	mama
miu	emu
mai	mimi
mimi	imi
mami	miu
mama	umu

Junte cada palabra de la primera fila con la misma palabra de la segunda fila, trace una linea.

12

pa'imʉ	pa'imo	pa'ime

Emu pa'imʉ. Miime mai. Mame. Ma pa'ime. Meame. Mea pa'ime.

13

Laubach's syllable method and the each-one-teach-one approach

Dr Frank Laubach began his literacy work, using a syllable method, in the Philippines in 1929. Since that time his method has been used in over 96 countries of the world. During the great depression of the 1930s, a time when money and jobs were hard to get, it seemed that his successful literacy work would come to a halt. It was then that a Filipino chief declared, "Literacy is the best thing that ever came to my people—everyone in my village who knows how to read must teach someone else." This was the beginning of the each-one-teach-one idea.

The each-one-teach-one approach is still appropriate for today because of (1) the high number of illiterate adults in the world, (2) the many things which stop busy adults becoming literate, and (3) the huge costs and time involved in using trained teachers to run literacy campaigns.

> If it is necessary to have highly trained teachers and specially constructed schools, and to find time when the adults can be brought together between their working hours and sleep, the immense cost and the problem of finding a time are almost insurmountable. If, on the other hand, adult volunteers can be organized to teach their illiterate friends at home at any hour of the day—each one teaching one—the cost is very small. (Laubach 1960:1)

Laubach says that if people are to use this each-one-teach-one approach then it is important to have a special type of lesson which requires a minimum of skill in teaching.

Laubach used his literacy method in many different languages in the Philippines. The languages were all easy to work in because their alphabets were all based on the languages' phonemes. A phonemic alphabet is one where each letter stands for just one sound, and each sound is always represented by the same letter. Laubach says that teaching someone to read with this kind of an alphabet is easy. As soon as students can learn the sounds of the letters, they can then pronounce any new word without help. The Filipino languages were also easy to work in because their syllables all ended in a vowel.

Laubach later travelled to many other countries and adapted his method to suit their situations, but some of the languages were very hard to work in, particularly those in India. But over the years he kept experimenting and learning from his experiences. He would try again the next day or the next week or with the next language, trying to come up with a method that worked well. He did this because he felt that, "each-one-teach-one is a possibility only if the lessons are easy, swift, pleasant to learn, and easy for any untrained person to teach. . . . we are still making changes and additions to our method, but they are not drastic changes" (Laubach 1960:10–11).

Laubach's method starts off by introducing the letters of the alphabet. Each letter is associated with an object, and the name of that object begins with the letter. The symbol for the letter sometimes resembles the shape of the object. In the first box below, *s* is the first sound in snake and the letter *s* looks something like a curled up snake. In the second box, the letter *p* is drawn over *papa*'s head to help connect the sound with the letter.

The letters and words are then used in sentences. See the following sample Hindi primer lesson (from Laubach 1960:12–13).

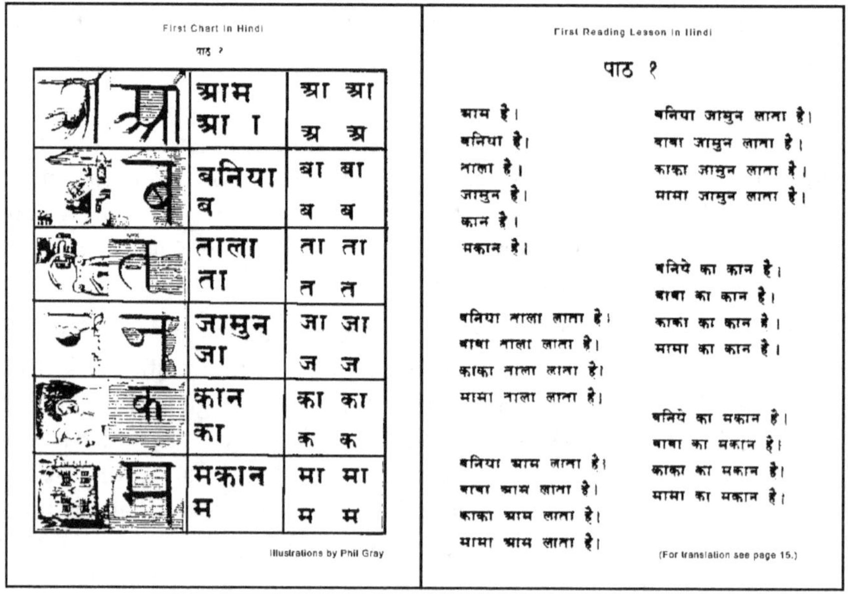

First Chart in Hindi

पाठ १

	आम आ ा	आ आ अ अ
	बनिया ब	बा बा ब ब
	ताला ता	ता ता त त
	जामुन जा	जा जा ज ज
	कान का	का का क क
	मकान म	मा मा म म

Illustrations by Phil Gray

First Reading Lesson in Hindi

पाठ १

आम है।
बनिया है।
ताला है।
जामुन है।
कान है।
मकान है।

बनिया ताला लाता है।
बाबा ताला लाता है।
काका ताला लाता है।
मामा ताला लाता है।

बनिया आम लाता है।
बाबा आम लाता है।
काका आम लाता है।
मामा आम लाता है।

बनिया जामुन लाता है।
बाबा जामुन लाता है।
काका जामुन लाता है।
मामा जामुन लाता है।

बनिये का कान है।
बाबा का कान है।
काका का कान है।
मामा का कान है।

बनिये का मकान है।
बाबा का मकान है।
काका का मकान है।
मामा का मकान है।

(For translation see page 15.)

All the lessons in the primer are similar to this sample. The left page of the lesson is the picture chart. There are four columns down the page. The first vertical column contains the pictures; the second shows how the pictured object and the letter look alike; the third has the name of the pictured object and below it the first letter of that name; and the fourth column contains a review of the letter for practice. The words and pictures on this chart are: mango, shopkeeper, padlock, an Indian fruit, ear, and house.

On the right page of each lesson is a story. The story should contain not more than four new words. Every word that appears on this story page is used at least five times.

Following is a translation of the story page of the above lesson.

This is a mango
This is a shopkeeper
This is a padlock
This is a cherry
This is an ear
This is a house

The shopkeeper brings a padlock
Grandfather brings a padlock
Father's brother brings a padlock
Mother's brother brings a padlock

The shopkeeper brings a mango
Grandfather brings a mango
Father's brother brings a mango
Mother's brother brings a mango

The shopkeeper brings a cherry
Grandfather brings a cherry
Father's brother brings a cherry
Mother's brother brings a cherry

This is the shopkeeper's ear
This is grandfather's ear
This is father's brother's ear
This is mother's brother's ear

This is the shopkeeper's house
This is grandfather's house
This is father's brother's house
This is mother's brother's house

The pictures, words, and letters on the left side face the story on the right side so that the student can find the word he wants with little or no help. In the story there are four people doing the same thing. The teacher only needs to help the student with one quarter of the reading. The stories are kept in this simple form to keep the reading easy for the student and also make sure he has a sense of achievement. Laubach says that interest should never be attempted at the expense of simplicity.

Here is an example of a Lauback primer lesson in Spanish.

		a	a	a a
		papá pa	pa	pa pa
		mamá ma	ma	ma ma
		dama da	da	da da
		vaca va	va	va va

a papá mamá dama vaca

papá llama a la vaca
mamá llama a la vaca
la dama llama a la vaca

papá va a la vaca
mamá va a la vaca
la dama va a la vaca

papá da agua a la vaca
mamá da agua a la vaca
la dama da agua a la vaca

papá ama a mamá
mamá ama a papá
la dama ama a papá

papá va a mamá
mamá va a papá
la dama va a papá

As each letter is introduced, the teacher points out the similarity between the letter and the illustration, for example:

This man is saying ah.

Here he is again, saying ah. See his open mouth and big chin.
Say ah.

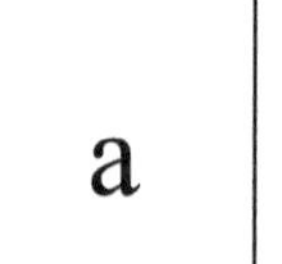

Here is ah again. See how it looks like the open mouth and the big chin.
Say ah.

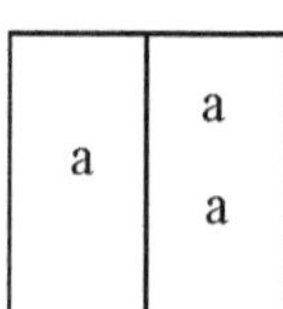

Here it is again. Say it.
What is this?

The number of lessons in a primer is determined by the number of letters in the alphabet. Usually five or six letters are taught each day. As soon as the sounds are well-known, teaching from the primer ends, and the student is ready for other readers. These readers follow similar patterns to the primers. The sentences are short and the words are all familiar. Five to ten new words are used in each lesson; each new word is repeated at least five times as soon as possible after being introduced, so the student will become familiar with it. "By the time the student finishes the graded series of approximately 100 lessons he has a sight vocabulary of about 1000 words, and also the ability to pronounce every new word slowly" (Laubach 1960:30).

Many people have found the Laubach method helpful. Many would prefer that fewer letters be introduced in each lesson, and the stories be more like real language rather than primer talk.

Laubach's idea of keeping all the lessons the same—easy, pleasant to learn, and easy for untrained people to use in order to teach others—has been very important for many people as they have constructed primers.

7.3 Word and sentence approaches

In the first part of the 1900s, psychologists were studying how people recognized things that they were seeing. They discovered that in most cases when people recognized words they saw the word as a whole object, not as a collection of separate letters. They found that people who were good readers often did not stop to look at the letter details of any word. They also found that the learning reader does not really begin to read until he knows by sight most of the words in the text.

From these discoveries, a new approach to teaching reading was born. It is talked about as the "look-and-say" approach. People using this way to teach reading start by teaching students to recognize whole words. They teach them to look at the word, the teacher then tells them the word, and they say the word. I was taught to read using this method. As children at school we were shown cards with words written on them. These cards matched picture and word cards that were hung around the room. In this way we learned all the words of our first reading book. Once we knew all the words, we were given a copy of the book so we could learn to read it. I can remember playing all sorts of games with the word cards.

These cards were sometimes called flash cards, because the word would be flashed in front of the student and he had to call out what it said as quickly as possible. One problem with this method was that students who could not quickly work out the word would be shamed in front of other students. Unfortunately, there was no context shown which could help the students to work it out.

During the time that the look-and-say approach was popular with teachers, teachers started doing two new things. One was to teach the new words separately from a meaningful context and separately from real reading. The other was to use controlled vocabulary in readers, that is, using only certain words in stories. This change made the language used in those books unnatural and uninteresting. Some contemporary educators would say that those were not very helpful developments (Holdaway 1979:28).

Some people who use look-and-say approaches teach their students to break down the words into smaller parts later on, once they know a lot of words.

Some people combine the look-and-say approach with the syllable approach, especially in early reading lessons. This means that students will already know some of the words in the primer and they can figure out the rest using sounding out strategies. People who insist that students be able to read every word perfectly the first time in reading lessons (working with a controlled vocabulary) find that by combining these two methods they can use more interesting stories in the early primer lessons.

Gwen Gibson and Joy McCarthy, working with the Kanite people (PNG), combined sentence and word approaches with a syllable approach in their reading programme. They designed the literacy classes in such a way that the teachers would begin by using two stories. Each story was on a single chart. Once the students knew how to read these stories, then the teachers introduced the syllable primers (workbooks). Note the page below.

mako ʋiemo'a nama hekahe ne'ʋikeno
kalamo'a ʋiemona a'kaʋe
kesi u'mainekeno ʋiemo'a
ati hekahe aye'ke'ke nehikeno
kalamo'a nama aketeno hau hau
nehie.
hau hau nehikeno
namamo'a haleho
ʋikeno ʋiemo'a tusi ke
ʋaim'ai'ne.

(Translation: A man went to the bush. A dog followed him. The man saw a bird in a tree. He drew his bow. The dog barked and the bird flew away. The man was angry.)

In the first lesson, the students are taught to read the story by using repeated readings. In lesson two, after they have read the chart story together, they are introduced to the sentence strips. They read these and build the story using pocket charts. (A pocket chart is a chart with strips stuck on, so that the strips form a pocket for the sentence strips to sit in. Word or syllable cards can also be put in the pockets.)

In lesson 4, the sentences are broken down into words, and by lesson 6 some of the words are used to form other new sentences. Some of these words are then broken down into syllables. In lesson 8 the second chart story, given below, is introduced.

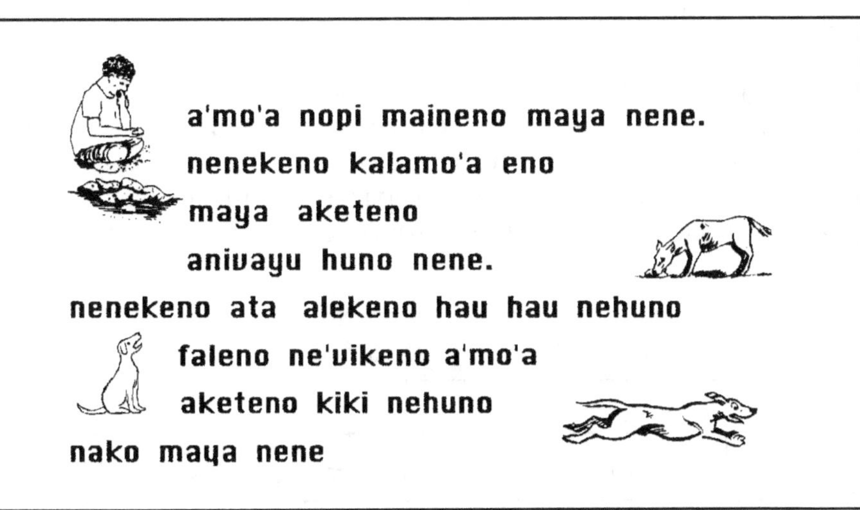

(Translation: A woman was sitting in her house eating some sweet potato. A dog came in and stole some sweet potato. He burnt his mouth and barked and ran away. The woman laughed.)

The students are taught to read this story using the same procedure as above. By the time students have completed the work with these two story charts, they have learned several sight words and some of the syllables of the language. They have also learned to blend some of the syllables into words. Along with these charts, the students are also introduced to the vowels of the language. These lessons are the introductory lessons. Once the students have mastered the charts, they move on to the first workbook (primer) and learn the rest of the syllables. The words from the charts are also used in the workbook to make interesting stories for the students to read.

This combination approach uses the sentence and word approach to introduce students to reading and to teach them some words and syllables of the language so that the early primer reading lessons can contain more interesting and natural story material.

When the look-and-say approach had become popular, other researchers began to think that the smallest meaningful unit was the sentence. They felt that real reading should begin with the sentence because real reading is getting meaning from print. They felt it was important for students to be able to use the clues in the sentence to help work out unknown words. The sentence approach also made it possible for teachers to use natural language instead of controlled language.

This approach, however, had several problems. One was that some teachers did not understand the sentence method very well, so they did not do a good job with it. Another was that students would often memorize the sentences in order to pass a test or to be allowed to read the next book, but they might not be able to read the sentences they memorized if they saw them somewhere else. And another problem was that some teachers went back to using the word method, drilling each word separately from the sentence, and so they were not really using a sentence method at all (Holdaway 1979:28–29).

There are some teachers who still use the sentence method today, usually combined with other methods. For example, they would help the students to read the sentence below. Then they would break it into parts and rearrange the parts (as shown), and then have the students remake the original sentence. Then the students would look for words from the sentence that are in other sentences.

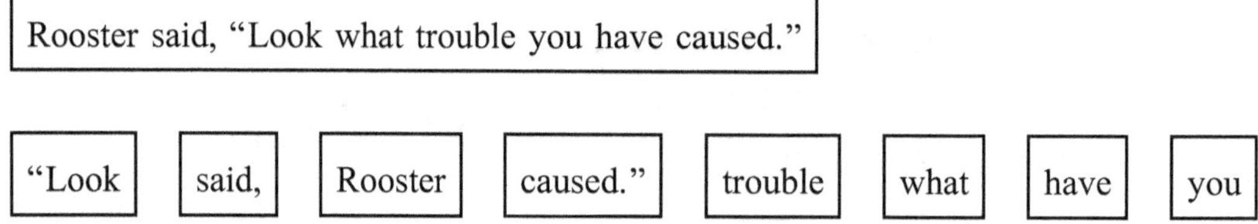

Many years later the sentence and look-and-say approaches led to the "language experience" approach and to approaches that used whole texts and whole books to teach reading. These are discussed in chapter 8.

8

Whole Language Approaches

8.1 What is the whole language approach?

Teachers who use the whole language approach try to encourage learning by involving students in doing real language activities. Students are taught to read by reading and taught to write by writing. While they are trying to carry out these tasks, teachers help them learn the things they need in order to become successful independent readers and writers, that is, readers and writers who can use their abilities in everyday situations as necessary.

Whole language teaching is supported by four strong posts. "It has a strong theory of learning, a theory of language, a basic view of teaching and the role of teachers, and a language-centred view of curriculum" (Goodman 1986:26).

Theory of learning

The LEARNING POST of the whole language approach says that:

- Learning is easy when it is whole, real, and relevant.
- Learning is easy when it is something that is owned and controlled by the learner.
- Learning is making sense of things in the learner's context and culture.

For example, think about learning to ride a bicycle. You can talk a lot about the laws of balance and about laws of motion, and you can give demonstrations. But it is only when you give the bicycle to the learner and he tries to ride it for himself that he puts all the separate skills of bike riding together and becomes able to ride. Riding has to be learned as a whole. It also has to be learned by doing. Just talking about it, watching films or videos about it, or reading about it does not mean a student will learn to ride. He needs to do the real thing.

The learning must also be relevant. There is no point in teaching someone to ride a bicycle if he does not have a bicycle, or if he lives in a mountainous area that is not suitable for bicycle riding, or if he lives surrounded by flooded rice fields. The learning must be related to the needs of the learner. The learner must accept responsibility for his part in the learning process. There is no point in teaching someone to learn to ride a bicycle if he is not willing to be part of the learning, or if he is not willing to get on the bicycle, or if he is not willing to risk making a mistake and falling off. The learner must realise he has a part to play in the learning and must take responsibility for that part.

The learner must also make sense of what he is learning, within his own social context. For example, when someone learns to ride a bike in Australia, he learns that cars have to stop and give way to him. In some other countries of the world, however, the context is different. If the rider does not take the different context into account, he could soon be dead. Learners learn how to do things and how to make sense of things in ways that make sense in their own culture.

Whole language teachers say it is the same with reading and writing. If students are taught to read and write using whole texts that are real and relevant, and they take ownership of their learning, and are willing to take risks, then learning to read and write will be easy. What the learner is doing will also make sense to him within his context and culture.

Theory of language

The next post is the LANGUAGE THEORY post. This post tells us that:

- All language is good language. One dialect is not better than another. The way some people speak is not better than the way others speak.
- Whole language is "whole."

As Goodman says, "Language is language only when it's whole." Whole text or connected speech is the smallest unit that we can look at on its own—the unit that makes sense.

> When teachers and pupils look at words, phrases, sentences, they do so always in the context of whole, real language texts that are part of real language experiences…Whole language teachers know, when they work with language that is whole and sensible, that all the parts will be in proper perspective and learning will be easy. (Goodman 1986:27–28)

View of teaching

The third post of the whole language approach is the VIEW OF TEACHING.

- Whole language teachers understand that learning takes place one child at a time.
- They see their jobs as creating the right kinds of situations to help the student with his learning, and to guide, support, monitor, and encourage him or her.

Many whole language teachers do not use primers that have unnatural stories in them. They tend to build their programs around interesting, whole stories, and often do this using themes.

Language-centered curriculum

The fourth post is the CURRICULUM post. This post tells us that:

- Language development belongs to all of the school curriculum.
- Speaking, reading, writing, and listening are all happening as students learn more about all kinds of things in their world.
- Language development is integrated throughout the curriculum—it is part of everything that is done in class.

Things to remember in teaching reading and writing using a whole language approach

- Reading and writing communicate meaning by means of print.
- Readers construct meaning during their reading as they make sense of texts.
- Readers use many ways (strategies) to make sense of print. They predict, sample, check, and self-correct. They use sounds and letters (grapho-phonic cues), sentence patterns (syntax or grammar), and meaning (semantics). It is difficult to separate the use of one strategy from another, so they should not be taught separately but as a whole, because they work together.

- Writers try to construct messages that will have meaning for readers. As they write they learn the ways of writing (conventions) that best communicate their message to the person who will read it.
- Learning about reading and writing develops from whole to part, and from what is known to what is not known.
- Learners are encouraged to take risks and to use language for their own purposes.

8.2 Shared reading

Shared reading is an important part of whole language teaching. What has come to be known worldwide as shared-book-experience was developed originally in New Zealand in the late 1970s. It was the result of much work, research, thought, and watching what children do with reading by many New Zealand teachers, teachers' college lecturers, and university lecturers over many years. Shared-book-experience is a way of encouraging children to learn the skills of reading by using favourite stories, songs, and chants in reading lessons. It provides children with opportunities to experience reading and reading-like behaviours in a supportive learning environment. It allows them to 'play' with reading, to predict (make informed guesses), to self-correct, and to control their own learning and the pace of that learning within a supportive non-competitive environment. Two people who are well-known for their contribution to the development of this way of teaching reading are Marie Clay and Don Holdaway. They have written several books about their ideas and experiences.

> My experience of teaching…confirmed my belief in the potential of young learners…to teach themselves within a properly supportive environment. (Holdaway 1979:7)

> The programmes, techniques, and styles of teaching which arose [from the work of many New Zealand teachers and researchers] came to be loosely bound together under the term *shared-book-experience*. (Holdaway 1979:8)

> Out of early reading and writing experiences the young learner creates a network of competencies which power subsequent literacy and learning. (Clay 1991:1)

Shared-book-experience uses the strengths of what happens when parents take children on their knee and share favourite story books with them. By using books with enlarged pictures and big print, often called Big Books, teachers can create the same kind of warm, encouraging atmosphere as they share books with their class. They can group students around them as they read the story. Everyone can see the words and the pictures because they have been made large. Students are encouraged to follow along with the teacher because the teacher uses a pointer to point to each word as he reads.

The stories shared together are usually ones that are known to be favourite stories with children. For beginning readers, stories are chosen that are fairly simple and easy to understand. Stories with a lot of repetition are good for beginning readers. Often well-known folk tales are used. Choose some of these good, well-loved stories and make them into Big Books. Write the print neatly, clearly, and large enough so it can be seen by the students in the back row. It is not necessary to put illustrations in every book. The students will enjoy making illustrations for some of them.

Once the story is introduced and talked about, time is given for rereading the story. As the story becomes well-known, the children are encouraged to join in with the reading. In later lessons they will be able to take turns at reading certain parts together. For example, the boys can read the parts of the story where the frog speaks and the girls can read the parts spoken by the other animals. Or children can take turns at being the teacher leading the group for one page at a time. The books can be reread in later lessons over and over again as long as the children stay interested. Rereading stories many times helps the children learn the words in those stories and builds their confidence in reading.

While someone is reading, the teacher or the student should point to the words being read. Pointing helps the student to see that each spoken word matches one written word. Pointing also helps to show the direction that the eye moves when it reads the print. In most cases this is from left to right along the line, then back and down. Careful matching of spoken word and written word by pointing helps the students learn these things (Holdaway 1979:75–76; Clay 1972:71–73).

As well as giving the children a lot of experiences with books and the print in books, the New Zealand teachers also encouraged the children to use "language-saturated and personalized experience of the outside world with all its real purposes for writing" (Holdaway 1979:71). They did many language experience activities with the children (see §8.6), and encouraged them to use the reading and writing skills they learned from the shared-book-experiences in other class activities.

As the students grow in their reading and writing abilities, they can begin to help make Big Books for the class about experiences they have had. Each student can help illustrate a page. The teacher prints the text clearly. Big print charts can be made of songs, chants, and poems, and these can also be used in shared reading times. In this way a good selection of reading materials can be created.

The following table gives a summary of the format that Don Holdaway developed in doing shared-book-experience in schools in New Zealand.

1. Beginning the session
   Begin with a verse, song, or chant, both favourite ones and new ones using enlarged print and charts.

2. Favourite stories
   Re-read stories that have been read before. Choose some stories beforehand to read, and read some that the students ask for. Students join in the readings.

3. Language activities
   Look at sound patterns and do games that come from these stories.

4. New Story
   Introduce the new story for the day. As the teacher reads the new story, he talks about how he works out new words. He also mentions words which are similar to key words that have been recently taught.

5. Independent reading
   Have children read books which are old favourites, in groups or on their own. Encourage them to point to each word as they 'read'. Some children may take turns to play at being the teacher. Children teach each other.

6. Expression
   Do something which is related to the new story you have read. Each person can do something, or groups can work together. Things like art, drama, puppets, and miming are good activities for this.

   [Note: You can do 6 before 5 if you wish; the order is not important.]

Some people think that whole language teaching is merely reading a lot of stories together. But that is not so. Good teachers use the opportunities that come up in the sharing times to support the students in learning what they need to learn. The teacher also watches to find out what the students already know, and what they can already do (evaluate). The teacher also does some positive teaching of things that he knows will be helpful for the students. Holdaway shares in his book about how phonics teaching is included in the lessons.

> A few children have caught on to the idea of letter-sound relationships after three or four explanations, but the majority haven't seen it. We decide to take the matter very carefully and introduce two highly contrastive letter-sound associations: *m* because the children can hum—and we have an extroverted Molly in the class—and *f* because it has a primal slippery sound and feel. Then we go looking in the familiar books we know, and keep our eye out for *m* and *f* in new stories.
>
> Some of the little rascals scan the text way ahead of where we are up to and shout at inappropriate times, "There's an EM!" We learn how valuable it is to know how to start saying a word that we're expecting. We get into that delightful *Fun on Wheels* by Joanna Cole and find quick confirmation in 'four' and 'five' wheels for our beginning *f*. Then comes 'f... on wheels' with a picture of a parading carnival animal on wheels—"Wow! FLOATS on wheels!"...Careful pairing of letter-sound relationships through *b, g, s,* and *t*—all contrastive—brings insights for many of the children. The rest of the initial consonants and blends are learned rapidly by those children in the following weeks without specific instruction. For those remainder, a continuing programme of contrast and use brings insight at varying rates. (Holdaway 1979:74)

As the students increase in their ability to read print it is important that they have a lot of easy readers available for them to practice reading for themselves. For children, books like caption books and other simplified stories are good. In choosing simplified stories, however, make sure the texts are clear, and that natural language is used so that words are easier to predict.

The programmes Holdaway was involved with used language experience type activities as well as shared reading. Gradually these two experiences became more like one another, and each influenced the other.

> As the programme develops along as natural a line as possible, the distinction between language-experience procedures and book-experience procedures gradually diminishes. Book experience generates the thrust to use written language and to arouse new interests and curiosity, to explore the real world more deeply. (Holdaway 1979:77)

Children dictated stories to their teachers and these were displayed in the classroom and used. Class stories were written about things the class had done.

Holdaway noticed that from time to time book language would become part of the classroom language and would help build special feelings within the class.

> For instance, the saying "No harm in that!" from *Just in Time for the King's Birthday* had a popular run for two or three weeks as a humourously exclusive answer to any request to be allowed to do something. Sendak's distinctive locutions for the passage of time in *Where the Wild Things Are* keep cropping up in the stories that the children dictate—"In and out of weeks and through a day." "It's time for me to be on my wa-ay" from *The House of Hay* has become a favourite farewell, and "I guess she'll die!" is a common comment when someone has been hurt or has done something shocking. (Holdaway 1979:77)

Adaptations of shared reading for various languages, cultures, and age groups

In the early 1980s the shared-book-experience method of teaching reading was widely adopted by teachers who were developing bilingual programmes for Australian Aborigines. They found the method suitable for these situations because it fit the way Aboriginal children learned skills within their own culture—learning by doing, by imitating the real thing, and by successive approximations (see chapter 1). When this way of teaching reading was tried, both the students and the teachers found it easier to see the link between real reading and what was done in the reading lesson. When other methods of teaching reading were used, sometimes Aboriginal teachers and children were not sure how those lessons fitted in with learning to read. Later, Barry Borneman adapted the shared-book-experience method for use with Aboriginal adults. It was very successful. Section 8.5 gives some of the details about this.

In the early 1990s various literacy workers introduced the use of shared-book methods of teaching reading to vernacular literacy work in Papua New Guinea, both with adults and children. The method has been modified to suit various situations and has been very successful in teaching reading in PNG. Others adapted the whole language method to suit their situations in other countries. Linda and Randy Easthouse used it in Peru (see §8.5).

In PNG, several people have developed variations of the shared-book method. Yasuko Nagai (1990b) developed a simple five-step teaching plan for teachers of the Maiwala/Labe TPPS to use. It is now used by the PNG Department of Education. It is summarized next. (The teaching of phonics was included in the writing lesson.)

1. Talk

Give a short introduction related to the book or the main character or the theme of the story.

2. Read

Read the Big Book phrase by phrase following smoothly underneath the words with a stick (pointer) as they are spoken. Do not read word by word. Read with expression. Do not read too fast. As you read, draw the students into reading the repetitive parts.

3. Talk

Talk about the pictures page by page. What do the students see in each picture? What do they think about each picture? This helps the students to express themselves freely. Avoid "yes/no" or simple answer questions.

4. Read

Read the story again. Once the students know some of the parts, you can divide them into groups and have one group read the part of the main character and the other group read the other characters' parts.

5. Do/talk

Play a game or do an activity related to the story. This provides further opportunities for the students to talk and think about the story and its main points.

Daniel and Wei Lei Jesudason developed a six-step teaching plan for the Umanikaina and the Daga literacy programmes. They included the teaching of syllables and the teaching of writing in the six steps.

How to teach with Big Books and the syllable chart

Craig and Pat Spaulding developed a slightly different approach. There are three parts to their shared-book method, and each of those three parts is divided again into another three. They described this method very clearly for the local teachers in a colourful production called *Skulim Ol long Rit na Rait* (Teaching reading and writing) with a lot of good illustrations. The teachers are taught and observe the method before getting the teacher's guide. Craig explains how teaching reading is like a tree. The tree (pictured in 1 on the next page) is the Big Book story. The roots are the meaning of the story which supports the tree (text). The fruit (2) of the tree equals the key words of the story. And the seedling (3) is the use of the fruit of the tree to grow something new.

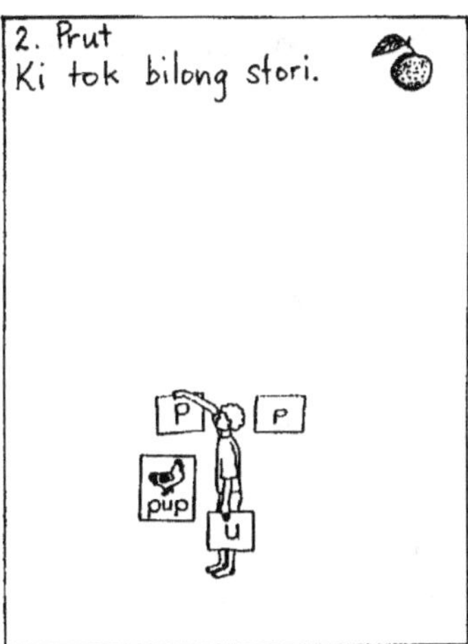

Craig told me, "We chose the picture of a tree because the language is full of organic metaphors. We thought a metaphor would help the teachers to remember the different elements more easily."

The tree, the Big Book story, has three parts as shown in the chart below. The Big Book stories are always stories that come from the students' world or from a shared class experience.

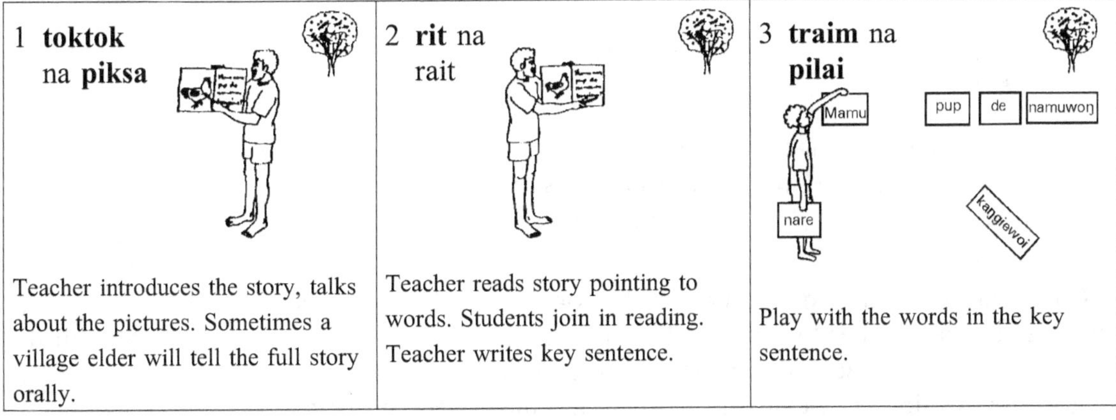

1 **toktok** na **piksa**	2 **rit** na rait	3 **traim** na **pilai**
Teacher introduces the story, talks about the pictures. Sometimes a village elder will tell the full story orally.	Teacher reads story pointing to words. Students join in reading. Teacher writes key sentence.	Play with the words in the key sentence.

The fruit, shown in the next chart, also has three parts to it.

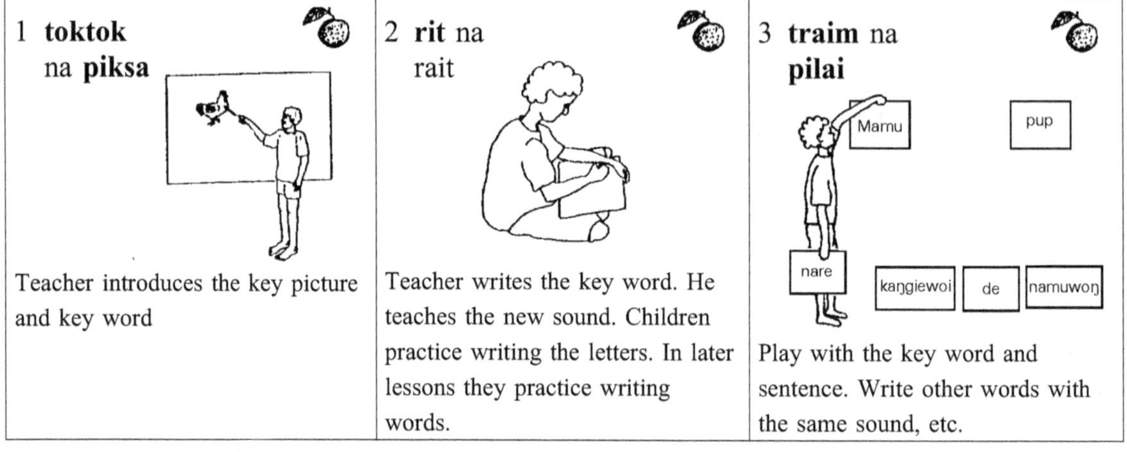

1 **toktok** na **piksa**	2 **rit** na rait	3 **traim** na **pilai**
Teacher introduces the key picture and key word	Teacher writes the key word. He teaches the new sound. Children practice writing the letters. In later lessons they practice writing words.	Play with the key word and sentence. Write other words with the same sound, etc.

Seedlings, representing new growth, has the following three parts to it.

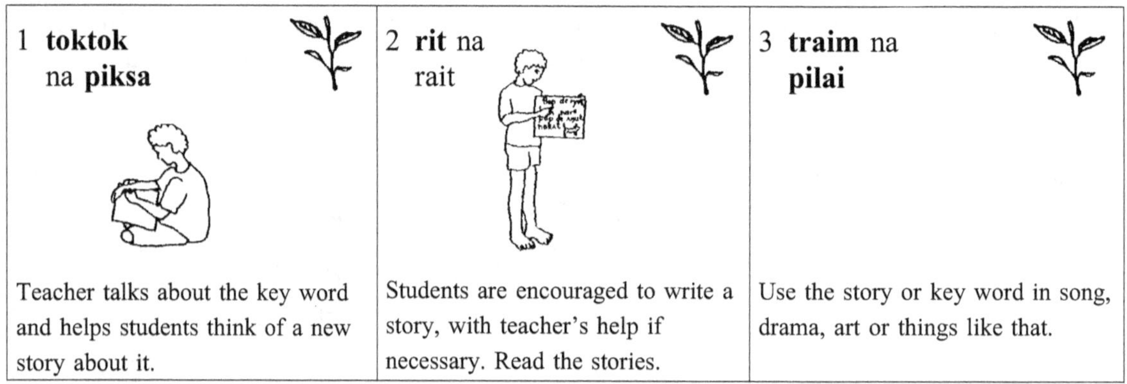

1 **toktok** na **piksa**	2 **rit** na rait	3 **traim** na **pilai**
Teacher talks about the key word and helps students think of a new story about it.	Students are encouraged to write a story, with teacher's help if necessary. Read the stories.	Use the story or key word in song, drama, art or things like that.

This is just a summary of Spauldings' booklet. It is full of pictures and has good ideas and examples for the teacher to follow. The book serves as a reminder to the teachers of all the things they have learned and experienced in their teacher training courses.

From this section, it is evident that there are many ways to develop shared-book experiences to help people learn to read and write. It can be adapted in many ways to suit different situations and ideas. But all of these ways have certain things in common. They provide experiences for the learner to learn from favourite stories and whole meaningful texts. They provide opportunities for learners to learn at their own pace, to take control of their own learning and to try reading and writing in a supportive non-competitive environment.

Versions of the next two sections, 8.3 and 8.4, have already been published in *Read* magazine in Papua New Guinea. I am including them here because they contain information that may be helpful in understanding the whole language approach and how it can be adapted to village situations in the two-thirds world. Both these papers were written several years before this manual was drafted, so some recommendations contained in them have been implemented.

8.3 Literature-based reading programmes for Papua New Guinea[15]

In 1979 Don Holdaway published *Foundations of Literacy* and *Independence in Reading*, two books which in the following decade were to make a profound impact on the way teachers approached the task of teaching their students to read. Holdaway's books are still useful resources in understanding the developmental learn-to-read-by-reading approach. Holdaway says that sharing books is the main ingredient in teaching children to read. He says that it is necessary to provide a supportive literacy environment for this task, one which includes a large supply of reading materials, regular opportunities to hear books read aloud, and an adult who enjoys reading and responds to the readers' questions about books and print.

In 1968 Kenneth Goodman published his book, *The Psycholinguistic Nature of the Reading Process,* and in 1971 Frank Smith published his thinking in a book called *Understanding Reading—A Psycholinguistic Analysis of Reading and Learning to Read.* These well-known educators, along with many others, questioned many things that teachers were doing in reading programmes at that time. They and others studied what readers actually do when they read, and the results of these studies have been applied to the teaching of reading. They found that new readers depend heavily on meaningful contexts. A teaching strategy based on the use of meaningful contexts is now the foundation of many different methods of teaching reading.

As a result of the research, practical applications, and writings of reading specialists like those mentioned above, many teachers have modified their approaches to teaching reading.

[15]This is the title of a paper I wrote and published in *Read* magazine in 1992. It is abbreviated and reprinted here with permission of the publisher.

Now teachers do not put as much emphasis on teaching word attack drills and games. They no longer use strategies which depend on heavy use of such drills, especially those which are not closely linked to the reading process. Inappropriate reading exercises have been severely cut back or removed entirely from most reading programmes. This means the removal of drills which convey no meaning, such as the following.

sa	se	si	so	su
ta	te	ti	to	tu

It also means the removal from the reading programmes of engineered unnatural texts that are sometimes found in vernacular reading lessons such as:

> This is Scottie. Scottie can run.
> See Scottie run. Run Scottie run.

These teachers also do not use reading games and activities where students are forced to decode print without having a meaningful context to help them work out the meanings of individual words. For example, many flash card games just have a single word on its own. Students who do not know the word have no context to help them figure it out.

Along with these developments, significant research in Australia on learning styles in pre-literate cultures has been done by Stephen Harris, Michael Christie, and others as they worked with the Northern Territory Bilingual Education Department. Although they worked with Australian Aborigines, many of their findings and conclusions are applicable to other pre-literate cultures. Learning by doing, learning by observation and imitation, and learning by approximating the real thing are learning styles that are central to many cultures. The strategy of learning to read by reading fits some learning styles better than some of the earlier approaches to teaching reading used in Western countries.

What do all these developments over the last ten years or so have to say to those involved in teaching vernacular literacy in Papua New Guinea in the 1990s? There are over 800 languages in PNG and the task of teaching people to read is often done by village people who have not had very much formal education.

The learn-by-doing approach to reading (Harris, Christie et al.) rather than the analytical and synthetic methods **must** be applied to literacy programmes designed for the PNG scene. The heavy emphasis on drills needs to be replaced by something more like real reading behaviour. Learning-to-read-by-reading methods are a good way to do that.

The task of implementing literacy programmes should be stripped down to the basic ingredients necessary. Village people need to design the materials and manage the programme on their own. The stripping down process, however, has to be done carefully, because there are many factors that influence the design of a literacy programme. The programme must still fit in with those factors. (See Waters 1992.)

Also, financial resources for vernacular literacy programmes are severely limited in Papua New Guinea. Therefore, the first priority for the use of available funds must be for the basic essentials.

What are the basics? If we base our methods on the advances in reading theory and practice of the last few decades, and if we also consider the dominant learning styles of the grass-roots people of PNG, there are three basic needs which need to be met. These needs are the same as those mentioned by Holdaway. They are as follows.

- a large supply of reading materials
- regular opportunities to hear books read aloud
- an adult who enjoys reading and responds enthusiastically to the reader's questions about books and print

The next section discusses the best way to foster the development of these three things in Papua New Guinea, given the limitations that exist in the country.

A large supply of reading materials

Where there is grass-roots interest in literacy programmes and a willingness to act, the starting point should be to develop a large supply of reading materials. Such materials are basic to any literacy programme and have been encouraged by many (e.g., Gudschinsky, UNESCO). These materials should be developed first, but often get overlooked in the rush to get programmes moving quickly. So the emphasis should be on holding writers' workshops and illustration workshops. Once the books have been well edited and tested, then they can be produced in large numbers in one or more literature production workshops.

Yasuko Nagai (1991b) says that the books that are needed for the start of a literacy programme must be enjoyable, good books. A book is 'good' if it is interesting to the learners, involving them in some way—often through touching their emotions, e.g., fear, humour, anticipation—and with good illustrations that help the learner to predict what the marks on the page say.

Nagai also believes it is necessary to expose the writers and illustrators to good books before getting them to write their own stories and the stories that are familiar to them from their culture. She does this by running workshops using Big Books (1991b), starting with sets of illustrations from books that have proved to be popular in other areas of PNG as well as in the Australian Aboriginal languages. She does not get the writers to translate the story which goes with the pictures, but rather encourages them to write whatever story they feel the pictures tell. In this way the stories become the writer's own and conform to the natural style of his own language.

Once the writers and illustrators have experienced good books and developed an appreciation of the types of books that are necessary for new readers, they can be encouraged to produce the body of literature that is necessary for a literacy programme. This can be done quite cheaply by running writers' workshops in local villages. Alternatively, people from villages speaking related languages can take part in workshops held in a local centre. In this way costs can be kept to a minimum. Writers' workshops have been held in many areas already and people have donated their time and effort because participants are keen for their own people to have reading materials. Such workshops need to be continued and facilitated in many more areas of PNG.

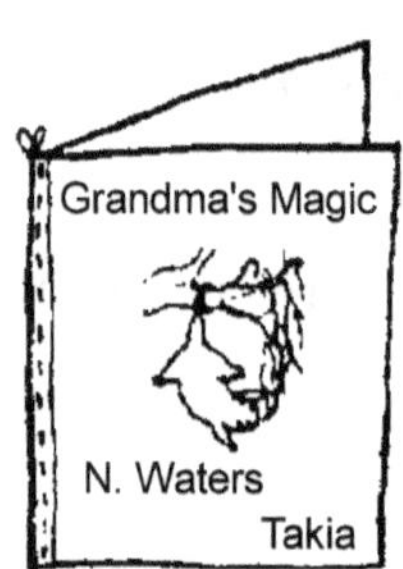

The core of books that are developed in this way can be added to continually. Often they can be handmade books or books made on village silkscreens. Big Books are an excellent way of providing inexpensive reading materials. (See §8.4 on how to make them cheaply.)

These large books can be made using scrap or cheap materials. Illustrations and print are hand done. Book sizes are quite large so that a whole class can read and enjoy the book together. Stories can be ones that are well-known or imaginative stories that appeal to the intended audience. For example, I have made Big Books of local folk stories, Bible stories, and repetitive stories as well as using stories from other places.

The advantage of Big Books is that you only need one book per class. Or you can share books between classes if you coordinate programmes with other teachers so that they use the books when you are not using them. You can make the illustrations very attractive by colouring them with paint, crayon, or pencil. You can even add other materials to bring the illustration to life. One teacher used bamboo meat skewers for the sides of the PNG hut and dried banana leaves for the thatched roof. Your imagination is the limit.

The reading class can also continually add to the supply of reading materials. The class can discuss, compose, and edit their own imaginative story with the teacher leading and directing. The teacher can write the text on each page, and groups of students can draw and colour the pictures themselves, if appropriate. Such class books can flow out of experiences the class has had together, e.g., "The day we collected galip nuts," or "When the possum came to class."

Or the class can add stories that are written in the same style as the story they have just read. Many times teachers use the story patterns found in favourite class stories and encourage the class to make up their own stories following these patterns.

For example, the story *Down by the Waterhole* by Beverley Randell (published by Thomas Nelson, Australia) is full of delightful repetitive phrases, such as:

I've seen a platypus,
I've seen a possum,
I've seen a big red kangaroo,
But I've never seen a bunyip down by the waterhole,
I've never seen a bunyip brown or blue.

Reading this book could lead to a discussion of things which the children have seen and things which they have never seen. The class can then make some new verses following the same patterns.

I've seen a laser,
I've seen a concord,
I've seen an astronaut walking on the moon,
But I've never seen a bunyip playing computer games,
I've never seen a bunyip playing games at noon.

Another example comes from activities that might follow reading the book, *Alexander and the Terrible Horrible No Good, Very Bad Day* by Judith Viorst. This is a favourite children's story book in Australia. The pattern of the original story can be used, and the class or individual students write their own version of the story.

When I woke up ....
I could tell it was going to be a terrible, horrible, no good, very bad day.
When I got up ....
I could tell it was going to be a terrible, horrible, no good, very bad day.
When I went to ....
I could tell it was going to be a terrible, horrible, no good, very bad day.
When I went to the garden ....
I could tell it was going to be a terrible, horrible, no good, very bad day.
When I came home ....
I could tell it was going to be a terrible, horrible, no good, verybad day.
My mom says some days are like that.

Or the reading class can write about experiences they have had that are similar to those that they have just read about, e.g.,

When I went fishing
Things I have dreamt about
Things that scare me
My favourite thing

As students become more fluent in reading and writing, they can begin to produce their own handmade books individually. The books can be made to look very attractive by shaping covers to match the main character or event in the story (see illustration below).

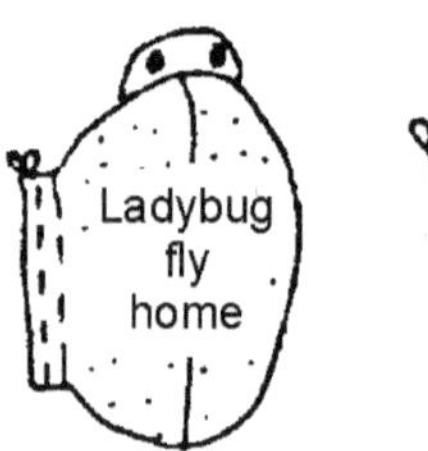

Handmade books often become class favourites because of all the shared experiences that have surrounded them—thinking about them, creating, and making them. They are often re-read many times and are well worth the effort put into making them.

Training adults to respond to readers' questions about books and print

Once a large supply of reading materials is available, the next ingredient necessary for a literacy programme is to identify and train adults who enjoy reading and who can respond enthusiastically to readers' questions about books and print.

There are many people in PNG who are committed to helping their own people in the area of literacy. Many do it not for money but because of their commitment. Because the majority of these people are village people with little or no formal teacher training, the methods that they are trained to use should be ones that fit well with their traditional learning styles. The methods should be ones with a minimum of fuss and ones that can be passed on easily to others. This is where the learning-to-read-by-reading approach is very acceptable and requires a minimum of training.

No matter what system teachers of reading are trained in, they should be trained to use the shared-book approach. This approach can be used with any method of teaching reading and will help students learn to read. Don Holdaway (1979:64–80) has taken an approach that many reading teachers have developed naturally and been using for decades. He has extended it and made it more formal. Several vernacular literacy workers have adapted this approach to suit the PNG context. Yasuko Nagai (1991a) developed an easy lesson pattern for people to follow when sharing stories. (See §§8.2 and 8.4.)

Once the sharer (teacher, friend, parent) understands how to share a book, they should be trained in ways of **drawing their audience into the story** and engaging their attention, interest, emotions, and participation in the event. This can be done in many ways.

- read with interest in your voice
- change voice pitch with different characters
- read with a sparkle in your eyes and interest on your face
- ask questions which require the audience to predict what may happen
- when there are predictable parts, once they have become familiar to the students, delay in reading until someone from the audience joins you
- when there are repetitive parts, after a while allow your voice to drop and the voices of the audience to take over
- turn a page near the climax slowly; this encourages predictions

Doing these things comes naturally to adults who enjoy reading.

The sharer should also be trained in ways of **drawing those in the group into discussion** during the talk times. This can be done in the following ways.

- talk about experiences the audience has had that were similar, or what happened when they met a frog, wild pig, or whatever the story is about
- give plenty of time in Talk times for different people in the group to give their responses or opinions; in some cultures children may not be used to doing this, but for their reading and language skills to develop they must be encouraged to feel comfortable doing so
- encourage the group to share what they thought was going to happen, or how they felt at certain times in the story
- talk about which parts of the story people liked best, which animal they would like to be, what it would be like to be in that part of the story
- talk about what would have happened if one part in the story had been different

Adults also learn to use the shared-book approach by watching others do it well, seeing it done several times, experiencing it, practicing it, that is, learning by observation, imitation, and doing. Good story sharers automatically do all the things mentioned above to involve the audience in the story and to encourage discussion of it. When the shared-book technique is modelled well in the training of new sharers, many of these tips can be passed on to them.

When doing shared reading, a story is shared many times (over a one or two-week period) until it is well-known. Each day the talk-read-talk-read-do pattern can be followed, but after the first day or so, the students can become more involved in the reading sessions. The teacher should encourage them to join in by:

- having the class read the repetitive phrases
- having the class read the part of one character
- having the class read the narration parts
- dividing the class into groups and having each group read one of the character parts
- having someone from the class, who feels comfortable and able, take the teachers role for one page at a time

There are a lot of activities which can be included in the "do" part of the lesson. Your imagination is the limit. These activities should, however, provide opportunities for discussion about the story or the characters involved in the story, or be activities related to the text of the story.

Some activities which can come from shared book experiences

The activities listed below can be used in teaching the shared-book method. This is not an exhaustive list; you will think of others.

1. Match character pictures with names.

sumsum

2. Match key sentence strips with actual text.

What do you give your children to eat?

Oh, is that so!

3. Make key sentences out of word cards.

give | eat | to | do | you | children | what | your?

4. Match characters with their actions, for example, in "Wide Mouth Frog" match them with the foods they eat.

5. Make stick puppets (or masks, or cards to hang around children's necks) and act out the story as it is read.

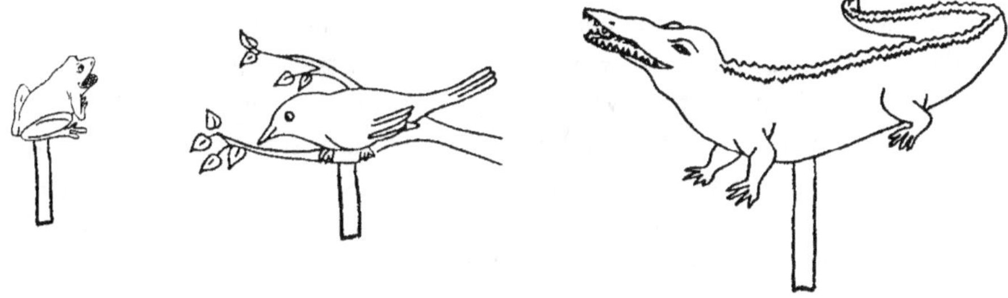

6. Retell the story in students' own words using puppets, masks, or character name cards.

7. Retell the story but change the ending.

8. Retell the story from another character's point of view.

9. Sequence the pictures from the story into the right order and tell what happens in each picture.

10. Who said it? Match quotes to characters by asking "Who said it?"

11. Do art work related to the story. For example, have the students paint, draw, or colour a favourite part of the story.

12. Make murals out of collections of papers, cards, or pieces of cardboard boxes joined or pinned together, hung, or stuck around the room. Murals can be as long as the children's or teacher's immagination. Each child can make part of the mural, or groups can work together on parts—drawing, colouring, or writing (in local language). When completed, join the parts together with tape or string and hang them from a string around the room or tape them along walls, so they can be read and enjoyed many times. A class mural may be about a story such as the "Wide-Mouth Frog" story shown in the first strip below; or a mural may extend the story such as the second strip below.

13. Make one of the class retellings (with the different ending or different characters) into a book.

14. Make a class book on a similar theme, for example, after reading the Dami story of "How We Got Mosquitoes," you could talk about something else in the environment and make up a story on how it came to be.

15. Read other stories about the theme.

16. Have a cooking session connected to the theme. For example, the story about the Cockatoo and Crow who decide to make sago would lend itself to a session on making sago. Talk about all the ingredients, label them, and talk about all the processes involved and what happens.

17. Plan an excursion connected with the story. For example, go and help gather sago palm, watch the men weave it into roofing materials, and try to do some weaving. Talk and write about the experience.

All these "do" activities help students think about the story, become familiar with the words that are used, and help them to think about the sounds of the words and the way they are written.

Some literacy workers may feel they need to do more than the things suggested above. Some feel they need to add a workbook to the collection of literature that is to be used to teach people to read. They think this will help unsophisticated teachers to use the books more effectively. They think it might be necessary to guide the teacher in helping students learn each sound of the language in a particular order. In other countries this guidance is normally given to teachers as part of their extensive teachers college training. These workbooks usually contain activities that are closely linked with interesting stories that have been read as a class, such as the lesson pictured next which goes with the Big Book *Strongpela Pik.*

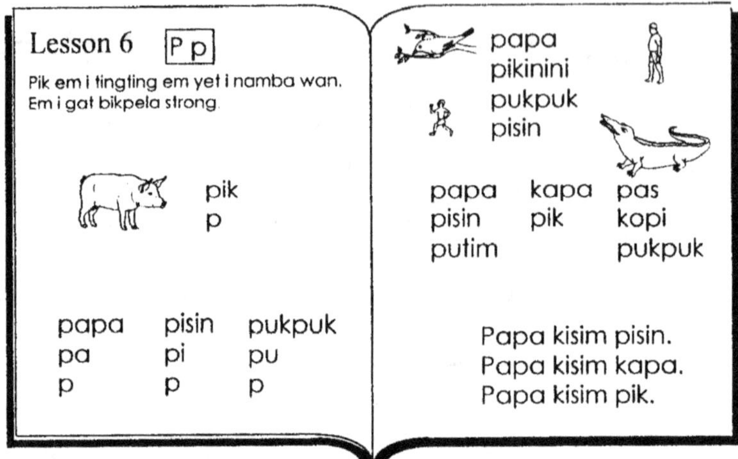

Workbooks can be designed in a variety of ways, and they have been used in various vernacular programmes in Australia (see Borneman, Nagai, Richards, and others).

In Papua New Guinea, Jesudason and Jesudason, Graham, Vollrath, Nagai, Waters, Waters and Elliott, and others have developed programmes using the learning-to-read-by-reading approach. All of these programmes are in various stages of implementation and/or design, but these people have demonstrated, or are in the process of showing, that it can and does work in PNG, for both children and adults. See chapter 9 for further discussion and examples of these.

The above-mentioned literacy workers have not all done the same thing. There is considerable variation in their approach, but none of their programmes have a strong emphasis on drills that lack meaningful contexts. The differences in their programmes depend on designer preferences, or the degree of belief in the reading theories on which a methodology is based, or because of a need to fulfill local expectations based on how reading has been taught in the past. Despite these differences, these people have each been able to develop effective reading materials with a minimum of effort.

Opportunities to read

Once a collection of books has been created and adults have been trained to share these books with others, then all that is needed is to create opportunities for students to read books, share books, and hear books read. This can be done formally through Tok Ples Preparatory Schools, through vernacular component lessons in community schools, through literacy classes held in the village, or informally as opportunities arise in the village, e.g., sharing on the front verandah (see §8.5). Teachers with a minimal amount of training can create and encourage such opportunities as can someone who is sitting next to a friend wanting to learn

(Jesudason). It can be done cheaply and appropriately, providing there is motivation and the reading books are available.

Given the research and development of the last ten years, literacy workers in Papua New Guinea should be able to present appropriate reading programmes to grass-roots level people. The reading process should be presented as a whole. Readers should be encouraged to use all of the decoding strategies that they have developed and to do so every time they read. If it is felt that workbooks are necessary, they should present reading opportunities that come from meaningful and interesting texts which mirror natural language patterns. Reading games and reading readiness activities also must be linked to meaningful contexts.

Summary of this section

To develop literature-based reading programmes in PNG it is necessary to:

- provide many interesting books with stories in natural language
- provide regular opportunities for reading and for being read to
- provide an enthusiastic adult who will demonstrate good reading behaviours and answer questions about books and print.

The advantages of this approach for PNG are:

- Learning-to-read-by-reading best matches the traditional learning styles, which are non-analytic and based on imitation of real behaviours.
- The learning by doing strategy minimises the need for specialised teacher training, complex curriculum, and complex literacy training courses. The development and maintenance of effective literacy programmes is thus simplified.
- This strategy allows financial and personnel resources to be used where they are most needed, that is, to provide good, interesting books for learners to read.

8.4 Big Books for sharing enjoyable reading experiences[16]

A lot has been said about different literacy teaching methods in the past. You may be happy with the method which you have been using (e.g., Gudschinskey method), or you may be bogged down and wondering if there are any other good ways of teaching. So when someone comes up with a new idea, you may feel you would like to use it in your programme. In this article, I am not introducing a new teaching method nor another

[16]This section is excerpted from an article by Yasuko Nagai, 1990, "Sharing Enjoyable Reading Experiences" *Read* magazine 25(2):23–29. It is used with permission of the publisher.

theoretical idea. I [Yasuko Nagai] am sharing with you my experiences as a teacher-linguist for the Burarra Bilingual programme at Maningrida in the Northern Territory of Australia.

The purpose of teaching literacy

Every person presenting a new method to literacy teachers has something impressive to say, but how do you determine if it is really a good method? Is the purpose of your literacy teaching for the student to perform well on an evaluation test? After I came to Papua New Guinea and observed a few *tokples skuls* 'vernacular schools', I became very concerned about teachers who focus heavily on literacy skills, as it seemed that is all they offer the children. In each class I visited, children recited mechanically what they were taught. Although they seemed to perform well in what they were asked to do, there was no excitement. On the contrary, there seemed to be a burdensome atmosphere in the class. What was wrong?

One literacy consultant shared with me that she did not enjoy reading. For her, reading always related to studying. My experience is similar, as the purpose of studying for Japanese students was to get better results in exams. We had no pleasure in learning. Everything I acquired was mechanical, just as those children whom I observed in *tokples skuls*. What was missing?

If you do not enjoy reading, you cannot teach others to enjoy it. You can give only what you have. To look back, I taught Aboriginal adults only the mechanical skills of literacy in my first two programmes (Yanyuwa and Garawa). It was not fun, it was agony—especially with many digraphs (sometimes trigraphs and quadrigraphs!) and very long words. Although they learned the skill of reading, it did not become a pleasure.

While making interesting books for Aboriginal children during my third programme, I finally came to appreciate the importance that pleasure has in the reading process. Literacy is only a part of the whole education programme, yet it is the key for learning other subjects. I want students to acquire the necessary mechanical skills, but those skills are only by-products of my main purpose: to train teachers that reading is fun and how to pass this attitude on to their students.

Why make Big Books?

Big Books are attractive chart-size books which are large enough to be seen by the whole class at once. They are designed so that the whole class can be involved in encountering literacy together. Many Big Books with large coloured text and colourful illustrations have been printed commercially in English and are available for schools. Even though the Big Books we produced in Aboriginal languages were hand-made, the ones made for the Burarra bilingual programme were very attractive, perhaps even better than the English ones. We chose stories with a lot of repetition and a good story line that engages the emotions of the reader.

> Children come to school knowing how to learn. They have learned about things familiar to them in their home environment. For example, some children know how to dance. They learned by watching adult models, imitating the actions, practicing over and over and experiencing it in a meaningful situation. (Gale 1983:4)

Children learn to read and write by using these same learning skills. However, reading activities are not always part of the home environment of the children who come to *tokples skuls*. Although school itself is a formal setting, Big Books can provide an informal learning setting that suits their learning style.

Learning as a group creates a nonthreatening atmosphere. It is a good way of sharing interesting books together, passing on the joy of reading. The children watch the teacher model the reading process. Later when they read it together, they can imitate the modelled reading behaviour by using contextual clues and prediction. This method enables children to focus their attention on repetitive phrases, words, sounds, and syllables within a meaningful context. They can learn to read by practicing it over and over, so that the children can feel in control of what they are doing. Also, many activities relating to the Big Book provide informal prereading and prewriting lessons in a meaningful context.

Most of the Big Books for the Burarra program were made in an adult literacy class. The first Big Book was made by the whole class, including the beginning students. It gave the participants pleasure, confidence, and pride in creating stories. We used those Big Books not only in a bilingual programme, but also in adult literacy classes.

You can make Big Books with children later, once they have caught on to the idea of how interesting books are. In order to draw out the children's hidden creative skills, you need to let them experience some good stories first.

How to make Big Books

For the Burarra programme we made most of the Big Books in A3 size [approximately 11.7 by 16.5 inches, or 29.7 by 42 cm] since it was easy to enlarge to this size on the photocopier. For the Tawala [Milne Bay] *tokples skuls* we were not able to use a photocopier. However, we made the Big Books A3 size by using butcher paper. (Half a sheet of butcher paper makes two A3 size pages.) Some of the original illustrations are in A3 size, and this size can be reduced later to A4 size for printing.

Big Books are made as cheaply as possible by using materials available locally: cardboard boxes for hard covers, butcher paper, fishing line [for sewing together], clear plastic bags to protect the front covers, etc. For the Umanikaina [Milne Bay] programme some Big Books were made from plastic flour bags. They can be rolled up for travelling from village to village in the mountains and are water-resistant for crossing rivers. There are many other ways to make Big Books (see Northern Territory Department of Education, "Making Big Books"). The above methods are just ways that I have used. You can make them whatever way best suits your programme. Following are detailed instructions for making Big Books.

(a) Using a cardboard box and butcher's paper

1. Cut two panels of a large cardboard box. Fold the centre twice for the thickness of the book.

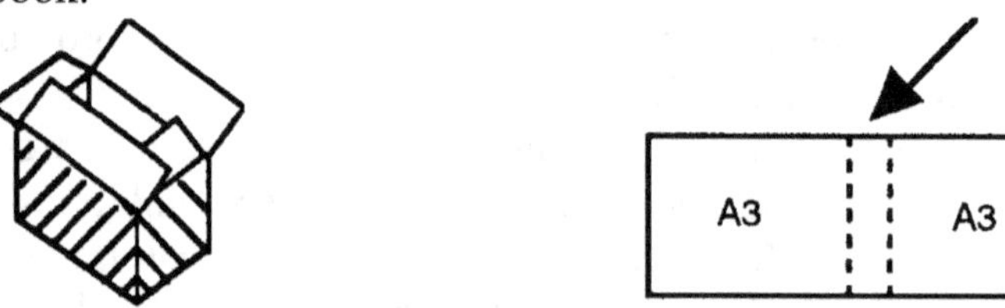

2. Cut a sheet of butcher's paper in half.

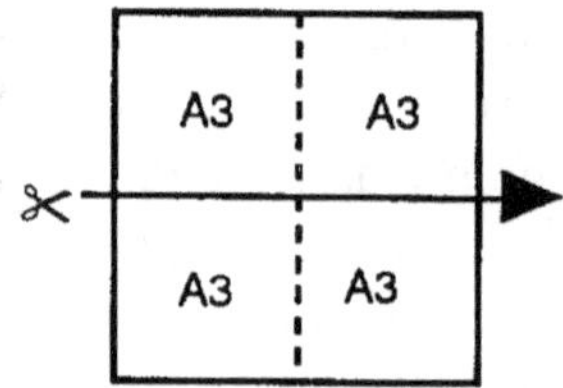

3. Allocate pages (double the sheets of paper for backed pages).

4. Trace illustrations, colour, and write text.

5. Paste the backed pages together.

6. Paste the cover page on the cardboard cover. Place a sheet of clear plastic (e.g., a half of a used plastic bag) over it and tape the edges with strips of masking tape.

7. Collate the pages and hold them on the cover cardboard with clothes pegs.

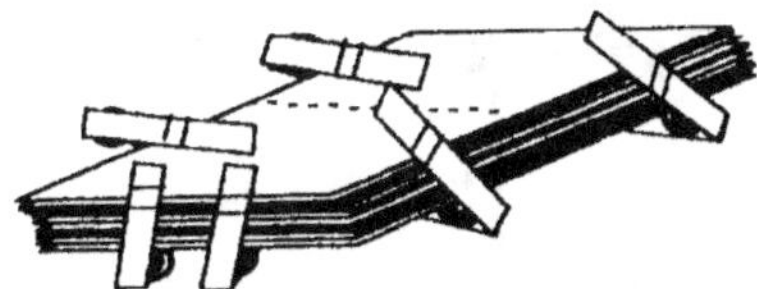

8. Sew the center with a fishing line and cover it with a strip of masking tape. Tape also over the spine of the cover.

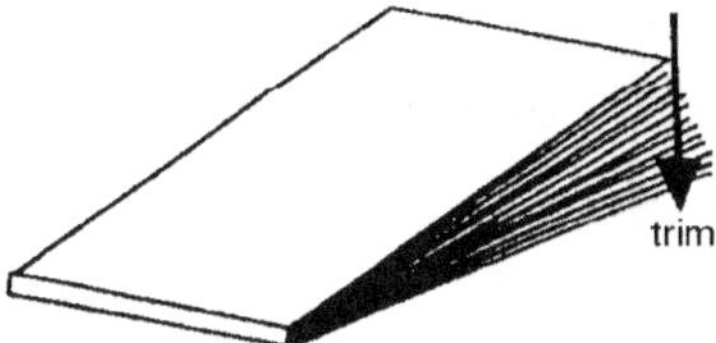

9. Trim the pages evenly to the cover.

To store the Big Books and other teaching materials, a cockroach-proof wooden box can be made. A plastic flour bag can be made into two bags for carrying Big Books, games, etc.

(b) Using plastic flour bags

1. Cut a flour bag into two.

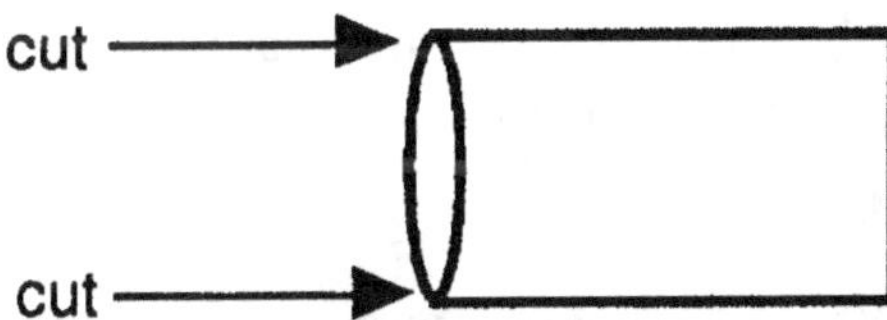

2. Fold it in half.

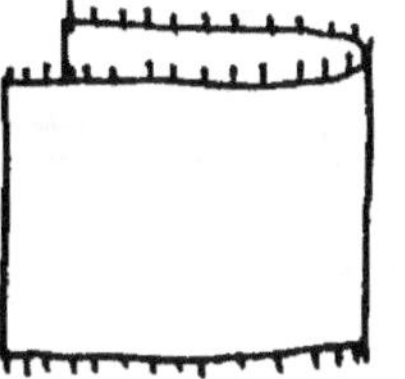

3. Trace illustrations and write text.

4. Sew over the rough edges folding inside.

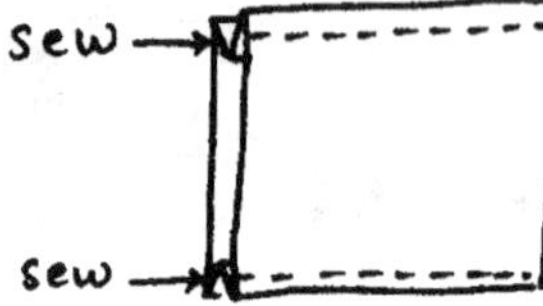

5. Collate the pages.

6. Place the spine between two sticks and nail them together.

7. Cover the sticks with strips of masking tape.

Conclusion

One literacy consultant told me that the teaching methods used in PNG have to be very simple so that teachers who have had hardly any education can handle them. That may be true. Some teaching methods may be easy to follow because they employ a mechanical way of teaching. Other methods may indeed be too complicated because they include too many different things. Big Books are an easy and effective way of teaching reading, without being too complicated, and make the reading process fun.

One important thing that must be remembered is that teaching is a gift. Only certain people are suited (gifted) to teach young children, while others are gifted in other areas. If you are a creative literacy worker, share your purpose and the kind of teaching method you would like to use (e.g., Big Books) with those who are interested in being involved in your literacy programme. You will be surprised to know that there are talented people around you who are able to handle the method beautifully.

8.5 Whole language approach case studies

The Hewa of Papua New Guinea

The material in this section was adapted from a report written by Karen Vollrath, November 1991.

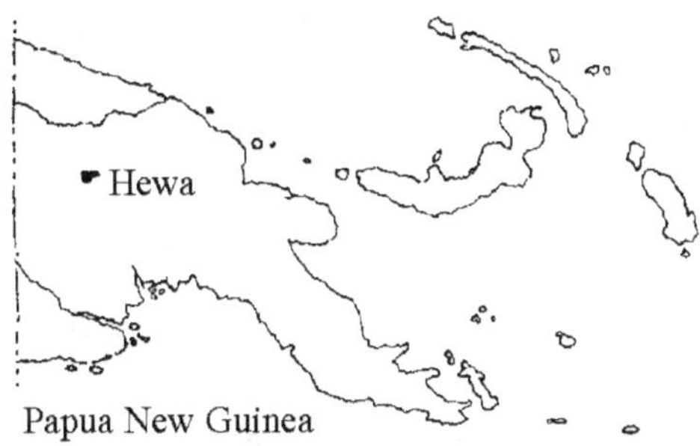

The Hewa language area is an irregularly shaped area 91 kilometres from east to west and up to 40 kilometres north to south along the Lagaip River. Most of the area is in the Southern Highlands Province but some falls into the West Sepik and Enga provinces of Papua New Guinea.

The Hewa area is characterized by steep-sided mountains climbing to about 2,194 metres. These are mostly ranges of mountains rather than separate, high peaks, and they tower as much as 1,524 metres above the rivers at their bases. The valleys are nothing more than river beds.

It takes at least eight hours of walking to go between any given non-Hewa community and its nearest Hewa neighbours. The area is very remote and isolated, and there has not been a lot of outside contact. The area was de-restricted by the government in 1972, and only occasional government or mission patrols enter the region. Although ecological exploration by oil and mineral companies and the construction of an airstrip during 1989–1990 has increased the area's contact with the outside world, a high level of traditional life has been maintained with few changes in traditional ways.

Hewa terrain is sparsely populated. The population of 2,000 people live in an area approximately 2,800 square kilometres (1,080 square miles). The people live in household settlements scattered across the ranges, rather than in hamlets or villages. Distances between these households vary in walking times from five minutes to eighteen hours. All travel involves walking over trails cut through the dense rain forest. Small rivers are crossed by using vine-and-cane bridges. The larger rivers are crossed using rafts.

There are no community (government) schools in the region. The government has set up medical aid posts at four locations and has trained village health workers to give basic medical care in six other places.

The Hewa economy is based mainly on subsistence agriculture, although the people do spend a lot of their time hunting and gathering in order to supplement the basic crops that they grow. Few people grow food to sell, and there is very little opportunity to earn money. Most of the time available to the average Hewa adult is spent doing things necessary for staying alive. There are no trade stores in the entire language area.

The smallest social unit that functions within Hewa society is the household, which is made up of a man, his wife or wives, and their children. Added to this core group may be elderly parents, unmarried male relatives, and other relatives. Households relate to each other for two main reasons: they have relatives in the other household, or the other household is nearby.

Major projects such as garden and house construction are usually handled by members of one household, with all members of that household joining in the work. Members of other households do not often help in such work unless they are paid which is done when the job is finished.

Traditionally, households did not join together except to help each other in times of war. This situation has changed a little in recent years, but in each case, cooperation between families has been encouraged by people from outside the language area, and the motivation to be involved has been payment, the promise of future services, or both.

The heads of households are the decision-makers. Those who are fathers or oldest brothers are the leaders. Decisions are made by everyone coming to have the same opinion and agreeing with each other, with every person being allowed to express his or her opinion about the topic under discussion.

The exchange of food is extremely important, and serves to establish, maintain, strengthen, and reestablish relationships between partners. It is one of the most important cultural activities, important in relating to other people, and to their dead ancestors.

The Hewa people do not accept new things from the outside world easily. They think about changes very carefully because they do not want to damage their way of life. They know that relationships with other people are the most important thing in their culture, so they are not willing to accept anything which could hurt those relationships. Gradually the Hewa people are becoming involved with literacy concepts, skills, and use, especially in areas that have more frequent contact with neighbouring language groups. It is estimated that one or two percent of the Hewa population is literate (that is, they are able to read and gain some degree of meaning from written material), either in Tok Pisin or in Hewa.

History of Hewa literacy. When we [Karen and Paul Vollrath] began to live with the Hewa in 1979, we found that very few people knew anything about reading and writing. Most of them were completely unfamiliar with paper, pencils, books, pictures, drawings, and any sort of written symbols. We introduced magazines for people to look at. Six months later a woman was looking at a picture of a man's head in one of the magazines, when, suddenly she cried out because she realised what it was she was looking at. She immediately shared her insight with others seated around her, and the whole group expressed genuine surprise and delight. It appeared that, until that time, people had been seeing only meaningless shapes and colours and had not been able to interpret the pictures. So we began to take photographs of everyday life and people and put them in photo albums for the people's enjoyment. People are still interested in photo albums, and these help them learn how to get information from a flat surface.

The use of literacy skills in our own everyday lives showed people the possible value of those skills. Because we had difficulty remembering everyone's name and our obligations to each one in the system of giving and receiving, we hung a clipboard where we could easily record people's names and details of our exchanges. My husband, Paul, also kept a separate notebook of people's names and any personal possessions which they wanted us to look after. They came to understand rather quickly that the marks on the paper carried information and were a good way of keeping that information correct over time.

As Paul worked with various Hewa men in drafting translation, he routinely read aloud the material previously drafted. The men expressed curiosity and interest in the fact that the recorded words always remained exactly the same as originally drafted or adjusted, no matter how long the period of time had been between readings.

In 1985, the people expressed a general enthusiasm and desire to learn literacy skills for themselves. They decided that some of the young men who had attended a Tok Pisin literacy class run elsewhere by another mission should be the first students in a Hewa literacy course. These young men were between the ages of fifteen and twenty, who could read Tok Pisin. Course materials included the primer lessons we had prepared with consultant help. The lessons were based on the Gudschinsky method. We also used syllable and word flash cards and song charts. Each class session included a story read to the students in Tok Pisin with discussion following. Basic mathematics skills were also included in the lessons.

The course lasted about six weeks. Results were generally good and showed us that the Hewa orthography was working well. One student kept practicing his Hewa literacy skills by writing letters to us and by writing down tape-recorded stories for us. The adult men said that they wanted to do the same kind of course at a later time. When the book of Ruth and the Gospel of Mark were published in 1985, most of the copies were bought by adults who could not read. They were all interested in Christianity and wanted to learn what the books had to say.

In 1986, a course was held for sixteen adults, five of whom were women. Their ages were from 25 to 60 years old. None of them knew how to read in any language and most of them spoke only Hewa. Course materials included a book of pre-reading exercises, the revised primer (including pre-writing exercises), song charts, an experience chart, and flash cards. (One page each from the pre-reader and the primer are on the next page.) Each class began with a reading from the Hewa Gospel of Mark. Then they discussed it together. Throughout the course, we often found it necessary to add extra drill and review and to slow down the introduction of new material. From the beginning, the question asked over and over by the students was, "When are we going to read?"

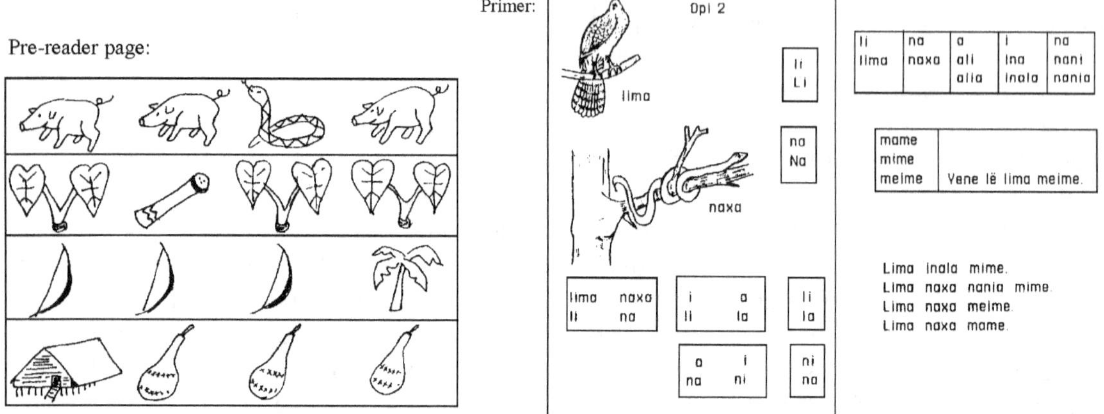

After five weeks we finished the pre-reader and began work in the first primer. By this time students were losing interest and were away from class for longer periods of time in order to handle their normal everyday responsibilities. The remaining students were happy to do the drills, but after only eight primer lessons, interest in continuing in class faded almost completely. The course had lasted eight weeks. It was obvious to us that the students were not seeing the drills as preparing them for reading.

Some of the goals that we had set for the course had been accomplished. The students were accomplishing things like:

- learning to read left to right and top to bottom
- being able to see things that were the same and different
- becoming familiar with writing instruments and
- being able to read and write their own names

But the students' goals of being able to read had not been met and there was no interest in having more literacy classes.

When we came back from furlough in August of 1989, we found that there continued to be a lack of interest in literacy, but the desire to know more about what the Scriptures said was extremely high. We were not too interested in getting back to literacy the way we had been doing it before, but we knew that the motivation to learn Scripture could be a powerful motivation for gaining literacy. In 1981 we had attended a literacy planning workshop and had seen the need for an each-one-teach-one approach for the Hewa literacy work. But we had no idea of how to use such a strategy when the people were not interested in the literacy materials we had made.

Late in 1989, we heard about a way of teaching that was being used by Daniel and Wei Lei Jesudason. They used several whole language methods to encourage literacy among the

Umanikaina people of Milne Bay, PNG. The materials they used were based on translated Scripture. So we attended another literacy materials workshop and developed Hewa materials using a whole language approach and using Scripture text as the foundation for the reading and writing lessons.

When we returned to the Hewa area at the end of May 1990, we silk-screened copies of the creation story from Genesis (see sample page below). This was used as the basic reader. We let everyone know that we would be teaching any interested adults how to read it, beginning June 12th. We also had an enlarged copy (Big Book) of the basic reader, large wall charts of the text with pictures from the basic reader, and a writing book which had text and pictures taken from the basic reader. Fourteen individuals bought readers showing that they wanted to be students in the class.

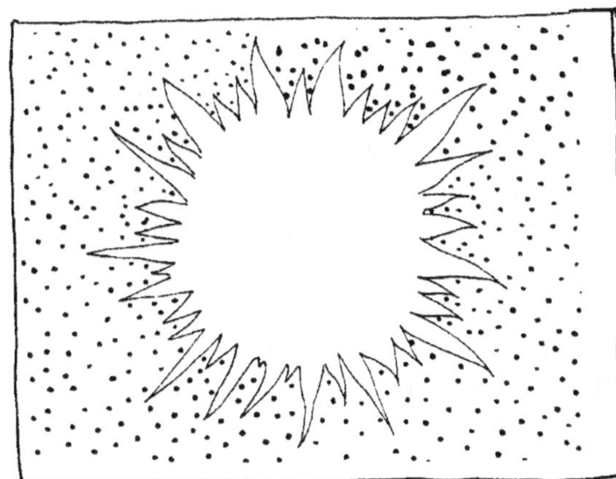

Kote lë kue nalume, "Nö alő maseáfenoyö," nalume. Änáme, nö alő meáfenome. Kote lë nö alő pina eiwepe, fäläma eme. Lë nö apipe, nö siláku mi, nö alő meáfeno eme. Lë nö alő wi wapa yaú naluweme, nö siláku wi wapa siláki nalume. Siláku lë yafenope ime, nö alő yafenome. Ele yaú ue na yafenome.

5

We used a shared-reading approach with the Big Book, and did repeated readings. First, Paul read through the whole story and then he did repeated readings of the page in focus for that lesson. The wall chart which matched the page in focus on that day was hung up on a wall. The students read that as well. Outside of class time, students were regularly encouraged to take their books home, or to spend time at our house whenever they wished, in order to practice their reading skills. In this way, several students completed the basic reader and began to read the book of Ruth.

Our house has a large enclosed area where people often come and visit. Some stay for several days at a time. The literacy lessons were held in this area and, as a result, large numbers of people who otherwise would have had no contact with literacy had the opportunity to observe the reading lessons. Many people who visited for other reasons gained knowledge about Scripture, and were exposed to literacy concepts and skills. We were amazed to find that some visitors as they talked among themselves were also following the students as they practiced their reading. Several times when students hesitated in their reading they would tell them what the word should be.

The wall charts proved extremely useful for encouraging interest in reading. They allowed people to practice reading familiar material whenever they wanted. The large format made reading easier, especially for older people with vision problems. The charts were hung on walls for all to see as the students progressed through their readers. This gave opportunities for visitors and students to try reading and to discuss the material.

Every single student improved in his or her literacy abilities. How much they improved in their reading depended upon how much they practiced. When students missed class and reading practice, it wasn't necessary to spend a lot of time on revision. Not one student was able to attend every class session, and some were away for seven to twelve days at a time during the twelve weeks of classes. In every case, however, the student was able to pick up where he had left off, after one hour of reading the text in class.

We found the basic teaching format quite effective, and we simply added or took out repeated readings according to the needs of the students at any given time.

We never knew just how many or which students would come to class each time, but we found the lesson format flexible enough to fit every situation. It was not difficult when new students joined the class; they joined into the group-learning situation easily. Students with strengths helped those with difficulties and they worked as partners during independent reading and writing. This was their normal way of doing things. Students of similar age tended to work together, or students who were related worked together.

We found that students did make use of their own books and the wall charts to practice reading at various hours of the day and night. Often, some of the young men would come to our house at night for one reason or another and would use the time to read independently from their books or to request guided reading practice. Students would help others as they tried to read the charts.

The whole language approach has been ideal in the Hewa context because each student can determine and control his own material, and learn at the pace which he prefers, in order to meet his own special goals. For example, an older woman student wanted to build a relationship with me, wanted to be able to write, and wanted to become familiar with Scripture material. She was not too worried about becoming an independent reader quickly. Two advanced students were wanting to increase their fluency. Another student, just as advanced as these two, wanted to read each text perfectly before moving on to a new one. Each student was able to meet his goals to his own satisfaction.

Additional practice in reading was gained by copying parts of the text into exercise books which also served as pre-writing lessons. (The dotted letters and diagrams were traced over by the students who needed pre-writing practice.)

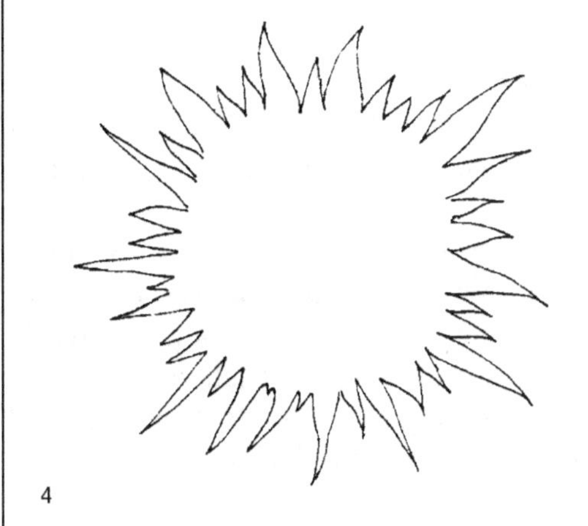

Kote le nö lëi na atetë meáfenome.

Kote lë nö lëi na atetë meáfenome.

Kote lë nö lëi na atetë meáfenome.

5

Hewa lesson format.

- Teacher reads through the entire Big Book once, commenting as necessary about the pictures.
- Teacher goes back and reads from the beginning, finishing with the page in focus for that particular lesson. He then reads the page in focus and the previous page at least twice.
- Teacher and students read through the basic reader as a group, with each student following in his own book. Teacher discusses pictures as necessary, pointing out how they match those in the Big Book.
- Teacher and students go back and read from the beginning as a group, finishing with the page in focus for that particular lesson. They read the page in focus and the one previous to it at least twice.
- Teacher and students read the cover, title page, and any text in focus in the writing book, as well as any text previously completed. Teacher discusses and explains any pictures in focus. He gives instructions about the exercise in focus; then supervises and helps students to complete the exercise.
- Teacher and students read the wall charts which are the same as the material they have worked on in that lesson and in previous lessons.

Remember: Repeated readings can be added or deleted according to the students' needs.

The Quechua of Peru[17]

The Quechua people live in Peru, a country of South America. For the last four hundred and fifty years the Quechua people have been oppressed by others. People used to say their language and culture were of no value. For centuries the Quechua have believed them. They are a very poor people who work hard to make a living. They are subsistence farmers and have little time for study or for learning to read.

The main language in Peru is Spanish and all of the government schools teach in Spanish. It is hard for Quechua students. They go to school but do not understand Spanish. In the rural areas over half of them drop out of school before they reach grade three; others leave in the next few grades. Very few Quechua children graduate from the primary schools and even fewer from the high schools (less than 10 percent). Any students that do learn to read through this system have also been taught that their language is worthless and so they are not motivated to learn to read it.

There have been a lot of Quechua literacy programmes tried over the last twenty years but few of them have been truly successful. They have met many problems such as the following.

- Problems with the alphabet and a lot of discussion about it—there are still problems with certain letter choices, how to write long vowels, and so on.
- Many of the parents have been against the programmes as they felt that their children must learn Spanish if they are to get ahead.
- A lack of government and community support.
- A lack of money for school, books, teacher training, and teachers wages.
- There are many different dialects of Quechua. Not one of them is accepted as a standard dialect, so each region needs to produce their own materials which is costly and time consuming. The government at one time tried to impose a standard Quechua but it caused many problems and was dropped.
- Quechua has long complicated words which have many small parts (suffixes) with different meanings (up to 18 parts in a single word); this has made it difficult to learn to read Quechua.

There have been various primers and a children's reader published by SIL and other people. But these have not been used very much. Some of the primers have not been very popular with teachers and most people have not been enthusiastic about using them to learn to read. These efforts have not produced many people who can read.

Since 1987, however, when the Ayacucho Quechua Bible was published, there have been many Ayacucho Quechuas wanting copies of the Bible and other religious materials. Many

---

[17]Adapted from Linda Orr-Easthouse (1994), "A Whole Language Approach to Quechua Literacy" Notes On Literacy 20(1):1–26.

of them can already read! It seems that the motivation to read the Scriptures has brought about this change.

Because of trouble with the terrorists in the area, during the 1980s and into 1992 it was not safe for national or expatriate teachers and literacy workers to move about to hold teacher training courses and literacy classes. Even community meetings were restricted because of these problems. This situation has since improved significantly and classes are being held.

The problem that confronted Linda and Randy Easthouse, therefore, was how to help people learn to read given all the problems mentioned above. The Easthouses chose to use a whole language approach and to work with family groups that could meet together each night in their own house around their own fires and a kerosene lamp.

Whole language and Quechua literacy. The Easthouses chose to use a literature-based reading programme. The stories and materials they developed used natural text. They started with local stories and later included Bible stories and other texts that the people wanted to read. They aimed their materials at mothers and their children, but they hoped that as the story books got harder others in the family who could already read a little bit would join in.

They had someone read each of the stories on to a cassette tape. They sold or lent the tape, sometimes with a handwind cassette recorder and 10 copies of the book. These teaching packets were often distributed with the help of respected community leaders. It was the leader's job to distribute the packages and to check one week later how the people were doing, and loan them a new tape and book set if needed.

The idea was that family groups would spend one night a week and listen to the tape and follow along in their books. Then they would practice reading that book at least once a day for the rest of the week. They would not go on to the next book until they could read the book fluently. Before they could go on to the next book, they should be able to read the story with natural intonation, speed, and expression. They should be able to read it with little hesitation.

The tape starts by asking three or four preview or prediction questions. The questions are not meant to be answered but are meant to start the listeners thinking about what the book might be about and what they might hear in the story that follows. Then the story is read at speed on the tape and people follow in their books. After the first listening, the tape asks the listeners three or four questions about the story to see if people have understood the story. The listeners are told to turn off the tape and discuss the questions.

Then the people listen to the story while following it in their books, over and over as many times as they need, until they feel comfortable and fluent in reading it. They are encouraged to practice reading the story each day in the coming week.

The levels of stories that were produced for the Quechua programme were as follows.

Level 1
- Books have one sentence per page
- One picture per page, that is large, clear but without too much detail; pictures are very important at this stage for giving clues to the meaning of the text
- Simple sentences
- Most of the stories were locally written

Level 2
- Two sentences per page, but may have more complicated sentences
- One picture per page
- Story ideas from other areas

Level 3
- Two to three sentences per page, may be more complex sentences
- Different kinds of stories
- Smaller pictures, not so important at this stage
- Could be translated information such as Bible stories

Level 4: Free reading
- Real Quechua stories, 50 sentences in the whole book
- One picture for every 3–5 pages
- Now people are not just learning to read, they are also reading in order to learn
- Stories about things that are not familiar; different kinds of stories

Advantages of this approach.
- The repeated readings encourage people to follow along and participate when they are ready to do so without fear of failure.

- The tapes enabled illiterate grandmothers to support and encourage their grandchildren in learning to read and it was no longer considered something foreign.
- Storytelling in family groups at night is something very often done in that culture.
- The method follows family patterns of interaction and instruction with no need for an instructor.
- The cassette gave opportunities for new readers to practice reading before they were ready to read on their own.
- The use of repeated readings is acceptable as it follows the cultural practice of retelling oral stories.
- Discussions about the story demonstrate that reading is understanding the message in the text. (Often when people read Spanish they do not understand what they read.)
- Regular class schedules are not required and the cassette player is extremely portable so classes and practice sessions continue when people need to move to their gardens.
- Books are shared and loaned because very few people can afford to buy them.
- Parents are involved with their children and are now encouraging Quechua literacy.
- Parents understand more about teaching and learning and they do not feel so ignorant when relating to the Spanish school teachers.

Problems with the approach.

- Initial technical difficulties in producing, duplicating and funding the tapes and books.
- In the past most families had at least one cassette player and enough batteries. No outside funding would have been needed to fund the programme. But now people do not have enough money to buy batteries; the economic situation does show signs of improving however.
- It has been hard to produce enough materials to keep up with the demand.

Assessment of this approach for the Quechua. Linda Easthouse described the results of the program as follows:

> The results have so far been encouraging. We can't publish books or produce tapes fast enough for the demand in the areas where we are providing cassette machines and/or batteries for trials. We are now experimenting with playing the tapes over a local radio station twice a week. This has been very popular.
>
> In one of the first trial programs with just sloppy photocopied mockups for books, we asked a neighbor to invite a few ladies from her family to listen. The first night we had six people including the two kids who took turns cranking the hand-crank tape recorder. The next night 18 turned up and by the end of the week there were forty ladies and a few extra children crammed into the tiny room sharing the 10 copies of the book.

> One of the young ladies that attended one evening came out of curiosity and informed us at the outset that it was impossible to read Quechua. She was in the Spanish high school and read reasonably well in Spanish. She sat at the back and didn't need to share a book as she was just there to listen. Half way through the tape she borrowed her friend's book and by the end, she was one of the first to volunteer to read the book to the group. Upon leaving she asked to buy a book and asked when the next one would be ready.
>
> In Ancash, the early books from Huanuco were adapted and five new local stories included. After hearing one of the tapes in a demonstration hour during a teacher training course, one of the students came and bought a copy of the tape and 20 books and is now teaching a class in his tiny rural community. Another of the co-translators was so excited that he came up with a solution for the problem of the cost for the tapes. He owns a large two-cassette tape deck that makes good copies. He now takes a master tape with him when he goes to a village. He takes along his big tape deck and plays the tape. Anyone who brings him a blank tape gets a free copy and then he sells the books to go with it.
>
> We are also introducing it into the primary schools in a six school pilot project using the same method but having the teacher teach instead of using the tape. It is an "enrichment program" during the language arts curriculum.
>
> Everywhere that [the program] has been introduced, it has been well received, produced new readers and increased interest in Quechua materials. (Easthouse 1994)

Recommendations for using tape cassettes.

- Record the same story on both sides of tape so that the tape does not need to be rewound each time.
- Plan ahead for how payment for the production and duplicating of the tapes and the printing of the books will be handled.
- Determine how many families have access to a cassette player and whether or not they can afford to keep buying batteries? Are there some hand-wind tapeplayers? Could a local radio station play the tapes?

For more information about this program, see the article by Linda Eastman in Notes on Literacy 20:1.

The Kriol of Australia

The following is an excerpt from Borneman (1992:7–17) which tells about a situation where the Kriol Holi Baibul was used as a reading textbook.

Charlie was around 50. He had not been to school and had little understanding of reading. It soon became clear that his primary motivation to learn to read was so that he could read the Kriol Bible. The literacy worker with the Anglican Church worked patiently with Charlie from the Kriol Bible. His progress was slow. The Kriol Bible seemed an inappropriate text for a beginning reader.

A reading specialist recommended that the literacy worker record a story told by Charlie and have it transcribed. This would be Charlie's basic reading material—personal, immediate, and interesting. After a couple days using this new strategy, Charlie began to lose interest and his reading seemed to regress. The literacy worker was about to give in to the common quip that *you can't teach old dogs new tricks*, interpreted in literacy circles as *don't even try to teach someone over 40 to read.*

Then Charlie provided the breakthrough. Charlie arrived and put his Kriol Bible on the desk and, pointing to his own story, said, "I don't want to read that story. I already know it. I told it to you. I want to learn to read the Bible." The literacy worker again took up the Kriol Bible as the basic text for Charlie's reading lessons. From that point on Charlie's reading ability progressed steadily.

Charlie was not alone in his desire to want to read the Kriol Bible. This story has been repeated several times by older Kriol speakers. There are several reasons for this. The Kriol Bible is the only significant adult literature in Kriol, is strongly identified as Aboriginal, and was translated by four Aboriginal people from Charlie's own community.

Kriol is spoken by many Australian Aborigines who live in the Northern Territory, Western Australia and in parts of Queensland. It is a language that has developed through the coming together of English and some of the local Aboriginal languages. It is now the mother tongue of many Aboriginal people. Other Aboriginal people have learned it as a second or third language when they worked on cattle stations or places like that.

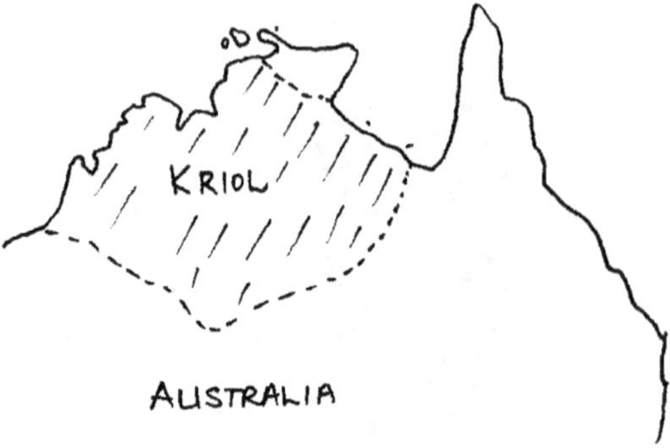

Given the strong motivations of the Kriol people who wanted to learn to read, Barry and Margaret Borneman decided to use the Kriol Bible as the reading textbook for these people. They started with the front cover and from there began with the creation story in the book of Genesis.

> This story not only had a form that lent itself to memory, to recital, and to predictablility, but also addressed the same type of questions that Aboriginal mythology endeavors to explain: Why is the world the way it is and how did it happen? In this creation story I was able to harmonize the conflicting factors of what the learner wanted to read and my belief that initial reading materials must be predictable, socially relevant, and meaningful.
>
> The components of the creation story are integral to the Aboriginal learner's world. The stars, moon, sun, trees, man and woman are all part of the immediate environment. These are all understandable and picturable concepts. The learner already has all the information necessary to make sense of this story.
>
> Furthermore, the creation story is characterized by repetition and balance, which are also specific features of oral tradition…In fact, approximately 40 percent of the Kriol text of the creation story is couched in repetitive oral refrain. For example, the refrain *Brom deya God bin tok* 'and God said', signifying God's creative activity, occurs on average at least once in every four verses. The phrase marking the end of one day and the beginning of a new day, *Brom deya naitaim bin gowei na, en wen imbin ailibala, imbin det namba (thri) dei na* 'and there was evening, and there was morning—the (third) day', occurs six times in the text. (Borneman 1992:11–12)

The motivations of the learners caused Barry and Margaret to design their literacy classes and materials for adults around the Kriol Baibul. They used four simple steps which are repeated throughout the reading session. These steps were represented by pictures in the Kriol reading book to reduce the amount of written instruction. They are pictured in the chart below.

1. The learner opens the story.
2. Reading. The helper reads the whole story expressively to the learner.
3. Talking. After reading, the learner and the helper talk together about what the story means.
4. Re-reading. The learner reads the story slowly with the helper, who points to each word as they read along.

These steps are repeated throughout the lesson at the story level, the phrase level, the word level, and finally again at the story level. For example, the first lesson starts with reading, talking about, and rereading of the first five verses of Genesis.

Yu garra luk dijan stori brom det Kriol Baibul.
Sambodi bin pudum mak langa detlot wed, 'Brom deya God bin tok'.

> God bin meigim ebrijing
> [1] [1,2] Orait, longtaim wen God bin stat
> meigimbat ebrijing, no enijing bin sidan. Imbin jis
> eniwei, nomo garram enijing. Oni strongbala woda
> bin goran goran ebriwei, en imbin brabli dakbala, en
> det spirit blanga God bin mubabat antop langa det woda.
> [3] Brom deya God bin tok, "Lait!" En lait bin kamat.
> [4] Wal wen God bin luk det lait bin gudwan, imbin
> gudbinji.
> [5] Bron deya God bin kadimat det lait brom det
>
> 1.3 2 Karin 4.6
>
> 3

Then the procedure is repeated again with verse 3.

Yu garra midimdanola mitwan wed iya.

> Brom deya God bin tok "*Lait*!" En _____ bin kamat.
>
> Wal wen God bin luk det ______ bin gudwan, imbin gudbinji.

Then the lesson focuses on the word *lait.*

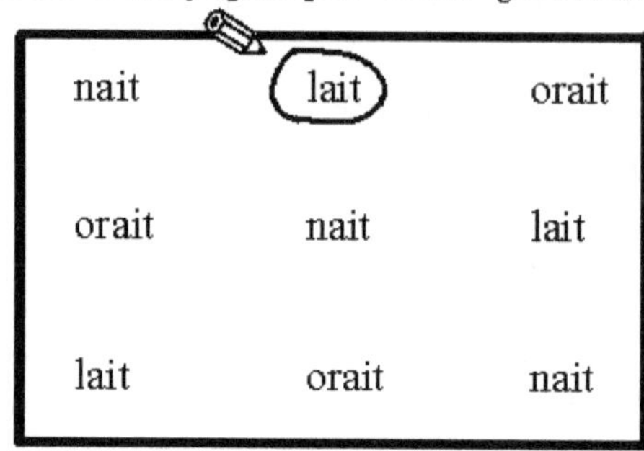

The lesson concludes with the whole story being read by the helper and then by the learner and helper together.

Barry says, "It is important that at each level the key concept is discussed so the learner realizes that reading is essentially about obtaining meaning from print. To assist this, comprehension activities are set after each story. Such comprehension questions are not meant to be primarily a test of understanding, but rather an activity to encourage the seeking of information from the text. Throughout the lesson, it is important to maintain a non-threatening environment." (Borneman 1992:15)

The Bornemans have found this method to be very successful. It has the following strong points.

- It is flexible and can be changed to suit the pace of the learner. The amount of rereading is determined by the needs of the student.
- Learners can be given the number of lessons they need. These have ranged from one half-hour lesson to four months on a daily basis.
- Learners can help each other.
- Family groups can work together.
- A learner who can read a passage can then help someone else learn to read that passage.
- There is always a feeling of success because of the reading together strategy.
- The method builds personal relationships because of the sharing of ideas about the text and the reading together strategy.
- It meets the needs and motivations of the learners.

8.6 Language experience approach

In the 1940s through to the 1970s, the language experience approach was a new approach to teaching reading and writing used in the western world. It was very popular with many teachers. It is similar to some whole language approaches because both encourage an abundance of books written by students about their own lives. The language experience approach made a major break with the teaching reading traditions of its time. It taught reading without using prepared sets of graded reading books (Altwerger and Flores 1991:106).

People started teaching this way as a reaction to the reading programmes that were in use at the time. The reading books used previously did not use natural language, and the people or animals in the stories were made to do all kinds of strange things just so the text would be able to use certain sounds and words.

> A generation had passed since "readers" contained natural stories which had not been mangled to serve some instructional purpose—it was almost as if children were being forced to learn to read a different language from the one they spoke so well. Language-experience methods arose in reaction to this sorry state of affairs. It was realized that a major insight for the beginning reader must be that written language is talk written down. By developing reading materials from the children's own language about matters of which they had real experience it was hoped that a bridge would be built between familiar language and printed symbols. (Holdaway 1979:29)

The major change in this way of teaching is that teachers use the stories of their students as their teaching materials. These stories are either told to the teacher who then writes them down, or written together by the teacher and the class, or written by the students on their own.

For example, when I was teaching a class of adults in Australia to read and write in English, I started by having the class talk about each student's story of how they came to Australia, and then we wrote it down. The following story is one of them.

> I was born in Greece in a small village very close to Thessaloniki, the second biggest city after Athens. Thessaloniki is a beautiful city with a population of one million.
>
> I lived with my parents and my brother in my village. We were a very happy family. This was before World War II started. I was a young girl during the war.
>
> The Germans came to my country in 1940 and they stayed for five years. Everyone was unhappy. We had a difficult life with them. We didn't have enough to eat, we didn't have enough clothes, they took everything from our country and they killed many people. When they left we had civil war for many years. My

> grandparents were killed and our house was destroyed. Many people lost everything they had, lives were lost too.
>
> This is the reason I came to Australia with my family, to have a better life and to live in peace. Emma

The students' stories became the texts that we read together and individually over the next few weeks. We also used their stories for other activities.

Cloze exercise

One of these activities was a cloze exercise. I used part of the story to make up the exercise. Then we did the exercise together. This is what it looked like.

> The __________ came to my country in 1940 and they __________ for five years. Everyone was un______. We had a difficult ________ with them. We didn't have ________ to eat, we didn't ________ enough clothes, they took everything ______ our country and they ________ many people. When they left we had civil ______ for many years. My grandparents were ______ and our ______ was destroyed. Many people lost ______ they had, lives were ______ too.

The students had to try to fill in the missing words. This made them think about the meanings of the sentences.

Making sentences

After that I had the students make up some sentences (shown below), using ideas and thoughts from the story. This helped them to think about some of the meanings and learn some of the words.

We didn't have enough to eat.
We didn't have enough clothes.
They took everything from our country.
They killed many people.

Having made up some sentences like these, the students can then write them on a lapboard or in an exercise book. This gives them practice with writing and copying the correct spelling of the words. Or the words can be put onto cards, and students can take turns making the sentence. Or one student can make a sentence for their partner to read.

Next, I had the students make up new sentences using words from the story such as those below, and then write or copy them.

I was born in a small village in Greece.
Athens is the biggest city in Greece.
The war came to my country when I was young.

Spelling activities

I also would have the students do spelling activities based on the story. The words I taught depended on what the students already knew, and what words were most often misspelled in their work. It is best to only teach two or three things in one lesson or it gets too confusing for the students.

Because the students in my class were all learning English as a second or third language, they often had trouble with past and present time words in English. So in the story shown above, I highlighted the word or part of a word that changed when something that happened in the present was talked about happening in the past.

For example, I talked about the use of 'was' and 'were'. I pointed out that 'was' is used if you were talking about something in the past that happened to one person, and 'were' is used if it was happening to more than one person.

I **was** born	My grandparents **were** killed
I **was** happy	We **were** happy

I talked about how *d* or *ed* is often added to words when talking or writing about things that happened in the past:

live	live**d**
kill	kill**ed**

We talked about other words in English that change their vowel sound when a person is talking about the past:

c**o**me	c**a**me
t**oo**k	t**a**ke

After looking at the smaller parts of the stories, that is, sentences, words, and spelling, it is always good to go back and re-read the whole story again to put these small parts back in their context.

Using students' stories

There are other activities that can be done with the words and sentences from students' stories that will help students learn to read and write. Encourage the students to write about different kinds of things that have happened to them. Or bring things into class or give them experiences as a class that they can write about.

After we had written each student's story of how each one came to Australia, we wrote and read other students' stories. These included stories on the following topics.

A time I was frightened
Cultures are different
Childhood experiences
How to cook special food from my country

The following is one of those stories.

Grandmother's garden

> When I was a young boy my grandmother was always trying to keep her garden looking nice. I used to go inside her garden and deliberately step on her plants. Other times I would take my cat with me to the garden and play inside until the garden looked very bad. After that my grandmother came looking for me and she was very angry.
>
> I heard her voice and I went straight to the tree and climbed it. But when I got up there, the branch I was on broke. I fell down and I was crying a lot. But my grandmother said, "That's not going to change anything. You are in big trouble."

Then we began writing stories about things that affect us now such as the following topics; another illustrative story follows.

Why is there so much war in the world?
My father is dying
Be careful whom you pick up in a taxi
I miss my sister

My father is dying

> My mother lost her health and she suffered for many years. On the 4th of August 1989 she passed away.
>
> From that day my father was very unhappy and very lonely. He lost interest in everything. He didn't want to see his friends, to go out or to talk to other people. He stayed home all day. He had a house close to my house, and he would visit me. We had coffee together and I tried to help him all the time.
>
> My children gave him a small dog for a companion. With his dog he walked to the beach and he enjoyed his companion. One day he got lost. He couldn't remember where his house was. That was the beginning. Every day he got worse and many times he walked around not knowing where he was. I was very upset. I feel sorry for him but I couldn't help him. He has dementia.
>
> We decided to put him in the nursing home. That day was for me, very sad. I cried for many hours. Now he has been there for two years. I visit him every afternoon. I try to help make him happy. Life for him is finished. I love him very much. He was a good father. I pray for him every day, that he will not suffer now at the end of his life. I will remember him and the happy days we had all together for the rest of my life.

There are several good reasons to use students' stories to teach reading and writing. It helps the students in a group to get to know each other. It relates the task of learning to read and write to the students' own lives, and students are dealing with words, sentences, and stories that are very familiar to them. It means that the students are reading and writing about things that they are interested in.

When the teacher uses stories the students have written, it gives a purpose to their writings. Students know it is going to be read and used in the class lessons, so they have an audience to write for. And when students start to ask questions of the writer about his stories to gain more information and understanding, the writer begins to see that he needs to put more information into his writings so that the readers will really understand the situation. For example, our class discussed Emma's story and underlined all the parts that we wanted to ask more questions about in order to get the right 'picture' in our heads. Because of this, next time we were writing Nick asked me if he should include in his story how it felt as a taxi driver to have four drunk men in his taxi. Two men were sitting beside him and two men sitting behind him in the taxi. He realised that if he talked about the thoughts and feelings he was having it would help the reader understand the situation better.

Also once students see their writings being used and enjoyed by others, they are encouraged to write more. Emma started by writing the story of how she came to Australia but went on to write her life story so that her children and grandchildren would understand her life better and understand what it was like living in Greece as a girl. Her children were born and grew up in Australia and do not understand about her earlier life.

Using student writings does have its disadvantages, and people who decide to use this way of teaching need to be aware of these. One is that it can be very time consuming because it is necessary to create or help create all the materials that are needed for the lesson on the spot or before each class, rather than using materials that have been prepared ahead of time as part of an overall literacy campaign. Stories must be written on charts or blackboards, or if students need to practice out of class time they need individual student copies which can be made by stencil. All of this preparation can take a lot of time. In Australia, photocopiers are readily available and so this is not a problem.

The best time to help students with spelling is when they are writing. This is not as easy as following a set programme. The teacher needs to keep a record of what has been taught in order to know what still needs to be taught.

Another disadvantage of using student stories is that students tend to use only the words that they know in their writings. If the only things students read are their own writings, then they do not experience new words or different styles of writing. Also, as Holdaway points out, the stories children write tend to become much the same—talking about coming and going, visiting, and doing things. Book stories often talk about things that are exciting, different from everyday kinds of things, and things that are worth thinking about over and over.

For this reason in my English class I always tried to include stories from other writers that I found in magazines and books. This gave students experience of many new and interesting words and different styles of writing. We also read different kinds of stories to gain information about things in our world, with titles such as:

The Rescue	Whales
The Cobbler	Migration
I'm All Right So Far	The Drilling Rig
Power, Good and Bad	The Hold-up

The level of reading difficulty was often much higher in these texts than in student writings, but by doing shared reading, cued reading, reciprocal questions, and talking a lot about the stories and about any words that were not familiar, the class soon enjoyed reading these stories too. They added an extra dimension to the class lessons. Often the students would use words they had learned from these stories when they were talking about other things, or use the words in their writings. Or they would bring stories on a similar theme that they had found in the newspaper or in magazines, or talk about things that they had seen on TV or in other places that had reminded them of the stories we had read in class. It also opened up the world to them. They could read about other people's lives, experiences, and opinions, rather than being confined to just their own. It gave them a valid reason to keep reading in their personal lives.

This way of teaching can also be used with children. Start by using stories the children dictate to you and gradually shift to having them write the stories themselves. Or write a story together as a class. Included below are parts of some of the dictated stories that the children at Midan Tok Ples Prep Skul did with their teacher in first term. The teacher then used these stories to teach the children to read.

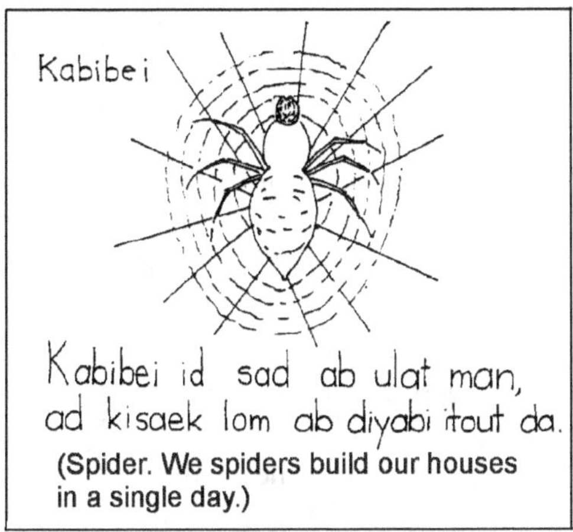

(Spider. We spiders build our houses in a single day.)

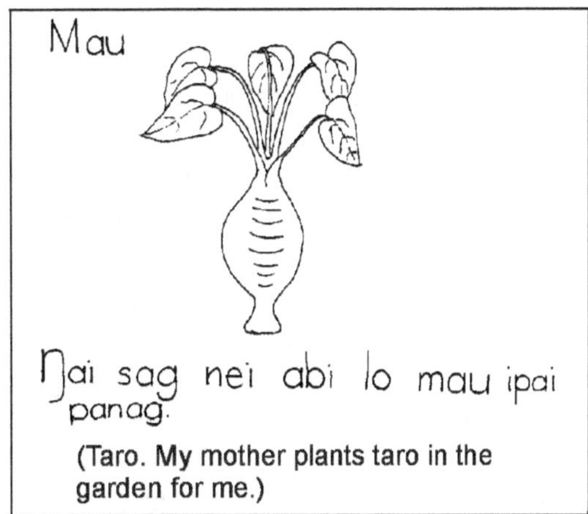

(Taro. My mother plants taro in the garden for me.)

The language experience approach is one way of teaching reading to students. It has both strengths and weaknesses, just like any other approach. Nevertheless, there will be times when it is very useful in teaching students to read and write.

8.7 Implementing a whole language programme[18]

Goodman says that "one major advantage whole language approaches have over others is that they don't require special instructional materials. What's required is a range of real materials in the language(s) of the learners" (Goodman 1986:43).

If you want to begin using the whole language approach to teaching reading and writing you can begin gradually. You can keep doing what you are already doing. Add a half-hour each day working with real stories and with songs and chants written on charts. If there are Big Books or large charts, then use them because they make it easy to work with a group. If not, use an ordinary-sized book but each day write one page out on a chart or blackboard and

[18]Many of these ideas come from Goodman's 1986 book, *What's Whole in Whole Language*? I have changed them and written them in my own way to apply them to vernacular literacy.

use that with the students. Help them learn to read it. Begin working in this way and soon students will begin seeing familiar words and phrases in new stories.

Goodman also says that "literacy development is a matter of getting the processes together: learning, in the context of reading and writing real language, to use just enough print, language structure, and meaning, and to keep it all in the proper personal and cultural perspective" (Goodman 1986:43).

Many teachers worry about changing their way of teaching. To worry is a normal feeling. But if you go carefully step by step a little at a time, it will work out all right. All along the way think about the students' reactions to the new things you are doing. Is it improving things? Do you need to make other changes? Do you need to do things a little differently. Work at change step by step, slowly, and as you get more confident and see things going better you can make more changes. Some of the things you have been doing for a long while have been good and are worth continuing. Do not throw everything out just because you want to try something new. Take small steps and change things slowly. If you find whole language ways of teaching are working better, then gradually increase the amount of time and the things you do using that approach.

You will probably find things will work better if you also encourage your students to help each other and work together on learning, rather than competing against each other. Let the strong help the weak and let the weak help in the areas in which they are strong. If you believe that all the children will be able to learn then they will learn. But they will learn at their own pace which may be different from others. And that is a good thing about whole language teaching. Each student can learn at his own pace.

Encouraging writing is also important. Give the students many reasons to write—letters to each other, to the teacher, to other people, reports, diaries, and stories. Writing helps strengthen reading and reading helps strengthen writing.

Planning a programme is very important in whole language. You cannot just stick to the primer lesson. You need to plan which books the students will read and what activities they will do related to their reading. Also plan what reading strategies you can teach with which books and activities. But always be willing to listen to the students. They will have good ideas of things they want to do with reading and writing, and ideas that are related to the books or themes that you plan.

At each step of the programme there are goals that you need to shoot for. These can be divided into three groups—when you are working with pre-readers, beginning readers, and developing readers. It is good to have these goals in mind when you are evaluating how things have been going, and when you are working out new plans for the future.

For pre-readers

- Build an awareness of print. Draw the learner's attention to print. Demonstrate the uses of print—reading for fun, writing letters and notes, reading for information, looking for print in the environment such as on boxes, rice bags, classroom walls, hymn books, and community notices.
- Make a lot of print for the environment—song charts, chant charts, notices, signs, and murals. Encourage students to take notice of these things.
- Teach students how to handle a book and make opportunities for them to handle many books.
- Read a lot of different kinds of stories to students so they come to see there are many different types of stories.
- Help students create their own stories. Start with dictated stories and then begin personal writing (see §12.2).

For beginning readers

When I talk about beginning readers I mean those students who are ready to begin a formal programme that is designed to support growth in literacy. For these students, you need to work on the following things.

- Continue to work on an awareness of print and its uses.
- Get the students involved in reading whole meaningful texts.
- Encourage them to join in or take over if they choose.
- Draw attention to words, phrases, and letters that are the same.
- Have a lot of books. Make books, signs, and murals together. Write class experience stories together.
- Continue to let students handle a lot of books.
- Help students build strategies (ways) for working out what words are in stories.
- Help students learn that each letter has a special sound and that sounds are used to help work out what certain words are.
- Do a lot of reading together and repeated readings with books that have a lot of repetition in them.
- Encourage students to try new stories (risk-taking). Teachers are there to encourage, support, and help—not only to correct mistakes.

For developing readers

Once students have begun to glimpse the idea of what reading is all about, they need to continue to develop their reading and writing skills. The teacher should work on the following things.

- Build students' confidence and willingness to continue to try. Encourage all their attempts at writing and work hard with them to understand what it is they are trying to say. Support them in their writing and reading attempts.
- Use different kinds of stories. Show them the many different styles of writing.
- Encourage them to write clearly and well.
- Help them to learn good ways of reading words they do not know. Help them to read more smoothly.
- Demonstrate how you can learn things through reading and help students to do that.
- Demonstrate ways of using reading and writing that suit their lifestyle and their community life.
- Build a love of reading and writing. Many students learn to read but will they choose to keep on reading and writing? Encourage them to read outside of class and have materials available that are worth reading.

9

Integrated Approaches

There are many skills involved in being able to gain meaning from a printed message. Some of these, taken from McCormick (1990:10–11), are listed below.

- being able to sound out words
- being able to recognize groups of letters
- being able to work out the main idea of the message
- being able to decode details in the message
- being able to think about the message (making inferences)
- recognising cause and effect
- comparing and contrasting ideas in the message

Some people say that many of these skills are being used all at the same time when someone is trying to decode print. They would argue that when people learn how to read they should use materials and methods which allow them to practice using many skills at the same time as they work out the meaning of the printed message. This approach would integrate several methods of teaching reading, that is, teachers would give opportunites for students to practice the things that each method stresses. Many primer designers therefore like to combine the use of a method that teaches sounding out (phonic or syllable method) with opportunities to read natural text—to read a story and not just sound out and say letters, words, and maybe a sentence or two.

There are many different integrated methods. I discuss briefly the ones suggested by Sarah Gudschinsky; Mary Stringer and Nicholas Faraclas; and by Paulo Freire. Then I give examples of integrated methods that I am calling whole-language-plus.

9.1 Eclectic methods

The Gudschinsky six-step method

For many years SIL has been doing literacy work among people groups in the two-thirds world. People within SIL have developed ways of teaching people to read in many different situations. Their methods have been strongly influenced by the linguistic work that SIL does and by the kinds of situations where SIL works. The linguistic work has influenced the style of the primers and the style of teaching. There is a strong focus on the syllable and on analysis (breaking down) and synthesis (building up) of words. Another factor in the development of these methods is that the teachers and facilitators of the reading groups or classes are often people who have not had much formal education because they live in isolated areas and they are working in areas where there are no books, charts, or printed papers of any kind unless the teachers and SIL workers make them.

Sarah Gudschinsky developed a six-step method of teaching in each reading lesson which came to be known as the Gudschinsky method. Primers using this method carefully introduce every syllable the reader is likely to meet while reading his language. The six steps are as follows.

- Step 1 breaks down the key word to teach the new item by positive or negative focus (depending upon whether the new item can be said in isolation or not).
- Step 2 builds the new element with known elements to form a larger unit.
- Step 3 compares the new syllables or grammatical items in vertical arrangement.
- Step 4 contrasts the new item with other known items used in the same context.
- Step 5, at the top of the right hand page, is word-building practice.
- Step 6 of each lesson is a story that gives practice in reading new material for enjoyment and promotes fluency and comprehension.

Every lesson should be followed by writing practice. The last pages of the primer often contain supplementary stories to give students added reading practice with longer stories.

This method thus integrates the teaching of sounding out syllables, recognizing groups of letters and words, as well as the skills needed to read and understand the story in step 6. Following are two examples of primers constructed according to this method. The first is from the Siane "We Will Learn to Read Book." (The Siane live in the Highlands of Papua New Guinea.) The second is from the Omie Primer, Oro Province PNG.

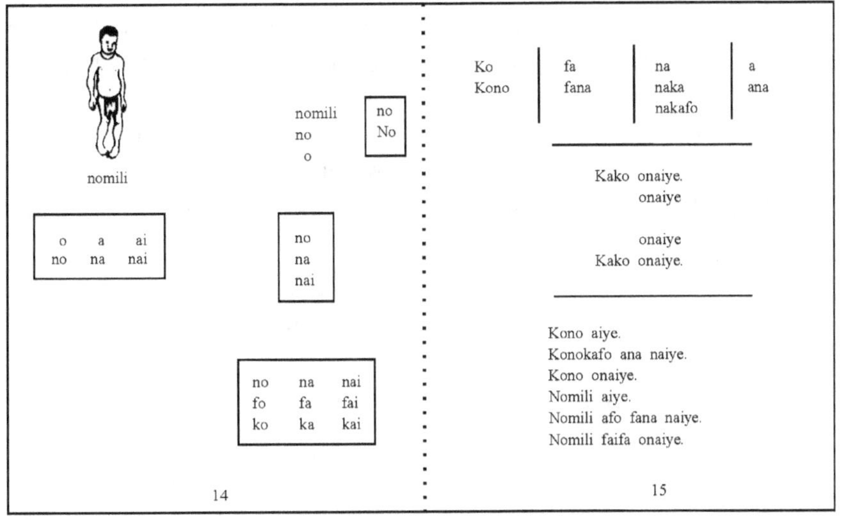

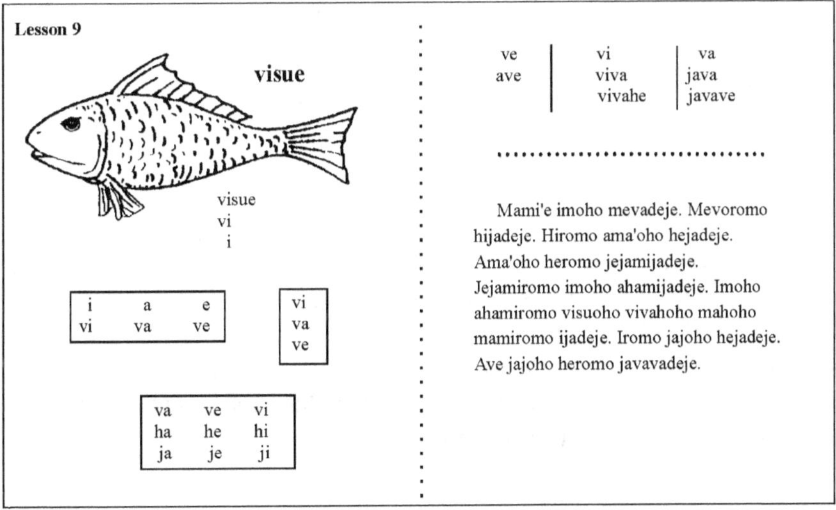

The multi-strategy method

Another SIL worker, Mary Stringer, worked with Nicholas Faraclas of the University of Papua New Guinea and developed the multi-strategy method. This method of teaching reading separates the teaching of reading and writing into two tracks which are deliberately kept separate. One track is called the workbook track and the other track is called the story track.

During the workbook track time, the students are taught to read and write using a syllable method and are limited to using only words that the student can sound out. During the story track time, reading and writing is taught using whole language approaches with no limits placed on the words used. The two tracks are often taught by two different teachers.

A sample of the workbook page is shown below. Story track books are similar to those used in whole language approaches or language experience approaches (see chapter 8 of this book).

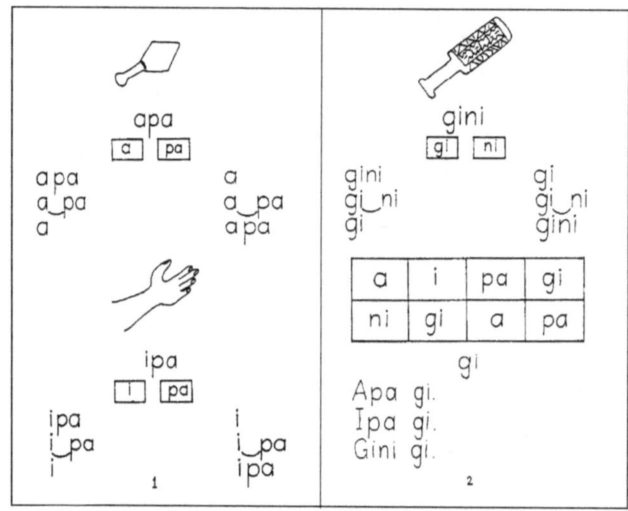

Manuals have been written that describe in detail how to prepare and plan primers and programmes using either the Gudschinsky method or the multi strategy method. They are: *A Manual of Literacy for Pre-Literate People* by Sarah Gudschinsky; and *Working Together for Literacy* by Mary Stringer and Nicholas Faraclas. These books are quite detailed in their descriptions and easily accessible; other books and articles have been published about them in various places, so I will not go into more detail here.

Freire's method

Paulo Freire is well-known throughout the world for his pioneering work in education, especially with the poor people of Brazil. Freire was born into a middle class Brazilian family in 1921 and he grew up in a household with plenty of money and opportunities. He was able to go to school and then to University. While he was studying at the top level of the University (Ph.D.), he developed his thoughts about education. At the same time he was aware of the needs and poverty of the people in the slum areas that surrounded his home area. Many people were living close together without enough food and land for each household. Their houses were often made of scrap materials. The areas where they lived were not good places to bring up families. Freire wanted very much to work with these poor people and help them educate themselves and improve their situation.

He began to make up reading lessons about things that were important to them. In teaching reading he chose to use words that people had strong feelings about. For example he would use the word *favela* 'slum' to teach the syllables:

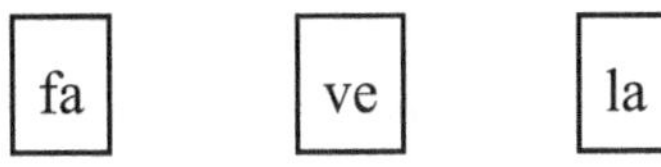

Then he would contrast these syllables with other syllables that had been taught. And he would get people writing words and sentences about the things that were troubling them.

Through his work and studies, Freire developed a philosophy of education that was different from those of other people. He became well-known for his literacy work from 1963 onwards (McCormick 1988:201). People still follow his philosophy today.

Freire encouraged the adults he worked with to think critically about their world and to actively shape it into something better. He did this by using cultural circles to take the place of classes, and he used group discussions instead of a teacher 'teaching'. He encouraged his students to fight against oppression and against those who caused them hardship.

He was critical of most teachers of his time for the view they had of students. He thought that teachers saw their students as empty vessels to be filled with knowledge and saw themselves as holding that knowledge and pouring it into the vessels. Instead, Freire argued, teachers should see their students as active human beings who already know a lot about their world and who are working hard at discovering and constructing new knowledge for themselves. He felt it was the teacher's task to encourage students to discover more and to help them organize what they already know.

His method of teaching was questioned by some people who thought his work was too political, and who saw it as stirring up trouble. But his philosophy of education has had an important influence on adult education today. Also, his literacy work showed the importance of working with the problems that concern literacy students. Freire pointed out that although literacy students could not read they still had many valuable experiences from life that could be used in furthering their education.

Freire's way of working with adults is still helpful today—choosing problems and themes that are of interest to the adults and using them as a basis for reading and writing lessons.

The two tables below list suggestions that were put together by different groups interested in doing adult literacy. The first group was a group of women who were thinking about doing literacy work with women. The second group was a group of prison officers who were thinking of doing literacy work with prisoners. Both of these lists show that the planners were thinking about the problems and interests of the people they would be teaching.

Suggested topics for adult literacy for women

Family life	Problems	Family security and welfare	Spiritual growth
	Not enough money Gambling Adultery No education Drinking Wife bashing Too many children *Wantoks*	Planning for children's education Protection from rape Looking after parents Divorced women with children Unemployment Saving money Family planning Helping each other Working with village police Rights and duties of family members	Going to church together Teaching children about Jesus Family praying together Visiting sick people Christian living and speaking Supporting the pastor Giving money to God
Health	Health problems	Nutrition	Community health
	Smoking Diarrhea Malaria Betel nut chewing Alcohol and drugs Immunizations Cavities in teeth Bottle feeding Sexual diseases	Breast feeding Food for growth Food for strength Food for protection Good ways to cook food Good food for baby Good food for a sick baby Good food for teeth	Keeping villages clean Animals in the village Clean water Water drainage Village toilet/latrine Rubbish pit Digging a rubbish pit Water wells and taps
Functional skills	Skills for village life	Earning money	Development projects
	Budgeting money Sewing Fishing Cooking Making string bags Taking care of animals Making drum oven	Baking Sewing Selling vegetables and fruit Handicrafts Village *singsing* Raising chickens to sell *Mumu*	Working with government for development Taking care of roads Taking care of the market Caring for the forests Building and construction Village committees

Community and nation	Law awareness	Culture and community	Community and nation
	Fighting Protection from stealing Protection from rape Working with the police Black markets Drugs Protecting each other	Traditional dances Traditional languages Writing about their cultures Learning from old people Weddings, old and new Worshipping God using traditional language and music Exchanging goods Funeral feasts Public holidays	Voting rights and duties Women and youth groups *Wantok* system Churches working together Many tribes but one nation Education of girls Supporting elected officials Radio, newspapers for communication PNG Constitution

Suggested topics for adult literacy in prisons

Rights and privileges	Constitutional rights	Prison rights and privileges	Code of conduct
	Lawyer at trial Free speech Right to appeal Right to trial	Visitation Medical treatment 3 meals a day Remission Mail Recreation Vocational training Newspapers	Good behaviour Decent language Cleanliness Discipline Care for issues Respect authority Obey instructions
Rehabilitation	Vocational training	Religious and spiritual life	Community involvement
	Mechanics Carpentry Gardening Cooking Literacy Handicrafts Plumbing Sewing Income earning projects	Counselling Church services Prison fellowship Praying together Supporting each other Sharing with each other Treating people with respect	Sports Outside assistance for materials After-care Churches Inmate/outmate programme

(continued on next page)

Life in prison	Problems	Health	Sport and recreation
	Security Escapes Overcrowding Fighting Homosexuality Smuggling Uniforms Riots	Balanced diet Dental care Sexual diseases Homosexuality Hygiene Smoking Alcohol Betel nut	Basketball Volleyball Soccer Videos TV Libraries
Life after prison	Money and work	Family life	Community and nation
	Plumbing Carpentry Cooking Gardening Welding Teaching literacy Getting a job	*Wantok* system Husband /wife relationships Taking care of old parents Husband support of wife and children Family planning Alcohol, drugs, and the family Family counselling Adopting children	Many tribes but one nation Voting rights and duties PNG Constitution PNG history

9.2 Interactive whole language

Primer lesson samples that I include under this category meet two main criteria. The first is that the story being used in the lesson is not restricted in any way to using only words that are already known or using words that contain only certain sounds or syllables. That is, the words used in the story or text are unrestricted. The second difference is that the beginning place (and often the ending place) of the lesson is with the story. The other activities in the lesson are linked as much as possible to the story. The integration of the various reading skills within the lesson is obvious.

There are different ways of doing this. I have chosen a few primer samples to illustrate approaches which use an interactive whole language approach. They are from the primers in Takia, Kandawo, Maiwaila, Umanikaina and Dami. I then discuss a modified multi-strategy method.

Takia primers, Madang Province, PNG

The following Takia primer samples give examples of primers in which I used the whole language reading philosophy, plus integrated activities which focus students' attention on phonic activities.

These primers were modelled on the Jesudasons' primers (see section below on Umanikaina) although I have adapted them somewhat so that I introduce the alphabet sounds and do not drill syllables. There are five primers in the series called "You can read God's word in Takia."

Book:	Title:	Letters Covered:
1	Creation	A, I, Y, T, D, U, N, G
2	The Fall	O, L, , W, E, M, F, B
3	Cain and Abel	K, S, P, R, VV sequences, revision
4	Noah	Revision
5	Christ died for us	(Text, pictures, and discussion questions only)

The procedure I followed is outlined below.

1. I determined the frequency of letters in narrative text. The frequency fell into five rough groupings:

(Most frequent)	1. A I O U
	2. B D G L N T
	3. Y E
	4. F K M
(least common)	5. S P R W

2. Then I broke the text into smaller chunks that can stand alone and make sense. Most of the time this was about three verses. If I needed to use more, I divided the text over two pages so it was not too crowded. Each text page was accompanied with an illustration on the facing page.

[9]Mulnag ulat nal utol an la Anut ago ibol: "You tan najan itumanip, aben kisaek mi yen dop, tan igos ak ilasa wa." Ago ilasa wo Anut ibol ak agomi ilasa ya. [10]Agogo tan igos ane yaŋan tan, Anut ago ibol dugo you yao go aben kisaek mi itumanig yendan yaŋan beig ibol. Agodugo Anut mel an fidian yil go ilon uyanan mok a.

25

3. I tried to pick key words from the text, e.g., 'light', 'God', 'ground', 'water', to match up with a letter from the frequency groups 1 and 2 for primer 1, from groups 2 and 3 for primer 2, etc. I used the key word to focus the students' attention on its initial sound.

4. After each text and illustration page I included four pages of phonic, word, and sentence activities, and writing activities that are linked with the text and with the sound in focus.

5. After the activities on these four pages are completed, the student and teacher go back to the first two pages of the lesson and re-read the text that the lesson is based on.

6. Some primers have a concluding activity on the last two pages. For example, primer 1 has a summary of the creation story for the student to read and/or write.

The sample pages (pp. 26–29) from the primers show examples of phonic, word, sentence, and writing activities.

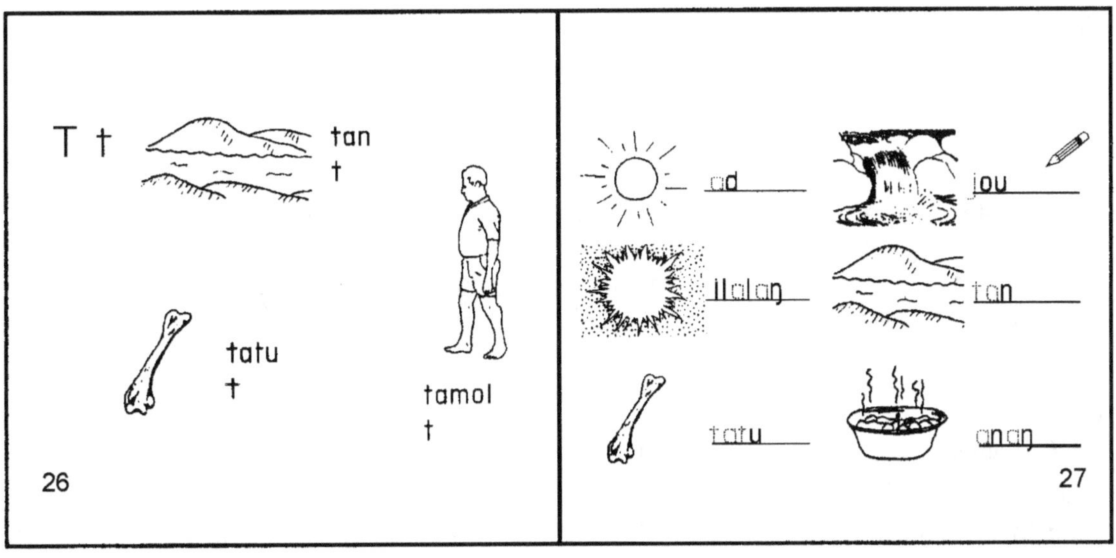

Agogo tan igos an jaŋan tan, Anut ago ibol dugo jou jao go aben kisaik mi itumanig jendan jaŋan beig ibol.

Anut ____ igos an jaŋan ____,
Anut ____ ibol dugo ____ jao go
aben ____ mi itumanig jendan
jaŋan beig ____

28

T

t

tidom tan

tan igos ak ilosa wa

ta

29

As each lesson is being planned I find it helpful to keep a summary of what I plan to cover in each lesson. A sample planning sheet is below.

Primer 1	Sound focus	Words to use
Lesson 1		
Anut 'God'	A, a	*Anut, ad, ab, ananas*
Lesson 2		
ilalaŋ 'light'	I, i	*ilalaŋ, ibol, ile, iagane, ilon*
Lesson 3		
you 'water'	Y, y	*yau, yeb, yok, yai,*
Lesson 4		
tan 'ground'	T, t	*tan, tatu, tamol*
Lesson 5		
did 'mountain'	D, d	*did, ad, dilasa, tidom*
Lesson 6		
urit 'octopus (sea creatures)'	U, u	*ubol, utol, uyan, urit, ut*
Lesson 7		
nai 'mosquito (land creatures)'	N, n	*nai, nal, nin*
Lesson 8		
galaŋ 'bush'	G, g	*galaŋ, gab, galuk, geg, guni, goun*

The format of each lesson is as constant as possible so that materials can be used for self-teaching or a simple each-one-teach-one approach, and teacher training can be kept to a minimum.

The first two pages of the lesson are the reading pages (sometimes 4 pages if the text cannot be cut down to a one page chunk). One page has the picture, the other the text. The text is read by the teacher with the student following each word. The teacher points to each word as he reads with a pencil or finger. This procedure should be repeated several times until the material presented becomes familiar to the student.

The next four pages contain the phonic, word, sentence, and writing activities, and each is explained on the page. At the conclusion of the activities, the teacher and student read the text for that lesson again. The lesson can be repeated the next time if needed, to correct students' errors and build their confidence in being able to read the passage independently. The lesson format is similar for most of the primers. This makes it easy for the teacher to know what to do.

Kandawo primers, Western Highlands, PNG

Mack and Doris Graham, working with the Kandawo people, had two main concerns in developing the Kandawo primers. They wanted to follow an each-one-teach-one approach (see §7.2). They also wanted the teaching approach to be one that taught reading by seeing and doing. They felt that this type of approach would fit well with the traditional learning patterns among the Kandawo. Mack thought that primers of this design could be used either in community school, or as transfer primers for literates, or as instructional materials for illiterates.

Mack also wanted to use stories that were already well-known to the people, stories that were interesting and popular, so that people were learning to read about something they already knew. He chose to use three Kandawo legends to provide the meaningful contexts from which to teach the sounds of the language.

Mack followed the same procedure in planning as I did with the Takia primers—breaking the text into meaningful units that could stand alone, looking at frequency counts, matching key words from the text units, and looking for other words that start with the same sound. Some were used in the text, others were not.

Mack made a Big Book (see §8.4) for each story and also printed small companion books that were half A4 size.

As already mentioned, Mack decided to use three legends as the basis for the Kandawo primers. The first legend is approximately 28 sentences long and divided into five paragraphs.

Lessons 1, 2, and 3 focus on paragraph one of the story and teach the letters *k, a,* and *i.*
Lessons 4 and 5 focus on paragraph two and teach *n* and *o.*
Lessons 6 focuses on paragraph three and teaches *w.*
Lesson 7 focuses on paragraph four and teaches *e.*
Lesson 8 focuses on paragraph five and teaches *ŋ.*

Beginning with lesson 9, the second legend is introduced using the Big Book. This story is again broken into chunks and used in a series of lessons to present new sounds. Lesson 15 begins with the introduction of the third legend which is taught in a similar series of lessons and covers the remaining sounds.

The lesson format is constant and repetitive to minimise teacher training and to make it easy to use an each-one-teach-one approach. Each lesson begins with the student (or students) and the person teaching reading the legend from either the Big Book or the companion books. Thus the primer lesson itself is surrounded by a lot of meaningful reading.

Pages 8 and 9 below are from one of the Kandawo lessons. Mack chose to use two A4 size pages per lesson. The page format changes very little throughout the primer.

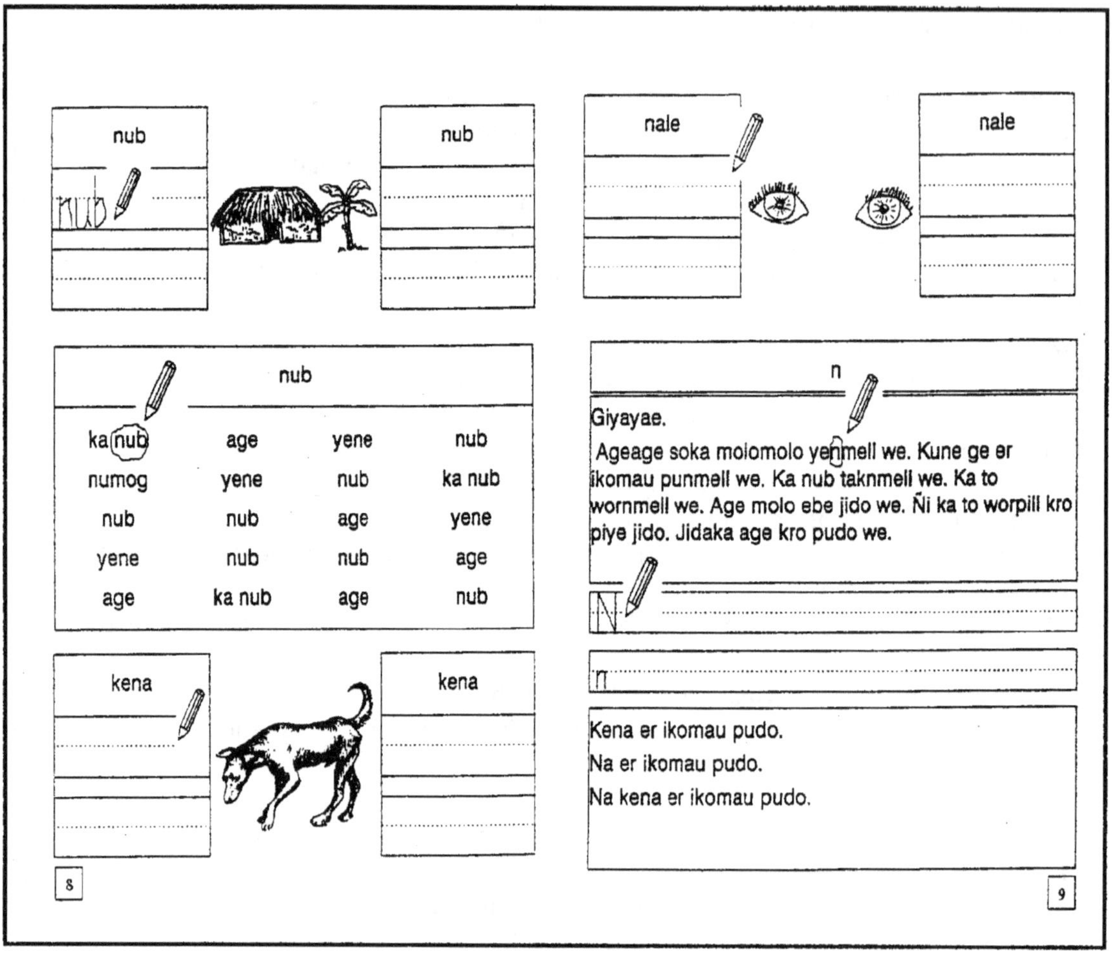

nub

nub

nub

nale

nale

nub			
ka nub	age	yene	nub
numog	yene	nub	ka nub
nub	nub	age	yene
yene	nub	nub	age
age	ka nub	age	nub

n

Giyayae.

Ageage soka molomolo yenmell we. Kune ge er ikomau punmell we. Ka nub taknmell we. Ka to wornmell we. Age molo ebe jido we. Ñi ka to worpill kro piye jido. Jidaka age kro pudo we.

N

n

kena

kena

Kena er ikomau pudo.
Na er ikomau pudo.
Na kena er ikomau pudo.

8

9

The lesson first introduces the letter which is to be taught in that lesson. The letter is introduced using a key word in the legend. Students are given opportunities to see the word, hear it, say it, and write it.

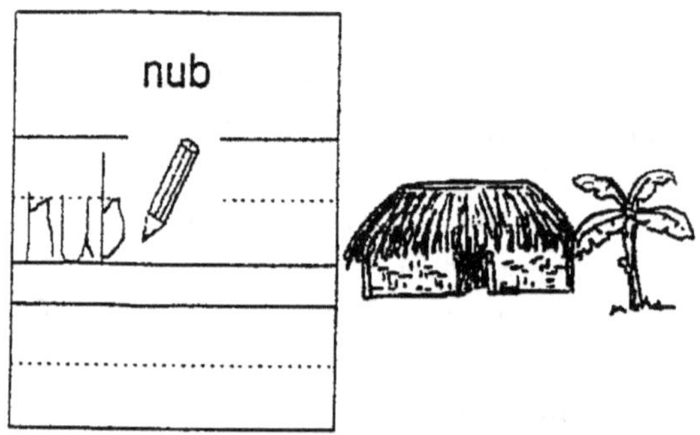

Then they are encouraged to find the word among other words.

nub			
ka nub	age	yene	nub
numog	yene	nub	ka nub
nub	nub	age	yene
yene	nub	nub	age
age	ka nub	age	nub

Next they are introduced to other words with that sound in it; sometimes the sound is in different word positions.

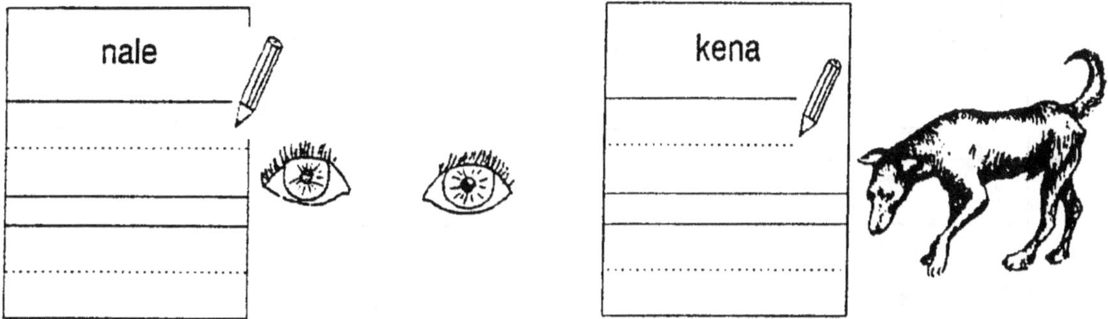

Then the lesson focuses on the main letter. Students look for that letter in text. Then they are shown how to write the letter, both capital and small.

The last element on the primer page is a small text for the student to try to read. The text is not from the legend, but is something new. It is something that is meaningful and includes words with the letters that have already been taught.

Mack designed these two pages as a "shell" on his computer and then adjusted them for each lesson.

Maiwala and Labe workbooks, Milne Bay, PNG

Yasuko Nagai developed workbooks for the Maiwala and Labe Tok Ples Prep Skul programme. In these programmes the teaching of reading and writing is centred around Big Books. The workbooks were designed to be used to check that students have mastered certain sound-symbol correspondences. The materials in the workbook lesson is drawn from the Big Book that is being used that particular week; see sample pages 8 and 9 below.

These workbooks were also developed as a shell on a computer and others have used a similar design for their programmes. The Maiwala programme no longer uses the workbooks

because the teachers found that they could teach the sounds and letters of the language more effectively using the spelling lessons as advocated by McCracken and McCracken (see §12.2) and 'fast phonics' to teach the sounds.

Umanikaina primers, Milne Bay, PNG

The following examples come from the Umanikaina primers, prepared by Daniel and Wei Lei Jesudason. Many people in PNG have found these primers to be a useful model to follow or adapt. I feel I should include them here even though you will have already seen a lot of ideas that have been taken from them. Good ideas often work well in more than one area and that is why it is good for literacy workers to share their ideas and successes with others. The Jesudasons share their ideas freely and they have been able to help and encourage a lot of other people by doing so.

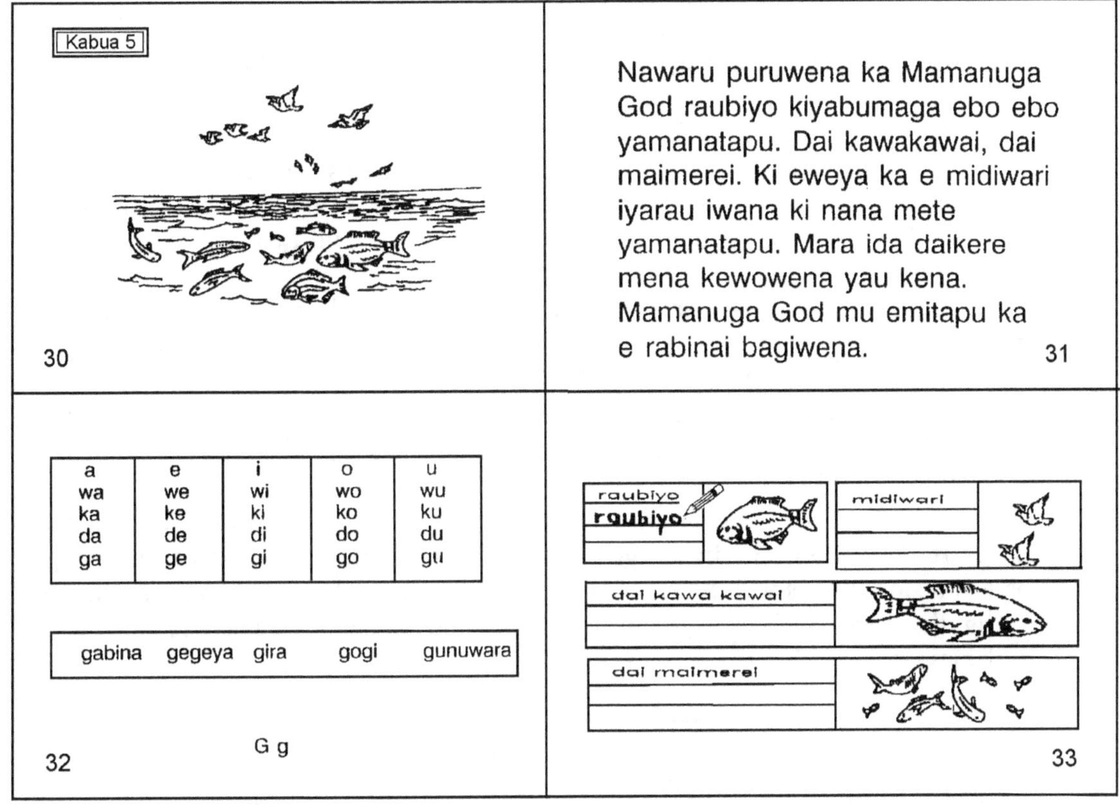

Kabua 5

30

Nawaru puruwena ka Mamanuga God raubiyo kiyabumaga ebo ebo yamanatapu. Dai kawakawai, dai maimerei. Ki eweya ka e midiwari iyarau iwana ki nana mete yamanatapu. Mara ida daikere mena kewowena yau kena. Mamanuga God mu emitapu ka e rabinai bagiwena.

31

a	e	i	o	u
wa	we	wi	wo	wu
ka	ke	ki	ko	ku
da	de	di	do	du
ga	ge	gi	go	gu

gabina gegeya gira gogi gunuwara

G g

32

raubiyo
raubiyo
midiwari
dai kawa kawai
dai maimerei

33

Dami reading and writing programme for TPPS

I helped develop the following programme for the Dami (PNG) Tok Ples Prep Skul (TPPS) in 1990. Some of it has been used. People who followed a different method of teaching have since been involved with the programme and now they are developing their own materials. I still think the programme we worked on gives a good framework for the PNG context. I share it here to give you an idea of another way of doing a literacy programme for children.

A one-week writers' workshop was held and the participants produced about 100 books in draft form for the TPPS. Approximately ten of these were rejected for various reasons. The rest are in various stages of being edited and illustrated. Many have been printed. First we worked on little story books where each one focuses on one letter of the alphabet. Then we worked on some instant readers where the sentence is almost the same on several succeeding pages with just one word changing on each page. The change is cued by the picture. Then we worked on story books for each term. Term one stories had one sentence per page. Term two stories had two sentences per page. For term three and four the stories were more complicated.

At the end of term four we had collections of stories together in one book. Some of the stories written at the workshop were also appropriate stories to make into Big Books which we did.

A separate committee, which included a local artist and two story writers, had worked on two primers before the writers workshop was held. The primers combined a whole language approach and a syllable approach. The primers included stories and activities about key words and sentences in those stories. After the workshop some people worked on translating some Big Books that had been popular in other areas. We also held two preliminary teacher training workshops.

The primer for term one consisted of the alphabet book and 18 small alphabet stories that went with it. Each letter of the alphabet had a little story written for it. These books introduced the children to each letter of the alphabet. The students learned to read each short story by repeated readings.

The primers for terms two and three followed a four page layout (see pages 10–13 below). The first page of the lesson contained either a small meaningful story or part of a story that is well-known from a previous term. The second page draws out a key word from the story which then isolates the letter which is being taught. The letter is then put into syllables.

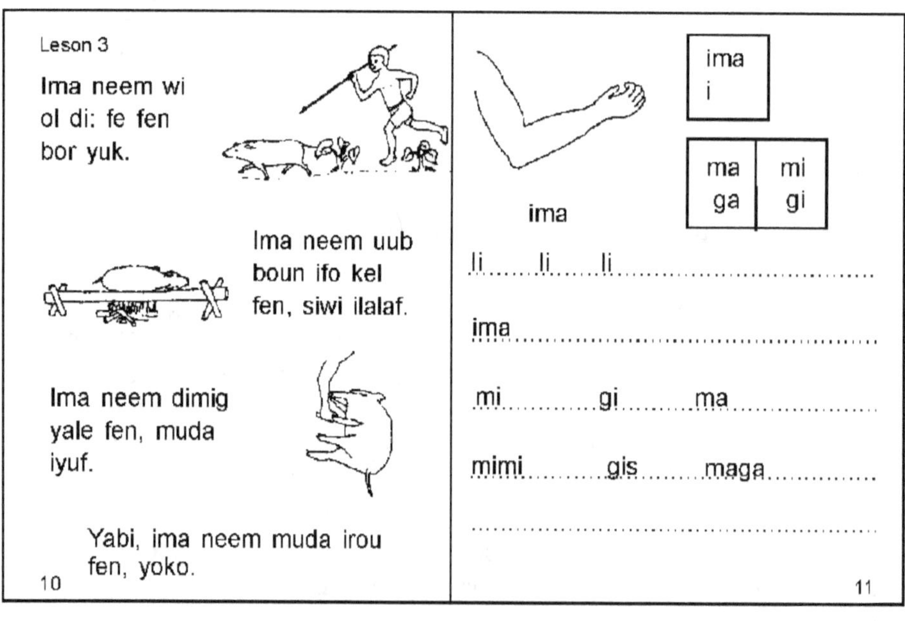

Leson 3

Ima neem wi ol di: fe fen bor yuk.

Ima neem uub boun ifo kel fen, siwi ilalaf.

Ima neem dimig yale fen, muda iyuf.

Yabi, ima neem muda irou fen, yoko.

10

ima
i

ma	mi
ga	gi

ima

li......li......li..................................

ima..

mi............gi...........ma....................

mimi...........gis.........maga..............

....

11

The next two pages (12 and 13) include a variety of activities, including opportunities to practice writing, activities that focus on words or sounds being taught, and so on. Each lesson concludes with the student and teacher going back to the beginning of the lesson and reading the meaningful text again together. (This is prompted by a shared-book picture at the bottom of the fourth page.)

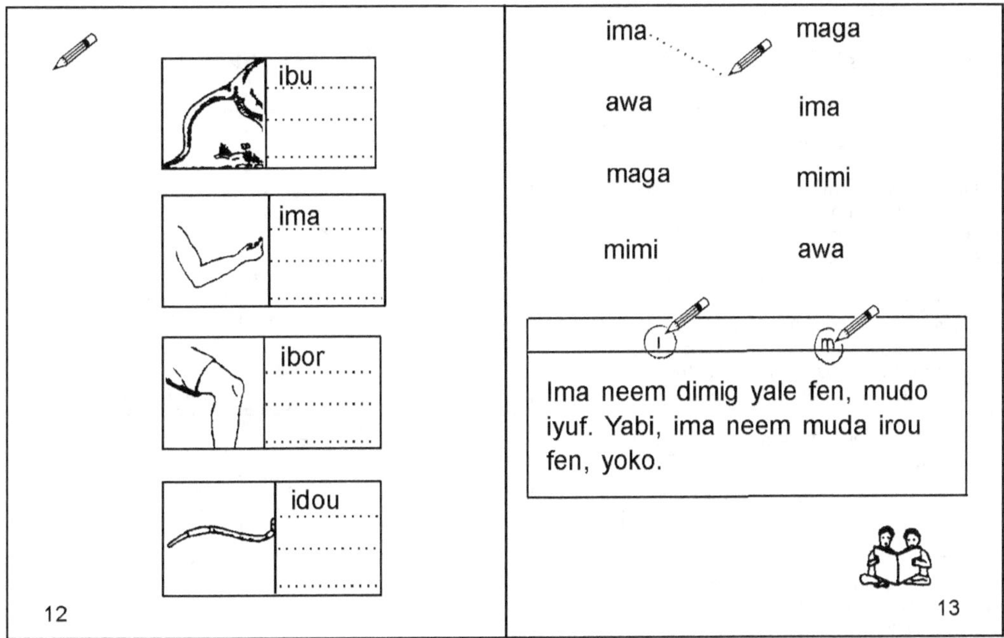

Each week the writing lessons focus on the same letter as do the reading lessons. Time is given in the programme for doing shared reading with a Big Book and for opportunities for individual reading of books from the library box. By term four the primers could be dispensed with and the focus be placed on teaching reading through shared-reading experiences and teaching spelling in the writing lessons. The programme has taken some different turns than planned, but design ideas may be helpful for other teachers.

Multi-strategy economy method

Robin Rempel has done a lot of literacy work with many languages in the Sepik area of PNG. She designed a method that she calls a multi-strategy **economy** method. At the time of writing, her method is being tried with three language groups—the Saniyo-Heyewe, East Sepik Province; the Lembena, Enga Province; and the Yade in Sandaun Province. This method has the following advantages over the multi-strategy method.

- It is easier for the teachers to teach
- The workbooks are easier to produce
- The programme can be run with less materials if necessary
- The workbooks are more interesting and attractive

Rempel also encourages the use of the experience story and creative writing as it is done in the multi-strategy method.

Below is an example of a lesson from the workbook (Rempel 1993:4).

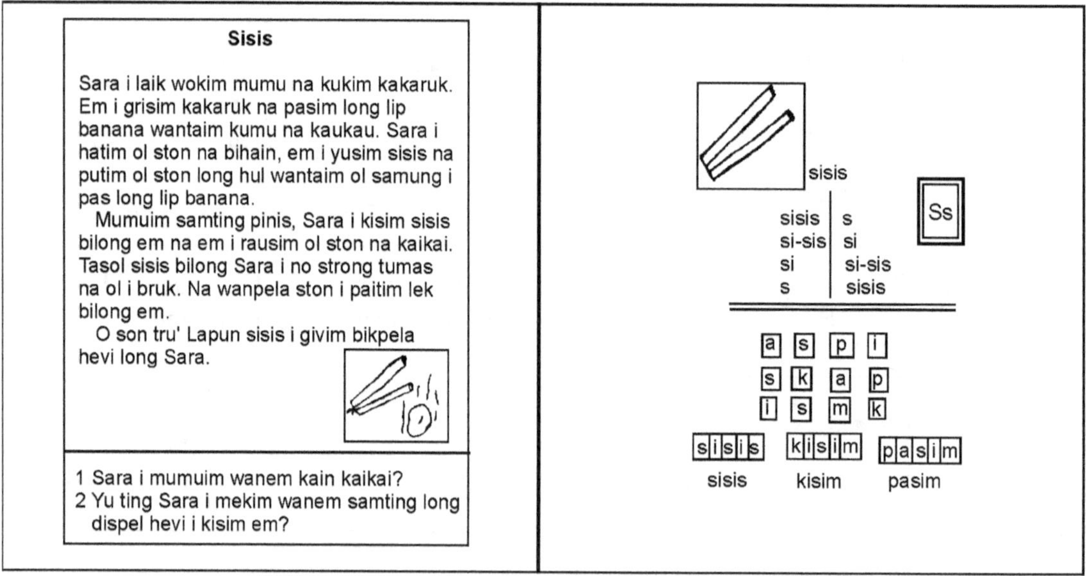

Sisis

Sara i laik wokim mumu na kukim kakaruk. Em i grisim kakaruk na pasim long lip banana wantaim kumu na kaukau. Sara i hatim ol ston na bihain, em i yusim sisis na putim ol ston long hul wantaim ol samung i pas long lip banana.

Mumuim samting pinis, Sara i kisim sisis bilong em na em i rausim ol ston na kaikai. Tasol sisis bilong Sara i no strong tumas na ol i bruk. Na wanpela ston i paitim lek bilong em.

O son tru' Lapun sisis i givim bikpela hevi long Sara.

1 Sara i mumuim wanem kain kaikai?
2 Yu ting Sara i mekim wanem samting long dispel hevi i kisim em?

The way these workbooks are set up allows teachers and students to integrate the various reading strategies they learn in the two tracks. Therefore I believe Rempel's method is similar to the methods I have already mentioned in this chapter, provided that those who use it give attention to integrating the two tracks, as the method intends.

9.3 Teaching language development using themes

Some teachers use a theme approach in their teaching. They or the children choose a theme for the week, the fortnight, or the month, and all their work during that time is based around that theme. Spelling, reading, writing, listening, maths, drama, art, and science are all about the theme that has been chosen. The theme can be about anything but should be one that can give rise to many different activities and interests.

Teaching by themes allows the teacher to use an integrated approach to everything taught. The teaching of reading links into and becomes part of the theme. In the reading times, books that have already been written and published can be used as well as murals, charts, class stories, and stories written on the blackboard. All these have been written as part of the theme work but can be used to teach reading and writing skills.

Some examples of themes might be: things that frighten me, house building, sago, frogs, going to town, canoes, chickens, dogs, malaria, spears, the moon, and pigs. There are many more. Your imagination is the limit!

On the next few pages are examples of themes that different people have developed and used. They give some ideas of the kinds of things that can be done using themes.

Theme: Fishing

Introduction

Role play: I really feel like going fishing
Poem: 1 2 3 4 5, once I caught a fish alive

Reading

Shared reading of a story (e.g. *Our Sides Ached*)
Follow the read-talk-read-talk-do pattern
Each day a different "do" activity:
- sequence the story and pictures
- retell the story from the uncle's point of view

Read other fishing stories

Writing

Each student writes a story about going fishing
- introduce the wordbanks, write key fishing terms that might be needed on them
- give each student part a large sheet of paper
- each student illustrates his own fishing story
- students write their name on their story

Collect the stories, make these into a class book and read it together
Have each student take turns in reading their own story

Science

Possible topics:
- Kinds of creatures where you fish
  - The different types of fish
- Parts of a fish
- How do they breathe
- How do they reproduce

Social studies

How our ancestors used to make fish traps, fishing nets, lines, and hooks
Different ways of fishing
How we work together to net fish

Health

Why fish is good for our diet
Which fish are poisonous

Sometimes it is easier to have a theme web to help in your planning of themes. It is a good idea to map out ideas for activities ahead of time and collect or make things that are needed for the theme. The following page is an example of a theme web constructed by Pat Spaulding 1994:27.

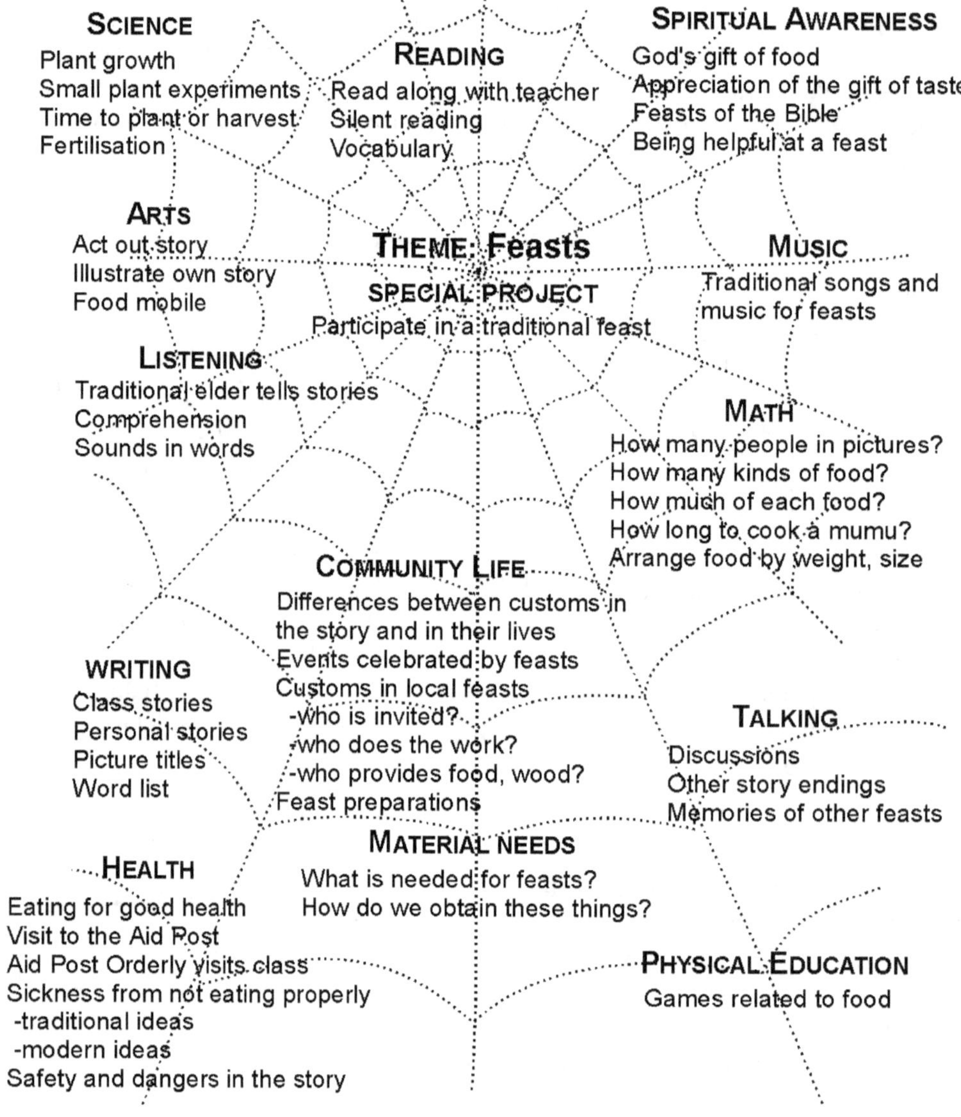

One day I was looking through some old Takia stories and I came across a few stories about canoes. They made me think of the theme "Canoes and working together." The main story that made me think about the theme was "The Rooster and the Wallaby" reproduced below. The theme web for it is on the next page. Following that there is a blank theme web that can be used as a guide for making a theme web of any topic desired.

The Rooster and the Wallaby

> A long time ago a Rooster and Wallaby lived in a small village by the sea. They were very good friends.
>
> One day the two friends decided to have fun sailing their small canoe. It was a fine sunny day and the sea was calm. The two friends pulled their canoe out and the wallaby started to paddle the canoe out to sea. Rooster stood at the front of the canoe looking down at the fish in the clear blue water.
>
> After a while a strong west wind started to blow. The canoe started to go faster and Rooster's tail shone as it swung to and fro in the wind. Wallaby was jealous of Rooster's beautiful tail, so he decided to change places with Rooster. While Rooster paddled, Wallaby stood up and tried to make his tail swing to and fro. His tail was strong and heavy and smashed a big hole in the bottom of the canoe, which sank.
>
> When this happened, Rooster flew to a small island and settled on the branch of a Mango tree. He was very sorry for his old friend who had to swim around looking for land. He sang out, "O friend, look what problems you have caused."

There are many other ways of planning themes. Once you have made your plans, do not feel that you need to stick closely to them as your students will come up with ideas while you are busy with activities. Or you might think of other things that would be helpful to do as you go along. You might discover that the students find some of the planned activities boring, or not helpful, or that the theme is just not working out right. You have the freedom to change things and to finish the theme early if things are not working well. You might discover that there are more things that can be included in your theme and that the students are very interested in the topic. You may wish to work on the theme longer and do more activities. Your plan is there to help you, not to restrict you.

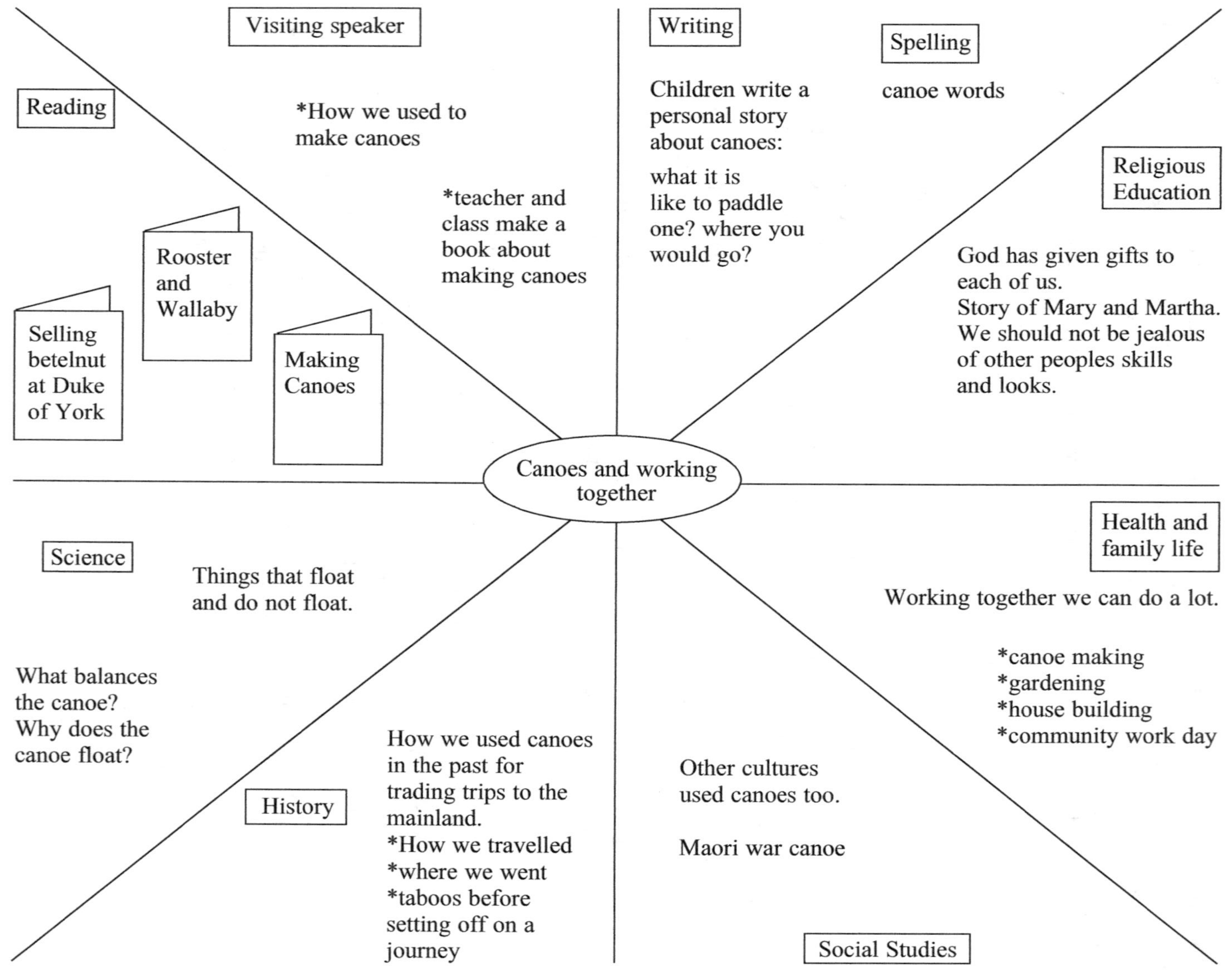
Visiting speaker
Reading
*How we used to make canoes
*teacher and class make a book about making canoes
Rooster and Wallaby
Selling betelnut at Duke of York
Making Canoes
Writing
Children write a personal story about canoes:
what it is like to paddle one? where you would go?
Spelling
canoe words
Religious Education
God has given gifts to each of us.
Story of Mary and Martha.
We should not be jealous of other peoples skills and looks.
Canoes and working together
Science
Things that float and do not float.
What balances the canoe? Why does the canoe float?
History
How we used canoes in the past for trading trips to the mainland.
*How we travelled
*where we went
*taboos before setting off on a journey
Other cultures used canoes too.
Maori war canoe
Social Studies
Health and family life
Working together we can do a lot.
*canoe making
*gardening
*house building
*community work day

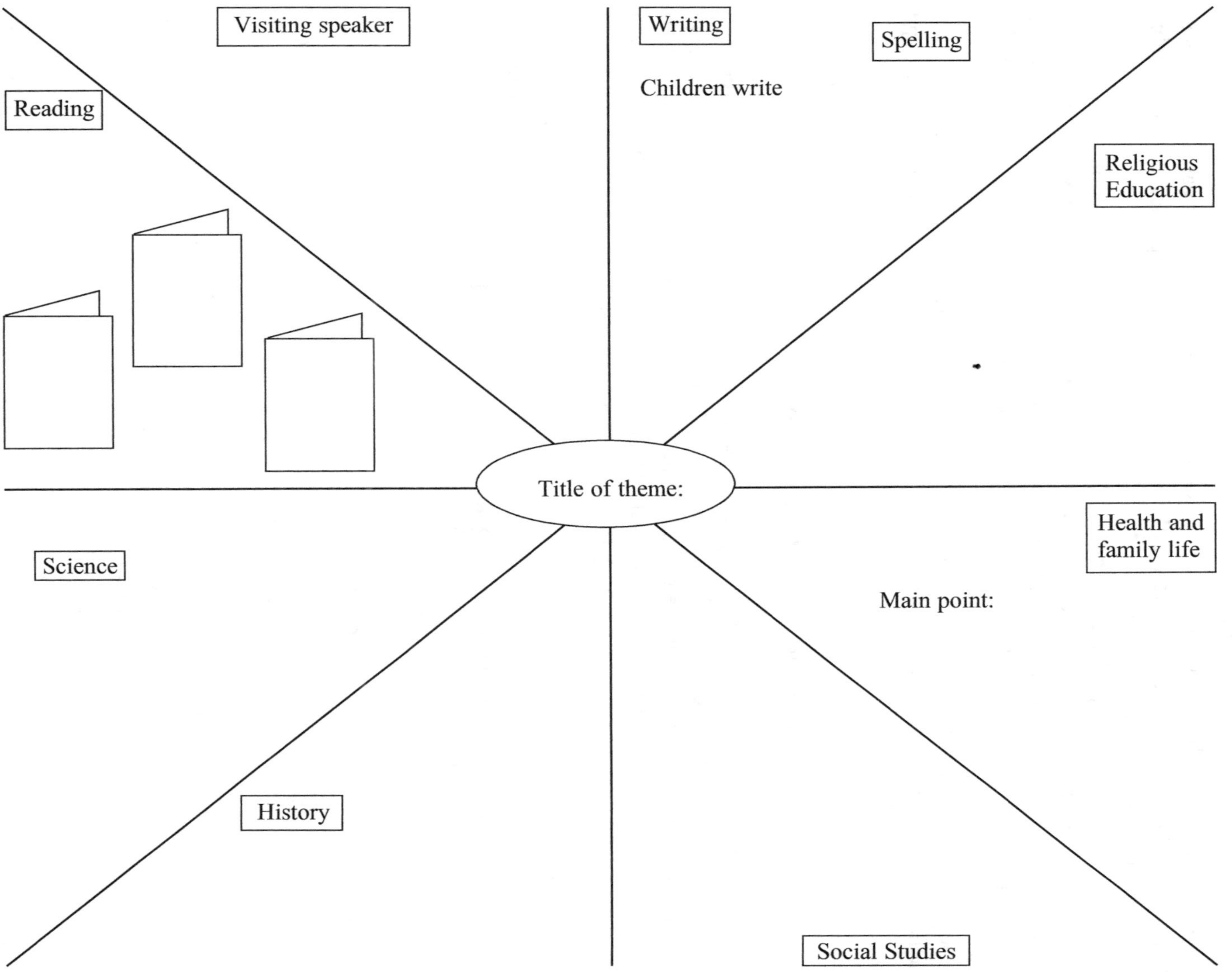
Visiting speaker
Writing
Spelling
Reading
Children write
Religious Education
Title of theme:
Science
Health and family life
Main point:
History
Social Studies

You do not have to be teaching in a school situation to use themes. You can use themes in informal situations too. Just make sure the theme and the activities are ones that are suitable for the situation you are working in.

Themes can be very helpful for teaching people. They can help get people interested in doing things together and learning together. People can be doing reading, writing, math, science, or other things without realizing it. Themes can hold people's interest in continuing to learn, and can make teaching more interesting for the teacher or the person helping with the learning.

Begin collecting a list of themes that might be helpful in your situation. Talk to other teachers about themes they have used that worked well. Look for ideas in other books and articles.

9.4 Samples of activities for primer lessons

In chapters 7, 8, and 9 many different types of teaching methods have been discussed. Literacy workers and primer designers often borrow and modify each others' ideas. They can grow and learn through this exchange of ideas. The following pages give examples of activities that can be used in primers, activity sheets, exercise books, on blackboards, or on lapboards. They can be modified to fit with the sentences, words, and sounds in any lesson and with any method.

Many of these ideas come from the following books: Karen Eliason, *Beginning Level Activity Book,* PNG: SIL, 1991; P. Spaulding, C. Spaulding, Anikap, Heforenuc, and Honemi, *Nankina Wam Sit Danam* PNG: Bambu books, 1991; Yasuko Nagai, *Maiwala Workbooks*., PNG: SIL, 1991; and G.Waters, *Takia Primers* 1–4, PNG: SIL, 1991.

Activities that focus on words

Draw a picture of the key word on the blackboard and talk about it.

Write the name of the key word under the picture.

Write the sounds of the word on some small backboards or on flash cards. Mix them up. Ask the students to put them in the right order.

Break the words into sounds, then build back to the word.

kulek kisaik
kalam kadai
kon kubam
kunum

List other words that start with the same sound.

Match the words that are the same.

ibol	oŋ
oŋ	dugo
ago	ibol
dugo	ago

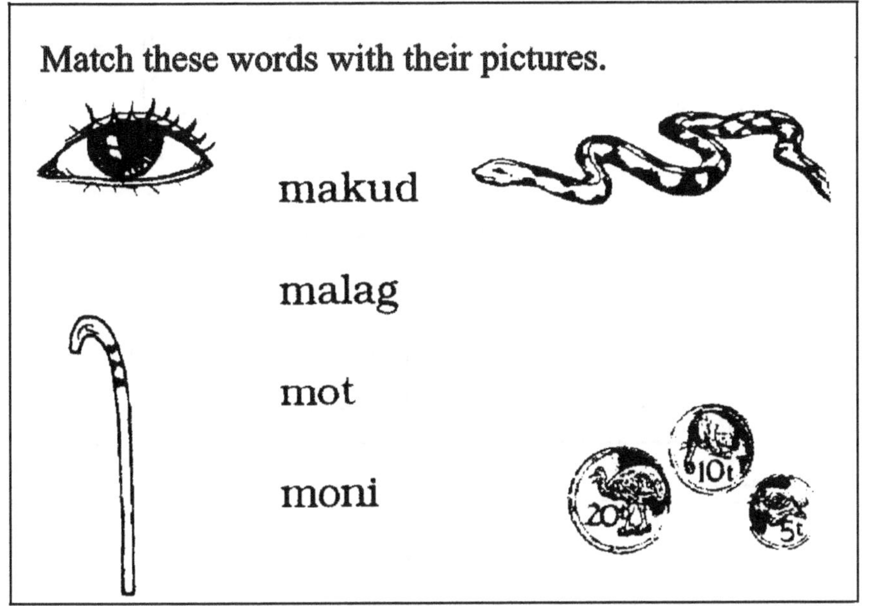

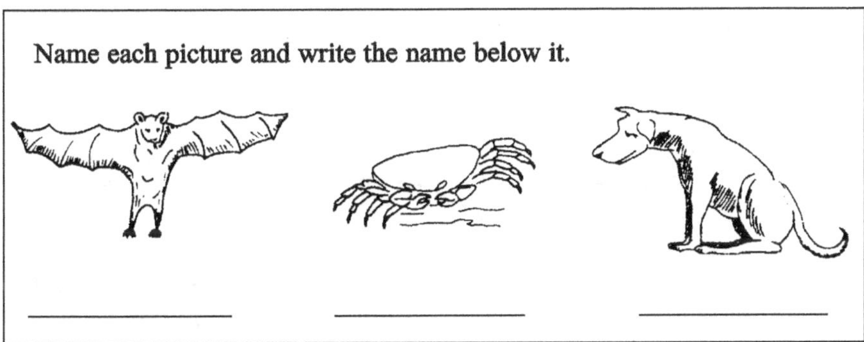

Have some key words written on cards and get the children to take turns in matching the words to ones that are the same in the text.

sis

nanuk

Have the student write a word on his lapboard and then draw the picture.

ŋai

Draw these words:
pein patun papai plagis

p ____________

____

____

____

Look at the picture. What is it? ________________

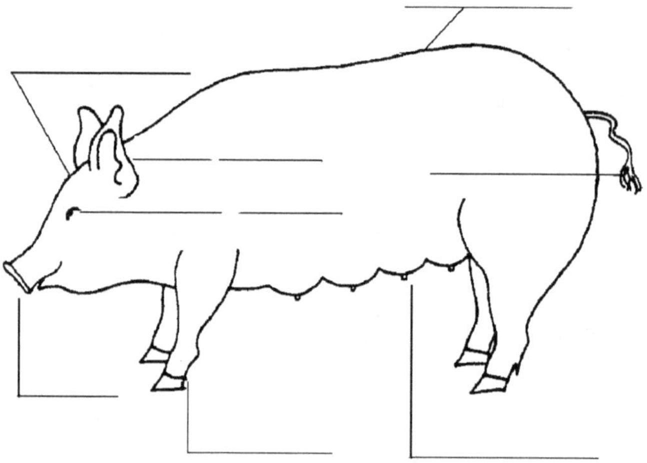

malan ŋen sun uyun patun nudun awan kudon gumulan

Write these body parts on the correct lines above.

Activities that focus on sounds and syllables

Think of all the words that start with the sounds. Put them on a chart or blackboard and illustrate them.

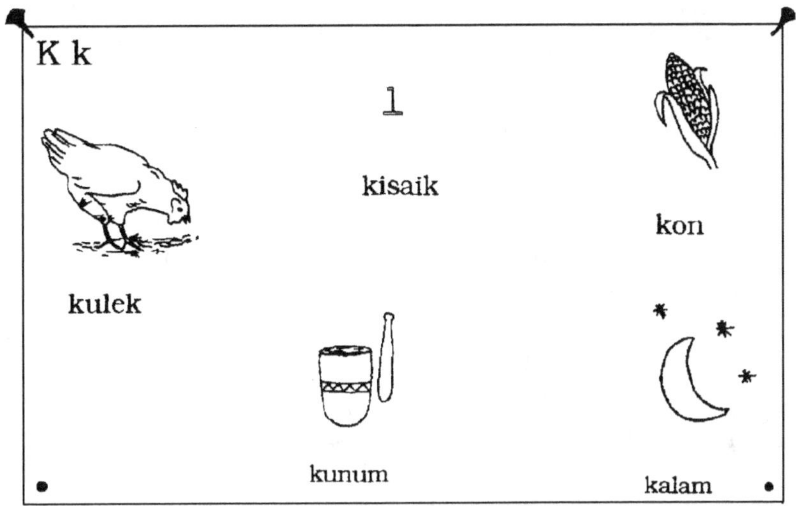

Show the sound in other words.

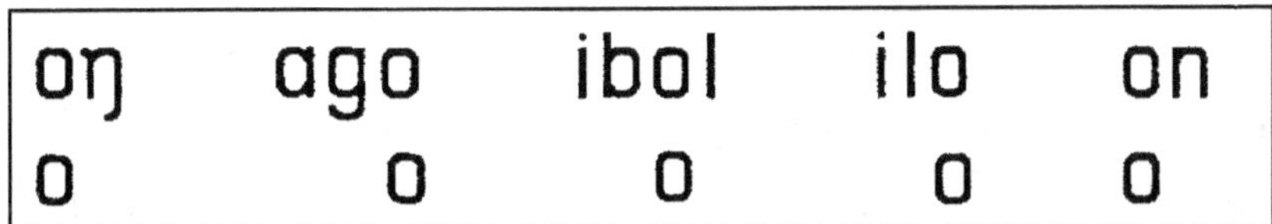

Find the pictures that go with each letter.

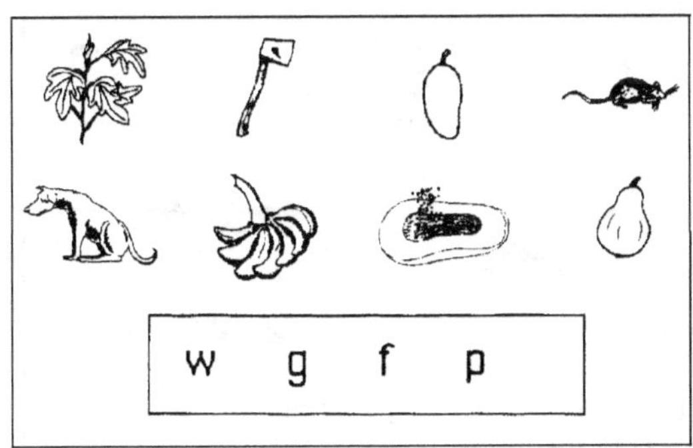

What is the missing sound? Have the students write the whole word on their lapboards or paper.

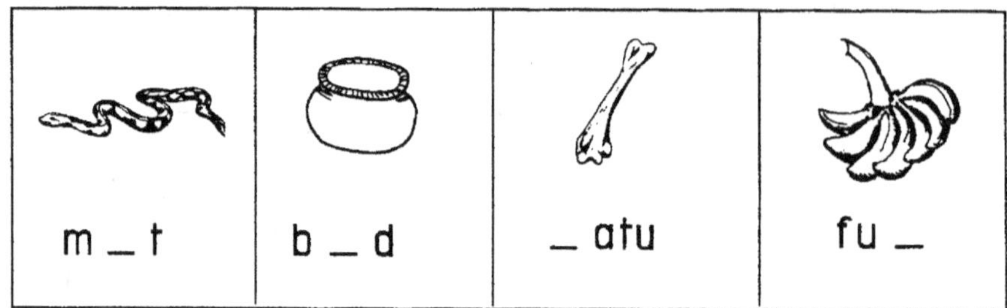

Have the students write the name of the picture on their lapboards.

Which letter starts these words?

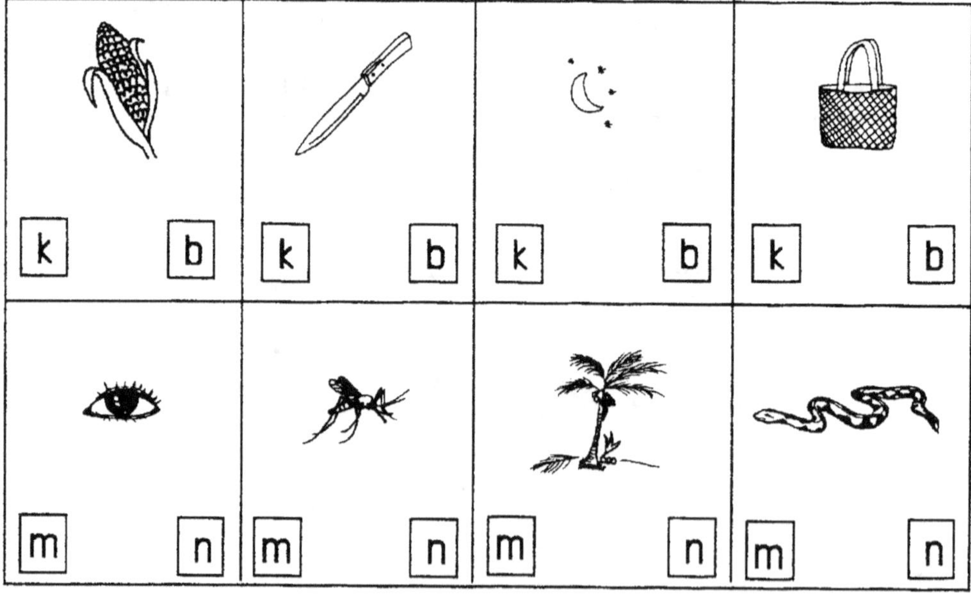

Look at the letter in the corner of the box. Find the other words that start with the same letter.

p pein	plagis	papai	tamol	patun
	kulek	ŋudun	badam	pein

w walu	fud	wao	weu	malag
	wos	ŋeo	wagai	bod

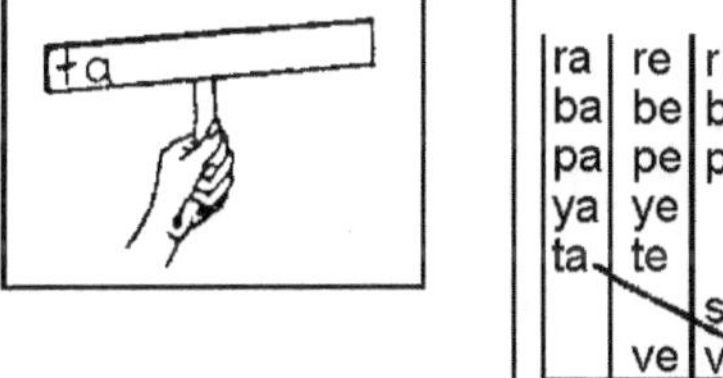

Teach a word by saying the word and showing the word on the page. Say the word again carefully and help the children work out the first syllable. Write the syllable. Find it on the syllable chart.

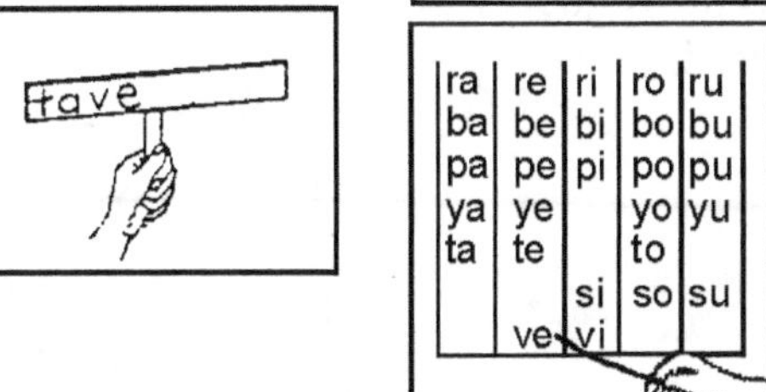

Say the word again and write the second syllable. Find it on the syllable chart.

Say and write the last syllable.
Find it on the syllable chart.

Activities that focus on sentences

practice writing some sounds and sentences from the story.

O o O o

oŋ iŋanen nuŋon wani dop

Oŋ wani tap, oŋ umat mok a.

oŋ mel uyan ak

Write the key sentence on the blackboard.

Malu iŋ Kaŋkoi da nug nukol a.

Write each word on cards or on lapboards and have the students put them in the same order as the sentence on the blackboard.

Make up some sentences that are similar to a key sentence in the story. Use picture prompts for the thing that changes in the sentence.

 Maŋ ai patun ka mani wa.

 Maŋ papai ka mani wa.

 Maŋ woi ka mani wa.

 Maŋ fud ka mani wa.

Maŋ ai kisaek man ta mani na wa.

Write some sentences on the blackboard. Get the students to choose the word that fills the gap and to write the complete sentence on their lapboards or in their exercise books.

galaŋ abi beig	Bol iŋ _____ ipitiŋini da.
ab abi anaŋ	Tinan iŋ _____ inei da.
kulek kuseŋ ŋeo	Pinein iŋ _____ ŋes digane da.

Cloze exercise

Write the text from the page on to the blackboard. After several readings of the text, have the students close their eyes. Erase about one word in every six, but make sure they are words that can be predicted from the words that are left. Have the children open their eyes. Read the passage together putting in the words that are missing. Or write a cloze exercise on the blackboard. Have a list of words that the students can choose from to help them fill the gaps.

Oŋ anaŋ urat ________dop, silali
ifuno wa. Ago dop urat ________
ganep yaup, __________ umat dop,
tan lo udu wa. Man dugo, ŋai oŋ
______ en lo ŋiginio ak ________ o fon
tini tan o ________ wa.

tan wagai gane murnap ibuli niŋen

Help the students write a class story about the key word. Write it on paper or on the blackboard. Read it with the class.

These are the primer activities I collected. Keep looking for more and add them to your collection.

10

Assessment of a Literacy Programme

It is very important to be able to observe, think about those observations (reflect), and evaluate literacy programmes, materials, and class and student performances. These assessments make it possible for the literacy worker to decide if things have been planned and carried out well. They are also helpful in deciding what to do next. If teachers are not trained to use the tools of assessment along with the other literacy tools they learn, then they may blindly follow whatever trail is set before them. This means that someone else is setting the direction that must be taken, and teachers are left in a state of continuing dependency on outsiders.

It is essential that teachers are taught to observe, reflect on, and evaluate all that they do so that they can improve their work and become independent in it. How can this be done?

It is important that those involved in training literacy trainers help teachers from the beginning learn about different kinds of assessment. The trainers should also involve the trainees in assessment experiences under their supervision.

10.1 Assessment of programmes

Often literacy programmes can be divided into several stages. At each of these stages it is good to stop and assess how the overall programme is running and see where there is need for improvement.

Usually programmes start with a small group of people where ideas and materials can be tested out to see if they are going to work. This would be called the trial stage of the programme and would involve only a limited number of people.

Once the literacy workers are happy with the materials and methods and can see that the programme is working alright for that situation, then a pilot programme is often the next stage. This stage may involve running the programme in several villages. By doing this the systems of training, supervision and encouragement of teachers, and the distribution of materials are tested fully.

Once the system is working well at that level, and the problems have been overcome, then the programme moves into the expansion stage. Now any villages or groups can request literacy programmes and there is a system in place which is able to help meet their requests.

Finally, programmes move into the stage where the programme administrators solve problems of keeping the literacy programme running indefinitely. This is the final goal of all literacy programmes and influences what is done and how it is done from the very beginning. But it is often not until this stage is close to being achieved that the local people can see ways and means of keeping the programme running.

At each point in these different stages, it is necessary for those involved in running and teaching in the programme to evaluate both what they are doing and how they are doing it. They need to look at what is working well and what can be done to overcome any problems that have come up.

Good communication needs to be established from the beginning between teachers and students, between supervisors and teachers, and between planners, trainers, and supervisors. As self-management is the ultimate goal, it is good to start the literacy programme with local people involved in its oversight, decision making, planning, and evaluation, and continue in that way all through the programme.

Uwe Gustafsson in the Adivasi Oriya—Telugu adult literacy and education programme (in India) found that it was very important to build communication and caring links between the learners and the teachers, between the supervisors and the learners and teachers, and between the project staff and the supervisors and teachers. In this way problems and concerns could be shared and dealt with sensitively. It also meant that the people who were involved in the programme were helping with its evaluation, and making decisions according to each one's ability.

> Staff members are also urged to contribute articles, suggestions, and comments on the program or project. This emphasis has gone a long way towards making each member of the project feel that this is 'his project'…
>
> The coordinator made it a point of inviting the staff to express their ideas and plans. This was difficult for them to do at first. They would not feel free to say anything different from what had already been suggested, and to bring forth a new idea of their own was not thinkable during the first year of literacy. But the chief language associates would express themselves in private to the co-ordinator concerning literacy matters. The coordinator then would draw them out during meetings and have them express their matters to the others. In this way, a free

> discussion time developed slowly in which the tribal staff would bring forward both short-range and long-range plans. (Gustafsson 1991:97, 98)

Another aspect of programme evaluation is assessing what has been done in regard to the total goals that were set for the programme. Various problems will have surfaced as people tried to reach the programme's goals. It is necessary to ask questions like these: Have the goals been met? If they have not been met, then why not? Are the goals realistic? Do they need adjusting or rewriting? How can the problems be overcome?

Programme evaluation should also look at the various groups that make up the language population and see if their needs are being met. It should consider the older people, the youth, the school children, the women. Does the programme adequately help each group? Do the people in each group continue to use the literacy skills they have learned?

Although the Adivasi project is a very successful literacy and development project, the planners are concerned about it because it is not reaching the women of the language area. They realise that there are several cultural reasons why this is so. One is that illiterate young men do not want to marry literate women. Other problems have been identified.

> Young men who are illiterate object to seeing their wives and relatives become literate while they remain illiterate...Traditionally, women in this tribal culture were thought not to be capable of learning to read and write....Even if a young woman would like to attend a literacy class, she may not have the time or the strength for it...Tribal women are less inclined to pursue the gaining of literacy skills in this male dominated environment...most organizers are reluctant to give equal attention to the young adult female learners....Tribal women, especially those who are married, may feel that their domestic responsibilities leave them little opportunity to make use of literacy skills even if they had them. Therefore they lack motivation to become literate. (Gustafsson 1991:124–25)

However, the project's strategy on this problem is to keep trying. They hope to encourage literate females to become organizers and teachers. They plan to establish separate literacy centres for women where they can come and bring their young children with them. They will also set up special women's groups—groups where students get a second chance at learning to read if they have not succeeded in the formal classes. The Adivasi's project evaluation showed that they were not meeting the needs of women, so this helped them plan future programmes to try and overcome these problems.

Literacy programme evaluation must also consider whether it has met the people's needs. This type of evaluation considers the transfer of literacy skills from the local language to the district or national language. For people who believe strongly in the use of local languages, it is often difficult to think positively of encouraging people to transfer their literacy skills to other languages. Sometimes people feel that this would harm the strength of the local language or give it lower status than the district or national language. Some communities, however, feel very strongly that they want to be able to transfer their literacy skills to other languages for purposes of trade, education, or gaining further information.

I heard of one language group who were upset with the translators in their area because the translators had concentrated on teaching literacy in the local language. The people felt that this had not helped them at all. Their attitude was: "We do not need literacy in our own language? It does not help us." They wanted to learn the national language so they could trade, and they thought it would help the children do better in government schools.

Others want to be able to read information that is only available in the national language. There are a limited number of books available in mother-tongue languages, and people want to be able to read more widely. Some of the things they are interested in reading about are: information about other countries, national news, world news, information about machinery and technology, information about health development and agricultural development, world and national history, sermon helps, and biblical reference materials. Some of these things can be translated into the local language, but the available materials will always be limited.

Recently I heard of a French-speaking country that made laws to limit all public speaking to French. They wanted to keep the French language strong. The French scientists spoke out against this law because it meant that scientists who do not speak French could no longer be invited to attend science conferences in that country. The French scientists knew that without these conferences they would find it difficult to learn what other scientists were doing. The new law would cause the French-speaking scientists to leave the country in order to work with scientists from other countries. So the law that was meant to strengthen the use of French may turn out to have some bad effects.

Feelings about national or trade languages can be very strong, and need to be considered. It is not the educator's job to make decisions on behalf of other people about which language they should use for reading and writing after they have gained literacy skills. It is certainly easier for the learner to learn to read and write in his own language first. But having learned those skills, it is up to him to decide which language he wants to use. In situations like these people will probably choose the language they use, depending on the purpose, the subject matter, and the audience.

Using a national or trade language does not necessarily weaken the local language. People have the power to make their own choices, and that is good. It may mean they use their literacy skills in the local language more often. The Adivasi programme was designed so that people would transfer their literacy skills to the Telugu language, but it actually made the use of local language literacy skills stronger.

10.2 Assessment of materials

A big part of a literacy programme is its materials. Often these can make or break a programme. As the Vollraths found with the Hewa, the people were still interested in learning to read even though they were not interested in literacy classes (see §8.5) They wanted to read what was in the book of Mark, but they had no interest in doing the primer lessons. Literacy materials need to be assessed all along the way in a literacy programme. A friend of mine in Africa told me of a programme where there had been primers for ten years but the programme had not run well. He said the primer needed to be thrown away and a new start made because the old one was not being used.

All literacy materials need to be carefully evaluated. First they need to be evaluated as trial materials. This means watching how people use the materials that have been designed and noticing any difficulties they have with them.

When I evaluated primers which I had made, I realised that changes were needed. I found that PNG teachers automatically do a lot of re-reading of stories, over and over until the students understand. This was the way they had been taught and so it is the way they teach. So after observing this practice, I changed the teaching instructions I had made for the programme. I took out a lot of the repetitions that I had put into the lesson plans because it made the lessons too long. I knew the teachers would do repeated readings many times anyway without me telling them to do it.

Another time I was reading books on my front verandah with some of the Tok Ples Prep Skul children. They had used the same story at school that week. I noticed when they were reading the story that certain parts kept tripping them up. This made me have a closer look at the story. I could see that what was written there was not what they were expecting. Probably the story needed improving in that spot.

Other times when people visit me, I often share stories that I am working on. I notice the places where they stop reading and go back and re-read. Often they do this because a word is not spelled correctly, or a word is missing, or because it is a word which they do not have in their dialect, or because the sentence is clumsy. Watching what people do with the materials gives clues about the things that need changing.

After evaluating materials as trial materials, the next step is to print a limited amount and get them into use. The experiences people have as they use them will then give you ideas for improvements and changes that need to be made. Also, as people become more confident in teaching, they will think of better ways of doing things which suit their situation better.

When I was on furlough, a TPPS programme started in the Takia area. The people organising the schools developed the primers. When I came back I asked the teachers what primers they were using. They had made primers themselves, they said, but they needed some revision. So they were not using them. Once the teachers had some teaching experience, the primers could be fixed so they would be more useful. The feedback from the teachers who use the materials is important for improving them.

I printed about sixty copies of the first two primers I designed in Takia. (In 1985 there were over 16,000 speakers of Takia.) The year I printed them some SIL trainees were on Karkar as part of their village living training. I had some of them try the primers out in the villages where they stayed. I got back varying reports. Some people had used the primers enthusiastically and were asking for the next ones. Others had shown no interest in them at all. Others had used them but they did not like the dialect they had been written in. Others had used them but changed some of the words because they thought they were wrong. You might think that printing all those books was a waste of time and money. But all the information that I got back would be very helpful when I revised the primers. I am glad I printed sixty copies so they could go to different areas and bring back different feedback. If I had printed fewer, I would not have gotten much feedback. But I am also glad I did not print 1,000 of them because I would have wasted money since there are mistakes that need fixing, they need to be printed in two dialects rather than one, and so on.

I was amazed at the number of drafts that I have needed to do of two stories in particular. The Takia editors keep finding mistakes or thinking of ways that the stories can be improved. There is an important lesson to learn from this: literacy workers should not think that their first efforts will be perfect and they should not make numerous copies of their early materials. Time needs to be given to test, evaluate, re-do and evaluate again. It has been a good lesson for me and one I needed to learn well, because I like to see the books rolling off the printing press quickly.

In evaluating the materials, it is necessary to assess whether or not the materials are achieving the purpose they were made for. Yasuko Nagai told me that she found out in the Maiwala programme (PNG) that the teachers did not need the primers which she had designed. They accomplished everything the primer was designed to do, but in other ways. So the next year they stopped using the primers.

I have asked some people who have made very long primers—some had over 150 lessons—when it was that people began reading fluently and the lessons were no longer needed. One person told me that, in their area by lesson 70 the students were reading well and no longer needed the primer lessons, but the teachers kept going to finish the primer anyway. Really, at that stage they just needed more reading materials.

Things are different in different areas. But these comments show that it is good to evaluate the materials in any literacy programme. It is good to learn what changes are needed by doing an evaluation, rather than to keep on doing things the same way simply because that was the way the programme was started. Good teachers are always looking for ways to improve their teaching and their materials.

Following are some things to think about when evaluating materials.

Reading

- Are the stories too hard or too easy at this level?
- Is there enough reading practice in the reading lesson?
- Are the students learning their sounds (or syllables) well?
- Are the students using the sounding out phonics strategies they have been taught?
- Are the students laughing in the right places when they read?
- Are the students wanting to read more?
- Are the students reading in their spare time?
- Which stories are the students' favourites? Why is this so? (Knowing this will help in writing other interesting stories.)

Writing

- Are the students happy to write?
- Are they learning to write well?
- Are they using the writing conventions such as capital letters, full stops, paragraphs?
- Are they sharing what they write with others?
- Are they enjoying each others' writings?
- Are they writing outside of class time?
- Is their spelling getting better the more they write?
- Are they writing stories like the ones they read?
- Are they using some of the words and phrases from their reading when they are writing or talking with each other?

Evaluation of literacy programmes and materials is very important. A good book which has more information on this topic is, *Evaluating "Literacy for Development" Projects, Programs and Campaigns* by H. S. Bhola.

10.3 Assessment of students' reading

The way in which students' reading abilities are assessed depends a lot on a person's view of how students learn to read and on what methods have been used to teach them in the early reading lessons.

People who teach initial reading programmes which focus on teaching sets of reading skills such as phonics or sound blending tend to test a student's reading performance using tests that check on the ability to read certain words in isolation.

pan	span	pit	spit	tab	stab	top	stop
pat	spat	pot	spot	tag	stag	tub	stub
pin	spin	tan	Stan	pun	spun		stud
sped							stem

Others test for a student's reading level by getting them to read a list of words. The words are graded as to level of difficulty and after a student misses, for example, three words in a row, the test stops. Scores can then be given to each student that is tested according to how many words were read correctly. The following example is one such test and is taken from *The Psychology of Teaching Reading* by Fred Schonell. These sample instructions are given to the student. "Well Jim, I have a lot of words here and I want to see how many you can read. The first words are fairly easy and then they get a little harder. Now let me see how many you can read, please. Read across the page." The instructor quickly runs his finger from word to word across the first five words where Jim is to start. The following chart is a copy of the first part of the test (Schonell 1961:255–63).

tree	little	milk	egg	book
school	sit	frog	playing	bun
flower	road	clock	train	light
picture	think	summer	people	something
dream	downstairs	biscuit	shepherds	thirsty
crowd	sandwich	beginning	postage	island
saucer	angel	ceiling	appeared	gnome
canary	attractive	imagine	nephew	gradually
smoulder	applaud	disposal	nourished	diseased
university	orchestra	knowledge	audience	situated

Others test students' reading abilities by asking them to read a passage and then answer questions about it. Students are then graded on their ability according to the number of questions they get right. A sample of this kind of test is given below (adapted from Schonell 1961:278).

Put a ring around the right answer

Dick is a boy.	Yes or No
Jack is a girl.	Yes or No
Dora sleeps in a basket.	Yes or No
Nip sleeps in a shoe.	Yes or No
You can wash a cat.	Yes or No
You can wash a dog.	Yes or No
Mother tied up Jack's knee with a rag.	Yes or No

Yet another way to test students' reading abilities is by asking them to read a series of passages carefully graded as to their level of difficulty. Students are then assigned the reading age of the level of the last passage that they read well. However some reading teachers feel uncomfortable relying totally on the above types of tests.

> Word knowledge tests, for example, do not seem to assess general knowledge of words at all, but children's ability to say a number of words on an arbitrarily selected list. Tests of comprehension do not seem to test comprehension, but usually the ability to use what one already knows or, alternatively, the ability to master an answering system...And tests which are given for establishing children's reading age usually fail to do so because reading age is relevant only to tests, not real reading of books, newspapers, magazines, advertisements and so on, which may demand varying reading levels, and certainly different styles. (Max Kemp 1987:vii)

Listening to and watching students read

Some teachers prefer to test students by listening to them and watching them read and write and by talking to them about their reading and writing. They do not give scores to each student. Instead, their observations and thinking about what they see gives them a more detailed picture of what the student can do, and also what the student still needs to learn to do in the reading and writing process. Some of these observations also give clues about the difficulties students are having. Then teachers can give them appropriate help.

When testing students' reading abilities by listening and watching, it is important to understand what is going on during the reading process. When someone is reading, a lot of things are happening at the same time. There are many ways that a reader can make mistakes. Look at the mistakes Nick made when he read the text in the following sample record. His misreadings and other comments he made are written above the word where the error was made. For an explanation of the other marks in the diagram, see "Running records," later in this section.

Suddenly the phone rang. I came to the office and
heard a man on the phone say, "Mum die, 8.30.
ring me and I will pick you up." I was very sad
when I heard this bad news. I tried to phone many
places to find my boss, but I couldn't find him.

Nick was in my migrant literacy class. Because the language he was reading was not his first language and he was just learning to speak it, Nick had trouble with words like 'suddenly' and 'mum'. He was not familiar with those two words. Sometimes readers have trouble reading words they do not know. (This is why it is easier to learn to read in your own language. You already know the words and thus have a good language foundation to draw upon when you are reading.) Nick's errors helped me to understand that when a person is reading he is constantly using the stored information about that language that is in head.

Readers often predict the word that is coming next. So Nick had trouble with the words like 'rang' and 'die' because he was not expecting these words to occur. He was expecting the word 'rang' to be 'ring'. He said to himself, "This is not ring!" Nick knew 'ring' but he did not know 'rang'. Readers often make mistakes because a word is not what they expect it to be.

A good English speaker would not have made the mistakes Nick did with the words 'heard' and 'places'. When good speakers read, they use their knowledge of the grammar of their language to help them work out what the words are going to be. So good speakers know that when talking about the action of hearing, at a time in the past, they would say 'heard'. And they know that after the word 'many', the next word has to be plural, so it would be 'places', not 'place'. They automatically speak and read that way because they know how their grammar works.

Another of my students had trouble reading because she often had trouble seeing the letters on the page clearly. She said sometimes they were fuzzy and blurred. Her comments suggest that there was something wrong with the way that her eyes and brain worked together, so she might need special help. One student I taught had trouble because his brain interpreted what he saw in unusual ways. While I could not tell what his brain was "seeing,"

I could tell from the unusual way his eyes moved, and the way he wrote letters and words and drew pictures, that he needed special help.

These examples show that there are many things involved in the reading process—the eyes, the brain, knowledge of the language, a good short term and long term memory, and good ways of using the printed information on the page, i.e., different kinds of reading strategies. Max Kemp has a chart in his book (1980:14) which illustrates how these things go together. It is a helpful guide for teachers when they are thinking about reading mistakes that students make. It is reproduced on the next page. If you want to understand the thinking behind his chart you need to read his writings about it (Kemp 1980).

When students have trouble with reading, teachers need to know where in the reading process the problems are occurring. Then they can look for a way to help students overcome their problems and help them along the road to confident reading.

The following pages give different ideas about how to observe students when they are reading and writing. Although there are many different kinds of activities listed, a teacher is not expected to use all of them, but to pick and choose. I list them here to provide a resource tool for when they are needed.

I am indebted to Max Kemp's book for many of the ideas presented in this section although I have presented them in different ways than he did in his book. I mention them here so that village people in third-world countries can have access to the ideas, since they are unlikely to have easy access to his book.

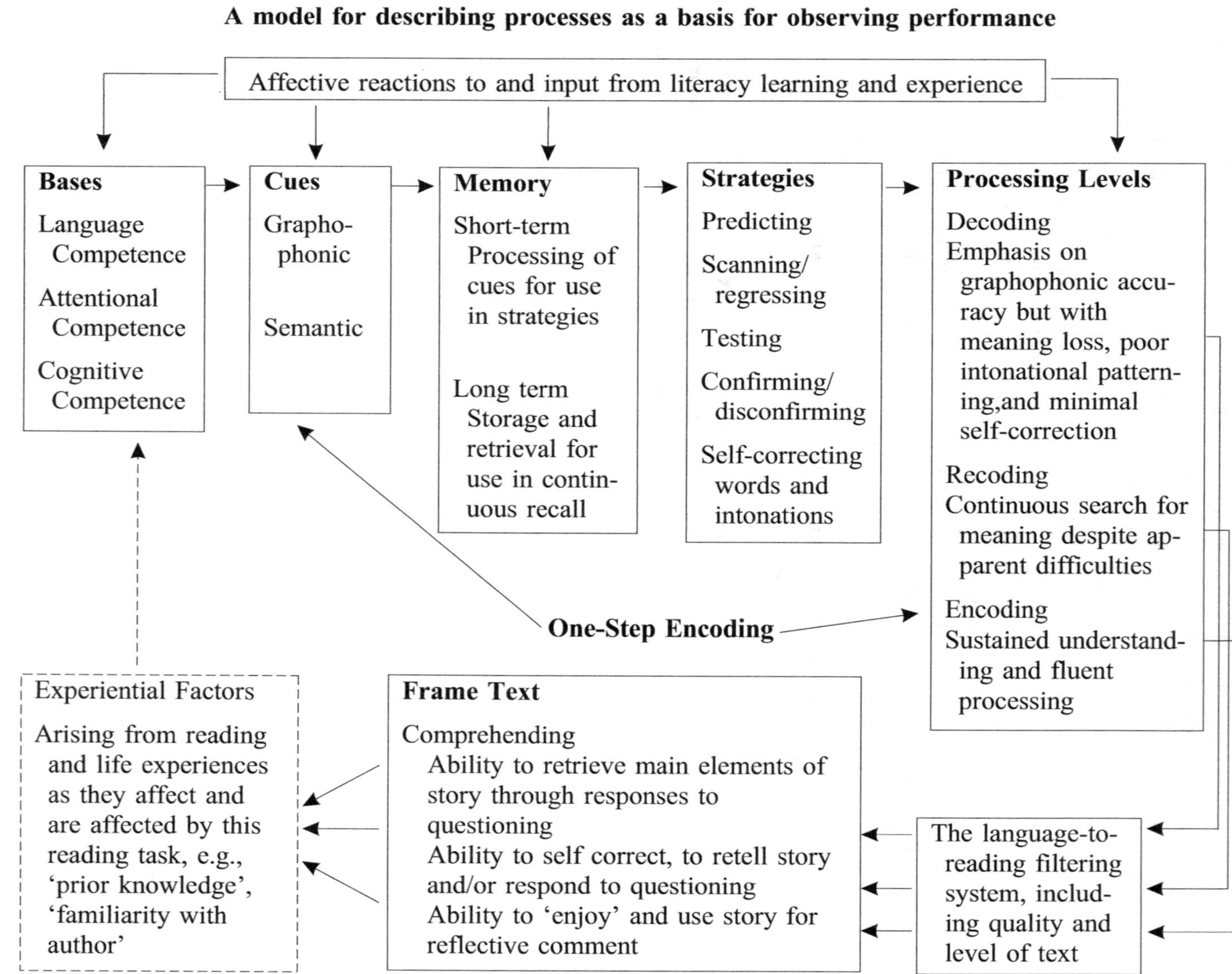
A model for describing processes as a basis for observing performance
Affective reactions to and input from literacy learning and experience
Bases
Language Competence
Attentional Competence
Cognitive Competence
Cues
Grapho-phonic
Semantic
Memory
Short-term
Processing of cues for use in strategies
Long term
Storage and retrieval for use in continuous recall
Strategies
Predicting
Scanning/regressing
Testing
Confirming/disconfirming
Self-correcting words and intonations
Processing Levels
Decoding
Emphasis on graphophonic accuracy but with meaning loss, poor intonational patterning,and minimal self-correction
Recoding
Continuous search for meaning despite apparent difficulties
Encoding
Sustained understanding and fluent processing
One-Step Encoding
Experiential Factors
Arising from reading and life experiences as they affect and are affected by this reading task, e.g., 'prior knowledge', 'familiarity with author'
Frame Text
Comprehending
Ability to retrieve main elements of story through responses to questioning
Ability to self correct, to retell story and/or respond to questioning
Ability to 'enjoy' and use story for reflective comment
The language-to-reading filtering system, including quality and level of text

Building a student profile

A combination of many different assessment methods can be used to build a reading profile of the student. Some of these methods are listed below with examples of activities that fit into that category.

Diagnostic tasks
- word differentiation
- sentence expansions
- running records
- dictation
- sequencing and re-telling
- story summaries
- interactive questioning
- reciprocal questions
- cloze test
- known words
- known sounds
- same meanings
- guided silent reading
- listening and watching
- visual difficulties

Annotated observations
- reading inventories
- running records
- print and book knowledge

Journal entries
- diary writing
- reflective journals

Student's self assessments
- personal reading inventory
- interview
- questionnaires
- learning journal entries

Using a combination of assessment methods helps teachers build up a detailed picture of a student's abilities which is far more helpful and meaningful than being able to say a student has a certain reading age or that a student is reading well because he got 7 out of 10 on a reading test.

In the village context, however, choices of how to assess students' reading must be made taking the local situation into consideration. It is important to consider the abilities of the village teachers and what they are able to manage given their own levels of education and training, the resources that are available to them, and the amount of time they are able to give to teaching reading and to assessment.

Following is a more detailed listing of some of the assessment activities listed above.

Word differentiation. A word differentiation test requires the student to listen while pairs of words with similar sounds are read aloud. The child listens to the pairs and says if they are the same or different. For example,

men	man
seat	sit
star	star

If a child is inclined to look at the tester's lips, tell him to look at a point behind the tester when the words are being said. The pairs should be spoken as evenly as possible. Keep a record of the student's responses. At the end of the session, correct the responses and list the sounds wrongly identified as the same or different.

If the numbers or types of error appear to indicate that there is a weakness in hearing differences between many sounds, then the student may need his hearing tested, or may need help with his speech.

If the errors are just a few here and there, it may be a good idea to retest. Make up additional tests with the error words included and retest. Should errors persist, the teacher may need to involve the student in activities that will help improve his listening or speech skills.

Sentence expansions. Working with students on sentence expansions can give teachers information about their language ability as well as their ability to remember words.

Step 1. Discuss a theme with the student and have him make up a sentence.

Step 2. Teacher writes the sentence on a strip of card.

We collected limbum and put it on the floor of the house.

Step 3. practice reading the sentence with the student, several times if necessary.

Step 4. Identify the phrases in the sentence and cut the strip into phrases.

We collected limbum	and put it	on the floor	of the house.

Step 5. Identify individual words and cut the phrases into words.

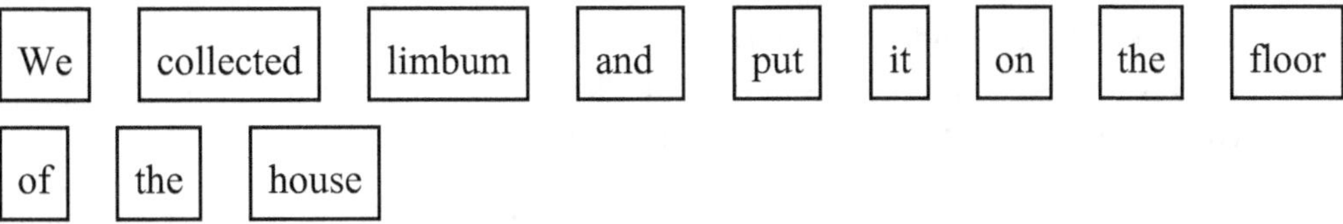

Step 6. "Play" with the sentence. For example, do a cloze exercise with some words.

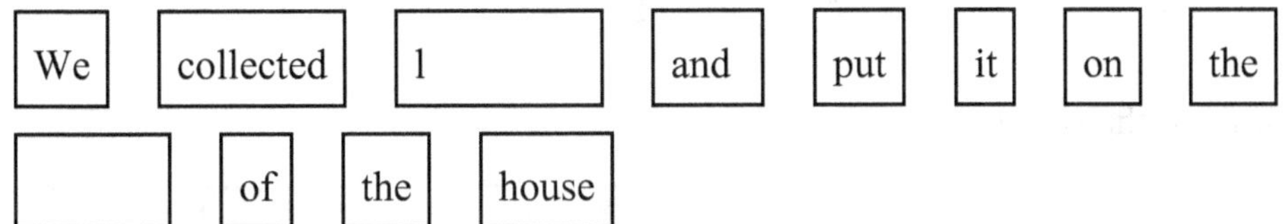

Or jumble the words and have the student put them back in the original order.

Step 7. Leave one or more open spaces to encourage the use of additional words or phrases.

1

	we collected limbum and put it on

2

the floor of the	house.

For example, the space at 1 could be filled by such words as:

One Sunday Yesterday Last week

and the space at 2 could be filled by such words as:

cook new Church government garden school teacher's

Step 8. Play with the new sentence which includes the additional words; jumble the words of the expanded sentence and re-make the sentence; or do cloze exercises similar to stage 6; or pick up named words by asking "Can you show me the word that says 'limbum'?"

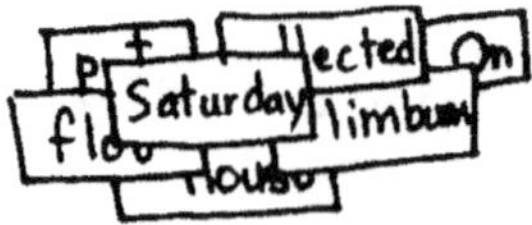

Step 9. Re-form the original sentence.

We	collected	limbum	and	put	it	on	the	floor

of	the	house.

Step 10. Place all sentence and word cards in a labelled envelope or pouch for use on other days when there is time to review the sentence and words.

Review Stage. Review the original sentence and make new sentences with the additional cards that are in the envelope.

Running records. Running records is a system that was developed and used by many people interested in studying reading. It was developed as a way of assessing children's oral reading abilities but is suitable for use in assessing adults as well.

> Clay recommends that three running records assessments should be made in close sequence, one using the child's current reading text, a second using an easier text and the third using a more difficult text. The current text should generate no more than 10% errors to be truly representative of the child's reading level.
>
> Sampling the texts in this way may help to reveal the processing strengths on the easier materials and weaknesses on the more difficult. (Kemp 1987:87)

When doing running records formally, it is normal for teachers to make their markings on a copy of the passage that they have either photocopied or typed from the text the student is reading. There are different kinds of markings that have been developed. I have made the following list from the writings of Goodman, Clay, and Kemp. A teacher should use those that are helpful for his situation, or develop his own marking system. As the student reads the teacher records on his copy of the text what the student actually says. He does this in the following way.

- Tick every word read correctly.
- Write every wrong response above the relevant word in the text.
- Write every attempted response above the relevant word, in ascending order.
- Write SC above or near every self-corrected error.
- Write a dash above every word left out.
- Write A or Appeal if the child cannot go on and looks or waits for help.
- Write TTA above any phrase where the reader becomes confused and the teacher needs to intervene.
- Write T above a word when the reader stops, and the teacher has to eventually tell the word. (Beware of helping when the child is moving close to solving the problem.)
- Write R above or next to any word or phrase that is repeated. Put a line above each word or group of words repeated. Each line represents one repeat and should appear above the whole word, words, or phrase that is repeated.
- Mark pauses by P or /.
- Write UC above an unsuccessful correction.

Included below is a chart which summarizes and illustrates conventions that can be used when doing a running record.

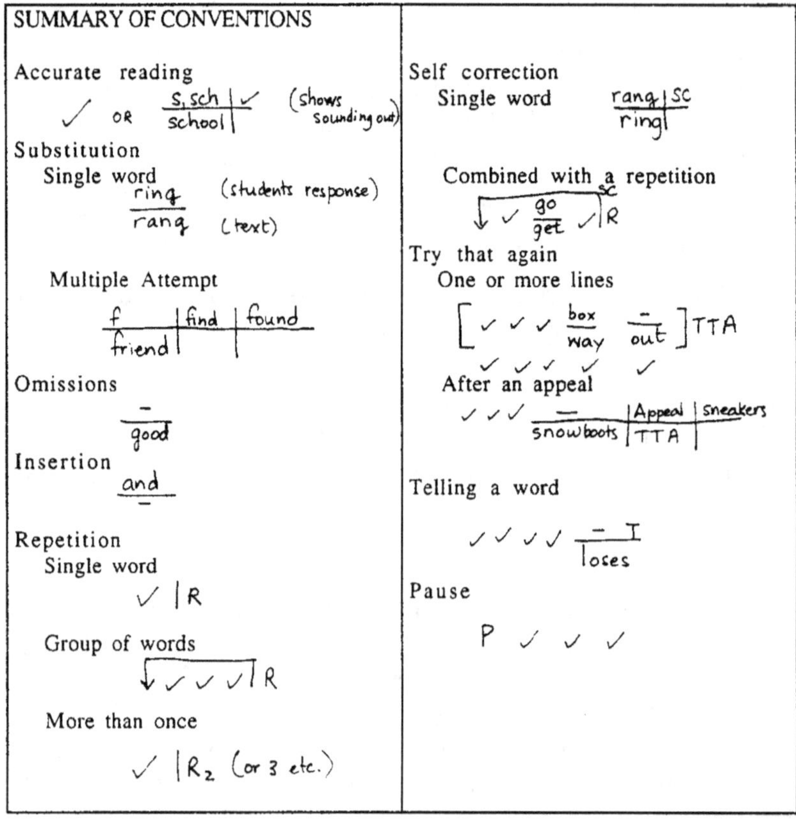

When a teacher is just learning to do running records, it is a good idea to have a copy of the text that the student is reading from. When doing running records, it is difficult to keep up with everything the reader is doing and still keep track of the words. By having a copy of the text, the teacher can mark his observations directly on to the copy. Part of a copy of one of my first attempts at doing a running record with Nick is on page 256.

After a few times of doing the running record this way, I soon felt confident enough to do the record without a copy of the text. I used a tick to show when the word was read correctly and wrote the other conventions when the reader made a mistake or correction; see below.

Migration p.11. 12-5-1993 Nick
✓ ✓ eels / seals ✓ ✓ ✓
✓ ✓
✓ ✓ ✓ ✓ ✓ ✓ ✓ ✓
✓ ✓ ✓ warm / water ✓ ✓ ✓ the / theirs ✓
✓ ✓ ✓ ✓ the / their ✓ ✓ ✓ ✓
✓ ✓ ✓ ↓Some place / same / same SC ✓ ✓
✓ ✓ ✓ ✓ ✓ ✓ ✓ ✓

Some teachers, when they become fast at using running records, use them at times when they are not doing formal testing. At such times they do not worry about copying the text separately but make notes on scrap paper they carry in their hand. They tick for correct responses and write down any mistakes. Any serious problems are noted in their daily journal or observational records.

practice a system of note taking that suits your situation until you become fast at it. Tape record students' reading and work from the recordings if you feel you are not fast enough. practice on children at home until you can do running records at speed. It is well worth the time and effort.

Once you have done a running record, the results need to be analyzed. Often this is done after the class is finished. However, when there are obvious problems that you can help students with straight away it is important to do so. Sometimes a few minutes pointing out helpful clues or things to watch for, or teaching a decoding strategy they are not using, will make a lot of difference to the student.

In the following paragraphs I discuss some things to look for when you analyze running records. These examples are from Nick's reading of the text "A funny story."

Error rate. A formula for calculating the percentage of errors is given in the first box below. (Self corrections are not counted as errors.) Question: Is the error rate less than 10%. If it is not, the text is probably too hard for the reader.

Error rate =	An example: Funny Story
$\frac{\text{No. of uncorrected errors}}{\text{No. of words in text}} \times \frac{100}{1}$ $= \square\,\%$	$\frac{14}{153} \times \frac{100}{1}$ $= \frac{1400}{153} = 9\%$

Self-correction rate. Question: Is the reader noticing his own errors and correcting them? A good reader will self-correct most of his own errors. If self-correction is not being done very well, you may need to work on this with the student.

Self correction rate =	An example: Funny Story
$\frac{\text{No. of errors}}{\text{No. of self corrects}} = \square$ That is, the reader is self correcting once every $\square$ errors.	$\frac{\text{18 errors}}{\text{4 SC}} = 4.5$ That is, the reader is self correcting every $\boxed{4.5}$ errors.

Grapho-phonic cues.

Look at the mistakes the reader made in the passage.
Is the reader using the look of the words (grapho) and the sounds of the words (phonics) to help him work out what the words say?
Is the reader using the beginning sounds to help him decode?
Is the reader looking enough at the ends of the words?

Grammatical correctness.

When the student reads a word differently than it was in the text, was the word he used one that fits well in the sentence? (Was it grammatically correct)?
Mistakes that good readers make are usually grammatically correct.

Attention to meaning.

Did the word the student used keep the meaning of the story correct or did it change its meaning?
When they corrected their mistake, were they trying to make the text make sense?

You may notice other things while doing the running records. These should be noted on your running record analysis sheet. For example, you may have noticed that the student depends on the teacher's reactions. The student may wait expecting the teacher to prompt him rather than trying to decode by himself, perhaps by reading on a bit and then going back. Or you may have noticed there were several times the reader did not bother to work out what a particular word was but just kept on reading. Or you may have noticed that a student keeps going back and repeating words, never too sure of what they are saying. These kinds of observations should be noted down.

If you notice some problem areas when you do running records, then you need to work with students on these things. You can do this by working either individually, in small groups, or as a class on activities that will give them practice doing the things they are finding difficult.

Sequencing and retelling. Sequencing and retelling activities help to assess students' understanding of texts they have read.

To do these activities, have an extra set of the story, both pictures and text. These could be photocopied if necessary. When duplicating or silk-screening books, there are often extra pages or discards left over. Do not throw these away. They can be used for reading activities about the story. Cut out the pictures, glue them onto cards, and jumble them.

Have the students read the original story, with text and pictures. Then give them the set of jumbled pictures and ask them to retell the story while putting the pictures in the correct order.

Other possible activities are:

- Ask the student to place the appropriate text with each picture.
- Ask questions about the text as they are matched with the pictures.
- Choose one picture and ask the student to tell what happens next in the story.
- Choose 3 pictures and their text portions. Jumble them. Ask the students to put them in order according to which came first in the story. Ask them to match the right text with each picture.

- Ask the students to choose their favourite picture and talk about why they like that part of the story best.

If students have understood the story or text they have read, they will find it easy to retell the story or put the pictures in the right order. While doing these things you can be talking with them and asking questions about the story to check their understanding. If a student has trouble with these activities, either the story is too hard for them or they do not understand that reading is getting meaning from text. They need to have a lot of stories read to them and need to talk about each one.

Following is an example of a sequencing exercise I did with some adult students. I typed out the telephone conversation that I had had with one of the students. We read through the entire conversation. Next I cut up the text into strips and jumbled the strips up as shown below. Then I had the students work together to put the strips into their correct order.

G: Oh, I am sorry to hear you are not well. Class starts next week.You should be getting a letter about it soon with the times. I think it starts at 11:30 and goes to 3:30. We will have a short break for lunch.

G: That's fine I look forward to seeing you then. Bye for now.

E: Hello Glenys, this is Emma.

E: I'm not too well. I have a bad flu. I am ringing to find out when our class starts again. Is it today or it is next week?

G: Hello, this is Glenys speaking.

G: Hello Emma, how are you? How can I help you?

E: Bye.

E: Oh, that's good because I want to stay home today because of my flu. I will see you next Monday. Thank you very much. See you then.

The same activity can be done with a story a student has written. Remember to read the whole text first before you cut it up.

Other times I would take my cat with me to the garden and play inside until the garden looked very bad.

Grandmother's garden.

After that my grandmother came looking for me and she was very angry.

But my grandmother said, "That's not going to change anything. You are in big trouble."

When I was a young boy my grandmother was always trying to keep her garden looking nice.

I used to go inside her garden and deliberately step on her plants.

But when I got up there, the branch I was on broke. I fell down and I was crying a lot.

I heard her voice and I went straight to the tree and climbed it.

Story summaries. Give the students some story summaries about a story they have just read. Have them decide which summary best fits the story. The example here is for the story called "Selling Betelnut," and the instructions to the students were to choose one of these four summaries that best sums up the story they have just read.

1. Rooster and Wallaby paddle in their canoe to different places selling their betelnut. They have trouble on their trip. People don't want to buy the betelnut and they have trouble with the canoe which eventually sinks leaving them stranded.	2. Wallaby and Rooster paddle in their canoe to different places trying to sell their betelnut. People buy Rooster's betelnut but not Wallaby's. This causes a big fight and Wallaby smashes up the canoe. Rooster flies away to safety but Wallaby is left to sink or swim.

3. Two friends decide to go on a trip to sell betelnut. At each place they stop they fight over something—where they will sit, who sold the most betelnut, and who will paddle home. Wallaby finally wins all the arguments and paddles home.	4. Wallaby and Rooster are selling betelnut in the Duke of York Islands. People do not like to buy Wallaby's betelnut because he is too smelly. Rooster and Wallaby work out a plan to trick people into buying the betelnut and then return home happily.

Although each of these summaries has some truth in them, summary two is more correct than all the others. Summary one talks about Rooster and Wallaby having problems on the trip but fails to mention the main problem of Wallaby's jealousy of Rooster and of his causing the canoe to sink. Summary three is incorrect because Wallaby does not paddle home. Although Rooster and Wallaby trick people into buying Wallaby's betelnut as summary four says, they do not return home happily in the end so this summary is incorrect also.

Giving summaries like these to students test whether or not they have a good understanding of the story they have read. It also is a good opportunity to talk about why the other summaries are incorrect. Such discussions show if students have gained the correct meaning from the story and how well they are able to talk about the meanings they have gained.

Interactive questions. Questions can be used to assess how well a student understands a passage. The easiest way to do this with poor or new readers is to discuss what is being read during the reading. It is also good to encourage the readers to talk about questions they themselves have about the material they are reading. Some teachers give students written questions to answer. I have found, however, that students often find these to be boring activities, and it makes them dislike reading. They become much more enthusiastic about their reading if the teacher talks with them about the books and discusses the questions with the student.

There are different levels of questioning and it is good to help the student to gradually progress in their abilities to dig into what is in the text that they are reading, rather than always remain on the surface. You do not want to do this with everything the students read; otherwise they will get tired of the questioning and become disinterested in reading if they always have to face a lot of questions after reading. Also, be careful to keep your questioning at a level that is right for the student and the passage. Some passages are full of hidden meanings or interesting things to talk about, others are not.

Who, when, where, what type of questions encourage the student to recall the basic facts that are presented in the story, such as:

- Who killed the little boy?
- Where did the accident happen?
- When did the accident happen?
- What was the little boy doing when he was killed?
- How did the policeman find out about the accident?

Other questions may ask for the student to remember finer points of detail, such as:

- What type of truck was it?
- Why was the little boy crossing the road?

Other questions will see if the student can use information in the text and think beyond what is printed on the page.

- Why do you think the driver did not see the little boy crossing the road?
- Why do so many accidents happen at that corner?

Other questions will try to encourage the student to make an evaluation or judgment about what they have read.

- Do you think it is strange that the little boy was left to cross the busy street on his own?
- What would you change to make the corner safer?

Other questions will try to get the student to become emotionally involved in the story to see if they were affected by the story in some way.

- How do you think the truck driver felt about the accident?
- If you had witnessed the accident what would you do about it?

It is important that the kinds of questions you use are ones that fit the level of difficulty of the passage being read, and that they are not too difficult for the student you are testing. A national translator friend of mine was doing a test which required him to answer questions about short passages that he had read. Although he could read the passages he could not answer the questions correctly. One of the questions required an understanding of quite difficult mathematics concepts that he had never been exposed to before. Another required him to understand what it was like to live in a place where it snows. He had grown up in a village in the tropics, so this was very difficult for him!

You will not want to ask all of these kinds of questions for every text. Also, in some cultures questions are not used very much as a way of stimulating responses from students. If this is true of your culture, you can do something more appropriate. For example, you might get a discussion going, so that the student gives you the same information that you would have tried to get using a question. Or you could tell the student to talk to you about the story.

The first set of questions above could be replaced by statements asking the student to tell part of the story.

- All right, the little boy died. Tell me who killed him.
- Tell me what you think the boy was doing when he died.

There is no "right" way to do this. Whatever works well in your culture is right for you to use. Remember that the goal is to get the student to talk about the story so that you can find out how well he has understood it.

Cloze exercises. Cloze exercises can be used for many things. They can test such things as the student's vocabulary knowledge, spelling, word identification skills, story comprehension, and language performance. They can also be used to teach the structure of texts or to encourage students to develop skills of prediction in their reading. They can be done individually, in small groups, or as a class.

Cloze tests are similar to fill-the-gap exercises. A cloze test is made by writing or selecting a text and deleting some words from it. Students are asked to read and fill in the gaps in the text with words of their own choices. The word chosen must match the story and the meaning of the text.

For example, I was using the following text in an English language class. After we had read it as a class several times, I made a cloze exercise out of it. Doing the cloze exercise helped the students think about the story more and read the words more carefully. I could also tell how well the students had understood the story by the substitutions they made or from the discussions they had with other students about what the right word was for a certain space.

Aman's story

I escaped from Vietnam in 1983 by boat. It was a small boat and there were 74 people on board. It took us about four days to travel from Vietnam to Malaysia. During that time we saw many Thai fishing boats.

We asked the fishermen for directions to Malaysia. When they came closer they saw that we were Vietnamese and not very strong. They took anything they could sell—gold, watches, clothes and money. They killed one person. He was sitting right beside me. They also took two girls from our boat.

When they left our boat, another boat came and did the same things. Until one night we didn't have anything left on the boat. One of the boats gave us enough oil to go to Malaysia.

Cloze exercise

I escaped from Vietnam in 1983 by boat. It was a ______ boat and there were 74 people on _____. It took us about four days to _____ from Vietnam to Malaysia. During that time we saw many Thai _______ boats.

We asked the ______ for directions to Malaysia. When they came _____ they saw that we were Vietnamese and not very ______. They took ________ they could sell—gold, watches, clothes and money. They _____ one person. He was sitting right beside me. They also ______ two girls from our boat.

When they left our boat, ______ boat came and did the same things. Until one night we didn't have anything ______ on the boat. One of the boats gave us enough oil to go to Malaysia.

When making a cloze exercise, the following guidelines should be considered.

- Use a text that makes sense on its own.
- Use a text that is not too long, and that matches the reading ability of the student, not too hard nor too easy.
- The text should have a beginning, a middle, and an end with reasonably predictable language.
- Do not change the introduction and ending; leave all the words in.
- Know what you are testing for. This will help you make decisions about what words to leave out.
- Decide how often you are going to leave out words. Some people try and leave out about every tenth word.
- Begin choosing words that could be left out using a pencil and think carefully about each choice. Does leaving that word out make the rest of the reading too hard? Do you need to keep that word in to keep important meanings clear? Is it too close to the last word that you left out?
- Check that the word you are going to leave out is predictable from the rest of the sentence if that is what you are testing. Or check that it is a word that is easily remembered from the original story if that is what you are testing.

- Decide if you want the student to have a wide choice of answers or if you want one particular answer. For example, in Aman's story, if I required the response **small** boat, I would need to indicate this in the exercise perhaps by giving the first letter of the word.

It was a s____ boat.

Otherwise answers such as "tiny" or "little," or "fishing" would also be correct. But with the sentence below, there is only one right answer. I cannot say "other" or "fishing" because the next word (boat) would have to be boat**s** (plural); so only "another" is correct here.

When they left our boat ___________ boat came.

- Give your test to a friend to do. Does he (or she) have any problems with it? Is his answer correct? Any places he was confused? Then make any changes that are necessary.

When you give the exercise, be sure to do the following:

- Tell the students to try to choose words that the author would have used in the gaps.
- Have the students read the whole text before trying to fill in any of the gaps.
- Have the students re-read the completed story from start to finish. Allow them to make any corrections.

The following suggestions as to when cloze exercises should be used are adapted from Hornsby, Parry, and Sukarna (1992:8):

- When students do not realise that the important thing about reading is making meaning out of the text.
- When students do not realise that an essential reading strategy is using what they know to help them predict what is coming next.
- When students need to gain confidence in using what they know to make meaning of what is coming next.
- When students are not aware of the reading strategies that they use.
- When students only use one strategy of decoding text.
- When students read word by word and do not understand much of what they are reading.
- When students are careless readers and often leave out things or add in things.

- When students do not think carefully and critically about what they read and need to learn to discuss what they read.
- When students do not realise that reading is more than just seeing letters and that in reading they need to combine what they are reading with information they already know, or with information they are building mentally as they read.

Same meanings. Have the students read a text. Then give them a list of words taken from the text. Underline these words. Beside each of these words list three words of similar meaning. Have the students choose which of the three words has the same meaning as the underlined word has in the story.

<u>file</u>	sharpen	smooth	line
<u>grasped</u>	caught	took	held
<u>father</u>	daddy	boss	pastor
<u>trade</u>	buy	sell	exchange
<u>boat</u>	canoe	dinghy	sailboat

Or use a cloze exercise that students have already completed. This time go through it together and have them think of as many different words as they can that could fill the gap and still have the story making sense. This will show who has a good level of language use.

For example, the following sentences from Aman's escape story have other possibilities.

It was a ______ boat.
tiny
little
wooden
fragile

When they came _________ they saw that we were
closer
alongside
onboard

Vietnamese are not very _________.
strong
aggressive
fierce

They __________ one person.
shot
murdered
slaughtered

Watching students working on tasks such as these helps the teacher to see how well the students language ability is developing.

Watching (Observing). When I was teaching primary school children, I found that I could assess children's abilities very easily by watching them at different times and during different activities. Their body language, attitudes, and knowledge were easily seen.

I will never forget Paul. Paul was in the first class I taught. It was his third year at school. Paul was in the bottom group in reading, writing, and math, and he really struggled with all of those subjects. Yet in other things he seemed to me to be very clever. His drawings were extremely good and very detailed and complex. He could tell a story and keep the entire class gripped as they followed along. Andrew, his best friend, was the brightest person in the class. He was a boy who read encyclopedias for fun. From my observations of Paul, his being in the bottom group just did not make sense. Yet he could not copy a word from the blackboard or from his page without making mistakes. He also had great difficulty reading despite his thick glasses and careful concentration. Two teachers before me had put him in the bottom group.

It turned out that Paul was extremely bright, he just had a severe problem. The squiggles on the page never stood still for him and got all confused in his brain. If I had given Paul a series of tests he would have stayed in the bottom group, perhaps for the rest of his life. But I could tell by watching him in many situations that he was not the kind of child you would expect in the bottom group, but one that I would expect to be sitting next to Andrew and joining in all the work with no difficulties.

Watching students is very important and can tell many things that tests do not show. But teachers need to focus their watching and know what they are looking for. I have listed some things below for teachers to watch for. I am sure there are many others that you might add.

- responds with interest to tasks
- listens to comments and instructions
- concentrates well on tasks
- remembers things well
- keeps trying when difficulties come up
- uses decoding strategies well
- uses picture clues to help decode for meaning
- responds to books with enthusiasm

- laughs in the right places when a story is funny
- answers questions about the text easily
- talks in well constructed sentences
- communicates well with fellow students
- shares enthusiastically about things that have been read

Visual difficulties. It is important for teachers to be aware that some students may have visual difficulties (problems with their sight) which are making the task of learning to read and write difficult. The following is a check list for teachers who suspect a student may have problems with their sight. It is adapted from a list made up by the Australian Optometrical Association.

Appearance of eyes

- one eye turned in or out
- frequent blinking
- frequent lumps, sores, or infections of the eyelids
- excessive watering of eyes or sensitivity to bright light
- squints or screws up eyes
- red eyes or lids, crusting on eyelids
- excessive eye movements

Behaviour

- holds book very close
- loses place when reading, skips lines
- closes, covers, or pulls at one eye when reading or doing close work
- confuses similar words
- has a poor or unusual sitting posture when reading
- rubs eyes frequently
- thrusts head forward to see distant objects
- has an obvious tendency to favour one eye more than the other
- avoids close work
- omits words or makes errors when reading or copying
- reverses letters more often than expected for his age
- has a short attention span when reading or writing
- squints or frowns to see blackboard clearly
- is rigid or tense when looking at distant objects
- is nervous, irritable, tense, or restless after maintaining visual concentration

Complaints

- headaches
- blurring of vision while reading or writing
- seeing double
- difficulty seeing clearly at a distance
- eyes burning or itching during or after close work

Reading inventories. An inventory such as the following will help to build a picture of a student's general attitude to reading at school and at home and help determine if he tries to use his reading skills outside of class. Students who come from homes where reading is valued or encouraged usually learn to read much better than those who come from homes where reading is not valued, used, or encouraged. The inventory will also highlight areas where the student feels he needs further help and will be a guide for teachers in structuring the student's reading programme. A sample reading inventory follows.

	Yes	No	Don't know	Comments	Teacher's notes
I was read to at home when I was young.				Has the student seen many instances of reading and print?	
We still have stories read to us at home.				What kinds of things to read are available in the home?	
I read a lot at home myself.				If not, why not?	
My parents read at home.				Is reading a value in the home?	
I like being read to at school.					
I like the reading activities we do at school.				Which ones do they like most? Why?	
I can think of several favourite school books that I would enjoy reading again.				What did you like about them?	
There are things that I still need to learn to help me read better.				What kind of help is needed?	
There are some stories I would like to read but I need help.				What things are difficult for the student?	

Inventories such as this sample are usually used with students who have already been part of beginning reading programmes. To get the most from the inventory, discuss the questions with the student and note any comments that are worth following up. Use questions that suit the situation.

Similar inventories can be designed to get information about students' attitudes to writing.

Print and book knowledge. The teacher may find the following activities useful in assessing what level of understanding the students have about reading and what knowledge they have about books and print at the beginning levels of reading. The teacher may ask a student to point out different things in a book, or may watch a student when he or she is handling books on their own, or may use the following questions and directions.

- What is a book for? What is in a book?
- Open the book up ready to read to me.
- Show me the back cover. Show me the front cover.
- Show me where the name of the story is.
- Run your finger along what the title says. (Does the student point from left to right?)
- Where is the story-writer's name?
- Turn to the first page of the story and ask, "Where does the story start?"
- Turn to the last page of the story and ask, "Where does the story end?"
- Turn to the first page again. Show me the first sentence in the story.
- Show me the start of the first sentence. Now show me the end of the first sentence.
- Run your finger along the sentence from beginning to end.
- Show me a sentence that has two lines or more.
- Show me a full stop.
- Show me the first word in the sentence? What letter does it start with?
- Show me the talking marks on a page. What do talking marks show us?
- Show me with your finger how you would read the page. Start with the first word and point to the rest of the story.

By observing how well the student can respond to such instructions, the teacher will know if the student understands things about reading and print such as:

- which way up the illustrations go
- that you read from left to right
- what a word is, what a sentence is
- how to hold a book properly and turn pages
- what to expect to find on covers of books
- where to find information about authors and titles of books

A teacher can find out a lot of these things by just watching children when they handle books or by spending time with them and asking them questions.

Journal entries. A journal is like a diary of the things that happen. Teachers often keep a journal when they are teaching. There are no set ways and rules for journal keeping. Each person must develop his own way of keeping a journal and own way of organising it. Each person has his own preferences of style and own purposes for keeping a journal. So each journal will be different.

A journal is a personal document. The writer is usually the only one to read it. But sometimes teachers share what they have recorded in their journal with others so that they can discuss the things that they are observing and thinking about, and get the help and opinions of others about the situation that is concerning them.

For example: After working with students on such activities as sentence expansions you may want to write down some of the things you noticed in order to keep a record of them. You would write the day and the date at the top of the page. You may note that Jane had a good control of language skills at that level, but Mark needed help to expand his phrases. Jillian may have found it really hard to come up with a sentence independently. Simon may have had trouble completing the cloze exercise with his simple sentence and trouble remembering the extra words in his expanded sentence.

Such dated entries in your journal will help you pinpoint problems students are having and also serve as a reference for the future. Later on you can note if they have improved in this area or still need work. You can use this information along with other information to build up a picture of the students' strengths and weaknesses.

Reflective journals. A reflective journal goes one step further than a daily journal. In this kind of diary you note down your observations but you also spend time thinking about what you have observed and trying to understand what was happening and why.

You write down your thinking about these things. Then you start to think about things that you may need to do to help with the problem that you noticed and write down a few ideas to try.In a journal the writer can carry on a discussion with himself about different experiences. Mary Louise Holly has this to say in her book about journals.

> In a journal, the writer can carry on a dialogue between and among various dimensions of experience. What happened? What are the facts? What was my role? What feelings and sense surrounded the events? What did I do? What did I feel about what I did? Why? What was the setting? The flow of events? And later, what were the important elements of the event? What preceded it? Followed it? What might I be aware of if the situation recurs? (Holly 1987:6)

Then you start to think about things that you may need to do to help with the problem that you noticed and write down a few ideas to try.

For example when I was teaching Nick to read I noticed that he often did not correct his own mistakes but just kept on reading as long as he was picking up the main ideas of the story. I knew if his reading was to improve he needed to correct his mistakes more often. I began to wonder why he did not self-correct more. I wrote this down in my journal and the next few times he read to me, I watched to see if he was still not correcting his own mistakes. I thought it might be because he did not know English well or because he was used to making sense out of very little bits of information. He was just learning English but he was a taxi driver in Australia. So he had to learn quickly where people wanted to go and how to deal with the fares, complaining customers, and the police when he had to report people who had not paid their fares and so on. All day he was working at making meanings when he only understood a little bit of what people were saying. He might be doing this with his reading. I wrote my thinking down in the journal.

After a while I thought of some ways that I might try to encourage him to correct his mistakes more. I thought we could discuss how good readers often go back when they are reading and re-read something to check the meanings, or they go back over a word and re-read it to make sure they have it right. Maybe Nick thinks that when he is reading to me he should not do that as it is not right. He may just need me to encourage him to do that. He may need to know that I expect him to do that. Or perhaps Nick does not understand what he is reading enough to be able to tell when he is making mistakes. Or perhaps he does not know enough English to be able to work out what his mistakes are. He might know that what he has read is not quite right but not know enough English to be able to correct it. I wrote my thinking down in my journal. Then over the next few weeks I tried each idea out and wrote about how things went.

So the journal not only helped me keep a record of Nick's progress but helped me to organise my thinking about one of the problems he was having and to think about some solutions. Thinking about something that has happened is called reflecting, so researchers call this kind of journal a reflective journal.

10.4 How to do case studies

A sample student profile

The following material is part of a student profile that I built up when working with Nick (not his real name), an adult literacy student that I worked with in 1993 in Australia. Nick came to Australia from Lebanon. At the time that we worked together he was a single male in his mid-thirties and he worked part-time as a taxi driver. Nick had gone to school in

Lebanon and had learned to read and write in both Arabic and French. In Lebanon he did an electrical apprenticeship, did his Army service for eighteen months, and then worked in Saudi Arabia, Africa, and Lebanon before coming to Australia to live in 1989.

When Nick joined my adult literacy class, he said he could read and write in his own language but wanted to learn to read and write in English. I asked him to choose something that he wanted to learn to read from a range of easy reading materials. His comment was that he would not be able to attempt to read any of them. So he chose three adult readers (level 1) and I read them onto tape for him to use as repeated readings at home. He later commented that I had read too fast for him. (And I thought I had read them slowly!) In the literacy class, the students did readings of texts that had been written by other students in the class, or texts that I had modified from magazines, books, or newspapers. At the beginning of the course when we did group readings, Nick often lost his way, so I made sure I sat near him and helped him, pointing to words when he got lost.

In the time that I worked with Nick I collected and observed a variety of things that had to do with his reading and writing. I did this by using such things as those below.

- Marie Clay's test of known words
- an alphabet test
- known words test
- writing vocabulary inventory
- sound accuracy sample
- book inventory
- collections of writing and reading text samples
- journal observations
- running records and analysis of these
- case-study journal and lesson plans

By the end of three months I could look back over all my records and make observations and descriptions of what Nick had learned about reading and writing, what he was able to do when he started, what he can do now, and what he still needs help to do. The following is a sample student profile written at that time.

Student Profile: Nick March to June 1993

Reading

From the outset, Nick has always understood that reading was gaining meaning from text. He was willing to go to great efforts to do this. For example when he was reading "A Funny Story" it wasn't until he read down to almost the bottom of the page that he worked out the words 'answering machine'. Then he went back and reread the section where it was first mentioned and he had not been able to get the meaning from it. He did this rather than gloss over it and keep reading to finish the article.

In the past three months Nick has progressed from someone who didn't feel confident to choose a Level 1 reader to read (March 3rd), to someone who in April read his first book, *Inspector Holt and the Fur Van*, independently with understanding and is now (June 2nd) on to his fifth book. He has built up quite a collection of texts that he can now read easily and use for practice reading.

It has been hard to find materials that are at a suitable level for Nick to read, for example: *The Rescue* 87% accuracy, *The Cobbler* 87.5%, but recently (19/5/93 *The Hold-up*) he read a page with approximately 98.5% accuracy. This has been a great encouragement to us both. Recently he borrowed an electrical engineering text from the library.

It is good to see Nick's accuracy levels slowly increasing, or staying in the 93–95% area, even though reading materials are increasing in difficulty. He does however need to read more during the week to consolidate gains and we have talked about that.

In continuing his reading Nick needs to work on his fluency and on using self-correction strategies more. It is extremely hard for a non-English speaker reading English to self-correct unless the word being dealt with is familiar to him. Any self-correction that is done is usually because of semantic (meaning) cues, rather than due to grammatical or graphophonic (sound/symbol) cues. This shows up in Nick's low self-correction rates—many times he knows the word is wrong but he has no alternative to try, and his use of graphophonic strategies is poor probably because he has learned through experience that English is not always phonetic!! However, I have encouraged him to realize that often the word can be sounded out and to at least try using sound-symbol cues more.

When reading a text to find out specific information Nick always manages to find the answers to questions that he has been given even when the texts have been too difficult for him. Over the weeks as we have talked about texts he has read, I have increased the difficulty of the questions I use with him, moving from questions of pure information recall into interpretive questions—from what?, how? and who? questions to why? and what do you think? type questions.

When talking about texts we have read, Nick has always been able to think of good questions to ask me about the texts and to frame his questions well. His progress can be seen in the following two extracts from my lesson notes.

7/4 Framed his questions well. On a few questions he caught me. Both of us needed to consult the text at times! As his background is in electrical engineering he understood it very well.

28/4 It's getting too easy for him so I deliberately was difficult in answering his last question, 'Why do they put the ring on the leg of the bird?', 'So it won't fall off!' He was unhappy with the answer but wasn't sure what to do about it. We talked about the need to clarify my answer by re-framing the question.

Writing

Text response:

Nick is good at summarizing the main points of texts that we have read. He sometimes needs help to frame sentences that are grammatically correct. Writing text responses has been very worthwhile for Nick as it presents opportunities to practice his spelling strategies at the point of need. He uses the practice page well.

It gives him confidence to make an attempt at any spelling problems that arise, and the opportunity to try several times until he can spell the word right.

Word analysis:

Nick uses strategies of stretching the word out and listening to what sounds he can hear in the different word positions. He often uses the strategy of using words which he knows how to spell in order to spell others: 'ing' from 'ring' to help spell 'missing'. When Susan was trying to spell 'material' he said it would be like 'arterial' from 'South Eastern Arterial'—the taxi driver coming out in him. He also goes from the look of things; he writes 'because' to see if it looks right before using it. If he remembers seeing a word in a text or list he will search for it, or he will ask for help. Sometimes if he doesn't know a word and it does not conform to known patterns then I immediately show him how to spell it. If I start to tell him a word that he wants to try out for himself he will tell me to let him try first.

Creative writing:

Initially Nick was hesitant to start writing as he did not feel confident to make an attempt. We talked a lot about not being overly concerned about spelling, just getting thoughts on paper etc. His initial attempt had some classic reversals, but it was interesting to do a sound accuracy check and find that almost 86% of the time he was spelling accurately.

In his second and third writing pieces, Nick used a wider range of vocabulary and was more enthusiastic about the writing task. When working with Susan on a letter to a newspaper about war, he was determined to finish it even though class was finished. Also he was very confident in his spelling attempts. Since his arm was fractured other people have had to write for Nick. I have noticed an improved confidence in Nick when he is presented with writing opportunities.

Concluding comments:

Over these past three months there has been a marked improvement in Nick's reading fluency and his accuracy. Also he is beginning to self-correct more and repeat and reread when necessary. His writing is improving. Before he broke his arm it was still a mixture of upper and lower case, but more lower case than in early texts. Above all, his confidence in his ability to be able to read and write has increased significantly. He will now tell others in class how to spell words. And he has been able to read four books and understand them with little or no assistance. He is now able to participate fully in class and help his classmates.

Doing a case study

Sometimes it is helpful to do a detailed study of a particular student's reading and writing. This study could be mainly for your own information. Case studies are an excellent way of coming to a good understanding of the things students need to learn when they are learning to read and write. Or you might be aware of a particular student who is having a lot of difficulty with reading and writing. By looking at their work in depth it may give you clues as to the areas they need to focus their attention on. It may also give you ideas of methods and strategies you can use to teach them skills that will help improve their reading and writing.

Individual case studies take a lot of time and if you have many other responsibilities they can be difficult to maintain. Case studies can span periods of 3, 6, or 12 months. Some teachers have done case studies over several years in certain instances. Some case studies require weekly meetings with students, others require lessons 3 to 5 times a week. It all depends on your purpose in doing the case study.

When I did the case study with Nick, I had two goals in mind. Firstly, I wanted to give Nick some extra help with his reading and writing because he was having difficulties. Secondly, I wanted to see what it was like to follow someone's progress closely over several months to see if there were gains and improvements in their reading and writing by following the suggested programme.

The things that I learned when working with Nick were very helpful to me, because they strengthened my understanding of the processes involved in learning to read and write. It was also helpful in giving me ideas for improving my teaching of the whole adult literacy class. I am sure what I learned doing the case study will affect the way I teach literacy classes in the future.

When I did my case study with Nick, I used the following lesson framework. It is taken from a reading tutoring programme that was developed in Australia known as "Making a Difference."

Familiar reading

The student chooses two short texts that he is familiar with and reads them aloud to the tutor as a 'warm up' exercise. (Readings that are used in the shared reading segment of the lesson can be added to the familiar readings collection as the lessons progress.)

Running records

A running record (see §10.3) is taken of part or all of the text that was used as shared reading in the last lesson. (If this is the first lesson and there are no previous shared readings available to work with, choose a text you think will be at the right level of the student—one that he is familiar with and one that he is not familiar with. With Nick, I used a story that he had written himself and a story that a fellow student had written and he had not seen yet.) It is the aim of the programme that the texts that the students deal with are in the 90–95% accuracy level range so that students are always operating at a level of success.

Guided silent reading

In this segment the student is asked to find the answer to a question by reading a text silently to themselves. (As they become proficient with this, you may want to give them two questions or have them predict what the answer might be before they read.)

Shared reading (see §8.2)

This is a time when student and teacher share a reading together. The teacher cues the reader to the text, reads the text to the student, then teacher and student read the text together, and then the student reads the text.

Reciprocal questioning

The teacher and student now ask questions of each other based on the shared reading text. In the early stages questions will probably be ones that deal with information contained in the text—who, what, when, how; and then move on to questions which require some interpretation or interaction by the reader with the text—why type questions (see §10.3 "Interactive questions").

Text summary

The student is asked to write a text summary of the shared reading text. This is done in an exercise book with the left hand page used as the page for writing the text summary correctly. The emphasis on correctness on this page is so that the texts can be used as familiar readings. The right hand page is used as a practice page where teacher and student can interact on words that the student needs help with. Students can use this page for multiple attempts at words. Teachers can use this page to write other words that sound the same. Writing in pencil allows for erasing of errors if desired and is less threatening.

This lesson framework encourages students in many good reading and writing strategies. Good readers spend a lot of time building meanings from text. They do this by asking questions of themselves and the text, by using the knowledge that they have to make predictions about what is coming next, and so on. In this lesson framework, there are a lot of opportunities to ask questions, to build meanings, predict outcomes, and so on. The running records pinpoint what strategies the reader is using and help teachers see what strategies need to be given more emphasis.

A good way to learn spelling strategies is for students to do so while they are involved in writing. Students learn spelling in real situations and will be able to apply immediately what they are learning to the task at hand.

If time permits, it is also good to add to the above lesson framework some time for the students to do some writing for their own purposes. They can write for self-expression (personal experiences or perspectives), for practical purposes (for example, filling in forms, doing the kinds of writing tasks needed in everyday life), for public debate, or to inform others. Again this is a good time to teach spelling—at the time when it is needed and in a real writing context.

From the students' writings you can observe what words they can already spell correctly, and what words they want to learn to spell. You can see what strategies they use in spelling words and help them learn other strategies—stretching out the words or using knowledge of known words that have similar sound combinations.

Analyzing student writings will give information about things that are causing them problems. It also gives you an opportunity to look at things like the following:

- Is the writing well formed?
- Does the writer use a common sound pattern?
- When words are unknown does the writer use an invented sound pattern?
- Are punctuation, capital letters, and paragraphing used with confidence?
- Are misspellings related to hearing or saying the word incorrectly?
- Are misspellings due to visual confusion, that is, transpositions (the right letters but in the wrong order), omissions (letters missed out), or additions (extra letters added in)?
- Does the writer use a wide range of vocabulary or stick to a small set of common words?
- Do the ideas flow together?
- Does the beginning of the story relate meaningfully to the middle and the end?
- Are the tenses used consistently throughout the text?

The following pages give some samples from my case study with Nick. They may provide some helpful ideas of things that can be done. In the two tests below, Nick was asked to circle any sounds or letters that he knew and to say them. The emphasis here was on finding out what he already knew.

Marie Clay's letter test

A	F	K	P	W	Z
B	H	O	J	U	
C	Y	L	Q	M	
D	N	S	X	I	
E	G	R	V	T	
a	f	k	p	w	z
b	h	o	j	u	a
c	y	l	q	m	
d	n	s	x	i	
e	g	r	v	t	g

Marie Clay's known words

List A	List B	List C
practise	practise	practise
the	said	is
I	and	Father
Mother	to	come
are [our]	will	for
here	look	a
me	he	you
shouted	up	at
am	like	school
with	in	went
car	where	get
children	Mr	we
help	going	they
not	big	ready
too	go	this
meet	let	boys
away	on	please

In Nick's vocabulary inventory I kept a list of all the words he was using correctly. You can see that as time went by he was writing more and more words correctly.

Vocabulary inventory (words written correctly in Nick's stories)							
24/2/1993 I came to Australia				7/4/1993 I was in the army			
in	Lebanon	I	to	I	was	in	the
the	for	then	left	Army	and	only	been
came	worker	Australia	new	six	month	then	ask
life	food	taxi	job	us	to	job	is
				stop	get	some	went
11/3/1993 Word inventory and dictation				we	my	do	under
				after	blew	front	
cabs	give	way	ring				
I	was	went	came	28/4/1993 Grandmother's garden			
can	he	airport	book				
key	king	car	bus	when	boy	garden	trying
sing	my	me	into	keep	I	was	a
fishing	so	got	line	looking	my	other	would
we	taxi			take	cat	after	step
				very	with	me	that
				and	she	came	for
				she's	very	angry	heard
				tree	but	got	up
				branch	on	play	the
				grandmother			

After doing the running records on Nick's reading (see §10.3), I analyzed his accuracy rates and self-correction rates. I kept a record of these so I could compare Nick's progress over time. I also kept a list of the books he read. It was encouraging for him to see that he moved from not being able to read books in the beginning to being able to read books after three months. It was interesting to notice that even though the difficulty level of the reading texts was increasing, Nick's accuracy levels were staying high. He still needed to work at his self-correction rates.

Running records summary	
10/3 I was born in Tripoli (self-authored) 92.5% accuracy Self-correction 1:5.5 Funny Story (fellow student) 90.5% accuracy Self-correction 1:4.5 The Rescue (adult booklet) 87% accuracy Self-correction 1:8 7/4 Power—Good and Bad (magazine article) 93.5% accuracy Self-correction 1:9 28/4 The Cobbler (Readers Digest) 87.5% accuracy Self-correction 1:4 5/5 Migration, pt. 1 (reader) 93% accuracy Self-correction 1:3.5	12/5 Migration, pt. 2 (reader) 94% accuracy Self-correction 1:8 19/5 The Hold-up, pt. 1 (reader) 98.5% accuracy Self-correction indeterminate (1 error, not corrected) 26/5 The Hold-up, pt. 2 95.5% accuracy Self-correction 1:3 2/6 The Island of Helos, (pp. 10–13, Jim Hunter Books) 93% accuracy Self-correction indeterminate (9 errors, not corrected) Book record Migration (5/5–12/5) Inspector Holt and the Fur Van (5–19/5) The Hold-up (12/5–26/5) The Island of Helos (26/5–2/6)

For each lesson I kept a summary of what we did and my observations.

Lesson summary: 28/4/1993

Familiar reading: The Rescue

Nick read it well.

Running records: The Cobbler

Nick hadn't read anything since our last lesson, so taking that into account he did very well on this difficult piece.

Accuracy: 87.5%, Self-correction: 1:4, i.e. one self-correction in every 4 miscues.

Goes for meaning, does not attend to ends of words, needs to improve use of phonic strategies.

Also it is hard to correct when English is not his mother tongue.

Talked about the need to look at the ends of words.

Guided silent reading: Shearing

Q. How long does it take a shearer to shear a sheep?

He estimated 5 minutes and was amazed it was only a couple of minutes.

Shared reading: Migration, pp. 2–7

This followed on nicely from the "Whales" we did in G.S.R. last week.

I was worried it was too hard but in context N. seemed to cope well.

Reciprocal questioning:

Done well, a challenge to trick me!

So I was not clear with my answers.

He wasn't sure what to do. We talked about follow up questions.

Text summary:

Done well and quicker than usual.

Good at summarizing now.

Needs help to get sentences grammatically correct.

Talked about words:

migration, immigration, migrant; built: another, weather

reason season, son, sea

baby babies; lady ladies

General:

Tried to get Nick to read at least 5 minutes a day. He will try taking his book in the taxi and reading while waiting for his next customer.

I also wrote my observations and reflections after each lesson in my journal.

Feb 24th: Nick arrived at class with his mobile phone. Chris arrived and offered me his business card. Two stark reminders that I am teaching adults who are whole people who function well in this society without the skills of literacy in English.

I encouraged each student to choose a book that they would like to learn to read from the sections in the shelves marked level 1–4. Nick said it was not worth him choosing any of them as he would not be able to read them. So I encouraged him to chose an easy reader booklet and I read it onto tape for him.

When we did group readings Nick often lost his way so I made sure I sat near him and helped, pointing when he got lost.

March 3rd: Nick had listened to the tape at home of "Bush Childhood" and said it was not slow enough. I encouraged him to re-read and re-read until he could keep up to speed. (I thought I had read it slowly!)

Nick had a go at writing his story and did quite well. He asked me to help him with spelling 'boarding'. Word accuracy was interesting, but more interesting was the sound accuracy—very high for those he attempted.

March 11th: Nick did really well on the running records. The group readings have obviously built his confidence and willingness to have a go. He is highly motivated to learn.

He also brought along the crime-watch section of the local paper. He wanted help to read it so that he did not pick up the wrong people in the taxi. He went to amazing lengths to understand the text even though it was too hard for him. He wants help to get to the end of the article but also to make sure he understands its message.

I also kept copies of Nick's writings. By looking back on these I could see he was writing more and using more complicated words, and writing more words correctly as our lessons continued.

TRIPOLI
I am bRON iN LeBANON iN 1966. I WiN. To THe
LacoL SCHoL and THeN I WiN To THe priaviTe
SCHoLl boARdinG X I complet arisHip eLecTRic I FiNcH
SCHoL iN 1984 I WiN To THe Ame I LeFT LeBANON iN
1986 To sudi ARbe and THan Bak To LeBANON
FOR SORT Time and THen Bak To Niajer LAGOS
AFRICA
and I came To AUSTRALiA iN 1989 and STRAT New
LiFe. Iam WORkeR. iN Tak wAy Food and SATiNe
TAXi DRiVeR. iN Iam Loking For
a JOB secRuty

24 Feb. 1993 (after editing)

I was born in Tripoli in Lebanon in 1966. I went to the local school and then I went to a private boarding school. I completed an electrical apprenticeship and finished school in 1984. Then I went into the Army for 18 months.

I left Lebanon in 1986 and went to Saudi Arabia then back to Lebanon for a short time, then to Lagos in Nigeria in Africa.

I came to Australia in 1989 and started a new life. I am working in a Take-away Food shop and sometimes as a taxi driver. I am looking for work as a security guard and have done a course about crowd control, patrolling, protecting property, and being a guard.

When I Was a young boy my grandmother
she Was trying To,keep The garden Looking Nice.
IUsed GO in said Hre garden. and sTep
On Hre plaTs. oTher Times I Would take my
CaT WiTh me toThe garden play insid TiLL
when The garden. Looking very bed.
and AFTer That my grandmoTher she Come
Looking For me and she's very angry
I heard Hre voice and I Went shraight
To the tree and cLimbed iT.
buT When I GoT up There
The branch I Was on broke.

24 April. 1993 (after editing together)

When I was a young boy my grandmother was always trying to keep her garden looking nice. I used to go inside her garden and deliberately step on her plants. Other times I would take my cat with me to the garden and play inside until the garden looked very bad. After that my grandmother came looking for me and she was very angry.

I heard her voice and I went straight to the tree and climbed it. But when I got up there, the branch I was on broke. I fell down and I was crying a lot. But my grandmother said, "That's not going to change anything. You are in big trouble."

The examples in these last few pages show just one way of doing a case study. There are many other ways it could be done. A lot about reading, writing, teaching, and learning can be learned by doing a case study.

10.5 Involving students in assessment

So far in this chapter, discussion has centred on the teacher doing the assessing and building the student profiles. Education specialists today are moving more towards doing what they call collaborative assessment.

They say assessment should be owned equally by the teachers and the students. It should not be something done to the students but something students do themselves. Students should be helped to reflect upon their own learning (Department of Employment, Education, and Training Handbook, 1993).

Collaborative assessment means the teacher and learner(s) work together to build up a picture of what they know, what they have learned, and what they need to learn next. Much of their assessment activities are grounded in discussion between teacher and learner or learners, and between learners themselves.

For example, in my first lesson with a new adult literacy class I talk about how we learn new things. In the Australian situation we talk about things like learning to drive, sew, knit, swim, or ride a bike. Each student talks of how he learned a new skill. From that we talk about the things that are common to our learning experience such as:

- someone to help
- opportunities to practice many times
- practicing the real thing
- making mistakes
- learning from mistakes
- taking risks
- feeling nervous
- being embarrassed
- gradually getting better and faster

We talk about how learning to read and to write are the same. We need to practice doing the real thing many times. We need people to help, encourage, and support us in our learning. We need to take risks and try new things and make mistakes. We need to keep going and learn from our mistakes. It is not easy. We will be nervous and embarrassed a lot.

In working with students it is important for teachers to tell them what they are doing right, always relating their behaviours back to learning behaviours. "That was good, you went back and corrected yourself there when it didn't make sense. Good readers do that often. It is the right thing to do."

It is also important to take time to reflect back and see progress every now and then because learning is often slow and hard and students often do not feel they are improving When I worked with Nick, I taped one of his early readings for an assignment. Several months later we were taping something else. While I had the tape running I went back and played his earlier reading again. Nick himself commented on how slow he was reading, and on several of the mistakes he made. He could tell from the tape that his reading had improved in speed and in accuracy, and that he was reading more fluently.

Emma talked about her writing progress. She said that when she first wrote her stories she used a dictionary all the time and it was very slow. Her husband told her to give up trying, but now she is not using the dictionary and is writing longer stories and is more confident. Her husband can even see the change in her writing and has told her she must keep up her lessons.

It is important to involve students in the assessment of their progress, to help them understand where they are making progress, what they are doing right, where they have improved, and what they can do now that they could not do before.

Students can be involved in building their own progress file. Have them select samples of their work to go in their profiles at regular intervals. Have them keep a record of the articles or books that they have read and how long they took to read them. Have them keep a list of the words that they used correctly. Have them write a regular entry in their learning journal. Encourage them to think about and talk about their learning progress at regular intervals.

11

Materials Production

In order for people to learn to read they need access to many books so they can practice their reading skills. There are different ways to build up a large supply of reading materials. Some of these are mentioned in chapter 8. Running a writers' workshop is another way of producing reading materials.

11.1 Writers' workshops

There are many ways to run writers' workshops and a lot depends on personal preference and style. Also you must consider local factors such as how long people can take off from their work at one time. Can they take off one or two weeks, or only mornings, or maybe a few days per week? Workshops can be run very differently, depending on what is in focus.

Most workshops I have been involved with were needed because village people wanted to prepare local language reading books for schools. I usually require that people participating in writers' workshops already know how to read and spell their language, but this is not always the case. If there is a mixture of abilities, put the participants in groups—good writers may be partnered with slower writers so that they can help each other. Talk to the writers themselves and see which way they prefer to work.

I prefer to teach writing skills separately from book production skills. I run two different workshops. They require different skills and abilities. Often people who are good writers are not good artists. People who are good at working duplicating machines are not necessarily good writers. Although it is good for each person involved in literature production to understand all the areas involved in it, I do not think it is right to expect that every person should have to develop skills in every activity unless he wants to. Circumstances may require, however, that all these skills be covered at one time.

Following is a sample timetable for a one-week workshop with participants coming every day. The length of the lunch break needs to be agreed on by participants, depending on heat, work, family needs, and so on.

Monday	Tuesday	Wednesday	Thursday	Friday
Welcome or thoughts for the day or devotions				
Spelling issues and practice				
Writing conventions				
the writing process	the need for re-drafting	audience reactions and the unexpected ending	a beginning, middle, and ending	plot, climax
repetitive stories intro	well known stories intro	funny stories intro	animal stories intro	personal experiences intro
break				
writing repetitive stories in groups	writing well-known stories in groups	writing funny stories in groups	individual writing—animal theme, build a word bank	individual writing—personal experience
lunch				
reading editing discussing	editing	editing	editing	show and tell
collect stories from elders	share your two stories with friends	write your own funny story		what next? encourage writers to continue

There are other ways of running a writers' workshop. This is only one suggestion. Design a timetable to suit your situation and purposes. When I did the Dami writers' workshop, we were writing books for a specific purpose so the timetable was different from the one above. We had certain kinds of books we wanted to write for terms 1, 2, 3, and 4 with specific requirements about pictures and the approximate number of sentences per page. We wrote the alphabet stories first, then the longer stories for terms 2 and 3. If some stories grew longer than planned, we considered them for term 4, depending on their topic (see §9.3). Other writers' workshops I have run were not done specifically for the writing of school materials, so we followed a timetable similar to the one above.

Regardless of the workshop timetable, make sure that you expose the writers to good stories of different styles before you expect them to write. The first thing I do is to read several good stories that others have written and that fit in with the theme for that day. I also discuss what it is that makes those stories good ones.

When writers are just starting, it is often better for them to work in groups rather than to work individually. This allows people to work together on the project and works well, especially if it is the first time people have done anything like this in their own language. In some workshops the young men partnered the older men. The older men had a lot of good stories to tell, and the younger men were more comfortable with the task of writing the stories down. Having them work together meant each person could contribute in their own area of skill. Some wonderful stories resulted.

If time and opportunity permits, some workshop leaders like to involve writers in interesting experiences, and then have the writers write stories about those experiences. Some of the best stories that my daughter wrote grew out of her own experiences of life—being brought up among the Djinang people in Australian, living in a small village in Papua New Guinea, mixing with people of different cultures at a mission high school. Writers need a lot of interesting input in order to produce good output. But do not forget they probably have a wealth of experiences to write about already.

A story about a vacuum cleaner

Encourage the writers to think of the audience that they are writing for. Sometimes stories about experiences the writer has had away from the village are not very popular because the village people have not had similar experiences, for example, "A story about a vacuum cleaner," or "Floating down the river," or "A visit to a sheep farm." The writer can often make these stories more interesting. For example, if he writes about his feelings or what he was thinking, it can add interest. But when the people have not had the same experience they may not be interested in reading about it. Or if he writes about unexpected things that happened or gives an unexpected ending, then the readers will find it more worthwhile. Just writing about comings and goings, and what was seen, does not have much interest.

I have found that using the following chart in a writers' workshop helps the writers understand the process they are involved in. I stress that it takes many drafts to get to the finished product.

THE STORY ROAD

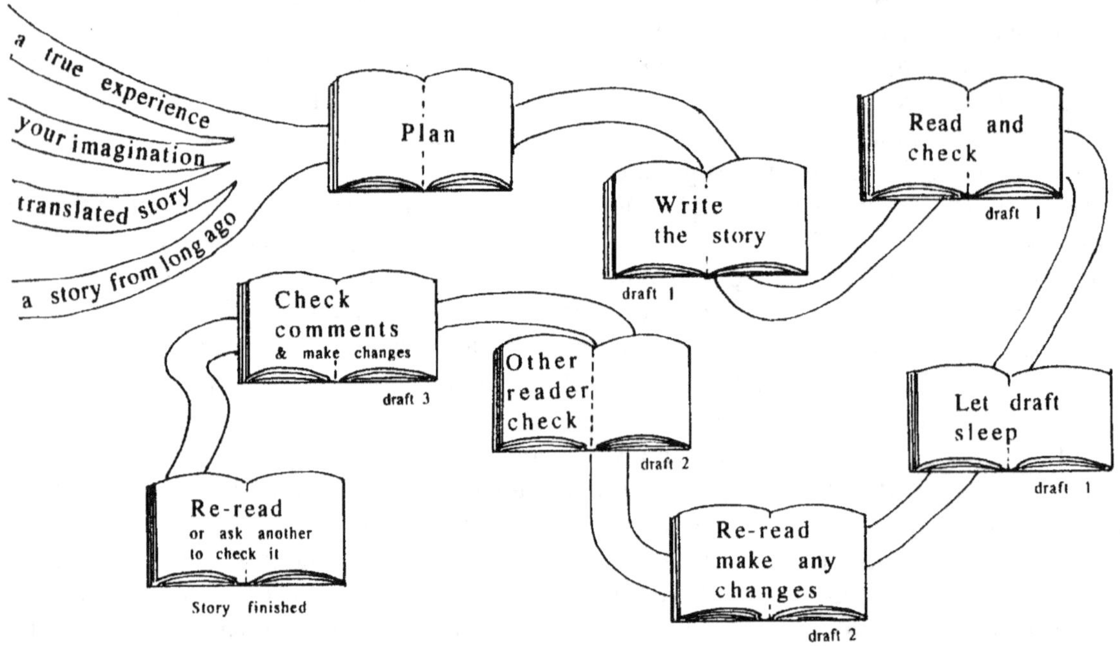

11.2 Writing good stories

When preparing reading materials that are going to be used to teach students to read, there are many kinds of stories that can be written. Some of these are discussed below.

Familiar stories

Familiar stories are ones that are known to the students. People of all cultures have stories that they tell their children or stories that they pass down from generation to generation. The Djinang, Australia, had many stories like this. There was one which told how the moon came into being. The Angor, PNG, have a story about how the crow came to be black and the cockatoo white. The Dami, PNG, have a story about how there came to be so many mosquitoes in their area.

Using these well-known stories in reading classes has advantages such as the following.

- The students already know something about the passage they have to learn to read so that makes it easier for the students to learn. Starting with something that is known and then working towards something which is unknown is a good teaching strategy.

- The students can use what they know to help them work out what the words are. They can use their knowledge to make predictions about the word that is coming next.

For example, look at the Angor story about Cockatoo and Crow (see 6.2). When an Angor person is learning to read the story of the Cockatoo and Crow, he will use all that he already knows about the story to work out the print on the page. For example, when he reads "After Cockatoo finished scraping sago, he..." he expects the next part to be "washed it." And where Cockatoo calls out "Bring the..." the reader expects the next word to be "water!" because that is what people do when making sago. When I read this text for the first time, I had trouble understanding it because I had never seen people making sago. But the Angor have a good knowledge of sago making. Every Angor has this background information in his mind because sago is the main food of that area. So it is easy for the Angor student to get the correct meanings from this text.

Meaningful texts

Stories that are used to teach others to read should make sense. It should not conflict with facts which the students already know.

For example, in one story a butterfly looks for friends to play with. Finally Frog says he will play with butterfly, but as he plays he eats it!

This story did not make sense to the Maiwala people, PNG, because they said frogs do not eat butterflies. So they changed the ending of the story so that it made sense. Instead of the butterfly being eaten, it was captured by a little girl and played with.

Another example was a story about a possum who wanted to fly. In the story the possum was wearing shoes. The people found it difficult to understand why a possum would wear shoes. So make sure that the stories you write make sense to the people who will be reading them.

Stories that use correct language

The language used in the story should be the kind of language that students expect. It should be written in the way they themselves say things and what they hear others saying. When I was testing the fifth draft of the "Big Mouth Frog" story in Takia with some pre-school children, I noticed that they always got stuck in a certain part of the story. This made me look more closely at that part of the page and to listen to what the children were wanting to say instead of the words that were written there. This gave me the clue that there was something not quite right, i.e., the language was not what the children were expecting. When I changed it in the next draft, the children had no trouble with that part and read it without stopping.

When some people write stories for new readers they try to limit the kinds of words they use. They try to use simple words that they think the student will be able to read. This actually may make it harder for the reader. For example, the reader often cannot predict what the words are going to be, or he reads the word that he thinks should be there and then becomes confused when he sees it is different from what he expected.

When writing stories for early reading lessons, be careful to make sure you use real language.

Repetitive stories

Repetitive stories are good for new readers. It is easy for them to learn the repetitive parts and this builds their confidence quickly.

There are many good children's stories that are repetitive. Listed below are some which are used in Papua New Guinea. Some are adapted from English stories, some are adapted from Australian Aboriginal stories, and many were written in PNG. There are many more of these types of stories. If you show people examples of repetitive stories they soon think of stories from their culture that can be written in a similar way.

- Are you my mother?
- I shone the torch
- It's raining
- Children like to play
- Whose friend is he?
- Who sank the boat?
- The very hungry caterpillar
- A big-mouth frog
- Strong pig, Pugi
- Crocodile daydreams

- Let's play
- Selling betel nut
- Will you help me carry the bananas?
- Hide a little further in

Finding repetitive stories suitable for adults is not as easy. If adults wish to learn to read scripture stories, then many of the following stories could be modified and made into repetitive stories.

- The creation story. This story repeats the following words several times: "On the _____ day...and it was good."
- The animals go into the ark
- Abraham asking the Lord not to destroy Sodom
- The plagues sent on Egypt. When each plague happened Moses said, "Let my people go."
- Joshua and the walls of Jericho
- Jesus calls the disciples

If you cannot find repetitive stories for adults, then you can accomplish the same thing by reading the same story several times (repeated readings). Using repetition helps the students learn the words easily. They gradually begin to break the repetitive sentences into parts and they recognise words from those sentences in other parts of the story.

Humorous stories

Humorous stories are always popular. They hold the reader's interest and make the reading experience enjoyable. Humorous stories can be about real experiences or about things that have happened to people in real life. For example, the story of the night Luwe woke up and went outside to relieve himself. He met a buffalo unexpectedly and ended up riding it naked through the village! Or a story about the time the first missionary came to an area and while on patrol he went into the bush to relieve himself. He was so ignorant he sat down on a stinging nettle. The story is still told with glee. Or the time that Grandpa encountered the wild pig yet again! He found out when he was up the tree that this time it was Grandma tricking him. He was not impressed!

Some cultures have a particular style of funny story. The story is not true, and it is so unbelievable that people think it is funny. "How to catch a pig" is one of these stories.

Remember, things that are funny in one culture are not always funny in another culture. You need to have the local people write these stories in a way that fits with their sense of humour.

Stories that involve the emotions

The stories written for students to read should involve their emotions. Maybe they have had similar experiences to those of the main character in the story. Maybe the reader can predict what is going to happen next and wonder what the main character's response will be.

"Our Sides Ached" is a story of two girls who decide to go fishing at night. Their uncle saw them going and decided to play a trick on them. Down by the river he frightened them. They ran away. As they were crossing the river, one of the girls held her bush knife up high in the air, instead of her coconut torch because she was so frightened.

The torch dangled in the river and went out. They ran the rest of the way home in the dark. When they told their uncle what had happened, he told them it was he who had frightened them. When they realized what had happened, they laughed and laughed until their sides ached.

This story involves the reader at several levels. He knows that the uncle is up to something but he wonders what it is. Being frightened in the dark is something everyone is afraid of, and doing something silly when we are frightened is something we can all identify with. And everyone certainly would laugh with the girls at how silly they were to be frightened over such a little thing. Involving the emotions of the reader is important for good story writing.

Stories that build interest

Interest can be created in a story by making sure the story has a good beginning, a middle, and an interesting ending which may be unexpected. Stories should build up to an exciting event, and often the event is different from what is expected.

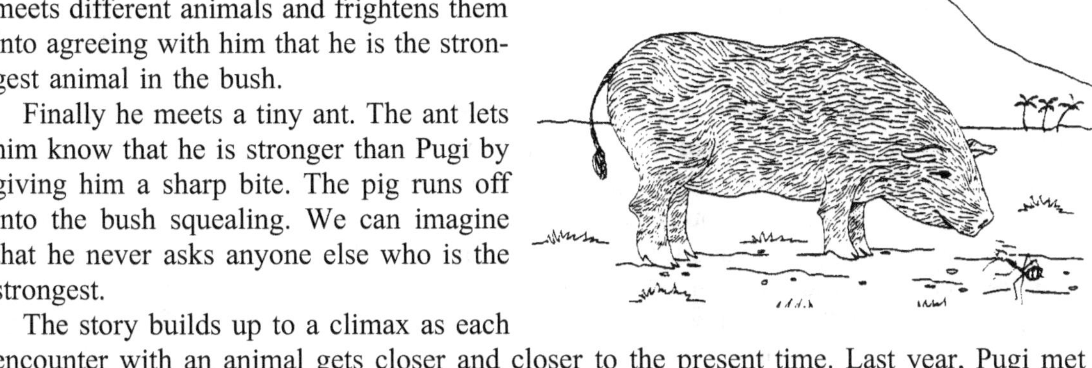

The story "Strongpela Pik, Pugi" takes us on a journey through the bush. Pugi meets different animals and frightens them into agreeing with him that he is the strongest animal in the bush.

Finally he meets a tiny ant. The ant lets him know that he is stronger than Pugi by giving him a sharp bite. The pig runs off into the bush squealing. We can imagine that he never asks anyone else who is the strongest.

The story builds up to a climax as each encounter with an animal gets closer and closer to the present time. Last year, Pugi met a cassowary. Last month... last week... yesterday... now... so the reader knows that something is going to happen and it is going to happen soon. What actually happens is the opposite of what the reader expects. A small animal ends up showing a big animal that he is not afraid, and so he can do something unexpected.

Stories with deeper meanings

There are some children's stories that I used to read to my classes when I was a schoolteacher. I read them to my own children when they were young and I still enjoy reading them. My daughters still remember some of these stories and if they see the book in a store they will buy it and bring it home to enjoy, even now when they are adults. These stories are still interesting no matter how many times you read them.

Usually these stories have more meaning to them than what is on the surface, and each time you read them you see something else that you had not seen before.

"Bossy Dog" is one of those stories. I knew this must be a good Takia story when Malio, the author, told me that the children liked the story and that he had seen them walking down the road acting the story out.

It is the story of five friends who go off to the bush. Dog takes control of the proceedings and starts issuing orders to everyone else. "You carry the knife, you carry the fire, you collect the wood, you get the breadfruit, you go up the tree and get coconuts for us to drink." Everyone obeys because they are afraid of the boss who is acting just like a 'white master' used to act, issuing orders while standing with his hands on his hips. While they are eating and drinking, a fight breaks out between two of the animals, and all the noise that they make brings people chasing after them. Bossy Dog and his followers are not so confident now, they become scared and run away into the bush.

But this story is not just a story about some animals. Malio shared with me that the story is telling about things that they used to do as children, and things that children still do today and ways they used to treat each other. So it has a deeper meaning.

No matter what kind of story you write, it is important to keep in mind the people who are going to read your story. Think about the kinds of stories they like to read. If you are writing for children, be careful to make the stories easily understood. If you are writing for adults make sure that they will not think the story is a children's story and therefore not worth learning to read. Write about things that are known to your audience and things that you know they can understand.

11.3 Materials production workshops

Once you have many stories that have been checked and prepared for printing, you may wish to have a materials production workshop and get groups working together to produce multiple copies of the stories. Some people like to do this at the same time as the writers' workshop, but I like to keep the two things separate (see §11.1).

One advantage of keeping the writing of stories separate from printing stories is that you give plenty of time for the written stories to be well checked with a variety of people. Some books I have worked on have taken six months to get to a stage where they are written well. Others may take only a few weeks. But time is needed between the first writing of the story and the printing for editing, changing, improving, and seeing how others react when they read the story. (See §10.2 for more details.) Following is a sample timetable for a one week production workshop.

Monday	Tuesday	Wednesday	Thursday	Friday
Devotions or thoughts for the day				
Before cutting the stencil: editing, layout, checking	Tips to remember on stencil cutting	Reminders about printing	Using a duplicator	Layouts: side stapled, centre staple Making mockups
How to cut stencils: writing and drawing	Cut the remaining stencils	Collating, trimming, covering and stapling	Print a book as a class using a duplicator	Cutting without a paper cutter
Break				
Cutting first stencil	Cutting How to use a silk screen	Complete printing, collating, stapling		Shells to follow Making a stencil guide
Lunch				
Preparing to print	Printing on silk screens		Maintaining and cleaning: duplicators and silk screens	Complete any printing jobs that need to be done Cleaning

11.4 Putting books together

On the side or in the centre?

There are two main ways that a book can be put together. One way staples the book along one side. The other way folds the pages down the centre, opens them out again, and puts staples in the crease of the centre fold.

There are advantages and disadvantages to both methods as shown in the chart below. These need to be thought about before you choose which way you are going to make your books. Ultimately it becomes a matter of personal preference which way you make books.

Advantages

Side stapled
- easier to design and collate
- better for thicker books
- better if printing only one side

Centre stapled
- sit flatter, so better for new readers
- can only be used for thinner books

Disadvantages

Side stapled
- do not sit open very well
- front and back pages can become loose, or get lost
- might require binding tape on the side, which is an extra expense

Centre stapled
- centre pages can become loose, or get lost
- can have problems with the previous page's print showing through

If you do not have a long-arm stapler or swivel stapler which allows centre stapling to be done easily, but you still want to centre staple your book, you can do so by using an ordinary stapler and a bunch of newspapers.

Put or fold the newspapers into a pile that is thicker than the length of the prongs on the staple. Open out the book you wish to staple on top of the newspapers face down. Open up the stapler you are using. Push the staples through the centre fold of your book into the newspapers.

When you have put in all the staples required for that book, pull the book away from the newspapers and turn it over. Fold the staple prongs down with a knife or a blade of the scissors. Place a piece of scrap unprinted paper on top of the staple prongs. Hammer the prongs tightly closed. Then remove the scrap paper. It is there only to keep the page clean when the hammer head hits the staple. Do the hammering on the newspaper pile so that you do not leave staple indents on your new tabletop or floor boards!

I have stapled all sizes of books, even Big Books, in this way. I would not recommend it, however, as a method to be used when there are many books to be stapled because it is very slow. Print shops usually have machines that centre staple so you can always pay to get the job done, or ask to use their machine when it is not in use.

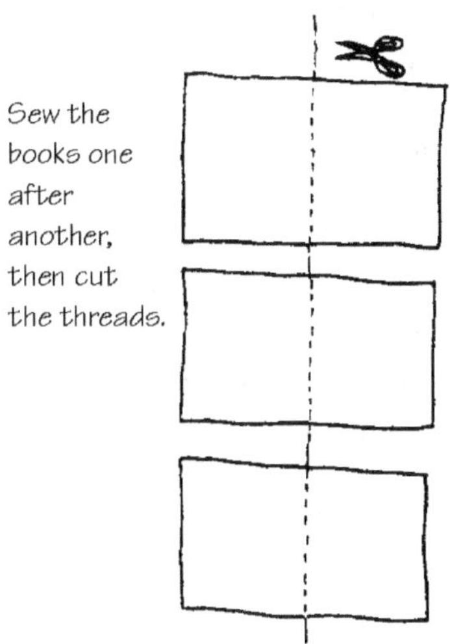

Another way of putting books together is to sew the pages together. Many literacy workers do this when they are working in moist, humid areas because staples rust very quickly. Print shops usually have machines that will sew books together. Some people have used a household sewing machine or a hand-wind sewing machine. Sewn books have the advantage that the middle pages do not fall out as easily when they are used a lot.

Size

The size of a book is largely determined by the purpose of the publication, the people for whom the book is intended, what its use is to be, and how much it will cost. For example, if you want to produce something that will be carried everywhere and used a lot you may wish to produce a small booklet. Some people like to produce such materials in 'pocket' size. Small books are also cheaper to make. However think carefully about the following things.

1. Do the people carry books in their pockets? In the village where we work, such things would go into string or coconut palm bags.
2. Do the readers have good eyesight, and are their homes well lit? Many pocket-sized books have very small print. Many people prefer books to have a larger sized print because they do most of their reading at night using a small lamp, candle, or torch light.
3. Is the book likely to be one that people will carry about? Many books that I have produced recently have been for class sets. Such books remain in classrooms, library boxes, or teachers' boxes.
4. Are the potential readers of the book new readers? When making books for new readers, I prefer to have larger print and more white space on the page. Therefore, the books need to be larger than pocket sized. Larger print is easier for a beginning reader to read. He also feels more confident to try and read what is on a page if there are not too many words on that page.

5. Are illustrations an important part of the book? What is the best size for those illustrations? I have seen some beautiful books that work well because of their illustrations, as well as their interesting stories. The illustrations are an important part of the book. To see these books shrunk to a very small size seems to ruin them.
6. Are the books to be read by individuals or groups? If the books are to be used by two or more people, then I think they should be no smaller than half an A4 size of paper. Books that are meant to be shared should be large enough so that all members of the group sharing the story can read it easily. This applies to the illustrations and to the print. If we want students reading together, classes reading together, or partners reading together, we do not want the books to be too small. Big Books (A3 size or bigger) are good for class reading, while full page A4 sideways is a good size for two people or more to read.

There are times when I would choose to use small-sized booklets, for example, things like the Sunday or weekly readings, small devotional tracts, books to go with cassettes, and so on. The Sunday readings books are mainly designed for people who can already read and are usually what I call 'quick and dirty' publications. They are put together very quickly, quite often without a cover and as cheaply as possible. They are designed to be read only a few times during that particular week only.

Sometimes it is good to choose a standard size for your books. This can be important for storage purposes in the classroom and elsewhere. A size that fits or stands well in library shelves or library boxes is a good standard size. If you are doing a series of books such as song books, primers, study guides, or pastoral helps, it may be good to make these books the same size so they can be sold and kept in sets and easily identified as belonging together.

Remember, also, that the page can be turned sideways. One day I produced a book for pre-school children and it looked all right. But my friend came along and turned the page on its side and said it would look much better that way! And it did!! "Of course," I said to myself, "that is the way it should go!" I had been so busy trying to meet deadlines and getting a lot of books on to the computer that I had not thought about changing the book to sideways print. But sometimes books look so much better when produced sideways. This is another option you should think about when making decisions about the size and layout of books. After producing a lot of books, you will begin to get a feel for what size and shape a book should be.

Setting up a page

Whenever you are making a book, you will find it easier to work on if you first make a 'mock-up' of the finished book. You can do this using any size of scrap paper. It does not have to be the same size that the book is going to be. A mock-up is different from a draft copy of the book. A draft copy is an exact representation of what the book will be like when it is finished.

A mock-up is a rough copy to help you make sure you print the right thing on the right page. A mock-up is particularly helpful if you are making a book that has printing on both the front and back side of the pages. Once you have made the mock-up you can pull it apart to find out what should be printed on each page.

If you choose to do some centre stapled books, you need to check carefully that the right things go on the right pages.

Remember, a centre-stapled book is made up of pages that are printed on the front and the back and then folded in half. Therefore each piece of paper becomes four pages of the book—two from the front of the sheet of paper and two on the back of the sheet of paper.

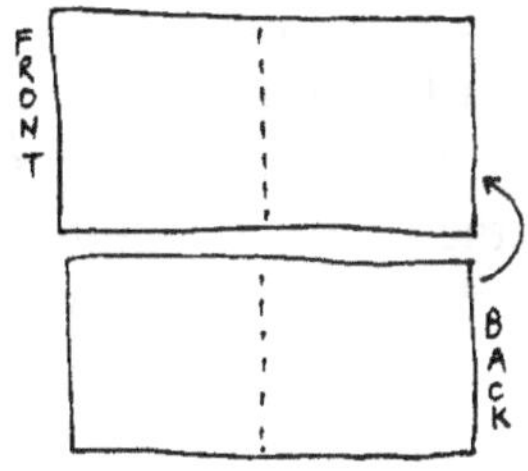

A stencil or camera-ready copy needs to be made for both the front and the back of each page. A 20 page book will need 10 stencils. There will be two pages on each stencil. If necessary, some pages can be left blank at the end of the book.

Because of the way the books are put together—folded in the centre—page 1 can be printed with say page 44, and page 2 can be printed with page 43 etc. It can be complicated trying to work out the pagination (how the pages go together) without a mock-up.

Checking pagination before stapling

No matter what system you use for putting the pages together after they have been printed, it is important to check that each book has all the pages and that they are in the correct order before it is stapled. It is easy to overlook this step because you are busy getting things ready, and printing and collating are time consuming jobs. But it is important that your products—the books you make—are the best you can make them in order to encourage people to want to read them. Sometimes books are put together by teams of people helping each other. It is easy to go ahead and staple a lot of books and then find some sections of those books are upside down, back to front, pages missing, and so on. It is very annoying for teachers to be using books with students and find pages missing or upside down. It is then time consuming to have to undo the staples and re-order pages, so it is much better to check that it is all correct first.

Preface versus postface

Sometimes the organisations that we work with require that we put extra information into books which is of no interest to the readers. Such information may include things like what language the book is written in, where the language is spoken, how many speakers there are of that language, who paid for the cost of printing the book, how the book is to be used, how many copies were printed, when, where, etc. This information is often printed in a language that the person using the book does not know. It is usually put in the preface of a book which is at the front of the book. Some people, however, choose to include the information at the back of the book (called a postface) because the information is often not important to the majority of readers, is in a language they do not know, and interrupts the lesson flow. I think a postface is the better place for such information. Before you decide which to use, you will need to find out if your organisation has a policy on how to handle this. You may need to explain your reasons for wanting to have a postface rather than a preface. Most administrators are willing to be flexible on this point, as long as the information they need to see is contained somewhere in the book.

Covers

Covers can be quite expensive and not every publication needs one. Friends of ours wanted to publish the daily readings of the church calendar and make these freely available to anyone who wanted one. People were not willing to buy one but they would take one and use it if it were free. So, in order to keep costs down, they produced them on cheap paper and did not put covers on them. I thought this was a great idea as the booklets only had a short life anyway. It also meant the scriptures were being read more widely and the translators could afford to pay for this ministry without it becoming a burden to them. It also meant the scriptures were not permanent and could be changed if people gave them feedback which indicated that changes to the text were necessary. Sometimes booklets that we put together only have a short life. A student writes in them so only one person uses them. There is no reason why such booklets need strong covers.

Another time I saw some children's books for a TPPS library corner without covers. They had been thrown together very quickly. The pages were uneven sizes and the covers had not been printed or used. Each book was stapled together poorly. I was very sad because I felt that this was saying to the children that "any old thing will do, your language is not as important as the national language, your village stories are not important." Also, these books were meant to last for several years and be used by many children. Taking the time and effort to put the books together well and give them the protection of a good cover in this case was very important if they were to have a long useful life.

12

Teaching Writing

12.1 Formation of letters

There are many different ways to teach writing, and students vary in their needs for formal programmes. It is important to determine what the students can already do and build upon that. It is best to start teaching printing first and transfer to "running writing" after students handle printing confidently and fluently.

Some years ago Des Oatridge made the following observations when he was working with the Binumarien people in the Eastern Highlands of PNG.

> The ability to write seems to reinforce the reading skill. Yet there are problems. The writing skill is different from the reading skill. There is the interference of:
>
> - pencil control
> - motor control of hands and mind
> - slowing speech down to writing speed
> - mind working faster than hand
> - fear of making bad letters
> - some letters being more difficult than others
> - applying a sound to each letter
>
> Some people in the village in which we live, especially women who had never been out in the wider world, began to get mental blocks against letters they found hard to write. Slight differences in letters on reading charts would puzzle the students. E.g., 'm' has only one more leg than 'n' and to a new reader this difference is hard to recognise. (Oatridge 1980:34)

Today the importance of the connection between reading and writing is widely acknowledged.

Some people like to teach writing ahead of reading. Oatridge was thinking along this line when he developed his pre-writing programme.

> If the pupil was completely familiar with each letter and could write it easily, then when he found it in the primer page, he would not only recognise it more easily but he could also write it without fear and treat it as an old friend. (Oatridge 1980:35)

I prefer to teach writing along with reading so that one is reinforcing the other. The teaching of one is supporting the teaching of the other. As the students are taught to read, they focus on a certain letter. They are taught how to say it, see it, and write it. The trial Dami prep school programme, in Madang Province PNG, was designed in such a way that in term 1 the students were introduced to each letter of the alphabet through stories and through the pre-writing lessons. In term 2 they met each letter more formally in primer lessons and writing lessons and their letter formation skills improved a bit more. Then in the third term all the letters were retaught and hopefully by that time their letter formation would be neater, tidier, and more fluent.

In his article (1980), Des shared how he did his early writing lessons.

1. Each student is issued a plywood chalk board (measuring about 46cm x 40cm), a piece of chalk, and an eraser or piece of cloth. All the students sit cross-legged, their customary way of sitting. With my back to them and facing a large blackboard, I say, in the students' mother tongue,

   "Now copy me and make a long mark with your chalk on this (left) side of your chalk board." I demonstrate and then check each student.

   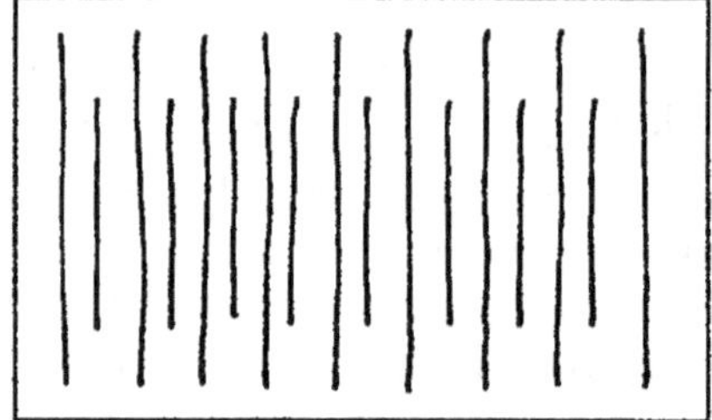

   "Now close to that mark and running alongside it (parallel) make another **short** mark." I demonstrate and check each student.

"Now draw next and alongside this short mark, a long mark and then beside it a short mark and so on till you get right across the board." I demonstrate and check everyone.

"Everyone erase!" This is enjoyed by all!

The only thing I require in this exercise is that one line is longer and the next is shorter, how short doesn't matter.

2. "Next draw a long line down the (left) side of the board and then a short one beside it near the top of the long line."

   I demonstrate and check each student.

   "Everyone erase!"

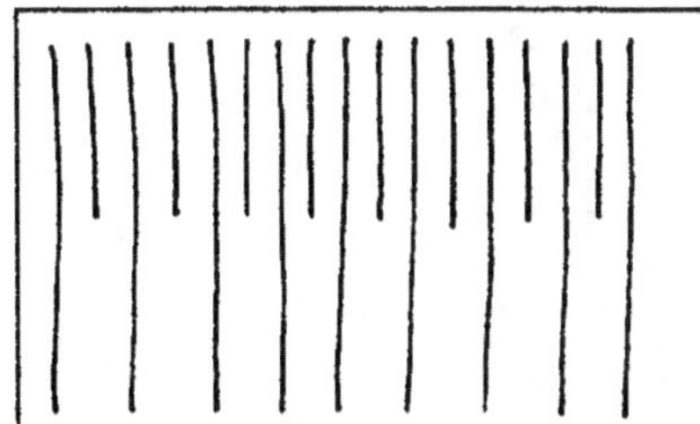

3. "Next draw a line down the left side of the board and a short one parallel to it at the bottom."

   I demonstrate and check each student.

   "Everyone erase!"

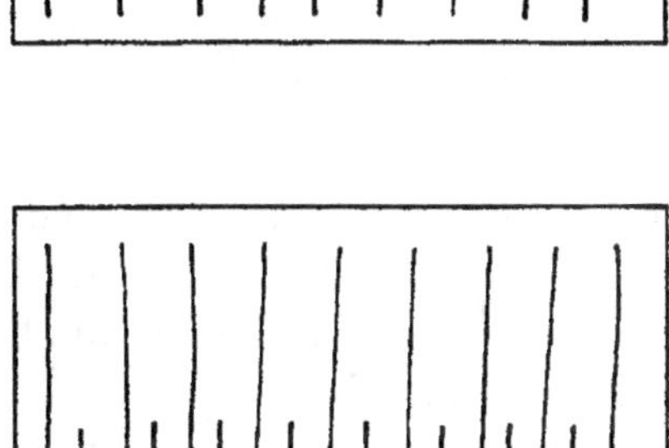

4. "Next draw a long line and then a short one parallel to it in the **middle**."

   I demonstrate and check each student.

   "Everyone erase!"

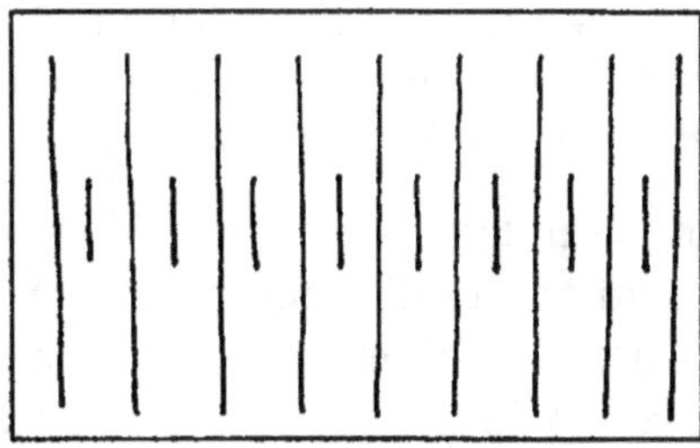

5. "Make a long mark down the left edge of the board and a short mark at the top. Next make a long mark followed by a short mark in the centre. Now a long mark followed by a short mark at the bottom."

   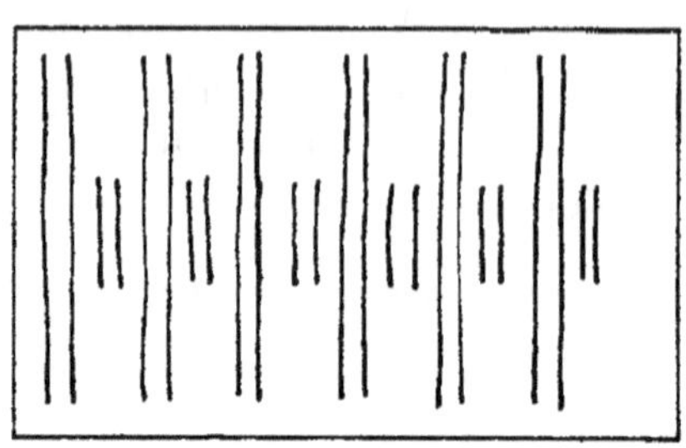

   I demonstrate and check each student.

   "Everyone erase!"

6. "Next draw two long lines starting at the left edge of the board, followed by two short lines in the middle."

   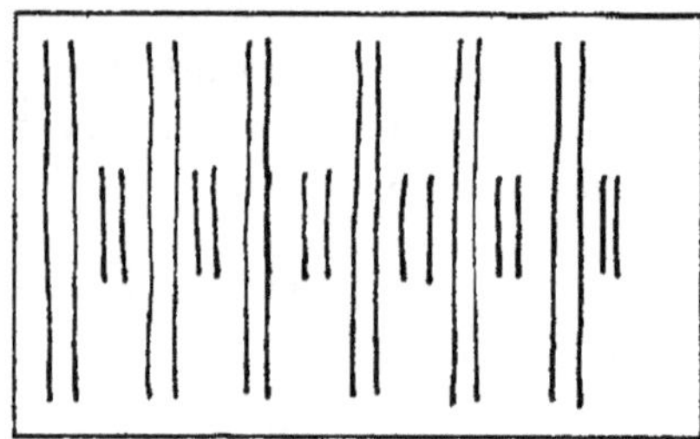

   I demonstrate and check each student.

   "Everyone erase!"

7. "Next draw three lines starting at the left edge of the board, followed by three short lines in the middle of the board."

   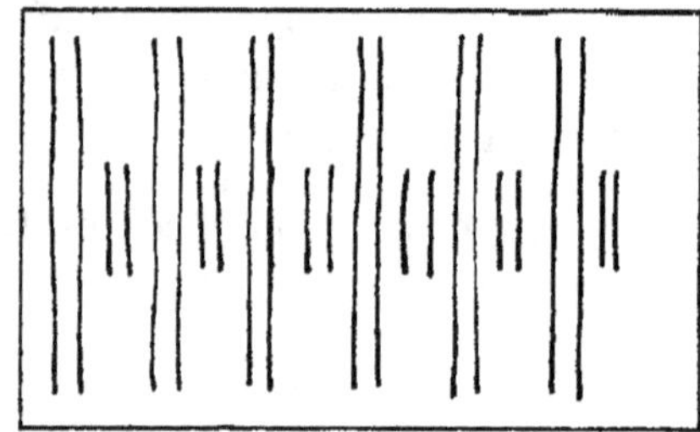

   I demonstrate and check each student.

   "Everyone erase!"

This is a little difficult for adults who are not number oriented but it prepares the way for talking about the different number of 'legs' in letters such as 'r', 'n' and 'm'.

Working in this manner, Oatridge was able to help the students feel comfortable with the blackboard and chalk, and they were beginning to realise what was meant by the top, the middle, and the bottom of the board and were able to respond accurately. They began to feel comfortable with trying to follow the examples, making mistakes and trying again.

After doing the above exercises, Oatridge did similar exercises but worked across the board moving from left to right, as in the diagrams below.

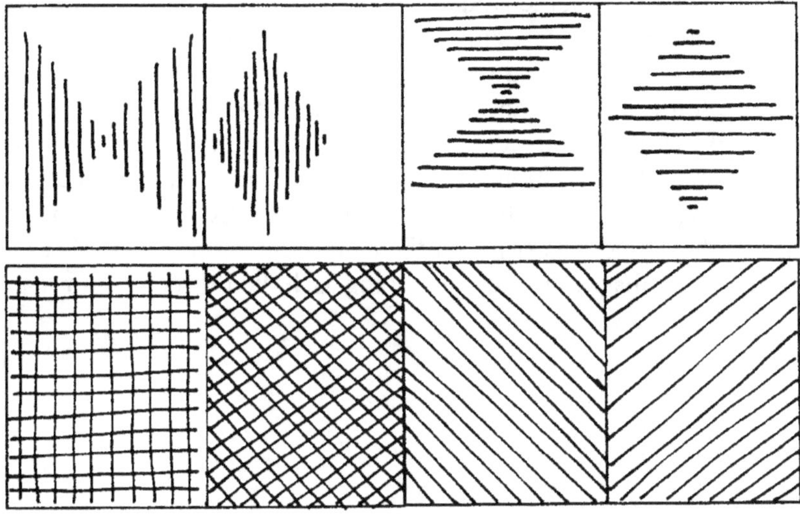

Oatridge also says:

> Exercises in creating designs can be endless. These give motor control and teach relative position within the area of the board...It is good to keep reminding students, especially adults, that these exercises are to make their hands agile...All vertical lines should start from the top. All horizontal and diagonal lines should begin from the left and move toward the right. It is best to teach direction by **example** and by **doing** rather than by saying it in words. (Oatridge 1980:38)

On the second day, Oatridge began to introduce exercises using shapes which are used in the actual formation of letters. Then in following lessons he gradually introduced every letter of the alphabet.

It is important to use the print script that is the standard for the education department in your province or country. This will vary from place to place. A sample of the PNG standard is included at the end of this section.

Also included are examples of some letter formation activities that can be done with students. Again it is important to match these activities to what is suitable for your area. Design your own set of exercises based on the alphabet of your area. For example, some languages do not have *f* in the alphabet so there is no need to teach the formation of this letter. If the letter is needed in the national language, then it should be taught when students are transfering their literacy skills to that language. Always make sure that any exercises you design are based on the way the letters of your alphabet are written.

What should you teach the students at the beginning? What approach to teaching should you use? The answer to these two questions depends on what stage of development your students are in their writing skills. Some students may be ready to learn to write the letters right away without practicing making lines, circles, and shapes. Others will need the practice to be able to learn to control their hand and eye in ways they are not used to.

In each writing lesson it is important that the activities that you do are meaningful. If the activity is meaningful it will link the actual practice of the formation of letters to writing real words and making real communication. Writing lessons should always end with the teacher and the students writing words that contain the letters that are being taught. It is important that the students see the connection between their practice activities and their writing of real words. They need to feel that what they are doing is linked directly into learning to write words.

Following are some examples of letter formation activities. Start with letters made up of lines.

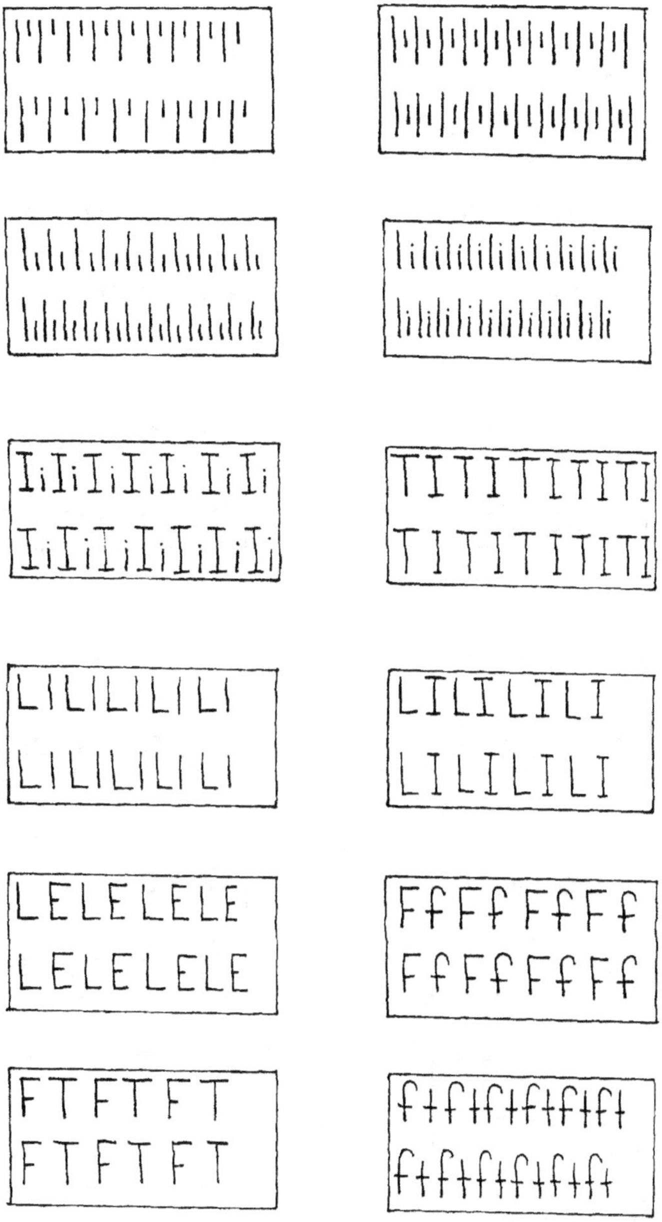

Next introduce letters made using circles, and then circles and lines.

oeoeoeoe
oeoeoeoe

OoOoOoOo
OoOoOoOo

esesesesese
esesesesese

aoaoaoao
aoaoaoao

adadadada
adadadada

agagagag
agagagag

odododod
odododod

dgdgdgdg
dgdgdgdg

ososososo
ososososo

SsSsSsSsSs
SsSsSsSsSs

OGOGOG
OGOGOG

Then introduce letters with ‘tunnels’ or ‘wings’. Find a way of talking about these shapes in your language. Do not forget to teach the capital letters too.

mn mn mn mn
mn mn mn mn

nr nr nr nr nr
nr nr nr nr nr

mr mr mr mr
mr mr mr mr

un un un un un
un un un un un

Uu Uu Uu Uu
Uu Uu Uu Uu

Ww Ww Ww
Ww Ww Ww

w y w y w y w
w y w y w y w

WYWYWYW
WYWYWYW

NMNMNM
NMNMNM

NANANAN
NANANAN

DRDRDRDR
DRDRDRDR

DBDBDBDB
DBDBDBDB

BRBRBRBR
BRBRBRBR

k<k<k<k<k<
k<k<k<k<k<

KkKkKkKk
KkKkKkKk

It is important to use the standard script used in the education system in your country. Below is the one recommended in Papua New Guinea, taken from *Prep School Teacher's Guide*, p. 8.

12.2 The process of writing

Writing is a process. It is a skill that will flourish only if students "are free to experiment with written language. Like reading, writing is an extension of spoken language and, like all activity in language, it is a process that will develop with use...the best way to learn to write is by writing" (Rowe and Lomas 1984:1).

In the last few decades the idea of students learning to write by writing has been more widely recognized. Also teachers have talked more about the writing process with their students as they are learning to write. Teachers explain that a writer does not take up pen and paper and write a piece of writing that is perfect from the start. He does not write a piece that is without errors, crossings out, mistakes, or reorderings. New writers often find this hard to believe, because they are always presented with other people's writing that looks perfect to them, so they presume that their writing must be perfect too, from the start.

New writers need to understand that writing is a process. They need to know that the skill of writing is something that is learned over many years. They need to know that people become good writers after many years of practice and hard work. They need to know that it is perfectly normal when writing anything to go through a process of drafting, editing, conferencing, rewriting, re-editing, reconferencing and so on, before it is satisfactory. I have definitely found this to be so in my own writing. Any piece of writing I do for an audience other than myself, except for personal letters, always goes through that kind of process.

Mem Fox, a famous Australian writer of children's storybooks, talks about her drafting experiences.

> The storyteller-in-me insists that the writer-in-me writes well. I know the importance of beginnings and endings so I try to hear an anonymous reader reading my words aloud: "Once upon a time but not very long ago, deep in the heart of the Australian bush lived two possums. Their names were Hush and Grandma Poss." For those of you interested in the writing process I re-wrote that first paragraph twenty-three times and literally cried with frustration in my attempt to get it right. (Fox 1986:39)

It is interesting to hear other writers speak about their experiences:

> Ernest Hemingway: "I rewrote the ending to Farewell to Arms, the last page of it thirty-nine times before I was satisfied."

> Robert Graves: "I wrote it (The White Goddess) in six weeks. It took me ten years to revise it. And I about tripled its length."

> Theodor S Geisel (Dr. Seuss): "To produce a 60 page book, I may easily write 1,000 pages before I'm satisfied."

> William H Gass: "I work not by writing but rewriting. Each sentence has many drafts. Eventually there is a paragraph. This gets many drafts. Eventually there is a page. This gets many drafts. And so on."
>
> John Steinbeck: "When I face the desolate impossibility of writing 500 pages a sick sense of failure falls on me and I know I can never do it. Then gradually I write one page then another. One day's work is all I can permit myself to contemplate."

Writing is not easy. It requires a lot of effort and reworking of words, sentences, and paragraphs before it can be shared in public.

Writing is communication. It is putting a message on paper for someone else to gain meaning from. As such, the writer needs to follow certain conventions (ways of putting the marks on the page) that have been agreed upon. These differ with different writing systems.

When I worked with the Djinang people in Australia, my 'Granny' would come to me with a page that looked like this:

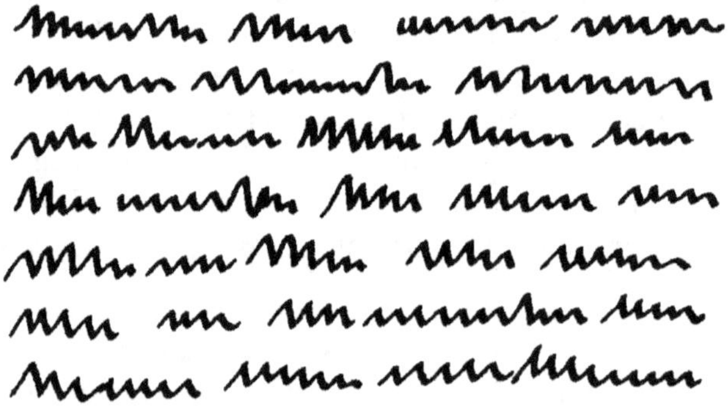

She would ask me to read the message to her. Well I guess she had learned that writing is putting messages on paper for others to read! She had also learned that you write from one side of the page to the other, and one line underneath the other. But there were a lot of other conventions she had not learned yet. She had not learned about the different letters in the alphabet and how to write them, that messages were put down on paper in groups of words, that she could decide what the message would be and put it there herself, that a certain word would always be written the same way and things like that. There were a lot of conventions she needed to learn about writing.

Steps in the writing process

The process of writing can be a fairly complex process. Good writing usually begins with something that needs to be recorded on paper or something that the writer wants to write about. The ultimate end in writing something is a successful sharing of the writing with a friend or other audience. There are many steps in between having something to write and a successful outcome to the writing. Following are the steps of the writing process.

Before writing. Good writing flows out of interesting experiences and observations of things in the real world and a desire to record some of these on paper. Some writing is purely imaginary and not true, but even these are based on understandings that the authors have built through their life experiences. The author may write about things he has experienced in real life himself, or has read about, or experienced through music, drama, video, film, or poetry.

It is important to have a wealth of experiences before you can write about them. It is difficult to write about horse riding if you have never experienced it, or never seen a horse, or never seen other people riding.

As well as experiencing what is going to be written about, writers need to feel comfortable with the basics of what is called the mechanics of writing, that is, how to form letters, knowing to write from left to right on the page, writing in sentences and paragraphs, starting with an attention-grabbing introduction, and working towards a conclusion that is satisfying to the writer and the reader. You may wish to spend some time each writing session talking about one of the mechanical types of things which writers need to learn.

Before writing sessions, it is good to spend time with students talking about things they might like to write about, because some students take awhile to get to the stage of knowing what they want to write about. Or you might read things that others have written and give students ideas of things they can write about.

Other students do not need to be encouraged to write. They already have stories they want to put down on paper

When talking about a writing topic, it is good to build wordbanks during the discussion. Wordbanks are lists of words or expressions that are central to the topic being discussed—words that may be used by the students in their writing. Wordbanks can be displayed on the blackboard, on charts, or on cards. Some teachers go to the extra effort of writing the wordbanks on cards cut into special shapes related to the topic. These are hung in the room for students to refer to as needed. Note the following examples.

Words that make me sick

worried	hungry	furious
nervous	hurried	surprised
hurt	sick	anxious
confused	angry	lazy

(from Rowe and Lomas 1984)

The pig got into the garden

One day we were reading Hwa's story about not being able to read the storybook to her daughter and then heard that her mother had been taken to the hospital and operated on for cancer. This turned the conversation to the difficulties migrants face when they come to Australia.

Our wordbank looked like the following:

After the discussion and making the wordbank, each student wrote their personal response to the difficulties migrants face. They checked their spellings of words with the words on the wordbank as needed.

When teaching writing it is important that the teacher creates an environment that encourages students to write well. Students should be encouraged to try, to take risks, and have their efforts accepted as valuable. They should be suppported when they experience difficulties and not left to struggle for too long. They should be free to ask for help from other students in the class and to give help to others.

Drafting. Students need to understand that their first writings are considered a draft and that these can usually be improved. I teach that the aim of the first draft is to concentrate on getting thoughts down on paper, not worrying too much about writing conventions, or spelling mistakes, or handwriting neatness. These things can be worked on in later drafts. I show students the numerous drafts of my own writings; each draft is an improvement of the previous draft.

It is important that students have plenty of paper to do their drafts on. This could be a problem in third world countries. Stockpile paper if possible—use the back of computer paper, the back of printshop discards, cut up butchers paper and brown wrapping paper from bales of sugar, etc. Ask the provincial education department for help in provision of exercise books. Make sure that both sides of the paper are written on before it is thrown away.

With young children drawings are an important part of their story writing and should be encouraged as part of the writing process. Students who are young may find it easier to draw their story first and write the text later.

In the first draft writers are concentrating on getting their thoughts on to paper. During this time they should be encouraged to use different strategies to cope with any spelling problems they meet. They can use invented spellings or leave a blank or a space and ask for help later. (See "Teaching spelling" and "Spelling strategies" later in this section.)

In early lessons students tend to write shorter texts using mainly words that they know how to spell. As they gain more confidence they write longer texts and will try using words they do not know how to spell. Students should be encouraged to not be afraid of words they cannot spell. If they keep interrupting the writing process because they get hung up on words they cannot spell, then they will become very frustrated and their writing will suffer.

Editing. Once the drafting process has been completed, the writer needs to self-edit his work. Some self-editing was probably done in the first draft. Once the first draft is completed, it is good for the writer to read through the complete draft to check that it is saying what he intended. Rowe and Lomas (1984:37) suggest the following process.

After writing:

- read it aloud
- read it to yourself
- read it to the wall

and ask

- does it make sense for me; for the audience
- does it say what I want it to say
- do I like it

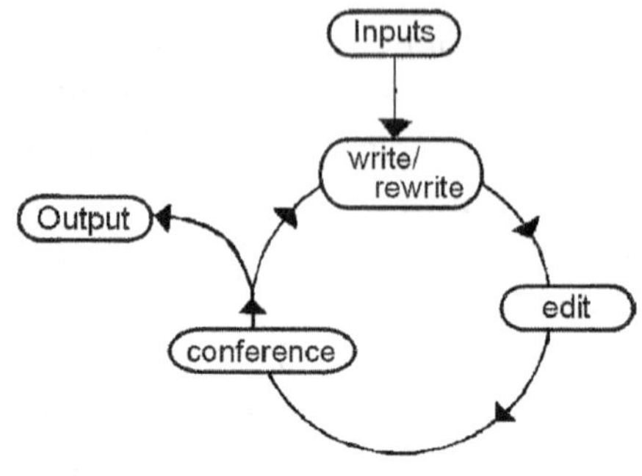

It is often good to let a piece of writing 'sleep' for a day or two and then come back fresh and edit it again. Or share the writing with a friend who may point out things that are unclear or parts where more information is needed.

While editing, the writer may find places where it is necessary to add more detailed information, to cut out some parts, cross-out, rearrange words or sentences, expand a simple sentence, choose a better title, change an ending, or tell more about the story. All these editing strategies need to be demonstrated and taught to the students.

In the process of working on a writing piece the writer may go through the write-edit-conference loop many times before being ready to publish.

Conferencing. Conferencing is the term used by writers and teachers for talking with someone else in order to improve a person's writing. It can be done between two people—the writer and a friend or a student and a teacher—or between one person and a small group, or between one person and a class. Most conferencing is done between a writer and a friend.

Conferencing helps the writer to see if the meanings of his message are the ones that he intended and to widen his knowledge about writing as he interacts with others over his work. It helps him to see alternative ways of presenting the message, improve his ideas of what should be said, and provides feedback or an audience reaction to his work.

When Emma finished her second draft of the part of her life story which told about her early childhood in Greece, we read it as a class. The class then asked Emma questions that had come to mind as they read her story. I was amazed at the questions they came up with, and we learned a lot more about Emma's childhood through her answers. Doing this helped Emma realise that people enjoyed her story and wanted to know more about the events mentioned in it. In her next draft she added more information, and the final draft was much more interesting for herself and for the reader.

Nick had a lot of questions about Emma's story. When he came to writing his own story, he was more aware of the need to add information to his story so the reader would understand the story better. He asked me: "Should I tell them about what I was thinking and how I was feeling when I had those men playing up in the back of the taxi?"

Conferencing with Emma about her writing had helped Nick realize that he needed to give more information in his own writing than just the details of people's comings and goings. Now he knew that if he was to involve the audience of his story, he needed to include information on his thoughts, fears, and feelings as well.

Conferencing must be handled well. Some people find criticism of their work very difficult to take. They already think they are no good at writing and if they receive a lot of negative comments they are likely to feel shame. It will confirm to them their feelings that what they have written is no good, just as they thought. So there must be a balance between talking about things that they have done well and areas where they can make their writing more effective. They must be involved in talking over these things in a nonthreatening environment.

Also some people when conferencing will take over the 'ownership' of the story and change it in such a way that the writer feels the story is no longer his own but someone else's. The other person may feel more comfortable in using certain phrases or a certain style, but it is important that the writer feels the end result is still his story written in his way.

Conferencing is a time when students should be learning about how they can improve their writing. A lot of valuable teaching is done during this time. In *No Better Way to Teach Writing* (Turbill 1982), the writers state that it was in conference "that Steven learned to insert sentences into his draft, that Merilyn learned to cross out and add new things to her draft, and that Gavin learned to use fewer 'ands' and 'thens' in his writing."

The authors of this book also point out, however, that it should be the student who is in control of the pen in these sessions and is the one who makes the marks on the page.

Conferencing, if done well, can be very time consuming. Teachers need to plan well to make sure they have time each day to work with the writers. Some teachers have found it impossible to work with every child every day. One teacher said, "I resolved to work with only one group each day" (Turbill 1982:21).

She found by planning things that way she was able to spend some quality time interacting with that one group of writers. Other teachers have asked other adults to help with the conferencing sessions. You will need to work out what will work best for your situation.

Rewriting. Because writing is a process, and because of conferencing and some self-editing, there comes a time when the first draft needs to be rewritten. This rewriting should only be done when it is necessary as it may discourage some writers because of the time it takes, particularly if it is a long story.

Learning to type and to use a computer is a boon to many authors because of the ease of making corrections without rewriting. This is not practical, however, in most situations where you are working. It is important to not require too much rewriting, especially if students do not want to do so themselves. The most important thing to do is to encourage the joy of writing. Limit the amount of rewriting needed by having students only rewrite pieces that will be read by others.

Some students, however, are happy to rewrite. My migrant English class wanted to rewrite most of their stories so they could practice their spelling and reinforce the English word order of the sentences they had written. Teachers need to be sensitive to how students feel about rewriting.

Publishing. Publishing can take various forms. It should be up to the students to choose how they are going to publish their writing. Will they make it into a book? Will they include it in a display of writing in the writer's corner? Will they take it home and share it with family and friends? The writer needs to be the person who decides if the writing will be read by others, read privately by the teacher, read aloud to the teacher, read aloud by others, read by other classes, read by their age mates, available to all who may like to read it, or a piece that is very personal and will be read only by the writer.

Writer's Corner

When making writings available to others to read, it is important that they be free of all technical errors. So if a piece is to be published, it will require extra work to get it to the standard required.

It should be stressed to the students and to teachers that it is not necessary to work on publishing every writing piece. Students can be put off by having to go through this extensive publishing process for every piece of writing that they do. Also it is unrealistic. Not every piece of writing that is done is worth publishing. In fact some say that only about one in every four pieces of writing are published. It should be up to the students to decide which are their best pieces and which pieces deserve the extra attention and effort to make them ready for publishing.

Record keeping (writing profiles). It is important to keep records of progress with the students. It is good for them to look back and see how they have improved because of all their hard work. Sometimes they are so preoccupied with today's frustrations that they feel they are not getting anywhere and want to give up. Looking back over previous writings helps the student see they have made progress. It is also important to keep records of progress so you can see what the student can now do, to see areas where the student is learning well, and to see areas where they still need help.

Keeping records can be done in a variety of ways and it can be done by the student and the teacher working together. Students can keep a record of the pieces they have written in the order they have written them, on the inside cover of their writing journal or exercise book. All drafts could then be done in the exercise books. Or, each student can have a writing folder in the classroom. Each month they can choose, with the teacher's help, a piece that represents their best work for that month. This can then be kept in their writing folder.

Teachers can help students evaluate their own writing by such questions and comments as:

- "Is this as good as your last piece?"
- "Is there any way you could improve this piece?"
- "Underline the parts of this piece of writing that you think need working on."
- "Underline the words you think you spelled wrong and want help with."

Teachers can keep a record book in which they note down observations they make about students' writings. Keep a double page for each student. Date each entry. These observations can be made while the student is writing, during conferencing times, or when looking closely at student drafts. They may read something like the following.

> Judy almost spelt people right, she had all the right letters but they were arranged differently. When I showed her the correct arrangement she was able to rewrite it without looking at my original and she spelt it correctly next time she used it.

> I am finding Gloria's invented spellings hard to read. I noticed she always uses a 'c' when it should be an 's' as in strong or smile. I need to do more work on words that start with 's' and words that start with 'c'.

When using an exercise book for their writing, I encourage students who are not good writers to write on every second line, allowing room for corrections and revisions to be made near by. I also encourage the students to have a practice page in their exercise books every now and then.

On the practice page they can make guesses at spellings and see if they look right, they can ask others to write in words that they want, or I can use the page to show them correct spellings of words and link them with the word family they belong to.

For example, when Nick was not sure how to spell the 'ing' part of 'missing', I told him he knew how to spell ring so he could work out the spelling of missing. We also listed other words that had the same ending under 'ring' on the practice page.

Teachers may choose to keep a checklist of objectives for each student and mark off each objective as it is observed. It is good for these checklists to be phrased in terms of what the student can now do well on their own. For example:

- good letter formation
- uses capital letters and full stops
- can decide where the paragraph breaks go when re-reading drafts
- good introductions
- good endings
- self-corrects as he is writing
- edits and makes changes while he is writing

Lists of objectives for each stage of writing would be different. Rowe and Lomas (1984) list objectives for the beginning phase (p. 33), the developmental phase (p. 55), and the composition phase (p. 71). Other teachers prefer to develop their own checklists. Some do not find this a helpful thing to do. As with everything you do, the way you keep records and assess student writings needs to be suited to your situation and you need to experiment and find out what works best for you.

In summary then, the teacher has to take on many roles in order to help the students learn the process of writing.

- The teacher needs to be there to support the students in their writing at every point where they need help so they can write in an environment where they know the teacher is there to ensure their success.
- The teacher must help the student have positive experiences with the process.
- Teachers must help provide experiences for students to write about.
- Teachers must give students opportunities to write in a creative and supportive environment.
- Students need to write every day to practice what they are learning.
- Teachers must develop honest relationships with the writers so they can share helpful ways in how to improve their writing.
- Teachers must be aware of the writers' development and talk to the students about the things they are now doing well and about a few things that need improvement.
- Teachers must understand that writing is a process and that progress will be made in small steps towards the larger goals.

As I mentioned before, my Djinang Granny did not know much about the special ways people have of putting their message on the page. The best way for students to learn these conventions is to start writing. They should be taught gradually as the need arises, a little at a time. Some of the things students need to learn during the writing process are listed below.

- use of capital letters
- use of full stops marked by a period (.)

- use of quotation marks (" "), sometimes called "talking marks"
- use of exclamation marks (!)
- use of commas (,)
- keeping tenses correct throughout the piece
- knowing where to put a paragraph break
- indenting for paragraphs
- importance of interesting first sentences
- special conventions for special kinds of writing, e.g., writing letters, addressing envelopes, and writing business letters

Group writing

Teaching writing as a group has many advantages. Firstly it is a good way of demonstrating the writing process in a way that does not cause anyone shame. Secondly it gives the students experiences with the writing process before they are expected to write independently. And thirdly, it shows what writing is like—that what we write is not perfect the first time, that writers need to cross-out, rewrite, reorder, and work on their writing until they are happy with it. Doing writing as a group will give people opportunities to experience all these things and hopefully will encourage students to try writing for themselves. They will know that what they are finding hard, others are finding hard too.

As I said in the previous section, it is important that before starting any writing the students have something worth writing about. The topic needs to be one that each person has experienced either in their own lives or as a group. For example, on Karkar Island most students would be able to tell and write stories from their own experiences about the following topics.

- Collecting galip nuts
- Going to Madang by boat
- Paddling a canoe
- Collecting breadfruit

But I would find it difficult to write about paddling a canoe or collecting galip nuts because I have never done those things.

Sometimes it is good to provide a shared experience for the group as part of the writing lesson. You can do this either by bringing something to the class and talking about it or you can take the class somewhere to see or do something. Then come back and have the students talk about it before writing about it together. It is good to do group writing sessions every now and then to deomonstrate different aspects of the writing processes.

The following pages give some samples of writing lessons. The first two samples take a common theme (teacher, football), the third is a sample of writing personal letters, and the fourth on writing business letters.

1. Our teacher

Goals

- demonstrate the writing process—that things are not written perfectly on the first try, that you draft, redraft, and conference about writing
- encourage students to talk about their writing before they write
- models how to plan paragraphs

Materials

- blackboard or chart paper to record group story

Session outline

- Choose a topic everyone knows about. In this lesson the class interviewed me.
- Record important words and phrases about the topic.
- Group the words and phrases that go together. These groupings can help decide content of each paragraph. Number the groupings as to what needs to be written about first and what follows afterwards.
- Ask for suggestions of how the story should start. Teacher writes the story on the blackboard or large sheet of paper. (Group works together on spellings, editing, reordering, and so on as the teacher writes.)
- Discuss the story as it grows.
- Rewrite the story on a clean sheet of paper or clean blackboard. Have the class read and re-read the story, making any further changes needed.
- Record the final copy on a chart or make a copy for each student. Read the story often as part of reading lessons.

Class notes:

Final copy:

Our teacher

Our teacher's name is Glenys. She is married and has two children. They are girls. One is 16 years old and the other is 19 years old.

Glenys' husband is a translator and she is a literacy worker. They work in Papua New Guinea with the Takia people. The Takia people are nice and friendly and they helped to build their village house.

Glenys is teaching us this year and then she is going back to work in Papua New Guinea.

2. Football

Goals

- encourage students to talk about their writing before they write
- give students lists of correctly spelled words to use in their writing
- shows how to plan the structure of your writing

Materials

- blackboard or chart to record word banks and discussion

Session outline

- Choose a topic everyone knows about and would like to write about.
- Talk about the topic and record words and phrases people are likely to use.
- Group the words that go together. These groupings can help decide content of each paragraph. (Students can do this separately—make their own groupings according to what they want to write about, or as a group.)
- Each person write about the topic in his own way.
- Read each other's written pieces.
- Discuss the pieces.

Word bank

umpires	players	ladders
whites	muddy	win
defend	draw	goal
freekick	banners	fans
streamers	football	score
lose	report	attack
coach	points	bottom
fair deal	top	biased
spectators	barrack	fans

Words organised into groups

umpire
- biased
- fair
- white
- flag
- report
- score
- free kick
- weather

football teams
- players
- muddy
- coach
- attack
- defend
- goal
- points

games
- goal
- points
- win
- lose
- draw
- ladder
- top
- bottom

spectators
- barrack
- fans
- streamers
- banners

This is just one suggested way of approaching writing on common themes. Many books have been written about this idea. You can also work out your own ways.

3. Writing personal letters

Goals
- teach how to set out a letter properly
- show the structure of letters
- encourage letter writing

Materials
- samples of letters you have received
- illustrated chart of letter layout and envelope layout

Session outline
- Talk about why people write letters and the special ways letters are written.
- Show the class examples of letters that have been received.
- Talk about the things that are important to letter format.

- Each person writes his own letter following the format.
- Read each other's letters, if they are not personal.
- Discuss the way the letters have been set out, and compare them to the chart. Talk about any improvements that could be made to the content of the letters.
- Rewrite the letters and post them!

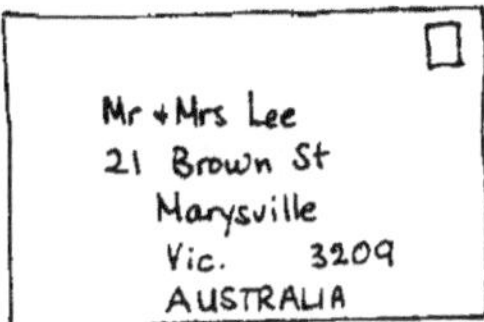

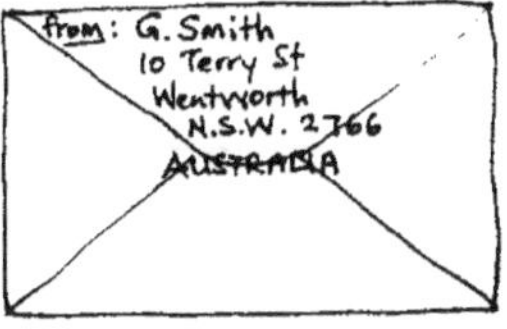

4. Writing business letters

Goals

- teach how to set out a business letter
- understand the structure of business letters
- encourage written communication skills

Materials

- samples of business letters
- chart of a business letter

Session outline

- Talk about why people write business letters and the special ways letters are written.
- Pass examples of business letters around the class.
- Talk about the things that are important to the business letter format.

- Pretend there is a need for each person to write to a bank about a problem with his account. Talk about how this would be done. Each person writes his own letter following the format.
- Read each other's letters.
- Discuss the way the letters have been set out, and compare them to the chart. Talk about any improvements that could be made to the content of the letters.
- Rewrite the letters.

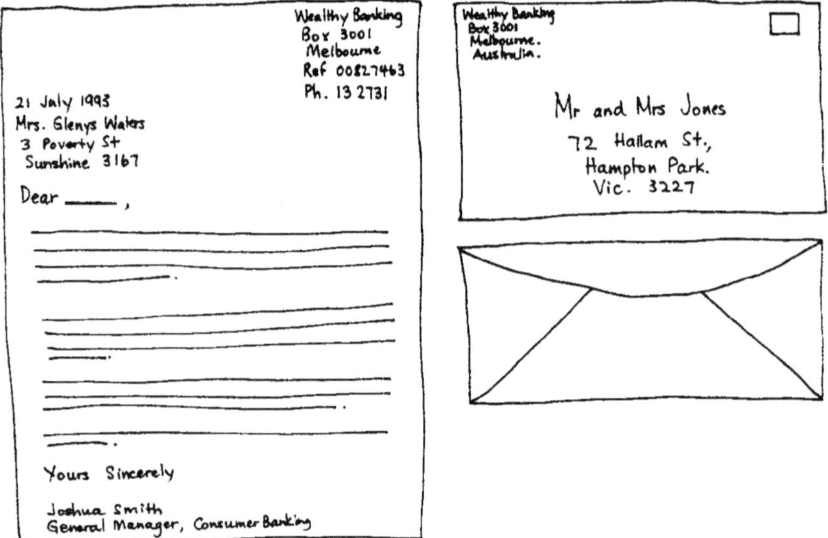

Personal writing

Once students feel comfortable with some of the conventions of writing and have taken part in the writing process in group writing times, they should be given opportunities to start some personal writing. They should start with small goals in mind, and have a lot of support during the writing process. They should be reminded that in the first draft they should concentrate on getting their own thoughts down on paper, and not worry too much about the conventions and other things. These can be improved on later.

Some possible topics:

- Childhood memories
- I was really frightened
- Horseback riding
- My first aeroplane flight
- Why the Rooster and Wallaby are enemies

- The canoe turned over
- Earthquake
- The great pig chase
- Fishing stories
- The tribe that was our enemy
- The first time I saw a white person
- When he sat on the stinging nettles
- Stories with animals treated as human characters
- The thief
- Humorous stories
- What it is like at school
- The car accident
- How we got mosquitoes
- When the cookhouse caught fire

Often things come up in class discussion that lead to other topics. For example, after reading about the refugee problem, the class wrote letters to the local newspaper about what they thought about war. And when Hwa's mother was being operated on for cancer, we all wrote letters to her to let her know we were thinking of her. When the class was closed down and students placed in other classes, they were all upset and wanted to write letters to the principal about it. These opportunities for writing were unplanned but provided good motivations for writing.

Writing for different purposes

Students who are just learning to write tend to write in a narrative style and to write about things that have happened to them. There are many other kinds of writing that they should be aware of. As they become familiar and confident with writing stories, they should be given opportunities to do other kinds of writings such as writing poetry, letters, or pieces to persuade someone to a particular point of view. They should learn how to write a text that explains to someone else how to make something. Some adults may want to learn how to write funding proposals, letters to provincial government officials, and so on. Try to give students opportunities to practice the types of writing that are appropriate to their situations.

The following are some of the different kinds of writing a Takia person living on Karkar Island might need or want to be able to write.

- What to do to treat someone for malaria
- How to bake bread in a drum oven
- How to fix a hand-operated sewing machine

- A report to the church circuit meeting
- Letters to family members studying away from home
- Letters to a bank about a banking problem
- Letters to a business about problems with supplies for the trade store
- Stories for children to read
- Bible study notes
- A sermon outline
- Sewing instructions for blouses, skirts, and shorts
- How to grow better vegetables
- How to raise chickens for market
- Why people should vote and how to do it

In each village there are needs for different kinds of writing skills. It is important that we do not just teach people how to write their personal stories but also teach the other different kinds of writing they may need to use.

Teaching spelling

Kids cn rit sunr thn we thingk

When young children grow up in a situation where they are seeing other people writing and they are encouraged to 'play' with paper and pens or pencils, they often start writing fairly early when they are beginning to learn to read. Because they do not know all the correct spellings, they use what teachers call 'invented spellings'. They invent or make up their own ways of spelling words. When adults are learning to read and write and do not yet know all the right spellings of words, they often do the best they can with what they know.

> The tome I have my fast jop in Magrobes to work I do not andesdent hot to do with the piece of chocol the people was work so fast no in showe how to work. The week I had ecxtra mone and I thot I gut in my work but I lost my jop and I fil so eparecet to tael my brother I was lost my job.
>
> [The time I have my first job in MacRobertsons to work I do not understand what to do with the piece of chocolate. The people was work so fast no one show how to work. The week I had extra money and I thought I got it for my work but I lost my job and I felt too embarassed to tell my brother I was lost my job.]

Often these invented spellings are easy to read for they follow some patterns the students are putting together in their own heads. The patterns just need to be refined to the ones that everyone else in that langauge uses. It is important to see the use of invented spellings as part of the writing process and to encourage people to continue to write using them while at the same time encouraging them to correct the spellings that they do know.

Some teachers have found that when they encouraged students to use invented spellings their 'known' spelling seemed to suffer. Evelyn Collaro reported:

> At first their 'known' spelling seemed to decline...I feared that "invented spelling" and 'rough drafts' were developing laziness. But perhaps their lapses were due to a change of focus—the children were concentrating on the meaning of their stories rather than their spellings. Soon I became aware of advances which more than compensated; not only did their skill in approximating to correct spellings develop rapidly, but they began to *use words they needed* where before they kept to words they could spell, and they rapidly developed confidence in attacking writing situations they were not familiar with. (Turbill 1982:53)

When students are beginning writers, do not place too much emphasis on correcting mistakes in their work as this can be discouraging. Focus on the parts of the words that they have spelled correctly while giving them the correct spellings that they ask for. Concentrate on the things they should know from other lessons and should have spelled right.

Also, show them the correct spelling of words they use often. Then they can see and use correct models as much as possible. When talking about the spelling of words, refer them to word families, that is, other words that have the same combination of sounds in them. Because I had taught Nick to do this, one day he said to Sophie that you would probably spell 'material' like you do 'arterial' and that he could spell 'king' because he could spell 'ring'. It helps students to learn new things if you point out connections with things that they already know.

If paper supply is not a problem, it is good for each student to have his personal dictionary. This is an exercise book with a letter of the alphabet on each page. The students build up a core of words that they want to use by asking the teacher or a fellow student to write in the correct spelling for words as they need them. They also add words themselves from their own stories, once they have been corrected, if they think they are going to use those words a lot.

As mentioned before, using a page in the writing journal as a practice page, and building wordbanks around writing topics will help students with their spelling.

Until students feel comfortable writing, it is a good idea to do a lot of dictated stories. The student dictates their story to the teacher and the teacher writes it for them, or with them. When working with school children, have them draw a picture. While they are drawing, go around to each one and have him tell you a sentence about his picture. Write the sentence under the picture (see sample below). As you write, ask him if he can tell you how some of the words start and involve him in working out some of the spellings. Read the sentence to him pointing to each word as you read. Read it again but this time have him read it with you. Do this for each student.

Adults are often not keen to draw their stories unless they are already good at art. Often it is best to just write their stories for them and practice reading them together. If you are teaching adults in a group, some of them can practice copying part of the story by themselves while you are writing the stories for others.

In languages that have alphabets which are phonemic (words are spelled exactly as they sound), teaching the sounds (phonics) of the language is an excellent strategy to use when teaching reading. It is also an excellent spelling strategy. But whatever the writing system, writers will not feel comfortable writing until they are beginning to understand the sound system of the language in which they are writing. Then they are not so limited and frustrated by not knowing enough letters to be able to write words. It is wise to delay students doing writing individually until the students are beginning to gain a basic grasp of the sound system.

Early spelling lessons should, therefore, concentrate on teaching sounds—how they are made in the mouth, how they feel, how they are written, and how they go together with other sounds to make words. McCracken and McCracken have an excellent five minute spelling segment that they encourage teachers to use daily with their classes.

> We consider phonics a spelling skill used when writing, so we begin phonics by beginning spelling and writing. We teach the children:
>
> 1. The name of the letter.
> 2. The sound the letter represents.
> 3. The way the letter is written.
> 4. The way the phoneme is made within the mouth, the way it feels. (McCracken and McCracken 1979:44)

The next few pages show how they teach spelling. Each student has a small chalkboard, 30cm by 45cm.

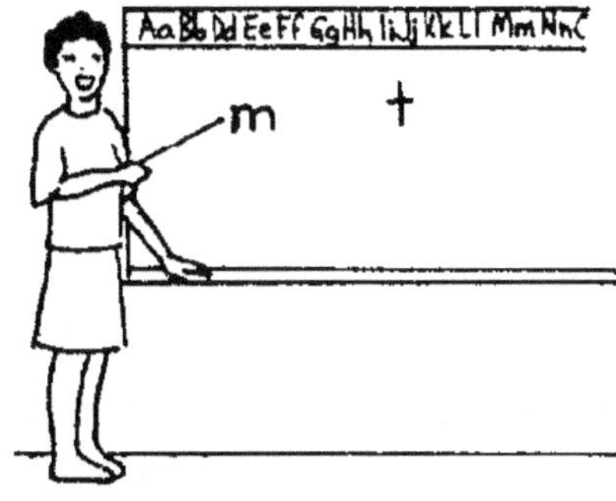

The teacher introduces the two new letters for the day. "This is the letter em. It makes this sound, 'mmm'. This is how you write the letter em."

"Alright, everyone make the sound of this letter 'mmm'. What parts of your mouth are making this sound?"

In this way you teach the students the name of the letter, the sound of the letter, how to write the letter, and how your mouth feels when making the sound.

Now have the students say the letter and write it on their own chalkboards and tell what its name is.

(Then repeat these steps for the other letter.)

> This is the first step in teaching the alphabetic principle, and the first step in developing the skill of spelling, getting children to understand that if they hear or feel a sound when they say a word that the sound is represented by a letter. (McCracken and McCracken 1979:45)

Once the sounds have been taught, give the students practice in hearing the sounds in words. The children must learn to spell their own speech so the teacher says the word once but encourages the children to say it as many times as they like.

The students are told to draw two short lines on their chalkboards. The teacher dictates a word. The students repeat the word. The children write an 'm' in the first space if they hear the sound at the beginning of the word, or they write an 'm' in the last space if they hear the sound at the end of the word.

When enough letters have been taught, whole words can be written.

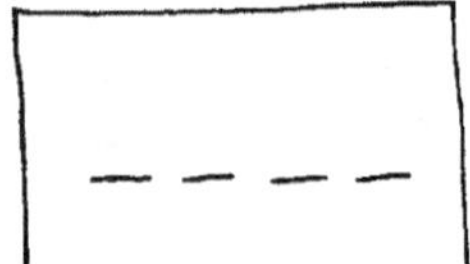

The teacher says the word and the students repeat it. The students then put a line on the chalkboard for each sound they can hear in the word.

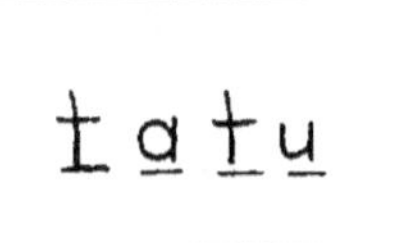

Then they fill in the sounds that they know.

The above three patterns are repeated until all the sounds of the language have been taught. It is important to relate the sound you are teaching to words that are well-known.

When the students are able to do these activities well, the spelling lessons change a little bit. The students are now told to divide their chalkboard into four areas. The teacher thinks of four words. Students should already know all the letters for these words.

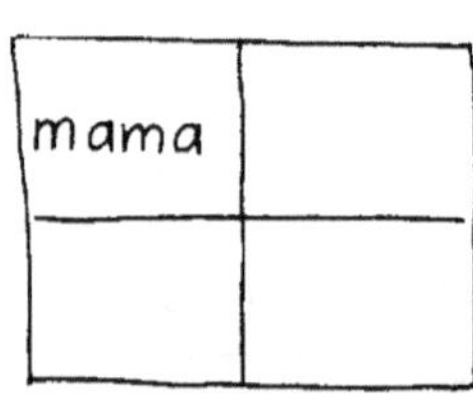

The teacher says one of the words once, the students repeat it as many times as they need to, and try writing it in one of the spaces on their chalkboard. The teacher makes sure that each student has written the word correctly. This procedure is repeated with the other four words. To erase the words, one student is asked to read one of the words. The rest of the class find that word, say it and erase it. This is repeated until all words have been erased, and the procedure can start again with a different set of words.

Remember, the spelling lesson is done quickly, just five minutes each day.

As well as doing this formal spelling and writing lesson, McCracken and McCracken stress the need for students to write every day, using what they are learning in the spelling lesson, using words from word banks around the classroom, and using invented spellings.

Spelling strategies

There are many spelling strategies that writers use when they come up against a spelling problem. Some of these are listed below. (For a more comprehensive listing see Kemp 1987:214–16.)

Spelling as it sounds. This method is phonetic spelling. The writer works with the belief that there is a way that each sound in a word should be written. In many languages, that is the case because alphabets have been designed that way. Some alphabets, however, are not designed that way or may have exceptions. English is one of those languages. In English, there are often many ways of spelling the same sound.

For example,

I / eye / my / tie / tight
pair / pear
ewe / you
two / too / to
here / hear

So beginning writers working with difficult alphabets (like English) often spell phonetically, that is, how it sounds, and once you work out their system you can often read what they write despite their errors. Note the following story.

Coming to Australia

> I cam too Australia 1967 whod may fammile may husband ent may san. I leve too may kazen house for few whik. After I rent a house ent start too worke. I do hart worke dukoz I'm not antisten Eglis. Ent I star lern lernit inglis - slou. Bat I am not have time too gou the scool bicoz is may kits is bery yieani. I am rait may store is never finis
>
> Kathy
>
> [I came to Australia in 1967 with my family, my husband and my son. I live to my cousin's house for a few weeks. After I rent a house and I start to work. I do hard work because I'm not understand English. And I start learn learning English—slow. But I am not have time to go the school because its my kids is very young. I am write my story its never finish]

Whatever the design of the alphabet, spelling as it sounds is an important spelling strategy that new writers use often.

Spelling as it sounds in slow speech. When sounding out words, we sometimes exaggerate the features in the word, so that sounds not normally heard are highlighted. For example, when I was learning to spell 'Wednesday' as a child, my mother would exaggerate its sounding out so that I would spell it right.

Wed-nes-day

Sometimes this strategy of exaggerated sounding out leads the new writer into error.

toew for toe *ellerfant* for elephant
sapoon for spoon *kazen* for cousin

Kathy spelled just like she sounded out her speech, but her Greek accent caused her to make some spelling mistakes: 'ent' for 'and', 'may' for 'my', and 'hart' for 'hard'.

Spelling as it looks. Many students check to see if their spelling is correct by writing the word in alternative spellings and seeing which one looks right. They do this because people often have a strong visual memory of what a word looks like. Sometimes this strategy only partly works as shown in the two words below. The letters are all there but they are not in the right order.

bycicle for bicycle *eigth* for eight

Sometimes visual recall also recalls other words that are similar. Often these words have been taught as a group, and this can lead to confusion. For example, I still have to stop and think about words such as lose/loose, principle/principal, their/there/they're, to/too/two and others. Also, I often find my hand has written or typed 'there' instead of 'their', when my **head** does know the difference! These types of words were always taught together when I was in school, so they still seem to live in my head in pears/pairs! However I still use spelling as it looks very often, especially when my children ask me "How do you spell…" I grab pen and paper and write it out to see if it looks right.

Spelling by reference to authority. This strategy involves the writer trying to find out the right spelling by using someone or something else. They might ask a teacher, a friend, or look it up in a dictionary, a personal words book, a classroom chart, or a text they have read. I have found that the dictionary is often the last thing that people use as a reference because they often need to have some idea of how the word is spelled in order to look it up. New writers find dictionaries very frustrating to use while they are writing. It slows the communication process down for them too much.

Using a different structure. Sometimes writers decide to use a different structure or word if they are having trouble with the spelling of one particular word. They avoid the spelling problem altogether.

Giving the problem to the reader. Sometimes the writer lets the reader sort out the problem, or try to hide the problem. For example, with the English possessive, the use of the apostrophe causes some writers problems, especially when the word already ends in an 's' as do both my names! Which should they write?

Glenys's or Glenys'
Waters' house or Waters's house

In cases such as these writers may conveniently 'forget' to put the apostrophe in at all, and let the reader sort it out. Or they mispell a word and hope that the reader will not notice.

There are many spelling strategies that can be used. These are just some of them. Watch and see what strategies your students use. Help them to improve the strategies they do use and introduce them to other strategies you think will be helpful. Knowing how a child tends to use a systematic if inaccurate way of solving a problem can, however, alert us to the need for finding an alternative track, such as discussions of meanings and word families (Kemp 1987:216).

Error analysis

Just as we can study the errors that students make in reading and can use what we learn from that study to help them improve their reading, we can do the same with writing. Looking at the spelling errors that students make in their writing and thinking about why they made those mistakes will help us to work out teaching programmes and strategies that will help them overcome their spelling problems.

Max Kemp (1987:227) uses the following categories to study spelling mistakes that students make in their own writings and see if there are any patterns of errors. Such patterns can give teachers ideas about things that need to be worked on with the students.

Spelling errors in students' personal writing can be grouped according to the following categories. Look at each mistake and ask "Why was the mistake made?" Was it because of a problem with one or more of the following.

1. phonetics (spelling as sounds), hed/head
2. sounding out (exaggerated sound), toew/toe, smoler/smaller
3. spoken (speech production), Wensday/Wednesday
4. meaning (generalising), holydaes/holidays cauliflour/cauliflower

5. patterning (visual memory), often used only with partial success, bycicle/ bicycle, buisness/business
6. analogy (influence of known words), hedding/heading, sumtimes/sometimes, hospitle/hospital
7. omissions (e.g., missing vowels), pensl/pencil
8. additions (e.g., doubling of letters), proffessor/ professor
9. transpositions (reversals, wrong sequence), donw/down, dee/bee

There may be more than one error classification applied to the same word. For example: if a student wrote 'ent' instead of 'and', this could be classified as a number 2 (sounding out error), i.e., 't' instead of 'd'. It could also be classified as a number 3 error (a spoken speech error), as the student says 'ent' and not the long 'a' sound of 'and' and 'apple'.

Look again at Kathy's story and follow the analysis of her writing.

Kathy. (24/2/1993) Coming to Australia Spelling analysis

> I cam too Australia 1967 whod may fammile may husband ent may san. I leve too may kazen house for few whik. After I rent a house ent start too worke. I do hart worke dukoz I'm not antisten Eglis. Ent I star lern lernit inglis - slou. Bat I am not have time too gou the scool bicoz is may kits is bery yieani. I am rait may store is never finis.

$$\text{accuracy: } \frac{\text{number of words correct}}{\text{total words}} \quad \frac{29}{72} \times \frac{100}{1} = 40\%$$

I cam too Australia 1967 whod may fammile may
husband ent may san. I leve too may kazen house for
few whik. After I rent a house ent start too worke. I do
hart worke dukoz I'm not antisten Eglis. Ent I star lern
lernit inglis - slou. Bat I am not have time too gou the
scool bicoz is may kits is bery yieani. I am rait may store
is never finis

Kathy wrote 72 words altogether and got 40 percent of them right. (She got a total of 29 words correct, but she only used 19 different words correctly). If we look at the sound accuracy of Kathy's story, however, we get a different picture. Even though 60 percent of her words were spelled incorrectly, 72 percent of the time she was spelling correctly and many times she was almost right (see the check chart).

Kathy's sample observation record may look something like the following.

Student's name: Kathy Date: 24-2-1993
Story title: Coming to Australia
Number of words in sample: 72
Words correct in sample: 29
Percentage correct in sample: 40%

Classification of errors and examples

1. phonetic (spelling as sounded)
   fammile/family, lern/learn, slou/slow, bicoz/because, kazen/cousin
2. sounding out (exaggerated sound)
3. spoken (speech production)
   hart/hard, ent/and, finis/finish
4. meaning (generalising)
5. patterning (visual memory)
   worke/work
6. analogy (influence of known words)
   too/to
7. omissions (e.g., missing vowels)
   cam/came; finis/finish; Eglis/English
8. additions (e.g., doubling of letters)
   may/my
9. transpositions (reversals, wrong sequence)

Summary
pronunciation needs work
knowledge of some sounds is weak
needs to listen to ends of words more carefully

Action
review the sounds of English
continue work with language families of 'sh', 'a-e'
teach 'go', 'my'
practice listening to ends of words

You may find the spelling observation record too detailed and too time consuming to use. It is included here for those who may be interested.

It is important, however, to do a spelling analysis of students' writings so you can help them at their point of need. You may not have time to do a detailed analysis like I did with Kathy but you can make these kinds of observations in your head as you are working with students. I find it helpful to do a periodic analysis with students who are struggling as it helps me focus my attention on what is causing them problems, as well as see what they can already do well.

12.3 The reading-writing connection

In the past reading and writing have often been treated as separate subjects and taught separately. Today research is showing more and more how reading and writing are connected. Researchers have looked at how reading can help improve students' writing and how writing can help improve their reading. More recently researchers have been looking at how learning is improved when the connections between reading and writing are taught. Improvements are measured in how well students read and write and also in the quality of their work.

Writing helps reading

Stellan and Eivor Lindrud, working with the Kol people in East New Britain (PNG), found that writing helped the students with their reading. In the early stages of their literacy lessons they do a lot of work on small handheld blackboards. They reported the following process.

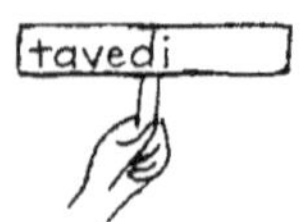

> With the handboard the learners focus on learning to write. Reading is learned in the process of learning to write. When we switched to the handboard, we could see that the learners remembered the facts and principles much better than they had before. This is to be expected because writing involves more physical skills than reading does. Therefore, more of the student's senses are activated in the process. Another result is that interest and concentration has increased noticeably during the lessons. This could be because students themselves must now work out the written forms of the words. Before, they were served finished words on the primer page. (1994:32–33)

The idea that children might actually learn to read by writing is not new. In 1908, Edmond Huey talked about using the sentence method (see §7.3) and students' writing to teach reading. This idea also fits with some of the ideas that underlie the language experience approach and other creative writing approaches (Tierney and Leys 1984:9). Some people say they learnt to read by writing. A third grade student in Tierney's study told of his learning to read as follows.

> I learned to write before I could read. I just wrote and then I started reading books because my mother taught me letters and how to spell and showed me all kinds of words. I started making words and I started making them spelled right, and then I decided to read books because I knew I could read right with the words all spelled right. So I started reading books and I could understand books more because I wrote first. (Tierney and Leys 1984:10)

Learning to write also helps the quality of students' reading. It makes them think like a writer. Sometimes they are more aware of the strengths and weaknesses of other people's writing when they have learned to write or are learning to be writers.

> Before I ever wrote a book, I used to think there was a big machine, and they typed a title and then the machine went until the book was done. Now I look at a book and I know a guy wrote it and it's been his project for a long time...After the guy writes it, he probably thinks of questions people will ask him and revises it like I do. (Calkins 1983:157)

When students learn to read, sometimes they apply what they have learned to the task of learning to write.

> When discussing what he did when he got stuck on a word he suggested: "What I do is I just think of what I do when I'm writing...I remember that mistakes aren't everything." (Tierney and Leys 1984:12)

This student has learned from his writing something that helps him in his reading. He had already learned that when writing he needed to take risks. So, in his reading, he was more willing to take risks and make predictions. Risk taking and making predictions are important aspects of reading.

Reading helps writing

Just as learning to write can help students learn to read, so learning to read helps students with their writing. By reading a lot of good stories, students see how other writers have written and they learn new words and ways of saying things. They also see the same words over and over and this helps them have confidence in their spelling. They begin to know the word is spelled correctly by the way it looks. They begin to learn good ways of starting and finishing stories. They pick up ideas about things they would like to write about and ideas about different ways of writing.

Similarly it has been found that students who read a lot of controlled text write using the patterns of that kind of text. These texts are written just for graded readers and are very formal. I found this to be true on Karkar when I was giving extra help to some children who were having trouble at the English school. They read and spoke very formal and controlled

English at school, so when I asked them to tell or write stories in English I would get things like:

Mother is in the garden.
Mother is digging a hole.
Father is in the house.

When I asked why was mother digging a hole? or what she was going to put in the hole? the answer was shy giggles. They did not know how to answer me. I had tried to break away from the formal controlled English, but because that was all the girls knew from their reading and speaking at school that was all they could write.

Reading and writing together

When students are writing they are also doing a lot of reading. This is especially true if they are doing process writing (see §12.2). As writers write, they are constantly going back and re-reading the sentence they have just written to make sure that what they have written is right and that it makes sense. As the number of sentences grows, the writer will take time out to re-read bigger sections of the text, again checking that the paragraph flows properly. As the number of paragraphs grows, writers re-read to check that the paragraphs are in the right order and fit in well with the overall way the story is developing. Writers do this re-reading whether they are just learning and writing one sentence, or are writing a letter to a friend, or are writing a book like this one.

The little girls learning English on my front verandah wrote me a story each afternoon. They first started with just one sentence. They re-read that sentence as they wrote each word checking they had it right. Their erasers were very busy! Then when they had it right they would read it to me. A lot of reading and writing and re-reading was going on. In writing this book I did a lot of reading—reading each sentence as I wrote it to see if it said what I wanted it to say; re-reading groups of sentences to see if they flowed well together; re-reading sections to see if they were right; and thinking about what should come next.

I have had to do a lot of reading of other people's books while I have been writing this book. While I am reading, I often write notes to myself of things that I agree with or disagree with. I write down ideas that come to my mind as I read about how other people have done things. If a friend gives me something to read that she has written, I will read and write at the same time. I will have written comments all over the page by the time I have finished reading it. Writing while I am reading helps me to understand the main points of what I am reading and how these ideas could affect the way I do things.

Thus, reading and writing are not things which stand apart from each other. They go together and help each other. Teaching them together will help the students. What they learn in reading will help their writing and what they learn in writing will help their reading.

Getting started with writing

Following is a list of ideas for getting started with teaching process writing.

1. Have a time each day for personal writing when everybody writes, even the teacher.

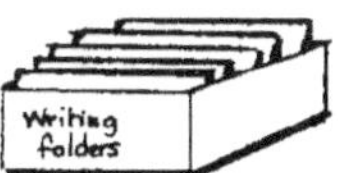

2. Encourage students to keep a writing folder. These can be made from strong brown paper, or can be an exercise book. Name each folder. In these folders students keep any writing papers. They can also keep records of stories they have written. Store all the folders together in a box and make sure the students return them after each lesson.

John's Folder

Stories I have written:
Feb. Crocodile hunt
Mar. Reptiles
April Fixing the house
April. My dream
May. Frightened to death

3. Encourage students to keep a list in their writing folder of stories they would like to write one day. They can write brief notes to remind themselves of key points.

Stories I'd like to write:
* Uncle's fishing story
* Grandpa and the pig
* Buffalo got away

4. Share other students' writings. This may give students ideas of things they would like to write about.
5. Read a lot of good stories to students so they experience the features of a good story:
   - structure
   - ways of expressing ideas
   - ways of beginning and ending
   - ways of building suspense
   - rich vocabulary
6. Have one place where all the materials are kept such as paper, covers for making books, etc. Have a different person each week in charge of making sure these things are kept tidy.

7. Discuss and establish rules with the class. For example:
   - no interuptions when people are conferencing about their work.
   - help each other when there are problems.

- respect another person's right to work quietly.
- before conferencing
  - read your story to a friend
  - circle words you think are misspelled
  - underline any parts you want help with

13

Mathematics

13.1 School mathematics versus real mathematics

Pictured below is a mathematics problem which you might come across in real life. If you were in a store, how would you solve the problem and make a decision about your purchases? (PNG currency has *kina* (K) and *toea* (t). One hundred toea make one kina.)

If I had K3.00 and a can of fish cost 78 toea, how many cans of fish could I buy?

What change would I get?

Think about this problem. If I were in a store deciding what to buy, I would choose a quick way of working this out. I would round the price of the tin of fish to the nearest ten toea. Then I would estimate that 3 cans would probably be all that I could buy with my money. I would do a quick times sum in my head, 3 x 80 K2.40, to check if my estimation was right. Knowing that 3 tins would cost approximately K2.40 I would then expect my change to be about 60 toea.

If it was really important that I know exactly how much change I was going to get because I had to buy something else for K1.63 at another store, and I only had another K1 in my purse, I might need to do a further sum. I would realize that in my estimating and rounding I had added on 2 toea to the cost of each tin. If I bought three cans, that would total up to an extra 6 toea. So my change from K3.00 would be 60 toea plus the extra 6 toea, making 66 toea altogether. I would then decide that with this money and the extra K1 in my purse that I had enough to buy the three cans of fish and still have enough for my other purchase.

Even though I have not done paper and pencil mathematics, I have used a lot of mathematics knowledge to help me solve my shopping problem. I used my knowledge of rounding numbers to get a simpler number that is easier to work with mentally. I also used estimating skills to guess how many tins I think I could buy for the K3 that I had. I used my knowledge of the 3 times table. I used my comparing skills, comparing K2.40 with K3.00. I also used my knowledge about money.

If I was asked to do this same problem at school, I would use a different strategy. I would know that the teacher would want an exact answer. So I would use paper and pencil and do a division sum as shown below.

```
     3
78)300
   234
    66
```

In doing the division sum I use my knowledge of estimation, of 3 times tables, of subtraction, and the knowledge that K3 is the same as 300 toea.

The mathematics done at school is often quite different to the mathematics we do in real life. School mathematics is usually done with pencil and paper and is concerned with getting an exact and correct answer. Real life mathematics is often done quickly in a person's head and deals with numbers and results that are approximate. When teaching students mathematics you need to decide such things as:

- what their purpose is for learning mathematics
- what kind of mathematics skills they need to understand and practice

If they are learning mathematics for school, then their mathematics will need to be the pen and pencil type that is taught there, and they will need to be more concerned with getting the exact answers and following the 'right' methods. If they are learning mathematics to use in everyday life, then the lessons should involve more real-life problem solving. Also the mathematics they do will, more likely, be the kind that is done in their minds—often involving estimating, rounding, comparing, approximating, and checking.

So before deciding what mathematics skills to teach in your programme you need to think about the situation (context) that your students are in. What are the skills they need in the place where they live and work? Once you have made a list of these skills then you can think about how to teach them. The following pages give you some ideas that may be helpful. Add to the collection any ideas that you have or that you find elsewhere. Change the activities to suit your situation.

13.2 Working with numbers

Getting to know the digits

The decimal number system is made up of ten symbols; each of these symbols is called a digit: 0 1 2 3 4 5 6 7 8 9. In the word "decimal," 'deci' means ten. With these ten digits we can make any number we want. Most numbers have more than one digit in them. For example, the number 21 has two digits, a '2' and a '1'. In a number, the place where each digit is written is important (see "place value" at the end of this section). The digit 7, for example, can take on different meanings depending on which place it has in a number. Consider the following numbers:

729   7   73   7500   K1.07

In the first number the digit 7 means "7 hundreds," in the second number it means "7 units," in the third number, "7 tens," in the next number, "7 thousands," and in the last number it means "7 hundredths of a kina," that is, 7 toea.

To be able to work with numbers, students need to be able to recognize the digits, to understand what they stand for, and to understand about place value. Once these things are understood, then students can learn to do operations on the numbers—to add, subtract, multiply, and divide. Then they can use their knowledge of numbers to handle money problems, read the time from clocks, read the weights of coffee or copra on the scales, and solve other mathematics problems that arise in everyday life.

The place to start with new students learning mathematics is to teach the numbers from 1 to 10, and later 11 to 20, and then 21 to100. If there is a local mathematics system, start with that first. Listed below are the Hewa (PNG) numbers from one to ten.

1	t p keli	6	maluenia
2	yoi	7	tokua
3	yumelea	8	al nia
4	kolua	9	al penia
5	k le	10	alia

Now look at the first five numbers in the Nii (PNG) counting system on the primer page below. Notice they count the number of fingers down, not the fingers which are up.

You can make a simple mathematics counting book for your students. The Hewa counting books show all the numbers from one to ten. Note the page for number nine. The next pages after teaching the numbers ask *fen me* (how many?), as in the page with the birds in a nest.

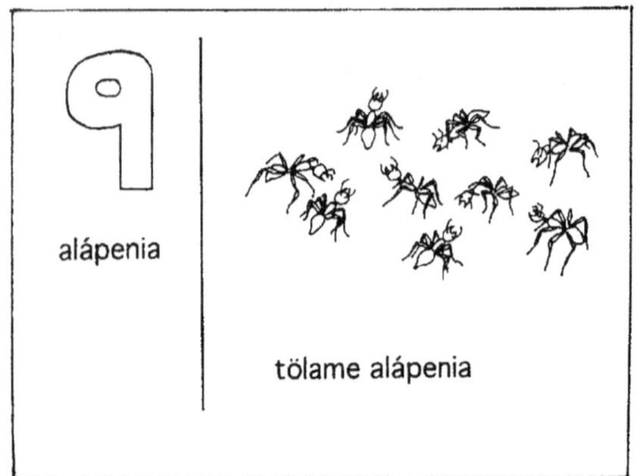

The last pages have space for the student to practice writing the numbers.

There are also many games you can play to help students get to know the digits. Some are listed on the pages that follow. Collect as many other games as you can find.

Matching digits to pictures of numbers. Make a set of number cards and a set of picture cards to go with them. Encourage the students to play games with the cards matching the number to the right picture card. Picture cards can be made using pictures of real things or can be made in the form of an array.

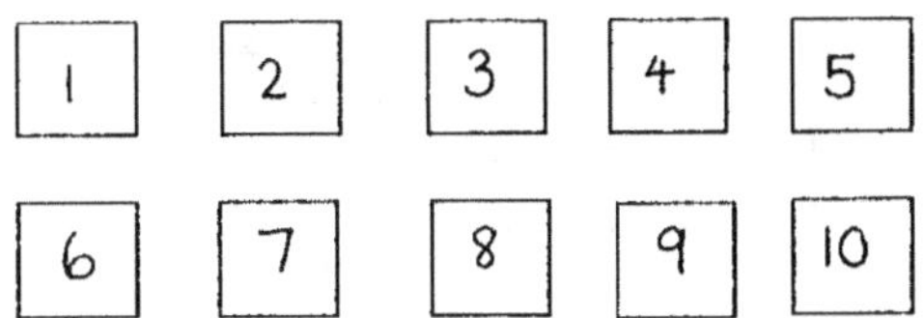

Sample picture cards (with their number cards next to them):

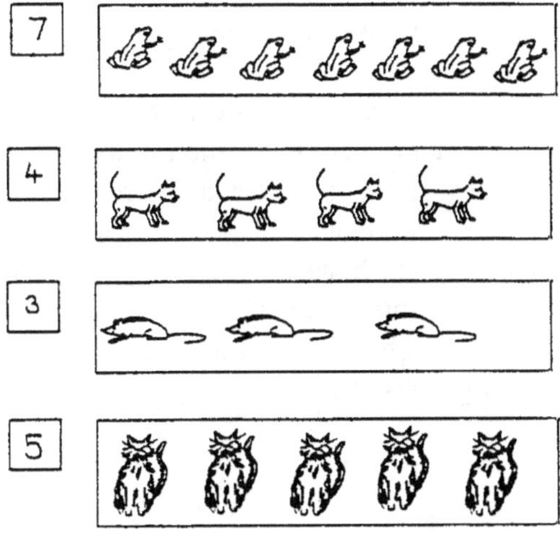

Sample array cards:

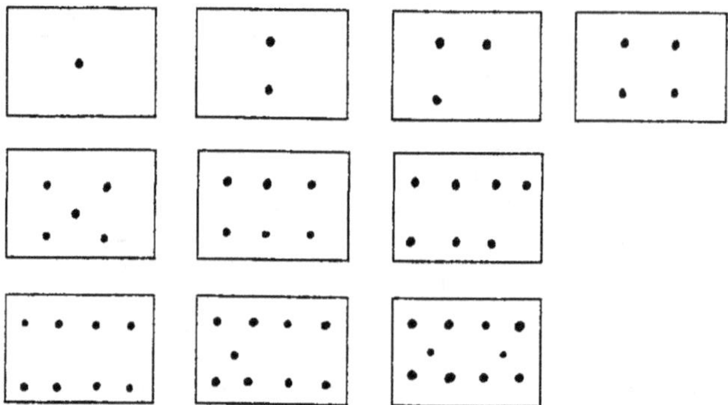

You can play several games using the number and picture card sets.

Number shuffle. Shuffle the number cards and deal one to each student. Have the student read the number on the card and then collect the same number of stones from a tin of stones. Or have the students draw as many circles on their lapboards as are needed in order to match the number on their card. Have the students put the number cards in order from 0 to 10.

Play other card games with the flash cards such as "fish," or "snap," or "memory." (These games are described later in this chapter.)

Following are some activities which involve guessing a number. Students have to work out what the number is by asking questions.

I am thinking of a number.

Skills developed

- use of more than and less than
- problem solving
- revising number order

How to play

The teacher thinks of the number and gives the students clues:

"I am thinking of a number that comes between 7 and 9. What is my number?"

"I am thinking of a number that is less than 5 and more than 3. What is my number?"

I am thinking of a number between.

Skills developed
- use of more, less, odd, even
- problem solving
- revising number order

How to play (same as above)

T: I am thinking of a number between 1 and 15.
Q: Is it more than 10?
T: Yes, it is more than 10.
Q: Is it less than 13?
T: Yes it is less than 13.
Q: Is it an even number?
T: Yes it is an even number.
Q: Is it the number 12?
T: Yes.

Once the students can play this game well, have them take turns at thinking of the number and answering questions about the number.

What is my number? (from Beth Marr)

Skills developed
- use of mathematics language like: less than, more than, even, odd
- practice remembering information
- developing strategies to solve problems

Materials
- sticky labels, or small pieces of paper and sticky tape

How to play

1. Write some numbers on small pieces of paper (or on sticky labels) and stick one number on each student—on their head, forehead or neck (where it cannot be seen by that person). Make sure the numbers are ones that the students already know. For example, you may wish to begin with numbers between 1 and 30. Before the game begins tell the students what range the numbers fall in to help narrow the field, "All the numbers are between 1 and 30."

2. The aim of the game is for each person to discover their own number by asking questions of the other people in the class or group. These questions can only be answered by 'yes' or 'no'. It is a good idea for the teacher to demonstrate the game first. Have a student write a number on a card and place it on your head. Ask questions of the group to help you work out the number. By doing this you can show that some kinds of questions are better than others. Some questions will eliminate many numbers at once and allow you to focus on just a few numbers. For example, you can ask questions like the following:
    - Is it an odd number?
    - Does it have 2 digits?
    - Are the digits the same?
    - Is the number more than 20?
    - Is the number less than 15?

3. Now divide the students into groups of 2 or 3 people, giving each person a number. Students take turns asking questions of other people in their group until they discover their own number.

If you want the students to compete with each other, the winner of the game can be the person who used the least number of guesses to find out his own number. Questions such as "is it 25?" are not very helpful until the last question, because it only eliminates one number.

The teacher can use this time to make sure that the students know:

- the meaning of odd and even (even numbers end in 2, 4, 6, 8, or 0)
- that less than 30 does not include 30
- that digit means one single figure in the number, i.e., one of the numbers from 0 to 9

What day is the birthday party?

Skills developed
- practice in the use of ordinal numbers—first, second, third etc.
- working together to develop strategies

Materials
- pieces of paper

How to play
1. Divide the students into groups of three.
2. One student thinks of a number between 1 and 31, writes it on a piece of paper and turns the piece of paper face down. The other two students guess what day the birthday party is by asking questions. The first student can only answer "yes" or "no."
3. The first student keeps a tally of the number of questions asked. The person that gets the correct anwer by asking the smallest number of questions wins the round.
4. Discuss the strategies used for solving the problem with the students when they have played a few rounds.

Note: Not all cultures remember birthdays, so this activity may not be appropriate.

Number patterns: fill in the missing numbers. Put problems such as the following on the blackboard and have the students fill in the gaps and continue the number pattern. Use easy number combinations to start with.

Skills
- encourage counting in 2's, 3's, 5's, 10's, etc., both forwards and backwards
- seeing patterns in numbers

What numbers are missing?
2, 4, 6, 8, 10, __
3, 6, 9, 12, __ , 18
12, 11, 10, 9, 8, __, __
20, 18, 16, 14, __, 10, __
5, 10, 15, 20, __, __, 35
10, 20, 30, 40, __, __, 70

As the students' knowledge and skills increase, make up harder number patterns for them to solve. Working with hundreds and larger numbers is more difficult. Also, leaving gaps at the beginning of the patterns makes it harder.

Fill in the missing numbers
2, __, 6, 8, 10, __, __
10, __, 8, 7, __, __, 4
31, 41, 51, 61, 71, __, __, 101, 111
5, __, 15, __, __, 30, 35
106, ___, 306, 406, ___, ___
___, 90, 80, __, 60, __, 40

Check in your location if it is acceptable to use cards in mathematics games. Because of the history of cards in Papua New Guinea, in some areas it may be best not to use them. However, cards do provide an ideal way of making up many mathematics problems and giving students extra practice. Cards are also good because they are usually easy to get or can be made by hand if necessary.

Looking for sames.

Skills developed
- recognition of digits

Materials
- cards: Ace(1)–10

How to play
Give the pack of cards to a group of students. Let them find bundles of sames, e.g., all the twos, all the fives, etc. Encourage them to talk about the cards as they gather them, naming the bundles. For example, here are all the twos, are there any more threes? How many should we have in each bundle? Students can also count the spots on the cards and see that they match the digits.

Fish.

Skills developed
- number recognition
- naming of numbers

Materials
- a pack of cards

Number of players
- two to four

How to play
- Shuffle the cards. Deal 5 cards to each person and then place the rest of the pack in the middle of all the players, face down.
- Players collect their cards and look at them and hold them in their hands. They must not let other players see which cards they are holding.
- Each player collects any two cards in his hand which make a pair, and puts them in a pile in front of himself.
- Then, players take turns asking the player to their left for a card that is the same number as one of the cards they are holding in their hand.
- "Have you got a five?," one player may ask. If the player asked has a five he must give it to the one who asked for it. The pair of fives is then put on the pile of the person who asked for it.
- Then he asks the player on his left again for a card that is the same as another card in his hand. His turn ends when the player on the left cannot give him a card.
- If someone is asked for a card and he does not have that card, he replies, "Fish." Then the player who has been told to fish takes the top card from the rest of the pack which is in the middle of the circle of players, and the turn passes to the next player.
- Play continues until someone has made pairs of all the cards in his hand. When this happens, play stops and each player counts how many pairs he has in front of him. The person with the most pairs wins the round.

Snap.

Skills developed
- rapid recognition of numbers that are the same

Materials
- a pack of cards

Number of players
- two to four

How to play
- The pack is dealt with an equal number of cards to each player.
- Beginning with the person next to the dealer, each person takes a turn putting a card from his hand on to a common pile, face up.
- Play continues until two cards that are the same number are placed on top of each other. The first person to see they are the same, puts their hand over the pile of cards, and calls out "snap."
- He wins the pile of cards and adds them to the bottom of his own pile of cards.
- The game continues like this until someone runs out of cards. Then the person who has the most cards wins.

Runs.

Skills developed
- number sequencing

Materials
- a pack of playing cards

Number of players
- four

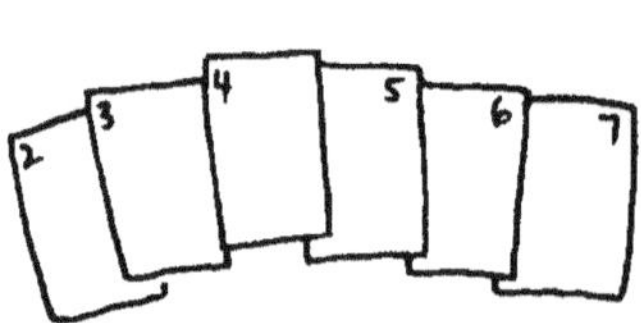

How to play

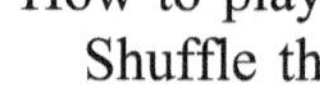

Shuffle the cards and spread them face up in the playing area. Have each person collect one set, that is, one person collects all the diamonds, another all the spades and so on. Then put the sets in ascending order. First to finish wins.

Variations: Try descending order

Flip.

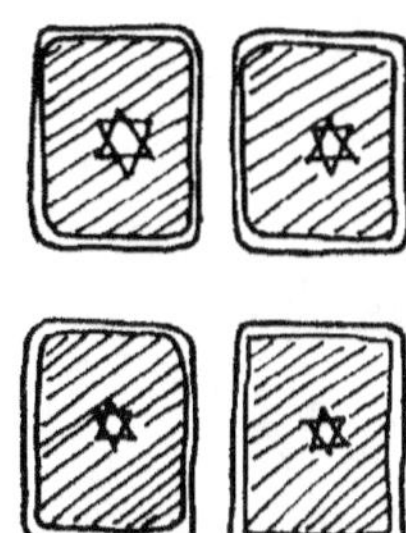

Skills developed
- number recognition

Materials
- a pack of cards, including a joker

Number of players
- two to four

How to play
- Each player is dealt four cards which they arrange face down:
- The rest of the pack is placed face down within reach of each player and the top card is turned over to make a discard pile. Each player has a turn to take a card either from the discard pile or the pack. This card can be used to improve any of the four cards in this hand, or it can be discarded.
- The aim of the game is to improve one's hand so that it makes the lowest score possible. The scoring is: Ace 1 point, King 0, other picture cards are worth ten, the rest of the cards are worth their face value.
- The player may only look at the bottom two cards in their hand, not the top two, although he can use the cards he picks up to replace any of his four cards.
- If a joker is played on the discard pile, the game stops immediately. Otherwise play continues until one player thinks his hand is better than the others' hands, and signals this by knocking on the table or ground.
- When someone knocks, play continues for one more turn each until the round comes back to the person who knocked. At this point everyone adds the total of his hand and compares it to the other players' totals. The smallest total wins the round.
- You can play several rounds and keep a running total to see who wins overall.

Rummy.

Skills developed
- number recognition
- sequencing

An example of a run: 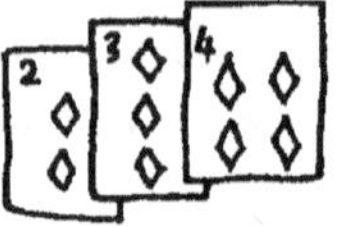

Materials
- a pack of cards
- score sheet

An example of a set: 

Number of players
- one to six

How to play
- Deal 5 cards to each person. The rest of the pack is placed in the middle of the players. The top card of the pack is turned face up and placed next to the main pack, to make a discard pile.
- The object of the game is to collect as many runs or sets as possible. A run is made up of three or more cards of the same suit that are in order. A set is three or more cards that are the same number, or the same picture.
- The player next to the dealer begins the play. He can either take the upturned card on the discard pile, or take the top one from the pile. The card taken can be added to the hand in order to improve it, or can be discarded face up on the discard pile. If the player wishes to keep the card, he must choose one of the other cards from his hand and discard it.
- If the player has runs or sets that he wishes to score from, he places these in front of him, face up, before he discards a card. Once a card is discarded, his turn is finished. If a player has a run or a set in front of himself, he then is allowed to add his cards to other players' runs. These cards, however, are not placed on the other people's runs, but are placed with his own runs.
- The game is over when one of the players has laid down all the cards from his hand as sets or runs, places one card on the discard pile, and has nothing left over.

[As the students will not know enough math to be able to total their score, just play that the person who finishes first wins. Normally at this point players count up how many cards they have in front of them, giving each picture card a value of ten and all other cards face value. If players are caught with cards still in their hands, the value of these is subtracted from their score. A running total is kept of each game and the player with the highest score when play is finished is the winner.]

Spoons.

Skills developed
- number recognition

Materials
- a pack of cards
- as many spoons as there are players, less one spoon. The spoons or sticks are placed in the playing area.

How to play
- Deal four cards to each player.
- One person operates the pack—he is the dealer.
- The dealer takes the top card off the pack and looks at it. He then decides to either discard it, or keep it and discard one of the other cards in his hand. The card is discarded face down to the next person. The next person's turn begins.
- That person either keeps the card or passes it on. Then the next person does the same, and so forth until the last person has received a card and decided to either keep it and discard another card from his hand, or to discard the card he received.
- As soon as the dealer is ready he takes another card from the pack, and decides either to keep it and pass on another, or to pass that one on. Each player who receives a card chooses what he will do with it, as explained above.
- The game continues until someone gets four cards the same. When this happens he quietly takes a spoon from the centre of the playing area. As soon as other people notice a spoon has been taken, they grab for a spoon also. One person must miss out on getting a spoon because there is one less spoon than players. The person who misses out loses that round.

Turn up two.

Skills developed

- reading 2-digit numbers

Materials

- pack of cards with tens and picture cards removed

How to play

Shuffle the cards. Take two cards from the pack and place them face up so everyone can see them.

Use the digits to make a number. Tell everyone the number. Pass the pack to the next person.

For example, you may turn up a 4 and a 2. You can make 42 or 24.

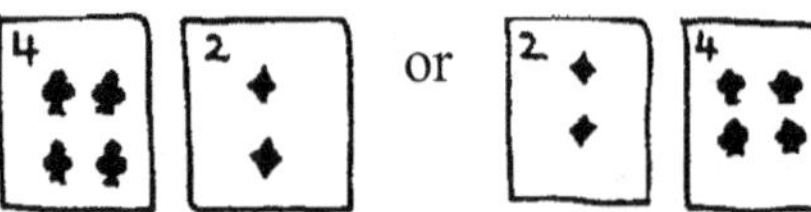

Addition and subtraction

Once the students are familiar with numbers and what they stand for they can begin learning about how to work with numbers. There are four basic kinds of processes that we do on numbers. They are: addition, subtraction, multiplication, and division. In beginning literacy classes, I concentrate on teaching addition and subtraction.

Start with simple addition problems. Using everyday mathematics problems so students can see the link between the numbers on the page and things that happen in real life. A simple addition problem from the Kanite mathematics book is reproduced below.

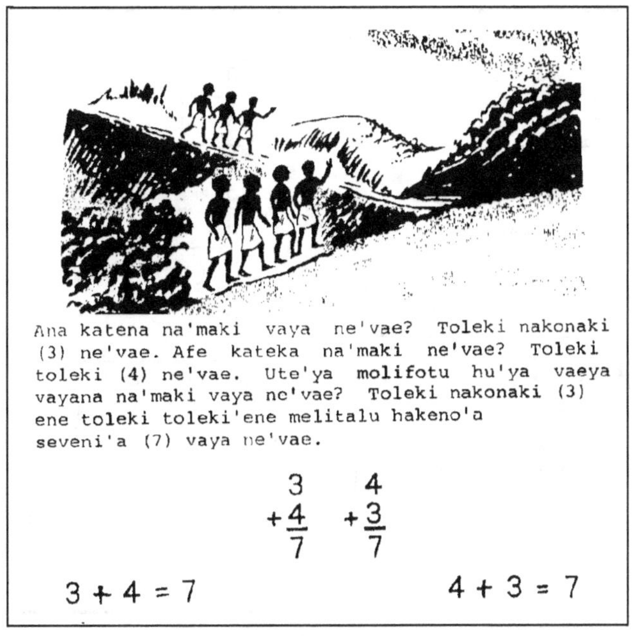

[Translation: Three men came on one road and two others arrived on another road. All the people met and went on. How many went on?]

In the book the 'plus' mark and the 'equals' mark are also explained in Kanite as follows.

> This mark is called plus. It means that all the numbers near it are to be joined together into one bigger number. Plus means join.
>
> This mark is called equals. It means that the things on one side of the mark are the same as the things on the other side of the mark. Equals means the same.

Have the students make up number stories using objects from the local environment—sticks, shells, leaves, and stones. After you have done problems like these, give the students a lot of picture problems to work with before moving on to problems that just involve numbers. Some examples from the Nii mathematics book are shown below.

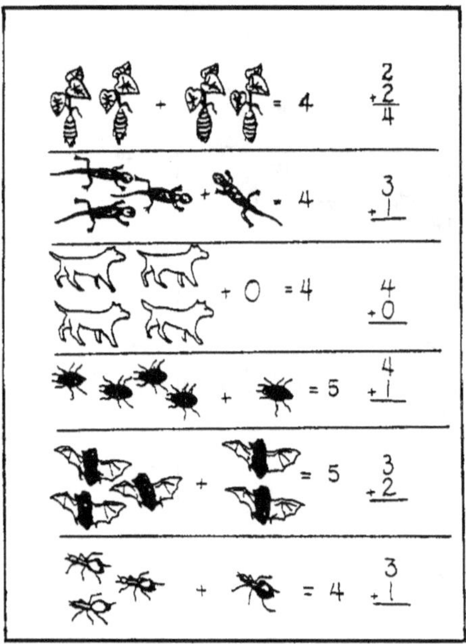

3 +1 4	2 +4 6	1 +1	0 +5	2 +1	4 +2	1 +0
3 +3 6	5 +1 6	2 +2	1 +4	0 +3	1 +3	5 +0
1 +2 3	0 +1 1	1 +5	4 +1	2 +3	0 +4	5 2
4 3 7	6 1 7	4 4	5 3	2 5	3 4	6 1
7 1 8	8 0 8	5 1	6 2	2 6	3 5	4 4

When the students have understood addition at this simple level then you can introduce them to subtraction. Again start by using picture problems, number stories using local objects, and then move to number problems such as the following.

2 -1	3 -1	4 -2	4 -0	5 -1	4 -1
7 -1	6 -1	3 -2	4 -3	5 -2	6 -2
10 -1	7 -2	6 -0	7 -6	8 -1	10 -9
8 -2	10 -0	7 -4	6 -2	7 -5	7 -6
7 -3	8 -1	10 -5	5 -4	6 -2	8 -4
10 -2	5 -3	5 -4	6 -3	6 -4	7 -0

Multiplication and division

Once the students have learned addition and subtraction, they can learn multiplication and division if they want to. Start with picture problems and number stories using local objects. Then move on to problems with just numbers such as the following.

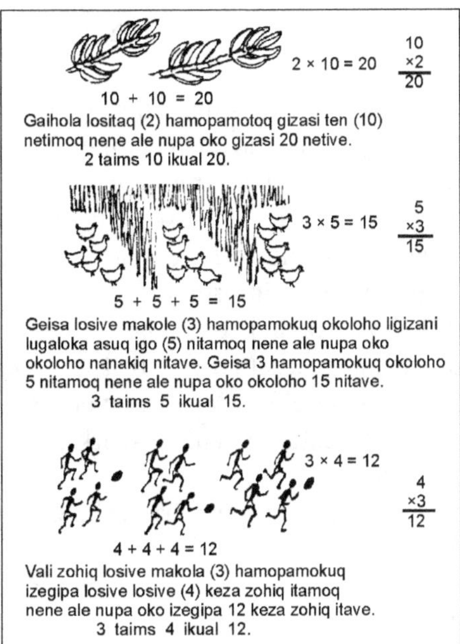

3	3	6	9	10	8	9
x3	x2	x3	x2	x1	x3	x2
6	7	6	8	8	4	3
x3	x3	x2	x1	x3	x2	x1
8	8	2	9	5	7	6
x2	x3	x1	x2	x3	x2	x3
5	2	8	9	7	3	8
x3	x3	x2	x1	x3	x2	x3
7	10	9	2	5	9	4
x2	x3	x2	x3	x2	x1	x3

Some people like to learn multiplication tables so they can do multiplication sums quickly. Tables for one through three are listed below.

1	0	0	2	0	0	3	0	0
1	1	1	2	1	2	3	1	3
1	2	2	2	2	4	3	2	6
1	3	3	2	3	6	3	3	9
1	4	4	2	4	8	3	4	12
1	5	5	2	5	10	3	5	15
1	6	6	2	6	12	3	6	18
1	7	7	2	7	14	3	7	21
1	8	8	2	8	16	3	8	24
1	9	9	2	9	18	3	9	27
1	10	10	2	10	20	3	10	30

When my daughter Rachel was learning her times (multiplication) tables, she enjoyed doing speed sheets for two minutes every lesson. The sheets were full of rows of sums like the following.

2	3	6	4	8	5	7	9	0	1	6	3	7	8	9
4	2	5	4	3	3	4	3	6	9	8	5	8	5	3

In class, the students were told when to start and when to stop. They worked along the rows as quickly as they could to see how many they could do in the time. Then they corrected them. They kept their own record and always tried to improve on their personal scores. They also knew the best record from the previous class and were trying to beat that. The emphasis, however, was on each student measuring himself against what he had done before, not against other students, to see how much he was improving.

Doing these sheets for two minutes each day helped Rachel revise her tables and become quicker at multiplication. Speed is important in mental mathematics, so it is good to have a session each day that encourages each student to work quickly. Because everyone is at a different level of ability, it is good for each one to set a realistic goal to work towards, a goal which he feels he can achieve with a little extra effort.

The last operation to teach is division. Below are some examples from the Gahuku mathematics book followed by a translation of them.

Luhuva imane ⟌ agulizaq tivaitet itoq intu nene neve. Neneqmo napaguq itekakaliqmini luhuva neve. Neneqmo noigo, nampa sogaloka minamoq neneqmo nampa lamagaloka minamoq neneqmini agikaguq iteko lelegiq okakaliqmini mogona lelepizekakaq noive.

2⟌4 = 2

Venaq makoliqmo goive losive losive aleneive. Aiq izegipala lositaq keza lelegiq iki alitaqimoq nene goive nanakiq alitaqive. Keza etoq etoq iki goive lositaq alitaqive.

2 intu 4 ikual 2

2⟌6 = 3

Ve makoliqmo mageq 6 aleneike lelegiq oko gona moloko izegipala lositaq kimitive. Izegipalate etoq etoq iki mageq nanakiq alitaqive. Keze etoq etoq iki mageq losive makole (3) alitaqive.

2 intu 6 ikual 3

4⟌4 = 1

Venaq makoliqmo loq losive losive aleneike ezagi mohola losive makolegi lelegiq iki loq aliki vitamoq nene etoq etoq iki loq hamoq aliki vitaze.

4 intu 4 ikual 1

2⟌14	2⟌8	2⟌10
3⟌21	3⟌15	3⟌30
5⟌0	5⟌25	5⟌10
1⟌9	1⟌5	1⟌7
10⟌20	10⟌40	10⟌30

> Translation: The name of this sign $\overline{)\quad}$ is divided into. It is a sign of going into something bigger. When it is there, it shows us the equivalent of the number on the left going into the number on the right.
>
> A woman has four sweet potatoes. If her children will receive equally, how many sweet potatoes will each get? They will each get two sweet potatoes.
>
> A man who has six arrows is going to apportion equally and give them to his two sons. How many arrows will each of them get? They will each get three arrows.
>
> A woman has four sticks of firewood; if she and her three girls carry them equally, how many will each take away? They will each take one stick of firewood.

Do not rush to teach all these types of math. Give the students plenty of time to understand them, one by one. Teachers in schools take several years to teach these things, and new students will need a lot of time to learn them too.

When the students are good at doing mathematics, it is also good to give them practice at rounding numbers up and down, because it is useful in daily life. Teach the student to use an easier number that is close to the value of the one he is working with, so he can work quickly. For example, it is difficult to multiply 29 by 3, but it is easy to round the 29 to 30, and use that instead. By multiplying 30 by 3, it is easy to know that the answer will be close to 90.

Another helpful mental strategy that people use in real life mathematics is called decomposing. This means breaking a number down to its parts. For example, when adding 7 to 57, I first decompose the 7 to 3 4. I know that if I add 3 to 57 the answer will be 60; that is why I chose to use a 3 when I decomposed the number 7. From there it is easy to add on the 4 that was left over, and get a total of 63.

Following are two more number games that can be used in class. (They are taken from *Growing in Numbers* by B. Marr and S. Helme, 1991.)

Number triangles.

Skills developed

- problem solving in groups or independently
- addition facts

Materials

- number triangles written on the black-board or on separate cards

How to play
Put numbers in the circles so that each pair adds up to the number between them.
For example:

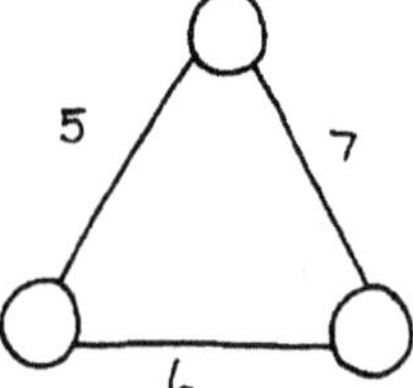

would be

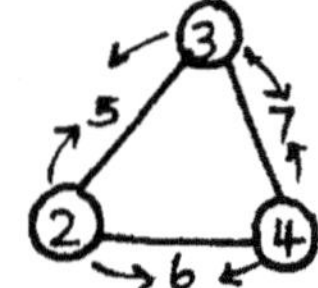

because:

2	3	5
3	4	7
2	4	6

Try to work out what numbers to put in the circles below.

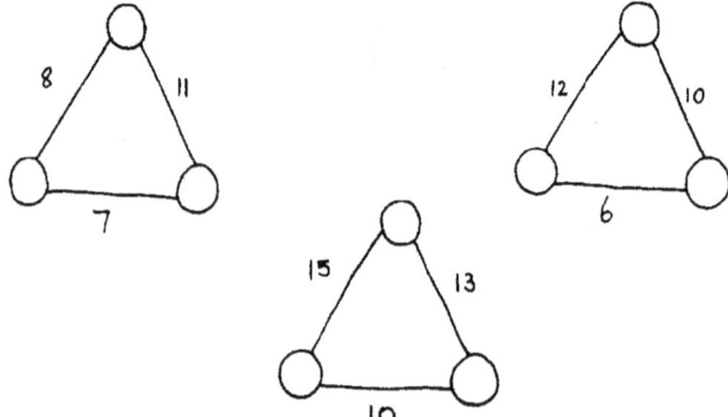

Make up one of these puzzles for a friend to work out.

You can build up a collection of problems like these.

Magic squares.

Skills developed

- addition
- problem solving

Materials

- lapboards and chalk, or paper and pencil

How to play
In all these squares all the **rows**, **columns,** and **diagonals** add up to the same total.

8		
	5	7
		2

Use all the digits from 1 to 9
They are: 1, 2, 3, 4, 5, 6, 7, 8, 9

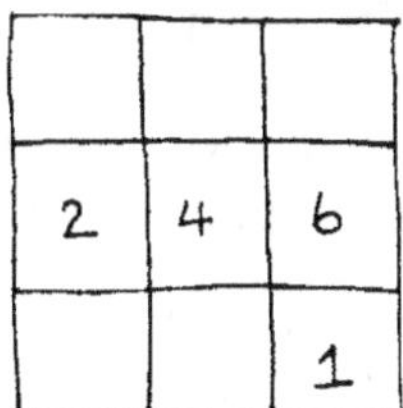

Use all the digits from 0 to 8.
They are: 0, 1, 2, 3, 4, 5, 6, 7, 8

	2	
	6	8
	10	

Use all the digits from 2 to 10

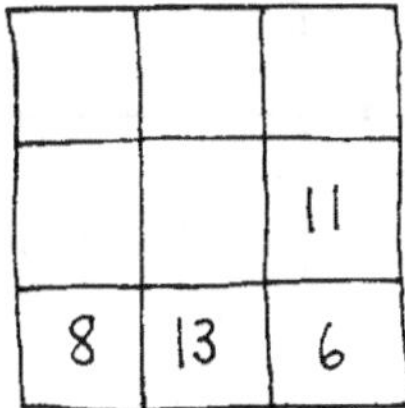

Use all the digits from 5 to 13

Place value

As mentioned earlier in this chapter, the position of a digit in a number changes its value. For example, the digit 7 can take on different meanings, depending on where it is in a number.

729 7 73 7500 K1.07 K7.00

Students need to learn to recognize the value of digits in the different places that they might see them within a number.

Making the number.

Skills developed

- understanding place value
- making, saying, writing numbers in the range 1 to 99, and then in the range 100 to 999.

Materials

- a card for hundreds, tens, and units.
- bundles of straws or sticks in ones, tens, and ten tens.

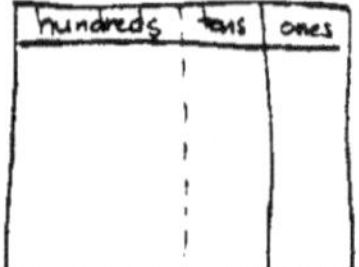

How to play

Using bundles of sticks or straws and working in pairs or small groups, practice making the numbers that the teacher calls out. As the number is called, place the right number of bundles or sticks in the correct column on the card.

For students who are just beginning, fold the card so that the hundreds column is out of sight and concentrate on numbers only from 1 up to 99.

Make sure each student practices making the number, saying it, and also writing it.

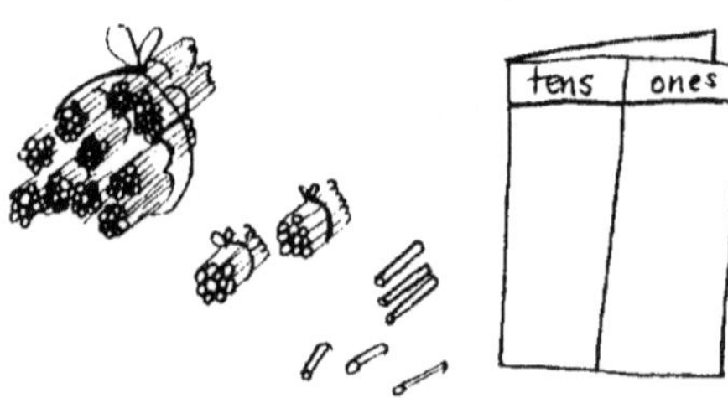

When the students are confident, fold out the hundreds column and practice making numbers that are 999 or less.

The same materials can be used to practice adding and subtracting numbers. Give people practice writing the sums, working out the answers and reading the answers. Have them practice both ways of writing sums.

$$23 \quad 36 \qquad \text{and} \qquad \begin{array}{r} 23 \\ \underline{36} \end{array}$$

When giving practice with subtracting numbers, start with the easier sums and move gradually to the harder ones.

Type 1.	23 – 13
Type 2.	32 – 7
Type 3.	43 – 16
Type 4.	100 – 45

Following are further games to help students learn place value.

Arranging the digits.

Skills developed
- understanding place value to three places.
- understanding place value to four places

Materials
- pencil and paper, or blackboard and chalk

Growing in Numbers, B. Marr and S. Helme 1991

How to play

How many numbers can you make with these three digits?

1 2 3

How many numbers can you make with these four digits?

1 2 3 4

Double digit.

Skills developed
- understanding place value
- a little probability
- addition
- reading numbers

Materials
- one pack of cards or ten-sided dice
- each person makes a scoresheet on their paper or kneeboard

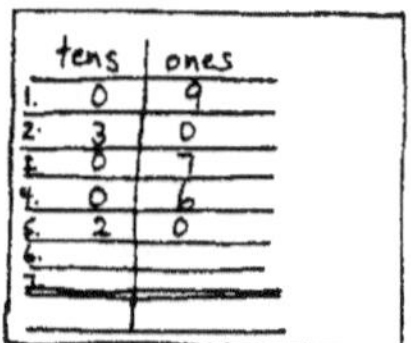

How to play

The teacher or one of the students uses a ten-sided dice or a pack of cards with 10's and picture cards removed.

Shuffle the cards and deal one. Call the number of that card. Or if you are using a dice, roll the dice and call the number that is on top.

As the numbers are called players must choose whether to put it in the tens **or** ones column. Once they have written it in one column, a '0' is written in the other column. This is done seven times.

At the end of the game the players add up the total of the seven numbers and compare them. The player who is closest to 100, without going past it, is the winner.

Multidigit.

Skills developed
- place value
- probability
- addition
- talking about big numbers
- comparing numbers

Materials
- frameworks drawn on kneeboards or on paper
- chalk or pencils

How to play

Use a ten-sided dice or two sets of cards with the digits 0–9 written on them. One person shuffles the cards and then deals them, (or rolls the dice). That person calls out the digits one at a time as they come up.

As the digits are called, students write them in the frameworks starting with row 1 and moving downwards. The aim of the game is to make the biggest number that can be made in each row.

You can make the framework any size depending on the level of difficulty.

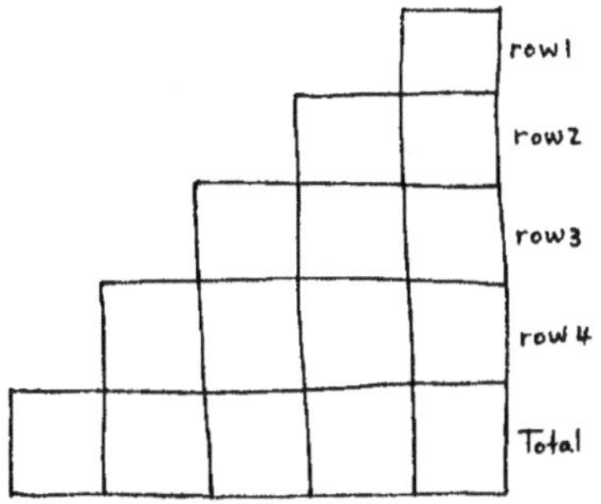

Beth Marr, lecture notes

At the end of each row, students compare their numbers and see who got the biggest numbers.

At the end of the framework all the columns can be added up. Each person reads out their grand total. Discuss who has the biggest number.

Have students line themselves up using their number. They should not show their number to others, but must read it to any other person who asks them. They should line themselves up in order, from highest number to lowest.

13.3 Telling the time

Some students may wish to learn to tell the time. Teach them what the numbers on the face of a clock mean. Talk about the big hand and the little hand, or the long hand and the short hand, and the jobs each hand has.

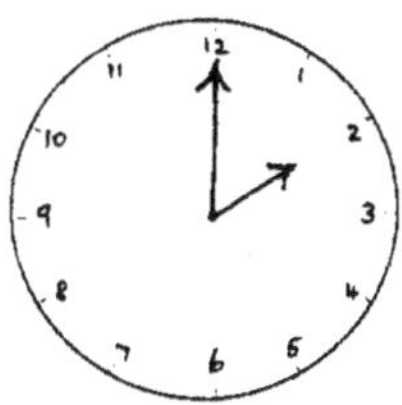

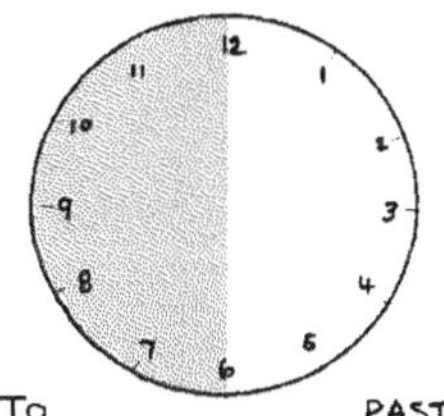

Then teach them the "o'clock" position.

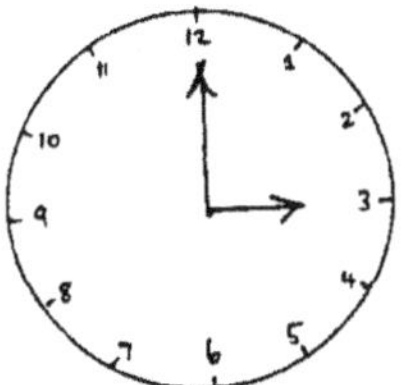

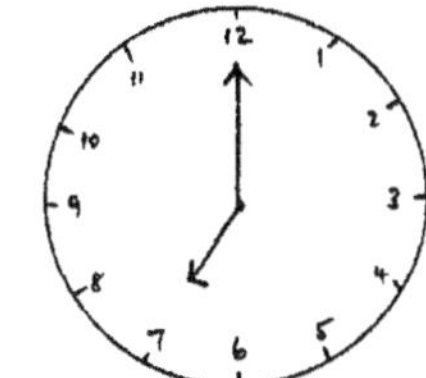

Then teach them the "half past" position:

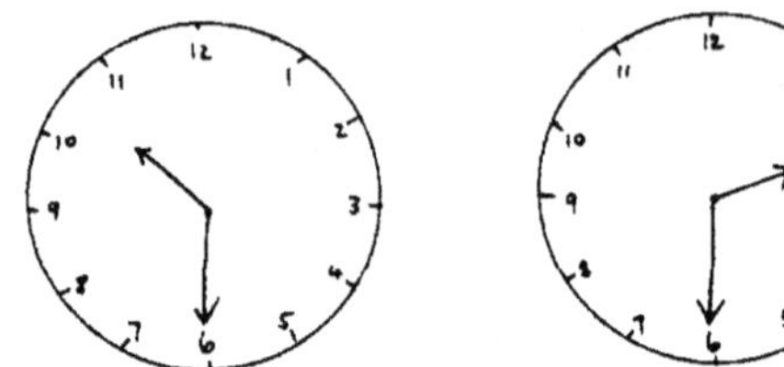
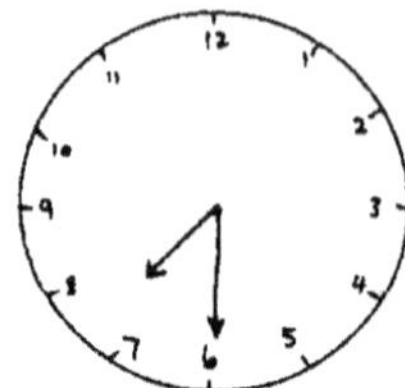

Then teach them the "quarter past" and "quarter to" positions:

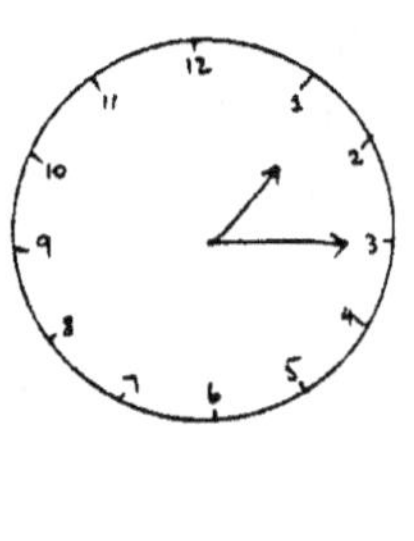

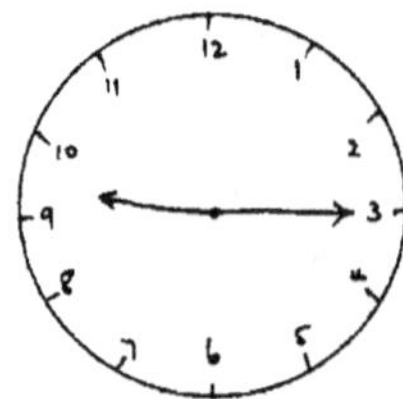

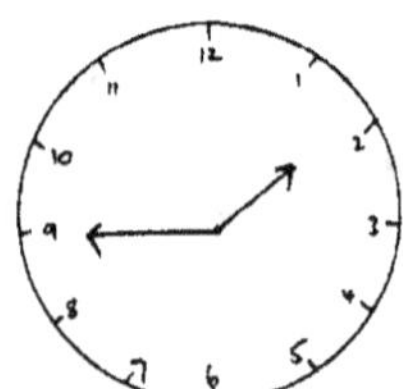

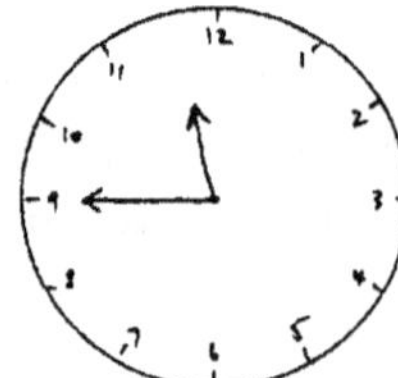

13.4 Practice problems using money

Some students may wish to practice adding and subtracting money. Teach them the value of all the notes and coins. The following examples refer to “toea” and “kina” which are currencies used in Papua New Guinea. The instructor will want to adapt these lessons to the currency used in his area.

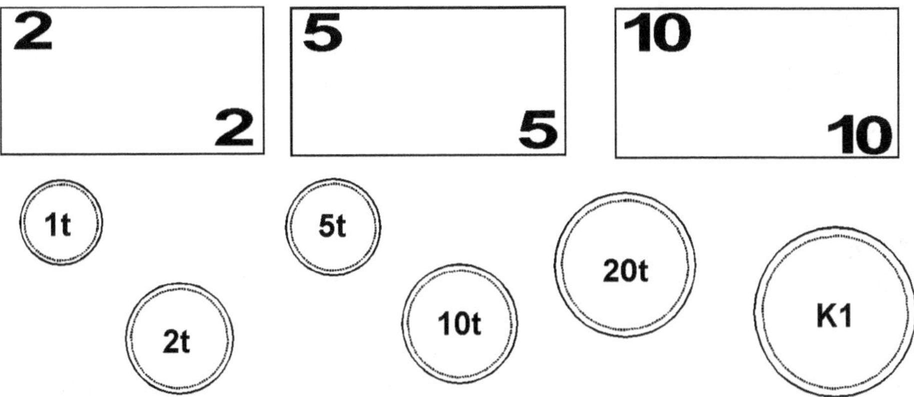

Teach them how to combine low value coins to equal the value of coins with a greater value.

2t + 2t + 5t + 1t = 10t

Making money 1.

Skills developed

- recognition of coins
- addition of coins

Materials:

- selection of smaller coins, or cardboard cutouts of coins

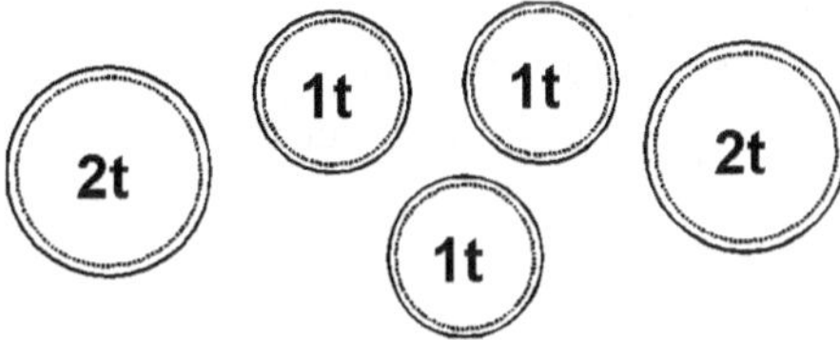

Use smaller coins to make exactly 5 toea.
Use smaller coins to make exactly 10 toea.
How many other ways can you do this?

Making money 2.

Skills developed
- recognition of coins
- addition of coins

Materials:
- selection of smaller coins, or cardboard cutouts of coins

Can you make 9 toea using exactly 3 coins?
then using four coins?
then using five coins?

How many different ways can you do each of these problems?

Making money 3.

Skills developed
- recognition of coins
- addition of coins

Materials:
- selection of smaller coins, or cardboard cutouts of coins

Use small value coins to make exactly 25 toea.

How many other ways can you do this?

Making money 4.

Skills developed
- recognition of coins
- addition of coins

Materials:
- selection of smaller coins, or cardboard cutouts of coins

How many different ways are there for making one kina using small value coins?

Keep a record of the different ways as you go.

Making money 5.

Skills developed

- recognition of kina notes
- addition of kina

Materials:

- a selection of paper kina play money and kina coins. These can be made by the class. They should always be marked as play money.

How many different ways can you find to make K20 using kina coins and other paper notes?

Keep a record of the different ways as you go.

There are many kinds of money problems you can make up to help people learn the combinations of coins that make up larger values. Begin making a collection of money problems like the above and keep adding to it. It is good to give practice with the coins of small value, because people who are not used to handling money often do not realise that the smaller value coins can join together to make larger amounts. One group of people I worked with called the small coins 'rubbish money'. They could not add up their value, so they did not use them. They gave them to their children to play with.

Shopping problems

Make up some everyday kinds of money problems related to shopping for your students to work out. Work these problems out in groups and have the groups discuss the strategies they used to get their answers. This gives a good opportunity for people to learn from each other, and to learn other ways of doing the same problem.

Below is a shopping problem from the Girawa mathematics book.

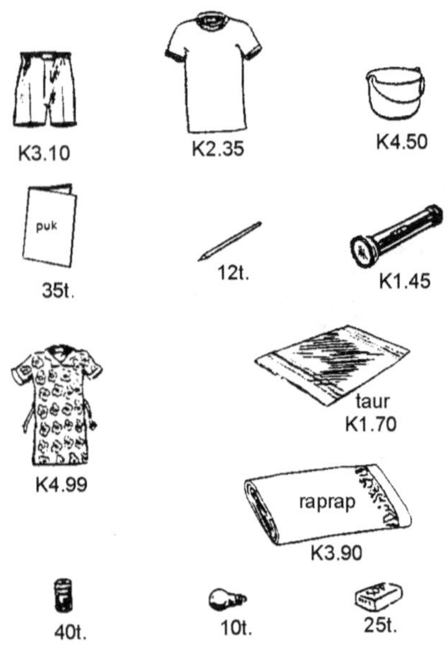

1. Mokoi bought a pencil and a book. How much did he pay?
2. A man bought trousers and a shirt. How much did he pay?
3. A woman bought a torch and soap. How much did she pay?
4. A man bought a battery, a globe, and a saucepan. How much did she pay?
5. Toni had 20 toea. He bought a pencil. How much change did he get?
6. Maria had K5.00. She bought a dress. How much change did she get?
7. Matiu bought 3 batteries. How much did he give the store keeper?
8. My mother has K1.00. She wants to buy 5 soaps. Has she enough money or not?

Following are a few more problems. Students should be encouraged to work these sums out in their heads, like they would if they were shopping. They might wish to start with paper and pencil if they are unsure about what to do.

Buying stamps.

Skills developed

- multiplication and division of money
- rounding and approximating
- problem solving in groups

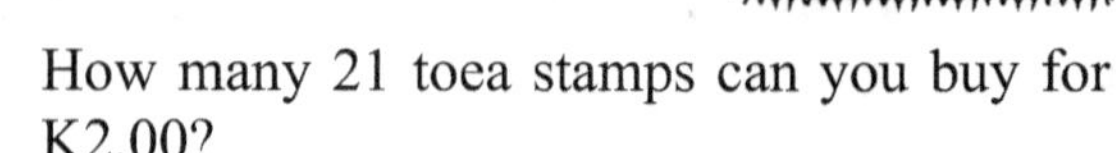

How many 21 toea stamps can you buy for K2.00?

Buying tinned fish.

Skills developed

- operating on numbers
- money knowledge
- rounding, approximating, checking
- problem solving in groups

If I had K4.00 and a tin of fish cost 78 toea, how many tins could I buy?

What change would I get?

Buying soap powder.

Skills developed

- operating on numbers
- money knowledge
- rounding, approximating, checking, comparing
- problem solving in groups

A 200 gram box of Omo costs K0.98.
A 600 gram box of Omo costs K2.95.
Which is the better buy?

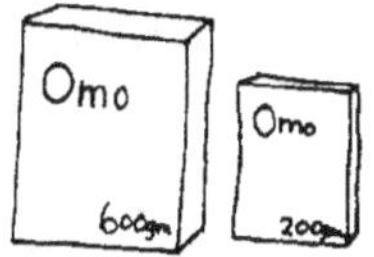

The following pages have some more card games you may be able to use in your mathematics lessons.

Ten combo, single deal.

Skills developed

- addition, subtraction, mental mathematics

Materials

- pack of cards, Ace (1) to 9

How to play

Deal each player 5 cards.

How many combinations can they make which add up to ten?

Ten combo, double deal.

Skills developed

- addition, subtraction, mental mathematics

Materials

- pack of cards, Ace (1) to 9

How to play

Deal each player 5 cards. Again players are looking for combinations which add up to ten.

Players can discard as many cards as they like, once, and get the dealer to replace the number of cards discarded.

How many combinations which add up to ten can you make?

Turn up two.

Skills developed

- addition

Materials

- pack of cards without picture cards

How to play

Dealer deals 2 cards to each player. They must add the two digits together and call out their answer. Dealer checks their answer.

When the pack is finished, it is the end of the game, or time to change dealers.

Facts turn up.

Skills developed

- addition facts to 20

Materials

- pack of cards without picture cards

How to play

Dealer chooses a number from 11 to 20, then deals each player a card. Players then choose what needs to be added to their card to make 20. The dealer must check their answers to make sure they are correct. The dealer then chooses another number and deals each player a card. Keep playing until the end of the pack. Then change dealers and start again.

Times turn up.

Skills developed

- times tables

Materials

- pack of cards without picture cards

How to play

Two cards are dealt to each player. These must be multiplied together and a total called out. Dealer checks their answers.

When the pack is finished it is the end of the game, or time to change dealers.

How close can you get.

Skills developed

- subtraction, estimation, addition, place value, mental arithmetic

Materials

- deck of cards, remove 10's and all picture card.
- paper and pencil

Number of players

- two to five

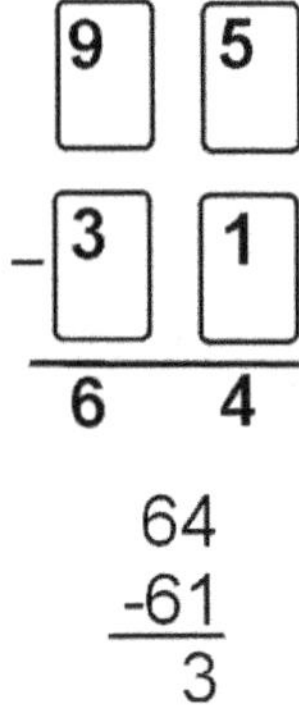

How to play

Deal each player four cards face down.

Turn up two more cards. The first card goes in the tens' place and the second in the ones' place to form the target number. For example, a six then an ace makes 61.

Target number

Round 1:

The players turn up their four cards and arrange them into two 2-digit numbers, so that when they **subtract** their two numbers the result will be as close to the target number as possible.

To count the score, each player finds how close he is to the target number by subtracting his result from the target number or vice versa, depending on which number is larger.

For example, if the target number is 61 and a player has an Ace, a 5, 3, and 9, the best she could do is 95 – 31 64. Her score for that round would be 3 (64 – 61 3).

You can go over or under the target number. 64 has a difference of three from 61, and a 58 also has a difference of three from 61, so either 58 or 64 would give a score of three from the target number 61.

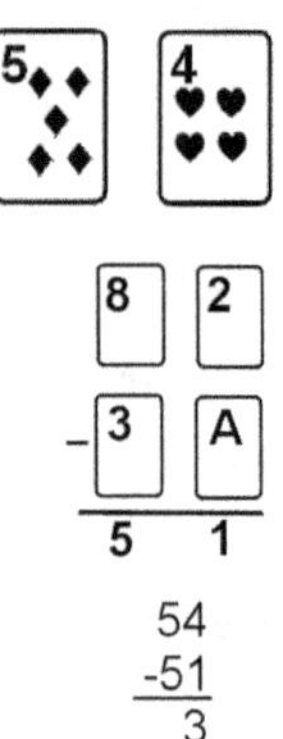

Round 2:

Turn up two new cards from the pack to make the next target number. Players can choose to use their same four cards and proceed as above, or have four new cards dealt out.

Play five rounds. The player with the lowest total score wins.

You might like to try a 3-digit target number and six cards for each player.

These are just a few maths activities that I have collected. Keep more and add them to your collection.

Literacy must help with better crops and help poor farmers improve their situation.
Literacy is learning to read & write anything I can say.
ka ke ku
ba be bu
What is Literacy?
Literacy must include everyday maths. People get cheated if they can't read the scales.
Coffee Export Quality
Literacy is being able to read & understand instructions.
THIS WAY UP!
DANGER EXPLOSIVES
Gardening made easy
Rooster & Wallaby
BIBLE
Malaria
Literacy is teaching people to understand and improve their world.
We want better housing
Health Care for our Children!!
STOP Political Corruption
To the editor on the issue of rent and tenants agreement
I think
Literacy is using reading & writing in everyday situations for real purposes.
Sarah is going to write to him. Maybe we should, too.
What chapter did he say to read?
I got a letter from Ken. He says, "Greetings, ..."
Here it is! I'll read it.
There's no Chapter 28. He must have meant Matthew 28.

14

What Is Literacy?

Many people think a book like this should start with a chapter that talks about what literacy is, rather than finishing with it. I wrote this as the last chapter because I wanted to first discuss things I think are at the core of literacy work and build up your knowledge about those things. This knowledge would then help you decide what literacy involves. It also helps you understand what others are saying when they offer answers to the question "what is literacy?" These answers are called definitions of literacy. So I have tried in the previous chapters of this book to build up your knowledge base first, before discussing the theory of what literacy is.

It is helpful for people involved in literacy work to have a good idea of what literacy work is about. This helps them to work successfully at their job. It helps them to decide what to do, what not to do, and sometimes how to do things. That is why many people over many years have struggled to come up with a good definition of literacy.

14.1 The many definitions of literacy

Before World War II it was thought that someone was literate if they could sign their name on a piece of paper. During that war people began to think that being literate was more than just being able to sign your name.

The problem came up when soldiers who were fit and able to serve in the war could not be used until they had learned to read and understand the written instructions for their basic army jobs.

In 1947, educators in the United States linked literacy ability with having some primary school education. They thought that people who had done at least five years of schooling would be literate and would be able to understand simple written instructions (Levine 1986:26).

Some people mentioned languages in their definitions of literacy. Because of UNESCO's work in trying to encourage literacy and development at the grass roots level in third-world countries, their definitions of literacy came to include an understanding that literacy would be carried out in the mother tongue. "A basic definition of literacy is the ability to read and write in the mother tongue" (Bhola 1992:12).

The definition put forward by Sarah Gudschinsky and adopted by the Summer Institute of Linguistics with its world-wide focus on vernacular literacy work also mentions the language of literacy ability. "That person is literate who, in a language that he speaks, can read and understand anything he would have understood if it had been spoken to him, and who can write, so that it can be read, anything that he can say" (Gudschinsky 1975:3).

Functional literacy

People who talk about functional literacy say that literacy is not just being able to read, write, and understand written instructions. Literacy should be linked more closely to the issues of economic and technological development and improved living conditions.

> Illiteracy is part of a tragic circle of underproduction, malnutrition and endemic disease. The circle cannot be broken by an attack on only one of these elements. (UNESCO 1951, quoted in Levine 1986:27)

Functional literacy links reading, writing, and development closely to the ways in which an average person uses literacy in his own culture. It says that literacy should help people to function well in their own cultures. UNESCO adopted the idea of functional literacy and their literacy programmes focused on teaching literacy while also teaching health, agricultural, or some other development programme.

> Literacy is no longer seen as an end in itself, but as a means of gaining useful knowledge and skills. Ideally, functional literacy is acquired by being used, and used while it is being acquired. It is essentially adult education and training, with literacy as a built-in component. So the substance of what is taught, the technical content, takes on a real importance. It determines and controls the method, the language, the media and even the selection and training of teachers and instructors. (UNESCO 1970:76–77)

The meaning of functional literacy has changed over the years. It has become more and more closely tied in with economics. Today, functional literacy programmes have three curriculum components: literacy, functionality and awareness; with economics still being the major focus. Bhola argues that the standard of literacy in these kinds of programmes should be one that helps the students to maintain their new literacy skills and not drop back into illiteracy. He also says that functional literacy is a life-long education when it is done properly (Bhola 1992:42, 60).

Some teachers and researchers did not like placing the strong emphasis of functional literacy on helping people to improve their money-making activities. They said that functioning in society is linked with more than just money and better crops, even though these things are important. They said literacy is also important for other things such as: communication and further learning, helping people become better parents or better citizens, and helping people find out about things they are interested in for themselves (Street 1990:32).

Social constructions and social contexts

In the 1980s, another group of educators began examining literacy from yet another direction. They felt that literacy has to do with people communicating with each other in social settings.

> Writing systems are cultural products...we don't pick them off trees like we do fruit, or hunt them as we do animals. And further, people do not learn to read just from interacting with objects in the world, but they learn to read from other people, and what they learn to read has been written by other people. (McCormick, Video 3)

Westerners tend to think of reading as something individuals learn to do on their own and something used for ourselves—an individual process. But this group of educators and researchers say reading is a "social interactional activity," something done in social settings where people interact with each other.

Educators began to look at the social interactions that took place in situations where students were learning to read. These interactions were between the teacher and the student, and between student and student. They looked carefully at things like how turn taking was controlled in the group, the kind of language that was used (school language), the hidden rules students had to learn about how to perform in the reading class, and the things that students did to each other in these situations (McDermott 1985; Cazden 1985).

Then people began researching about how attitudes and ways of doing things in the community where the learners lived affected what was happening in the class. McDermott looked at the attitudes of inner-city black children in the street gangs, and how these attitudes stopped some students from working hard and succeeding at their lessons. Heath, Au, and Ochs looked at how community ways and values were so different from school ways and values that the students were confused by these two different ways of behaving. Au found that when they used some of the community ways in the schoolroom the students progress was much improved.

Other educators have looked carefully at social interactions and use of literacy in different cultural settings. They looked at how people use literacy in their everyday living and the kinds of social interactions that are involved. The works of Heath, Street, and Wagner, Messick and Spratt, for example, show how people not only learn literacy in social ways but also use their literacy skills in social settings—constructing meanings together for mutual purposes.

These areas of research which involve the social interactions that occur when people are learning to read and write, or when they are involved in using literacy in their everyday lives, all make up the social perspective of literacy.

A 'critical literacy' perspective

Another group of educators are interested in viewing literacy from a 'critical literacy' perspective. They are concerned with teaching literacy so that the people learning the literacy skills can use them to understand their situations better, to study and think about their world, and to work out ways to improve their lives.

Thinking critically is an important skill. For example, some people think they need education but they never think through the reasons why they need or want it. A friend explained it to me this way.

> You ask people, "Why do you want education?" and they reply, "Because if you get educated, you get a job. And if you get a job, you get money. And money is good because it buys clothing, and salt, and kerosene and store food and soap, and outboard motors." But do they stop to think if they need an outboard motor? If they buy an outboard motor, they also buy the headache of maintaining it. Maintaining it costs more money. So they will need to work more to get money to pay for the headaches. Do they want to have to work hard to pay for headaches?
>
> Instead they could think, "Our brother down the road has a boat. And you guys in this clan you don't need to have a boat. Let's hire the other clan's boat. Let's support them." That's the other thing that is not available in the village, supporting one another. One clan supporting another clan. Let them have the headaches [of owning and maintaining a boat] but let's give them the money so that they can

> deal with the headaches. But people in the village do not think that way. (personal communication from a Papua New Guinean)

Using boats belonging to others instead of buying one for themselves is an example of using critical thinking applied to a particular situation. The speaker had learned that skill and was able to make use of it, but he felt that the people of his village had not yet learned it. Thinking critically about things can lead to better development of many aspects of one's life. This applies both to individuals and to communities.

Critical literacy workers define literacy differently than other literacy workers. They say it includes people learning to 'read' their own social and personal worlds so that they can intervene (take charge) in their own life and the life of their community in such a way that they become a responsible and creative agent of change.

For example, the same Papua New Guinean man told me of the time when his father died. The culture of his area required that he make five feasts to fulful his obligations and to set his mother free from obligations that his father's relatives might place on her.

> So I went through the process of thinking through that. And I only made one big feast, a very very big feast. I killed ten pigs, and the food was just plentiful, to the extent that when we finished, two days later my Dad's nephew came back and said, "What you've done on Thursday, covered every requirement for feasting in our own culture. And so there is no need for you to make any more feasts." Five years of feasting, that's a lot of gardening. Not only gardening but raising pigs, getting all the trade goods. That's a lot of hard work and it involves not just you but your whole clan. Not just your clan, but there's a whole network of relationships that you have to call upon to be involved. So if you can make one big successful thing and meet all the requirements that are necessary, that's better for everybody.

What my friend had done on this occasion was to critically think through one aspect of his social and personal world. He was then able to take charge of the situation and come up with some changes that he felt were needed.

Critical literacy is driven by the desire to free people from the things which are holding them back and are making integral human development difficult to achieve. It is, therefore, guided by a vision of what it means to be human, which includes political and economic realities as well as personal and social realities. Critical literacy is also inspired by the vision that it is possible for people's lives and society as a whole to be improved. Because of these ideas, critical literacy workers emphasize the importance of thinking and talking about teaching and learning in ways that recognize the problems that need to be overcome and possible changes for the better that could be made.

Critical literacy workers recognize that teachers are most effective when they function as "transformative intellectuals" rather than as agents who follow a set method. That is, they are people who think deeply and understand what it takes for the learner to be able to take control of his situation and they adjust their teaching accordingly. Because of this, critical literacy workers do not like to use pre-packaged materials that are "teacher-proof." They prefer materials to be developed within the situation—materials which address the problems and concerns of that situation.

Critical literacy workers see the languages and the cultures of their students as being very important. They work to preserve that culture and language and try and stop another culture from taking over or controlling its interests, history, and perspectives. Instead of blending cultural and personal differences so that everyone ends up conforming with the dominant culture, critical literacy workers prefer to see that personal and cultural differences are valued and maintained.

Critical literacy workers also believe that knowledge is a social construction. By this they mean that knowledge is built from sharing experiences and interacting with other people of the community. So they feel that schools should be places in which social relations and meanings are worked out by those involved. The people who are involved will often struggle with each other and may even resist what is taking place, but this is a normal aspect of the process of critical literacy. So what is done in schools (the curriculum) does not include just teaching knowledge and skills. It also includes teaching ways of learning and thinking that continue throughout a lifetime.

Critical literacy workers are also concerned with what they call "the hidden curriculum." A hidden curriculum is something taught without the learner being aware that he is learning it. It often involves the communication of someone else's different values, attitudes, or beliefs. This can be done in a variety of ways. For instance, the teacher might be dominant and not allow much interaction between the learners. He may use teaching methods and forms of evaluation that keep him in control; and the students receive the message that someone else is in control of their learning. Or the materials that are used may be biased and support the viewpoints of outsiders.

Critical literacy has much which is of value for those involved in vernacular language programmes. For example, it makes people more aware of the importance of the language and culture of the learners. It also makes people more aware of the struggles experienced by people who are dominated by others, or by other cultures. But certain key ideas of critical literacy must not be accepted without question. That is, anyone considering basing a literacy programme on critical literacy and its values needs to give careful evaluation and thought to it.

Critical literacy is correct to focus on the central aspects of human being's lives. But one person's understanding of what is central may differ significantly from another's. This is true of critical literacy workers: their understanding may conflict with yours, or with the understanding of the cultural group with which you are working. Many critical literacy thinkers are Marxist or socialist, and this may lead to conflict. Difficulties can also arise with those who value democracy highly. Many critical literacy workers vigorously promote democracy, but this may, or may not, be the preferred form of social organization for many groups. For instance, many groups may prefer some form of government by consensus, a council of elders, or a chief.

Finally, it is important to realise that some critical literacy workers hold strong beliefs of their own, and this affects what they teach and how they teach. Often such people have a strong anti-Christian bias, perhaps even a general anti-religion bias. Their views therefore may be in conflict with values and beliefs which the community feels are important and essential for good living. Also, some critical literacy workers have an idealistic view of culture; they view oppression as coming from outside the culture and ignore the things within the culture that oppress people and make their lives difficult. They often want to keep the culture the way it used to be, and not allow for things to grow and change unless such growth and change takes place in ways that match their ideas of what should happen.

Critical literacy has some worthwhile aspects to it. But it is important that you test the critical literacy worker's beliefs and ideas; test the hidden curriculum which they have, and see if their ideas, values, and beliefs match up with yours. But beware, it is also dangerous to assume that your own beliefs are always correct and so never need to be challenged. Values and beliefs which are different from yours should be allowed to challenge your own. That is a constructive process, not one to be feared. It is a strength of critical literacy that it encourages people to think deeply about what really is important in their lives.

There are, thus, many definitions of literacy; I have discussed the main ones. It is important to understand that literacy can be looked at from different points of view and what the implications are for any one viewpoint.

Literacy workers need to think about what kind of literacy they are promoting. Is it just a school type of literacy? Is it something learned but rarely used outside of class? Or is it helping people learn the literacy skills that will help them in everyday life, today and tomorrow? Or is it helping people to recognise ways in which others are treating them unfairly, and providing them with skills to help them take control of their situation? Or should the focus of literacy be to help improve peoples' living standards? Or should it be something else?

Answers to questions like these will determine the kind of literacy you want to promote. It will affect the kind of programme you develop with people, and the kinds of things that are done within that programme. It is important to think through these issues. Talk them over with others in your community and decide together the directions you want to take.

14.2 Literacy within the culture

I wandered around the PNG store in the heat and humidity, constantly wiping the sweat from my brow as I puzzled over what to buy the children for Christmas. The store was all decorated with Christmas tinsel, bells, stars, and other decorations. Christmas music was playing over the loud speaker. All of a sudden I had to laugh as I listened to the singing of the song "Chestnuts roasting on an open fire." That would be the last thing I would want to do this Christmas—sit by a fire warming myself roasting chestnuts. More likely I would want to sit under the fan or next to an air conditioner please! I thought how inappropriate some of the Christmas songs are for places like PNG—songs which talk of snow, sleigh-bells, and reindeer. Such things are never experienced at Christmas time in Australia either. There Christmas is a time for sun, surf, picnics, and beaches. Yet I knew the same songs were being played in the stores in Australia too!

Often when we teach literacy we do similar things to what the PNG storekeeper was doing. We use things and ideas from other cultures to achieve our goal without thinking too much if they really fit the situation we are in. How we teach literacy and what texts we use to teach it should fit in well with the culture and situation that surrounds the literacy teaching.

Often we teach a school kind of literacy—classes of individuals sitting in front of a teacher who is teaching the students to read and write.

But we need to look at the culture carefully and see where people really need literacy. In Australia a lot of literacy practices are tied in closely with school and university. Students like to learn to read well so they can handle the reading they need to do in the different school subjects in order to pass the exams. But some teachers find that the students never read a book other than the ones they have to read as part of their school course, and few of them even read the newspaper. Few of the students use their writing skills to write letters to friends, to write creative texts, to write poems, and so on. Many students in Australia think that reading and writing are only for school and work.

Literacy workers need to be careful to not think of literacy as simply teaching people to read and write in school. Otherwise, they will not bother to make the skills and the teaching of those skills relevant to the students' lives. Because of this, often students do not see that what they are learning is of benefit to them.

For example, people in a gardening culture might think that literacy is of no value to them. Some hardworking women may ask, "Will it help me to provide more food for my family?" Or they might say, "What good is a school education if students come home and do not know how to make gardens? After all, not everyone is going to get a job in the city. Most students will end up back in the village."

Recently I kept a diary of all the literacy practices I observed in the small village where we live on Karkar Island in the Madang Province of PNG. I found that people were involved in literacy practices a lot less than I expected. But when they did read or write, it usually had some connection to the church or community life and was done in a group or for a group. There the church and community life are intertwined. You cannot separate them from each other.

People used literacy to read scriptures, to find out what the daily readings were for family worship and Sunday services, and to read songs, and the liturgy. They used literacy to send and receive messages about church or community meetings. They also used literacy to send letters to people who were away from the island for some reason. Letters received were shared with others.

In some situations on Karkar, reading and writing were not used, but if I had been in Australia instead, reading and writing would certainly have been used. For example, the children could sing countless songs in Tok Pisin and in Takia without needing to have a song book in front of them. "But song books would help them learn to read," I hear you say. True, but most of the family devotions are done at night outside people's houses with very little light. So they would not be able to read the words anyway. And how do you do all the wonderful actions and dramas that go with the songs if your hands are busy holding a song book?

When I was keeping my diary I did not see many people reading or writing on their own. At night I often sit down and relax and read a good book or an article about something to do with my work. At night the Takia people visit their neighbours and 'story'. They talk about all kinds of things—about things that have happened that day or news they have heard, or they discuss things they are concerned about. Information is passed on to one another by talking.

To westerners, literacy is often an individual thing. Occasionally it is a shared thing. For example, Bruce loves to read all the jokes in the Readers Digest to me, much to my annoyance if I am in the middle of an exciting part of my own book. But usually, for Bruce and me, reading is an individual thing. He reads his book and I read mine, both of us reading silently. But on Karkar most literacy practices are a shared thing—something you do with or for others.

A literacy worker must consider these kinds of things when doing literacy work in other cultures. How do the people use literacy? How do they want to use it? It might be helpful to keep a diary, like I did, because how people actually use literacy might be different than how you think they use it.

Another thing that is important is the kinds of texts which you use in your literacy classes. It is often easier to use things that are developed from outside the culture. They can be prepared very quickly. There are a lot of childrens' stories that I love. Most are in English, some are from other languages spoken in PNG and by the Australian Aborigines. I am often tempted to encourage people to translate them into their local language and use them with the children in their area so they can enjoy them too. But the stories are not always appropriate in their culture, and this must be taken into account.

For example, the Nahu story from the cool highlands of PNG tells about the man who neglected his responsibilities. He should have been helping his family in the garden each day. Instead he stayed home, took off his arms and legs, and laid them on the ground for the sun to warm them. This story would not be very appropriate in the lowlands of PNG where it is very hot all the time.

Another example would be what kind of animal stories are appropriate. Some animals are totally unfamiliar to children living in parts of PNG. The texts that are used to teach reading and writing should be ones that the people are familiar with.

When developing literacy programmes, it is best to use mainly local stories, not just because these are familiar but because they carry a wealth of ideas, values, and attitudes that have been developed by the people as a result of their living in the local situation (C. Spaulding 1994a). By using these kinds of stories, literacy is strengthening their values and attitudes and building upon them.

In fact this is the way English children's stories first developed many centuries ago. They were the folk tales and legends of their times, written down for the purpose of teaching children to read. And they were not just teaching reading and writing, they were also teaching about the morals and values of their times and their cultures. The story which we know today as "Little Red Riding Hood" was actually a legend that peasants used to tell about three hundred years ago. In the original legend, Red Riding Hood was able to use her own intelligence and ability to outsmart the wolf. The legend had a meaning for society at that time. It showed how young peasant girls were very clever, which they needed to be in order to escape all the dangers that lay in store for them in their lives (Waters 1993).

Using local legends and folktales has many advantages. The list below is taken from C. Spaulding 1994a.

- They help connect the students' world with the new skills and things they are learning.
- They help students build on what they know.
- They strengthen ties with the culture and its values.
- They help students to appreciate the past.
- They reinforce community values and ideals.
- They are usually stories that are exciting and full of emotion for the local people.
- They are often full of extra meanings and leave the audience with a lot to think about.

Chestnuts roasting on an open fire? Sea, sun and surf? What is Christmas to you? The real meaning of Christmas is a little different from both of these pictures. What is literacy? What kind of literacy fits the culture where you are working? It should be a literacy that serves the culture well and reflects the strengths and values of the culture. It should not be out of place—like a reindeer pulling a sleigh along a beach under a blazing sun!

14.3 The literacy system

No matter what definition of literacy we choose in our literacy programme, if our programme is to be successful and keep going, it needs to become part of a working system, that is, a system that keeps working on its own no matter how big or how small the literacy programme is.

If you were working on Karkar Island, Madang Province (PNG) you might choose to place literacy within the church system that already functions well there. You might choose to work with the children through the Sunday school system, focus on the women through the women's work, and work with the pastors through the circuit conferences.

In order to have a successful programme, you would need to think about developing ways to do the following kinds of things:

- materials development and production
- teacher training
- supervision and support
- curriculum development

- planning
- mobilization of people and resources
- programme evaluation

These same kinds of things need to be considered if you are trying to implement literacy on a much bigger scale, for example, in a whole nation with many languages. The needs in this situation are similar to those for a single language, but the solutions would be worked out on a larger scale.

Bhola (1994) developed a picture of what an ideal system would look like. In it he shows the many subsystems that need to be involved in the literacy system in order for it to function well. He says that not all literacy projects, programmes, or campaigns are fortunate enough to have all these subsystems working properly. But in order for the total system to run well these subsystems need to be in place and functioning, even though some may function poorly.

Recently I have seen some enthusiastic attempts to introduce Tok Ples Prep Skuls into communities in PNG. Some of these have gone very well, others have had a lot of problems. Some programmes had many trained teachers, interested parents and students, and local school buildings had been built. But there were few books and no paper or lapboards for the children to write on. So the teachers found it hard to teach the children to read and write. The materials development and production systems, needed to feed these schools with reading and writing materials, had not yet been established. In other areas the needed books were printed, the teachers selected, the primers were ready, but there were no buildings to hold classes in. Mobilization of the resources within the community had broken down, and the whole system stopped before it had really begun to function.

When starting a literacy programme it is necessary for the total system to be working to help keep literacy going once it is started. Look closer at Bhola's picture of what a literacy system should be. He has explained his ideas in *A Source Book for Literacy Work*, 1994. See the diagram on the following page.

In the diagram you will note that there are several different subsystems. Each is a necessary part of the total system which delivers literacy to the people. The subsystems interact with and influence each other. They are all interrelated. It is difficult to talk about them all at once, so I will discuss them one by one. My discussion is based on what Bhola says on page 77 of his book (Bhola 1994). I have found his insights on this topic to be most helpful.

The ideological subsystem

This part of the system establishes the ideas on which the literacy project is based. These ideas may be cultural, economic, political, and so forth. This subsystem shows how these ideas (that is, the ideology) relate to the politics of the country. For example, the PNG

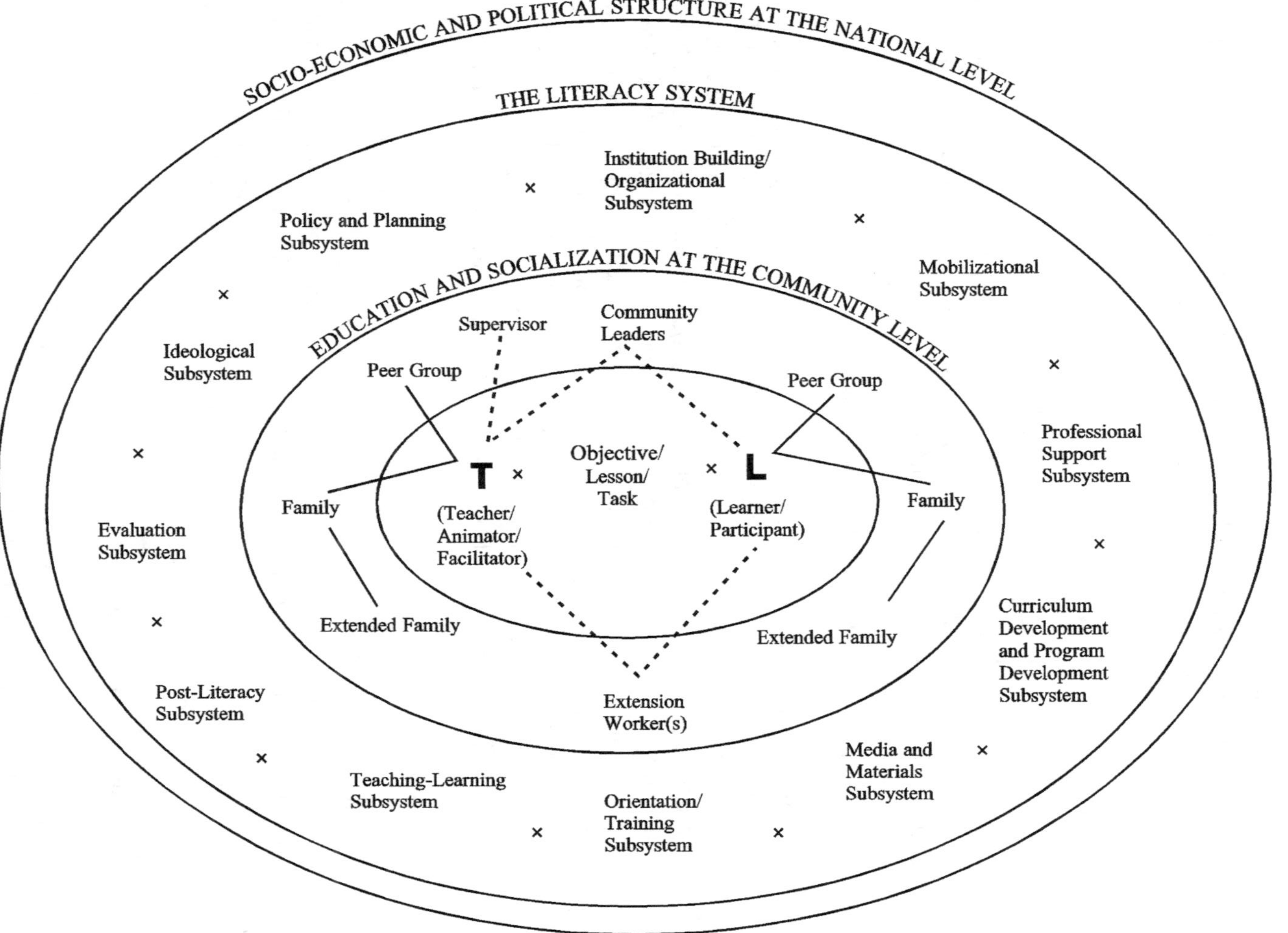

The basic teaching-learning relationship within the total social-technical system.

Computer graphic by Kenichi Kubota, 1991

constitution, the 1989 Ministerial Report on an Education Philosophy (Matane Report), and the current government education policy outline the kind of educational system and philosophy PNG wants. Any literacy programme carried out in Papua New Guinea needs to pay close attention to the ideas in these documents.

The policy and planning subsystem

The task of this part of the system is to link the basic ideology of the literacy project with concrete policies and plans, for example, planning which language or languages to work in, which groups to work with first (that is, adults, children, or youth), and organising the various tasks so that the most important ones are done first.

The institution-building and organizational subsystem

This part of the system makes decisions about sharing responsibility between those people, groups, or agencies that need to be involved in the literacy task. This could be a village literacy committee which would plan and establish several subcommittees to delegate the work to various groups of people. Or in bigger projects it might include figuring out how to work with regional, provincial, or national government agencies and nongovernment agencies. It includes taking into consideration things like how each group of people will participate in the running of literacy projects or campaigns. Decisions need to be made about what new organisations, committees, and jobs are needed in order to run the literacy project well. Also, how new groups and existing groups and committees can be encouraged to work together and share ideas. These are the kinds of things that come under 'institution building'.

The mobilizational subsystem

The word mobilize means to bring into use or prepare for active service. Mobilization means setting up a resource base. For example, whether a literacy programme is small or large, decisions need to be made about who will be the teachers and how they will be trained. Decisions also must be made about who should come to learn, and how they will be encouraged to be involved. The resources of communities and governments need to be made ready so the literacy project can go ahead.

The professional support subsystem

This area of the literacy system is concerned with providing professional support to the literacy system. Professional support needs to be done in several areas.

Firstly, provide support, training, and help for the teachers, supervisors, and officers involved in the literacy project. Secondly, provide support and training to those who evaluate how the project is going and what areas need strengthening. And finally, provide support and training for the people involved in research connected with the project.

The professional support system may be within the main literacy organization in charge of the project. But more likely it will also draw on resources and help from agencies outside of the main organization. Some training, support, and help may come from the teachers colleges, nongovernment agencies, universities, and research institutions that exist in the country. For larger projects some training may also be done overseas.

The curriculum and programme development subsystem

This part of the literacy system makes curriculum judgments, that is, decisions about what will be taught, at what levels, and in what order. It also involves decisions about programme delivery.

The media and materials subsystem

This part of the literacy subsystem makes decisions about writing and publishing materials—things like primers, follow-up books, visual aids, teachers guides, and manuals. It must also integrate the use of various materials and media available from a variety of inside and outside sources.

The orientation and training subsystem

This part of the literacy system prepares pre-service and in-service training programmes for teachers and supervisors, and orientation programmes for other workers. This subsystem is important in that it helps the total system to improve its quality of work over time.

The teacher-learner subsystem

This is the heart of the system. It makes sure that the core of any literacy system, that is, the teaching-learning event, is successful. If this part is not done well, all the other subsystems are pointless. The teacher, more than any other factor, determines the quality of education.

The post-literacy subsystem

This part of the system makes sure that new literates keep on reading so that they do not return to being illiterate. Decisions will need to be made about what needs to be done to make sure people stay literate. More importantly, the organizers of the post-literacy subsystem must make sure that new literates use the literacy skills they have learned in the economic, social, political, and cultural aspects of their daily lives.

The evaluation subsystem

This part of the system makes sure that all decisions are informed decisions. This means people will collect both descriptive and evaluative information. Evaluative information must be in terms of both numbers and quality. People need to evaluate how well learners have done, and also what impact the programmes have had on communities. All evaluations should be made with the people involved in the task (collaborative) and include self-evaluation by the learners (participative).

System summary

Each of the parts of the literacy system are interrelated and influence each other. In small literacy projects many of these things will be carried out by one person, or one group of people, and the tasks will seem to run into each other and be one thing rather than many. But in big literacy projects, like the introduction of Tok Ples Prep Skuls in PNG for many hundreds of languages, each area of the literacy system will need to be the concern of separate groups of people.

In order for the literacy system to function well, all parts need to function to some degree, even if poorly. For a while the system can work with a few weak parts, but there is a strong need for all subsystems eventually to function properly in order to have good interaction between the facilitator, the participants, and the task.

Papua New Guinea is in the middle of a lot of educational reform. Nationally they are trying to encourage the use of vernacular languages in education, particularly in the first few years of schooling. So it is a key time to be thinking about which literacy subsystems are already working well in PNG and which ones need strengthening

I have found Bhola's picture of a literacy system to be very helpful. It helped me to organise my thinking about literacy work in Papua New Guinea. I used his diagram to think about what a good literacy system might look like in PNG. I have developed my own diagram which is on the next page. I made some changes to Bhola's ideas. I have my own literacy philosophy. I have also made some observations about how vernacular literacy is done in this country. These things influenced the picture that I have created of this literacy system. Pat Spaulding and Colleen Oates also gave me some good ideas. Other people might draw a different picture for PNG which reflects their ideas. I am sharing mine as an example of how Bhola's diagram can help literacy workers to think about the literacy system. I am not saying

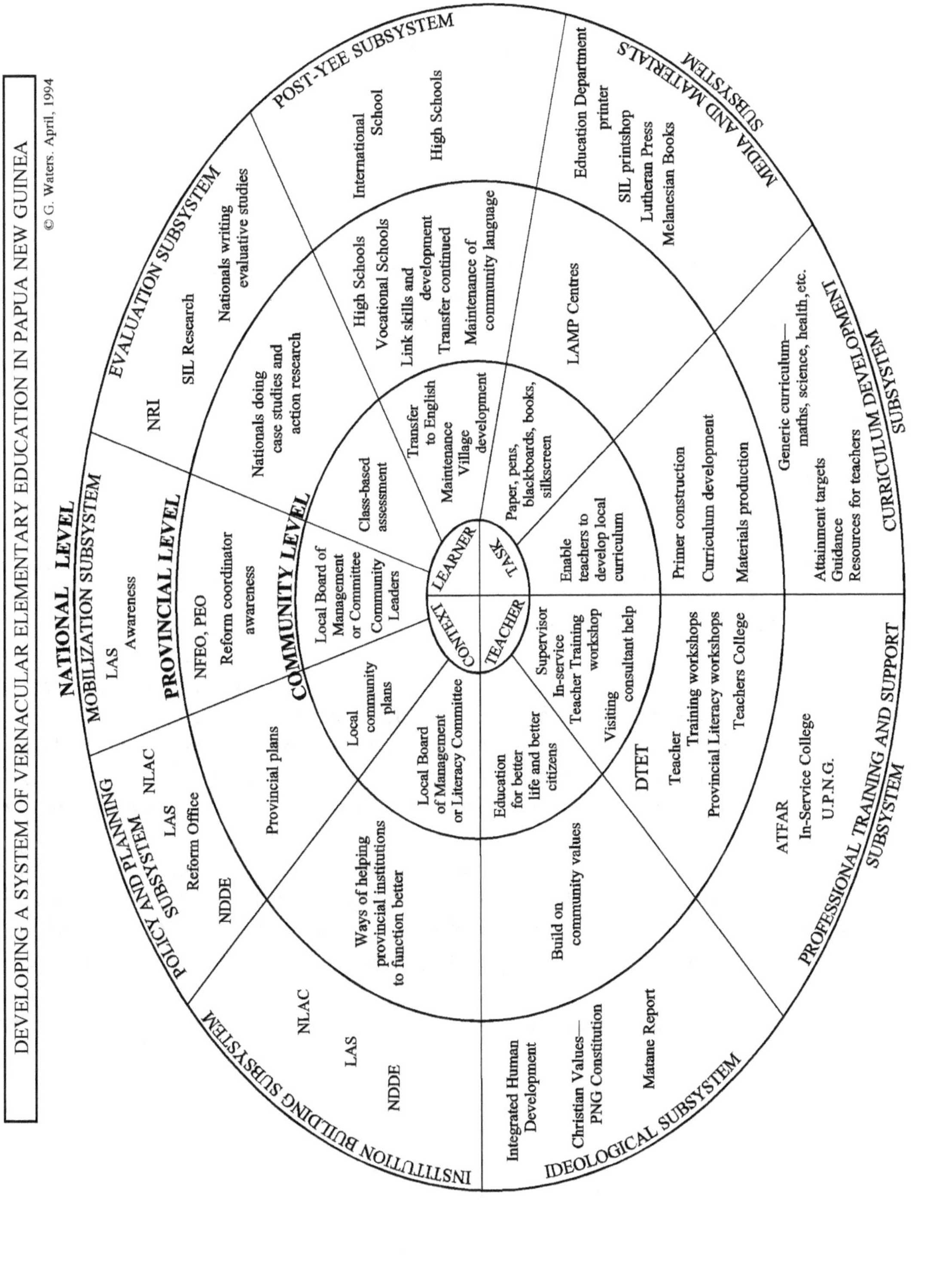

DEVELOPING A SYSTEM OF VERNACULAR ELEMENTARY EDUCATION IN PAPUA NEW GUINEA

NATIONAL LEVEL

PROVINCIAL LEVEL

COMMUNITY LEVEL

LEARNER
TASK
TEACHER
CONTEXT

MOBILIZATION SUBSYSTEM
LAS
Awareness
NFEO, PEO
Reform coordinator awareness
Local Board of Management or Committee
Community Leaders

EVALUATION SUBSYSTEM
NRI
SIL Research
Nationals writing evaluative studies
Nationals doing case studies and action research
Class-based assessment

POST-YEE SUBSYSTEM
International School
High Schools
High Schools
Vocational Schools
Link skills and development
Transfer continued
Maintenance of community language
Transfer to English
Maintenance
Village development

MEDIA AND MATERIALS SUBSYSTEM
Education Department printer
SIL printshop
Lutheran Press
Melanesian Books
LAMP Centres
Paper, pens, blackboards, books, silkscreen

CURRICULUM DEVELOPMENT SUBSYSTEM
Generic curriculum—maths, science, health, etc.
Attainment targets
Guidance
Resources for teachers
Primer construction
Curriculum development
Materials production
Enable teachers to develop local curriculum

PROFESSIONAL TRAINING AND SUPPORT SUBSYSTEM
ATFAR
In-Service College
U.P.N.G.
DTET
Teacher Training workshops
Provincial Literacy workshops
Teachers College
Supervisor
In-service Teacher Training workshop
Visiting consultant help

IDEOLOGICAL SUBSYSTEM
Integrated Human Development
Christian Values—PNG Constitution
Matane Report
Build on community values
Education for better life and better citizens

INSTITUTION BUILDING SUBSYSTEM
NLAC
LAS
NDDE
Ways of helping provincial institutions to function better
Local Board of Management or Literacy Committee

POLICY AND PLANNING SUBSYSTEM
NLAC
LAS
Reform Office
NDDE
Provincial plans
Local community plans

mine is the right picture. In my view I believe that the central point is the learning event. This event (see chapter 2) involves the interaction of:

- the facilitator, or person who is teaching
- the learner
- the task (in this case a literacy related task)
- the social setting

This learning event is surrounded by a community context, which in turn is influenced by district, provincial, national, and international contexts. My literacy system concept for PNG includes the following subsystems:

- ideological
- institution building
- planning and policy
- mobilization
- evaluation
- post-literacy
- media and materials
- curriculum development
- professional training and support

You can see that these are similar to Bhola's subsystems but I have joined some of his subsystems together and represented things a little differently in some areas.

In my system I see information and expertise flowing both **from** the central core and **into** the central core. However, the core or main concern of the system continues to be the successful interaction of the teacher and learner with the task in the grass roots community context.

What will your literacy system picture look like? Which parts of your literacy system are working well? Which parts do you think you need to strengthen? Which parts will need help from outside? You need to think what the literacy system picture might look like for the language group you work with, or for the nation that you work in. Develop your own picture just like I have done.

References

Adams, Marilyn Jager. 1990. Beginning to read: Thinking and learning about print. Washington D.C.: Department of Education.

Ahai, Naihuwo and Michael Bopp. 1993. Missing links: Literacy, awareness and development in Papua New Guinea. A report to UNICEF regarding a review of the National Literacy and Awareness Programme and related issues in Papua New Guinea. PNG: Educational Division of the National Research Institute of Papua New Guinea.

Allen, Margaret. 1985. Concentrated language encounters of the Kriol kind. Australia: Barunga School.

Anderson, Richard C., Elfreida H. Hiebert, Judith Scott, and Ian A. G. Wilkinson. 1985. Becoming a nation of readers: The report of the commission on reading. Champaign-Urbana, Ill.: Center for the Study of Reading.

Anderson, Richard. C. and David Ausubel. 1966. Readings in the psychology of cognition. New York: Holt, Rinehart and Winston.

Au, Kathryn Hu-pei and J. M. Mason. 1981. Social organisational factors in learning to read: The balance of rights hypothesis. Reading Research Quarterly 17(1):115–152.

——— and Alice J. Kawakami. 1985. Influence of the social organization of instruction on children's text comprehension ability: A Vygotskian perspective. In Carolyn N. Hedley and Anthony N. Baratta (eds.), Contexts of Reading Instruction. Norwood, N.J.:Ablex.

Ausubel, David. 1985. Learning as constructing meaning. In Noel Entwistle (ed.), New directions in educational psychology 1. Learning and Teaching, 71–82. London: Farmer Press.

Bendor-Samuel, Margaret. 1977. Paulo Freire: His use of literacy in social revolution. Notes on Literacy 21:10–18.

——— and David Bendor-Samuel. 1987. A manual for strategic planning and review for language programs. Dallas: Summer Institute of Linguistics.

Bhola H. S. 1994. A source book for literacy work. Perspectives from the Grassroots. United Kingdom: gentlemen. Kingsley Publishers.

Borneman, Barry. 1988. Holi Baibul riding buk. Jinasis 1:1–2:4. Darwin: Wycliffe Bible Translators.

———. 1992. Holding your reading theories lightly. Notes On Literacy 18(2):7–17.

Bruner, J. 1986. Actual minds, possible worlds. Massachusetts: Harvard University Press.

Bussis, Anne M. et al. 1985. A research focus on meaning. In Anne M. Bussis, Edward A. Chittenden, Marianne Amarel, and E. Klausner (eds.), Inquiry into meaning: An investigation of learning to read, 3–22. Hillsdale, N.J.: Lawrence Erlbaum Associates.

Calkins, Lucy. 1983. Lessons from a child. Exter, N.H.: Heinemann.

Campbell, Bev. 1991. More than life itself. Melbourne: Victorian Adult Literacy and Basic Education Council.

Cazden, Courtney B. 1985. Social context of learning to read. In Harry Singer and Robert Ruddell (eds.), Theoretical models and processes of reading. Third Edition, 595–610. Newark, Del.: International Reading Association.

Chall, Jeanne. 1967. Learning to read: The great debate. New York: McGraw-Hill Book Company.

Chomsky, Carol. 1975. When you still can't read in the third grade: After decoding what? In S. J. Samuels (ed.), What research has to say about reading instruction, 227–54. Newark, Del.: International Reading Association.

Christie, Michael. 1982. Teaching purposeful reading to Aboriginal children. The Aboriginal child at school 10:(2)11–26.

———. 1984. The Aboriginal world view: A white person's ideas. The Aboriginal child at school 12:(1)3–7.

Clay, Marie. 1972. Reading: The patterning of complex behavior. Auckland: Heinemann Educational Books.

———. 1979. The early detection of reading difficulties. Auckland: Heinemann Educational Books.

———. 1991. Becoming literate: The construction of inner control. Auckland: Heinemann Educational Books.

Cutting, Brian. 1982. Reading matters. Auckland: Shortland Publications.

Davidson, Judith L., ed. 1988. Counterpoint and beyond. A response to becoming a nation of readers. Washington, D.C.: National Council of Teachers of English.

Deibler, Ellis and Katherine Deibler. 1974. Gona molokakaq puku. Maths book. Papua New Guinea: Summer Institute of Linguistics.

Department of Education, Papua New Guinea. 1994. Maths for Prep. Teachers Resource Book. Papua New Guinea: Education Printshop.

———. 1988. Mekeo. Resource book for expressive arts.

———. 1988. Programming expressive arts. A guide for community school teachers.

———. 1993. Enjoy teaching in your own language. ms.
———. 1993. Using tok ples to learn how to read and write.
Dilena, Mike. The active reader.
Di Vesta, Francis J. 1987. The cognitive movement and education. In J. A. Golver and Royce Ronning (eds.), Historical foundations of educational psychology, 203–33. New York: Plenum Press.
Duranti, Alessandro and Elinor Ochs. 1986. Literacy instruction in a Samoan village. In Bambi B. Schieffelin and Perry Gilmore (eds.), The acquisition of literacy: Ethnographic perspectives, 213–32. New Jersey: Ablex Publishing Corporation.
Edelsky, C. with Bess Altwerger, and Barbara Flores. 1991. Whole language: What's new? In C. Edelsky (ed.), With literacy and justice for all, 96–111. London: The Falmer Press.
Faraclas, Nicholas. (in press). Critical literacy and control: Give praxis a chance. In P. Freebody, S. Muspratt, and A. Luke (eds.), Constructing critical literacies: Teaching and learning textual practices. London: Falmer Press.
Fowler, Phyl. 1993. Reflective piece. ms.
Fox, Mem. 1986. The fox in possum's clothing: The teacher disguised as writer, in hot pursuit of literacy. A paper presented at the National Conference of the Australian Reading Association, Perth, Western Australia, 2nd–5th July, 1986, 28–43.
Gale, Kathy. 1983. Encouraging children to write: The Kriol experience at Bamyili. Northern Territory, Australia: Bamyili Press.
Goddard, Ruth, Beth Marr, and Judith Martin. 1991. Strength in numbers. Victoria: Eastern Metroplitan Council of Further Education.
Goodman, Kenneth. 1968. The psycholinguistic nature of the reading process. Michigan: Wayne State University Press.
———. 1986. What's whole in whole language? Portsmouth, N.H.: Heinemann Educational Books.
Graves, Donald. 1983. Writing: Teachers and children at work. Portsmouth, N.H.: Heinemann Educational Books.
Gudschinsky, Sarah C. 1973. A manual of literacy for preliterate peoples. Papua New Guinea: Summer Institute of Linguistics.
Gustafsson, Uwe. 1991. Can literacy lead to development? A case study in literacy, adult education, and economic development in India. Summer Institute of Linguistics and The University of Texas at Arlington Publications in Linguistics 97. Dallas.
Guthrie Larry F. and William Hall. 1984. Ethnographic approaches to reading research. In P. David Pearson (ed.), Handbook of reading research, 91–110. New York: Longman.
Harris, Stephen. 1977. Milingimbi Aboriginal learning contexts. Ph.D. dissertation, University of New Mexico.
———. 1987. Aboriginal learning styles and formal schooling. In M. Christie, S. Harris and D. McClay (eds.), Teaching Aboriginal children: Milingimbi and beyond, 41–57. (First

published in Aboriginal child at school in 1984) Mount Lawley, Western Australia: Western Australia College of Advanced Education.

——— and Joy Harris. 1970. Napa kie haviho. Let's learn numbers. Papua New Guinea: Summer Institute of Linguistics.

Heath, Shirley Brice. 1983. Ways with words: Language, life and work in communities and classrooms. New York: Cambridge University Press.

Holdaway, Don. 1979. The foundations of literacy. Sydney: Ashton Scholastic.

———. 1980. Independence in reading. Sydney: Ashton Scholastic.

Holly, Mary Louise. 1987. Keeping a personal-professional journal. Australia: Deakin University Press.

Hornsby, David, Jo-Anne Parry and Deborah Sukarna. 1992. Teach on: Teaching strategies for reading and writing workshops. Portsmouth, N.H.: Heinemann.

Itzkoff, Seymour W. 1986. How we learn to read. Ashfield, Mass.: Paideia Publishers.

Jesudason, Daniel and Wei Lei Jesudason. 1990. Report on the Umanakaina literacy program. ms.

Kemp, Max. 1980. Reading-language processes: Assessment and teaching. Adelaide: Australian Reading Association.

———. 1987. Watching children read and write. Observational records for children with special needs. Melbourne: Thomas Nelson Australia.

Laubach, Frank and Robert Laubach. 1960. Toward world literacy. The each-one-teach-one way. Syracuse, N.Y.: Syracuse University Press.

Levine, Kenneth. 1986. The social context of literacy. London: Routledge and Kegan Paul.

Lillee, Pat. 1985. Namba puk. A Girawa arithmetic book. Papua New Guinea: Summer Institute of Linguistics.

Lindrud, Stellan and Eivor Lindrud. 1994. Why teach the word and the sentence first? Read 29:(1)30–34.

Litteral, Robert and Susan Malone. 1991. The sounds of your language. Papua New Guinea: Department of Education

Making a difference. Video. 1992. Victorian Education Department.

McCormick, Thomas W. 1988. Theories of reading in dialogue: An interdisciplinary study. New York: University Press of America.

———. 1990a. Phonics outline. ms.

———. 1990b. Primer lessons. Unpublished notes.

McCracken, H. and M. McCracken. 1990. The McCracken philosophy. Video. Canada: McCracken Educational Services.

McCracken, Marlene and Robert McCracken. 1979. Reading, writing and language. A practical guide for primary teachers. Winnipeg: Penguis Publishers.

——— and ———. 1982. Spelling through phonics. A practical guide for kindergarten through grade three. Winnipeg: Penguis Publishers.

McDermott, R. P. 1985. Achieving school failure: An anthropological approach to illiteracy and social stratification. In Harry Singer and Robert Ruddell (eds.), Theoretical models and processes of reading. Third Edition, 558–94. Newark, Del.: International Reading Association.

Ministerial committee report. 1986. A philosophy of education for Papua New Guinea. Port Moresby: Papua New Guinea Government.

Nagai, Yasuko. 1990a. Sharing enjoyable reading experiences. Read 25(2):23–29.

———. 1990b. Using the shared book approach to teach Maiwala and Labe prep schoolers in Milne Bay, Papua New Guinea. ms.

———. 1991 Writing good stories. ms.

National Department of Education. 1991. The sounds of your language. Papua New Guinea: Government printer.

Nelson, Arch. 1989. My dear ministers. N.S.W. (Australia): University of New England.

Northern Territory Department of Education. 1985. Making Big Books.

Oatridge, Desmond. 1980. Pre-writing. Read 15(2):34–48.

Orr-Easthouse, Linda. 1994. A whole language approach to Quechua literacy. Notes On Literacy 20(1):1–26.

Rayner, Keith and Alexander Pollatsek. 1989. The psychology of reading. New York: Prentice-Hall.

Rempel, Robin. 1993. A mini multi-strategy method? Read 28(2):3–9.

Richards, Eirlys. 1987. Pinarri: Introducing Aboriginal languages in Kimberley schools. Darwin: Kimberley Language Resource Centre and Summer Institute of Linguistics.

Rowe, Gaelene and Bill Lomas. 1984. A writing curriculum. Process and conference. Melbourne: Oxford University Press.

Rumelhart, David E. 1981. Schemata: The building blocks of cognition. In John T. Guthrie (ed.), Comprehension and teaching: Research reviews. Newark, Del.: International Reading Association.

Salmon, Phillida. 1988. Psychology for teachers: An alternative approach. London: Hutchinson Education.

Schonell, Fred. 1961. The Psychology of teaching reading, 255–63. London: Oliver and Boyd.

Smith, Frank. 1988a. Joining the literacy club. Further essays into education. Portsmouth, N.H.: Heinemann.

———. 1988b. Understanding reading: A psycholinguistic analysis of reading and learning to read. Fourth Edition. Hillsdale, N.J.: Lawrence Erlbaum Associates.

Spaulding, Craig. 1994a. Community directed development through literacy: Fact or myth? Read 29(1):14 –24.

———. 1994b. Missing links: Literacy, awareness and development in PNG by Naihuwo Ahai and Michael Bopp 1993. National Research Institute. A review, to appear in Technical Studies Memo, Papua New Guinea: Summer Institute of Linguistics.

——— and Pat Spaulding. 1994. Skulim ol long rit na rait. Olsem pasin bilong diwai. PNG: Bambu Books.

Spaulding, Pat. 1994. Community directed curriculum development. Read 29(1):25–29.

Street, B., ed. 1990. Literacy in development: People, language and power. Papers by the International Seminar, Commonwealth Institute and Education for Development, 6–7 April 1990.

Stringer, Mary D., and Nicollas Faraclas. 1987. Working together for literacy. Wewak, PNG: Christian Books Melanesia.

Stucky, Alfred and Dellene Stucky. 1990. Beltpin kinamin! Let's count. Ukarumpa, PNG: Summer Institute of Linguistics.

Tierney, R. 1992. Ongoing research and new directions. In Judith Irwin and Mary Anne Doyle (eds.), Reading/writing connections. Learning from research. Newark, Del.: International Reading Association.

——— and Margie Leys. 1984. What is the value of connecting reading and writing? (Reading Education Report No. 55). Champaign-Urbana, Ill.: Center for the Study of Reading.

Trelease, Jim. 1989. The new read-aloud handbook. 4th edition. New York: Penguin Books.

Treloar, Aileen. n.d. Debbie. ms.

Turbill, Jan, ed. 1982. No better way to teach writing. Rozelle, N.S.W. (Australia): Primary English Teaching Association.

UNESCO 1970. Literacy 1967–1969. Progress achieved in literacy throughout the world. Paris: United Nations Educational, Scientific and Cultural Organization.

Vollrath, Karen. 1991. An initial report of Hewa literacy methods. Read 26(2):13–26.

Vollarath, Paul and Karen Vollrath. 1990. Ana menemeyo. Counting book. PNG: Vollrath, duplicated typescript.

Vygotsky, L. S. 1978. Mind in society. Cambridge, Mass: Harvard University Press.

Wagner, Daniel A., Brinkley M. Messick, and Jennifer Spratt. 1986. Studying literacy in Morocco. In Bambi B. Schieffelin and Perry Gilmore (eds.), The acquisition of literacy: Ethnographic perspectives, 233–260. New Jersey: Ablex.

Waters, Glenys. 1992a. Is there one best primer/programme design? You bet! The one that is designed to fit your program. Notes on Literacy 18(3):17–36

———. 1992b. The implications of two theories of cognitive development for teaching in developing countries. ms.

———. 1993a. The development of vernacular children's literature in Papua New Guinea: History repeats itself. ms.

———. 1993b. Encouraging classroom-based assessment in vernacular reading classes in Papua New Guinea. ms.

———. 1993c. How did I "come to know" and how then should I teach? ms.
———. 1993d. Learning by clockwork versus coming to know: Phillida Salmon and James Britton in dialogue. ms.
Zipes, Jack. 1983. Fairy tales and the art of subversion. The classical genre for children and the process of civilization. London: Heinemann.

Index

www.ingramcontent.com/pod-product-compliance
Lightning Source LLC
LaVergne TN
LVHW061218100826
845148LV00004B/788

* 9 7 8 1 5 5 6 7 1 0 3 8 4 *